ADMINISTRATIVE JUSTICE AND ASYLUM APPEALS

How are we to assess and evaluate the quality of the tribunal systems that do the day-to-day work of adjudicating upon the disputes individuals have with government? This book examines how the idea of adjudicative quality works in practice by presenting a detailed case-study of the tribunal system responsible for determining appeals lodged by foreign nationals who claim that they will be at risk of persecution or ill-treatment on return to their country of origin. Over recent years, the asylum appeal process has become a major area of judicial decision-making and the most frequently restructured tribunal system. Asylum adjudication is also one of the most difficult areas of decision-making in the modern legal system.

Integrating empirical research with legal analysis, this book provides an in-depth study of the development and operation of this tribunal system and of asylum decision-making. The book examines how this particular appeal process seeks to mediate the tension between the competing values under which it operates. There are chapters examining the organisation of the tribunal system, its procedures, the nature of fact-finding in asylum cases and the operation of onward rights of challenge.

An   of administrative
justice   responsible for making
poten   he literature and will a
of val   um adjudication.

ONE WEEK LO

Administrative Justice and Asylum Appeals

A Study of Tribunal Adjudication

ROBERT THOMAS

·HART·
PUBLISHING

OXFORD AND PORTLAND, OREGON
2011

Published in the United Kingdom by Hart Publishing Ltd
16C Worcester Place, Oxford, OX1 2JW
Telephone: +44 (0)1865 517530
Fax: +44 (0)1865 510710
E-mail: mail@hartpub.co.uk
Website: http://www.hartpub.co.uk

Published in North America (US and Canada) by
Hart Publishing
c/o International Specialized Book Services
920 NE 58th Avenue, Suite 300
Portland, OR 97213-3786
USA
Tel: +1 503 287 3093 or toll-free: (1) 800 944 6190
Fax: +1 503 280 8832
E-mail: orders@isbs.com
Website: http://www.isbs.com

© Robert Thomas 2011

British Library Cataloguing in Publication Data
Data Available

ISBN: 978-1-84113-936-4

Typeset by Hope Services, Abingdon
Printed and bound in Great Britain by
TJ International Ltd, Padstow, Cornwall

PREFACE

This book is the product of an empirical legal research project into the procedure and determination of asylum appeals by the responsible administrative tribunal, the Asylum and Immigration Tribunal (AIT). In undertaking this project I have become indebted in a number of ways. First, the project would not have been possible without the generous financial assistance of the Nuffield Foundation (AJU/00124/G), for which I am extremely grateful. In particular, I would wish to thank Sharon Witherspoon, the Deputy Director of the Foundation, for her enthusiasm, assistance, and support. Secondly, the research grant enabled me to benefit from an excellent research associate, Dr Rute Caldeira, who ably demonstrated her commitment, efficiency, tirelessness, and good humour in undertaking with me the legwork of the empirical research and the analysis. I would also like to thank Rute for our extremely useful, though often inconclusive, discussions over asylum appeals. Thirdly, I would not have been able to undertake the research project without the agreement of the AIT, the Ministry of Justice, and the United Kingdom Border Agency which granted access to undertake the research, in particular, to have access to tribunal determinations which would otherwise had been unavailable and to conduct interviews. I am particularly grateful to Mark Ockelton, Deputy President of the then AIT for his receptiveness, assistance, and guidance when I first approached him with the idea of undertaking empirical research into asylum appeals. Fourthly, thanks also go to the School of Law, University of Manchester for affording me study leave to work on the project.

For some years, I have had an interest in the operation and functioning of administrative appeal systems and in the working of the asylum appellate jurisdiction in particular. This interest has several sources. First, there has, over recent years, been much academic and other debate over administrative justice which has accompanied various reforms to the administrative justice system and the tribunals system in particular. Much of this debate has been supported by institutions such as the Nuffield Foundation, the Economic and Social Research Council, and the Administrative Justice and Tribunals Council.[1] A second source of my interest stemmed from the particular difficulties of organising an effective appellate process for those individuals refused asylum. No other tribunal system has been as frequently reformed as the asylum appeal process. When the Government proposed in 2004 to reform the appeals process, I acted as a specialist adviser to a Parliamentary select committee.[2] The most notable aspect of this

---

[1] See, eg, M Adler, *Administrative Justice in Context* (Oxford, Hart Publishing, 2010).
[2] House of Commons Constitutional Affairs Committee, *Asylum and Immigration Appeals* (2003–04 HC 211).

set of reforms had been the controversial proposal to enact an ouster clause in order to immunise the tribunal's decisions from challenge in the higher courts. This aroused widespread opposition and focused attention directly upon the appeals process. After the Government backed down and the dust had settled, this interest quickly dissipated. Nonetheless, my own interest remained. Following the establishment of the AIT in 2005, I wanted to examine in detail how the tribunal was working in practice. I also wanted to demonstrate to my fellow administrative lawyers that tribunals are not, as often assumed, peripheral to their discipline, but are instead central to understanding the complex and dynamic relationship between governmental and legal processes. A third source of my interest has arisen from the particular challenge of investigating and researching asylum appeals. After all, most other large-scale tribunal jurisdictions have been the subject of academic study. However, the immigration and asylum appeals system—now the second largest—had, for one reason or another, either often eluded or been overlooked by the few administrative law scholars interested in administrative tribunals. Finally, as I examined the appeals process in more detail, I became interested in and perplexed by the nature of asylum decision-making and its peculiarly difficult demands.

The principal objective of the book is to examine the effectiveness and quality of tribunal adjudication through a case-study of the asylum appeals process. The book is, then, a study of a specific, and slightly unusual, adjudication system, in one geographical setting, over one period of time. It is not, therefore, claimed that the specific findings and analysis presented here on asylum appeals are generally applicable. The book does, though, offer a general way of thinking of about adjudicative quality. In this respect, the book might shed some broader light upon the role and function of administrative tribunals and the difficulties and problems that arise when we seek to assess and evaluate their work.

The study of immigration and asylum appeals, the legal rules, and their administration can be a challenging endeavour at the best of times, partly because of the incessant outpouring of judicial decision-making—tribunal determinations and court judgments—as well as policy and legislative changes, and new rules and regulations. Indeed, during the progress of the empirical component of the research project, there was a consultation on a further restructuring of the immigration and asylum appeals system to transfer the AIT into the new, two-tier tribunal system, the First-tier Tribunal and the Upper Tribunal (Immigration and Asylum Chamber). This transfer occurred in early 2010 and represents an important change to the organisation of the tribunal, particularly as regards onward appeals against initial tribunal decisions and the role of the higher courts in the decision-making process. The transfer is certainly an important reform, but it does not radically affect the handling of initial appeals; even less, does it alter the nature of the decision-making task involved in determining asylum appeals. The transfer does not, therefore, represent a wholesale reform of the tribunal, but another step in its evolution. For this reason, the analysis presented in this book remains valid and is not undermined by the transfer. Despite this structural change, I have, however, referred to the tribunal as the AIT at various sections throughout the book, where it has been appropriate to do so; for the most part, I have referred to it simply as the Tribunal.

In addition to keeping up with constant legal and policy developments, the empirical project involved the collection of masses of empirical data about the appeals process. The empirical component of the research involved three principal forms of data collection: the observation of appeal hearings; analysis of tribunal determinations; and interviews with participants in the appeals process. Some of the chapters draw upon this data, but it is neither possible nor desirable to present all of it. The book, therefore, draws selectively upon the data collected to illustrate how the asylum appeals process functions and to support the analysis presented here.

It is commonplace to note that people are more likely to come into contact with the legal system by appearing before a tribunal than a court of law. The task of observing tribunals at work and watching them operate in practice brings home their prosaic character as they discharge their quotidian task of delivering justice to people. Asylum appeals are, though, distinctive because of the nature of the issues involved. Appellants often give personal evidence of a kind that does not feature as regularly in other legal proceedings. The consequences of wrong decisions can have drastic consequences and the decisional task is highly challenging. As this book seeks to argue, decisional accuracy is one of the key values informing an adjudication system, but also one of the most imponderable. In the asylum context, it is virtually impossible to pin down something as elusive as decisional accuracy. Having observed around 200 or so asylum appeals, and having had access to the same documentary evidence as the judge, and heard the same oral evidence as the judge, I cannot really claim to be any the wiser as to whether the decisions were right or wrong. From personal experience, it seemed to me that, in a handful of cases, the decision reached was questionable—either because asylum might have been either wrongfully refused or granted—but whenever I felt this, it just seemed to be my own subjective point of view and that I was certainly in no better position to decide. In most of the appeals that I observed, the decision reached seemed to me to be within the bounds of what was reasonable and that some decision one way or the other was required—otherwise the adjudication process would fail in its primary mission: to adjudicate.

In undertaking this project, I have been fortunate enough to have received considerable assistance from a number of different institutions and people. The empirical component of this project involved immersion in the world of asylum appeals and I was able to speak with people holding positions at all levels within this world. Immigration Judges, Senior Immigration Judges, representatives, Home Office presenting officers and caseworkers, medical and country expert witnesses, tribunal interpreters, and Tribunal Service staff all generously spared their time to speak about their work and to provide the kind of insights that cannot be gleaned either from observing appeal hearings or reading appeal determinations. I am grateful to them.

Thanks also go to my academic colleagues at Manchester and elsewhere who provided guidance, assistance, and encouragement during the project. In particular, I would like to thank Charles Blake, Tom Gibbons, Andrew Sanders, and Hugo Storey. At an early stage of the project, I received valuable assistance from Alex Hermon, Jo Shaw, and Maurice Sunkin. I would also like to thank Sarah Craig, Richard Rawlings, Genevra Richardson, Neville Harris, and William Lucy for their comments on drafts. Thanks also go to Richard Hart and his team at Hart Publishing. Of course, despite the assistance provided to me, I assume sole responsibility for the book's shortcomings.

Earlier versions of some of the chapters have been presented in a number of academic conferences and seminars and I have benefited from the comments received. An early version of chapter seven was presented at a conference on the best practices for refugee status determination hosted by Monash University at its conference centre in Prato, Italy in 2008. A revised version of the conference paper appeared as 'Consistency in Asylum Adjudication: Country Guidance and the Asylum Process in the United Kingdom' (2008) 20 *International Journal of Refugee Law* 489. A different and extended version is included here. I have also drawn upon a chapter, 'Refugee Roulette—a UK Perspective' in J Ramji-Nogales, AI Schoenholtz, and PG Schrag (eds), *Refugee Roulette: Disparities in Asylum Adjudication and Proposals for Reform* (New York, New York University Press, 2009), that offered a UK perspective on empirical research by Ramji-Nogales, Schoenholtz, and Schrag which revealed striking disparities in asylum adjudication in the United States. An amalgamation of chapters five and six was presented at a conference on asylum and refugees hosted by the Centre of African Studies, SOAS, University of London in 2009. Presentations based on other parts of the book have been given to the Administrative Justice and Tribunals Council, the Nuffield Foundation, and the Sussex Centre for Migration, University of Sussex. Furthermore, together with the Nuffield Foundation and the International Association of Refugee Law Judges, I organised a roundtable discussion on the topic of country guidance in asylum decision-making systems in the UK and elsewhere, which took place in the summer of 2009, from which I learnt much.

Finally, I need to thank my family: my wife, Nicola, and our children, Penelope, Rosamund, Constanza, Edward, and Gwendolyn, for their support and forbearance.

Robert Thomas
Hartford
May 2010

CONTENTS

Contents

TABLE OF CASES

AUSTRALIA

EUROPEAN COURT OF HUMAN RIGHTS

REPUBLIC OF IRELAND

UNITED KINGDOM

Court Judgments

Tribunal Determinations

UNITED STATES

TABLE OF LEGISLATION

UNITED KINGDOM

Secondary legislation

1

Administrative Justice, Quality and Asylum Adjudication

E VERY YEAR ADMINISTRATIVE agencies, tribunal judges, and other decision-makers collectively make millions of decisions that both affect the lives of individuals and implement public policy. This field of activity is generally known as administrative justice and comprises a variegated range of individual decision-making systems that govern many aspects of our collective social life, such as social security, tax, education, transport, mental health, and immigration and asylum. Administrative justice concerns the overall system by which administrative decisions affecting individuals are taken, including the procedures and law governing such decisions and the processes for resolving disputes and airing grievances in relation to them.[1] This system utilises a number of mechanisms by which individuals can seek to resolve their disputes with administrative agencies that arise in the context of the implementation of policy programmes. These mechanisms include: internal reviews of initial administrative decisions; complaints processes both internally within the public agency and by external complaint handling bodies; investigations by ombudsmen into allegations of maladministration; tribunal adjudication; and judicial review.

A principal issue arising out of the operation of these decision-making processes is their overall quality. Ensuring that these processes are of high quality is important for those individuals directly affected by the decisions produced. It is also important for the general public interest in terms of the ability of such processes effectively to implement policy. A quality decision process is one to which we all aspire—both as recipients of decisions and as members of the general public. But what does the concept of quality mean in the context of administrative justice? And how, if at all, are we to evaluate and assess whether or not the decision processes that we have live up to our aspirations?

The task of seeking to assess and evaluate the operation of the various different techniques of administrative justice which function across the many different contexts of public administration presents administrative-legal scholars with a dauntingly broad research agenda. The objectives of this book are, by comparison, much more modest. Its principal aim is to examine the effectiveness and quality of one technique of administrative justice—tribunal adjudication—in one area of

---

[1] Tribunals, Courts and Enforcement Act 2007 sch 7 para 13(4).

1

public administration—asylum decision-making. This book presents a detailed case-study of asylum adjudication. In doing so, it draws upon empirical research undertaken into the procedure and determination of asylum appeals. In this way, the book sits comfortably within a discrete tradition of administrative law scholarship—that of undertaking detailed studies into the operation of particular tribunal adjudication systems. Other studies within this strand of scholarship have examined tribunal systems operating in contexts such as social security, mental health and education, but there have been few studies of immigration and asylum appeals.[2]

To examine and assess the effectiveness and quality of asylum adjudication, the book identifies a framework for thinking about and investigating adjudicative quality. This framework is constructed by identifying the criteria that together define the quality of a particular tribunal system; that responsible for asylum adjudication. It is then used to examine the degree to which those criteria are fulfilled in practice and the ways in which competing values are balanced against each other. While this framework of values is derived from the context of a particular tribunal and applied specifically in relation to that tribunal, it seeks to offer some insight into the operation of other tribunal systems and the idea of administrative justice more generally.

A second aim of the book is to examine in detail the nature of tribunal decision-making. The focus of this book is specifically upon one aspect of the work of the immigration and asylum appeal tribunal, that of asylum adjudication. In essence, asylum adjudication concerns the task of deciding whether or not a foreign national is entitled to asylum because he will be at risk of persecution, torture, or serious ill-treatment on return to his country of origin. The book examines how decision-makers, in this context Immigration Judges, decide who is and who is not in need of asylum and the inherent difficulties this task presents. This second aim is closely connected to the first since an appreciation of the problematic nature of asylum decision-making must inform an evaluation of the quality and effectiveness of the adjudicative process.

The purpose of this chapter is to set the scene in the following four sections. The first section considers the development of administrative justice, the role and function of tribunal adjudication, and the criteria that together define the concept of quality. The second section situates the study in the context of asylum adjudication by outlining its nature, history, and procedures. The third section details the research methods used to collect the empirical data which is drawn upon while the fourth section provides a brief explanation of the book's structure.

---

[2] See though S Juss, *Discretion and Deviation in the Administration of Immigration Control* (London, Sweet & Maxwell, 1997); M Travers, *The British Immigration Courts: A Study of Law and Politics* (Bristol, Policy Press, 1999).

Quality and Administrative Justice

The Development of Administrative Justice

Over recent years, the profile and importance of the administrative justice system has increased and is now a distinct area of governmental and legislative concern. Alongside the criminal and civil justice systems, the administrative justice system comprises a separate part of the broader justice system in its own right, the principal difference being that it concerns neither criminal prosecution nor civil liability, but administrative-legal decisions that affect individuals in the implementation of public policy. One reason for the enhanced position of administrative justice has been the impetus to reform and improve its processes and systems. Indeed, a persistent concern has been that administrative justice has long been viewed as a disparate collection of individual decision systems which lacked systematic design and were poorly organised. The reform programme commenced with the Leggatt Review of Tribunals in 2001 which proposed that tribunals should be brought together within a unified tribunal system.[3] This was followed in 2004 by a governmental white paper which broadened the policy focus beyond tribunals.[4] This wider strategy has been predicated upon the real world problems that people face, the aim being to develop a range of services and policies that help people, wherever possible, to avoid disputes in the first place, and, where they could not, to provide tailored solutions to resolve disputes as quickly and cost-efficiently as possible. The Tribunals, Courts, and Enforcement Act 2007 has subsequently established a simplified statutory framework of the First-tier and Upper Tribunals to provide coherence and enable future reform.

But how is administrative justice itself to be defined? Broadly speaking, there are two ways of understanding administrative justice. The first approach can be labelled a top-down perspective. It focuses on the external accountability mechanisms by which individuals dissatisfied with initial administrative decisions may challenge them. From this perspective, the role of the courts and judicial review in particular often take centre stage as the principal means of articulating general standards of legality that apply across the disparate range of individual administrative processes. A contrasting approach is labelled as a bottom-up conception of administrative justice. From this perspective, administrative justice concerns the justice inherent in administrative-legal decision-making and the focus is, therefore, the mass of front-line initial decisions and the processes necessary to ensure quality within such processes.

---

[3] A Leggatt, *Tribunals for Users: One System, One Service. The Report of the Review of Tribunals by Sir Andrew Leggatt* (London, The Stationery Office, 2001).

[4] Department for Constitutional Affairs, *Transforming Public Services: Complaints, Redress and Tribunals* (Cm 6243, 2004).

The relative standing of these contrasting conceptions of administrative justice has ebbed and flowed over recent years.[5] The dominance of the first approach focusing on the mechanisms of external control has, to some degree, given way to greater attention being devoted to initial decision-making and the ways in which administrative justice, in the sense of the justice inherent in initial administrative decision-making, might be promoted. There have been various reasons for this. It has increasingly come to be recognised that the impact of external judicial legality upon initial decision-making can vary dramatically. By contrast, a 'bottom-up' approach may promise a better perspective from which to examine the operation of administrative justice and how to ensure quality by focusing upon getting decisions right first time round in the mass of initial decisions rather than putting them right in the much smaller number of disputed decisions. Secondly, there has been a shift in governmental policy on administrative justice.[6] Furthermore, administrative law scholars have increasingly sought to re-orient and broaden the conception of their discipline moving away from a largely court-centred focus on the law of judicial review toward the myriad of administrative agencies with responsibility for the vast majority of official decision-making and the processes that resolve disputes and grievances that arise.

Given its broader focus, the bottom-up conception of administrative justice is clearly welcome, but it also raises various questions. First, where do particular techniques of administrative justice fit in within these two contrasting conceptions? Take tribunals, for instance, which provide the institutional focus for this book and are a well-established technique of administrative justice. They resolve disputes individuals have with administrative agencies by adjudicating appeals against initial administrative decisions. In doing so, tribunals replace the decisions of administrative agencies with their own. Do tribunals sit alongside the courts as another redress mechanism external to administration or are they part of the broader administrative process?

A second set of issues concerns the assessment and evaluation of the effectiveness and the quality of particular techniques of administrative justice such as tribunal adjudication. It can be assumed that the pursuit of quality is a central concern of such decision-making processes; few, if any, decision-making process would consciously aspire otherwise. After all, a quality decision process is one that is legitimate because it can command the confidence of the individuals concerned and of the general public. Indeed, administrative justice in the broader sense—the justice inherent in administrative-legal decision-making—has been defined as those qualities of a decision process that provide arguments for the acceptability or legitimacy of its decisions.[7] But how is quality to be defined? Which criteria

---

[5] M Adler, 'Tribunal Reform: Proportionate Dispute Resolution and the Pursuit of Administrative Justice' (2006) 69 *Modern Law Review* 958, 982.

[6] Department for Constitutional Affairs above n 4 at [1.7] and [2.2].

[7] J Mashaw, *Bureaucratic Justice: Managing Social Security Disability Claims* (New Haven, Yale University Press, 1983) 24–25; M Adler, 'A Socio-legal Approach to Administrative Justice' (2003) 25 *Law & Policy* 323, 329.

together define the desirable attributes of a quality decision process? And how is the operation of a particular system to be assessed against such criteria and what is the optimum balance between competing values? In other words, if administrative justice is to be understood as something more than a convenient label for those decision-making bodies which belong to neither criminal nor civil justice systems, then which normative values or principles might it embody? And how, if at all, can we assess the degree to which such values are fulfilled in any particular area? These questions are addressed shortly, but before doing so, we need to consider the role and function of tribunal adjudication.

Tribunal Adjudication

The development of tribunals has been one of the most notable features of administrative law over the last hundred or so years. The number of individual tribunal jurisdictions has proliferated and only recently have the First-tier and Upper Tribunals been established to provide a coherent framework for the tribunals system. The basic purpose of tribunals is to provide a means by which individuals can appeal against initial negative administrative decisions to an independent judicial body.[8] However, tribunals have suffered from a longstanding ambivalence and uncertainty as to how both their role and function within the broader governmental-constitutional system should be understood. Are they merely court-substitutes or part of the administration? Do tribunals belong to either the judicial or the administrative branch of government?

These questions have been discussed since the development of tribunals.[9] The long-term trend has been for tribunals to come to be seen as part of the judicial system. Tribunals have been viewed primarily as a means of protecting individuals' legal rights by providing them with a legal dispute resolution process. Consequently, the prevalent view has been that tribunals both are and should be informed by legal values and subject to the oversight of the higher courts. This trend has been advanced by influential developments affecting tribunals. In 1957 the Franks committee stated that tribunals were properly to be regarded as machinery for adjudication rather than as part of the machinery of administration.[10] More recently, the restructuring of tribunals into the First-tier and Upper Tribunals has been the principal means of completing this process of embedding tribunals firmly within the broader judicial system.

This differentiation between judicial and administrative functions, and the placing of tribunals firmly in the former domain as opposed to the latter, stemmed from a desire to placate concerns and suspicions over the role of tribunals. After

---

[8] The concern here is with tribunals that determine disputes between individuals and the state as opposed to those tribunals, such as employment tribunals, which adjudicate upon 'party and party' disputes.

[9] See P Cane, *Administrative Tribunals and Adjudication* (Oxford, Hart Publishing, 2009) 30–48.

[10] *Report of the Committee on Administrative Tribunals and Enquiries* (The Franks Report) (Cmnd 218, 1957) [40].

all, a court has no responsibility for implementing policy; it merely acts as an impartial arbiter deciding disputes between the parties involved. However, the distinction between adjudication and administration is suffused with difficulties, which may generate an incomplete or partial way of understanding the role and function of tribunals and provide a misleading basis from which to examine the quality of any particular tribunal system.

One such difficulty concerns the concept of adjudication itself. It has often been assumed that adjudication is entirely separate from the task of administering policy, a distinction supported by the traditional division between law, on the one hand, and politics and administration, on the other. However, adjudicating disputes between individuals and administrative agencies inevitably involves the adjudicator exercising some role in the process of administering and implementing policy. Unlike the courts in judicial review proceedings, tribunals do not merely review whether or not a particular decision is lawful; they are able, indeed obliged, to substitute their own decision for that of the initial administrative decision-maker, whether that decision concerns the entitlement of an individual to some benefit or status. The essence of adjudication is that it is a process by which a dispute between two parties can be formally resolved by an independent and neutral decision-maker. That decision-maker will normally proceed by making findings of facts as regards an individual's particular situation and circumstances, finding the relevant applicable legal rules, and then applying those rules to the facts as found. But the process of adjudicating upon the application of the law in any particular area will normally, if not always, involve the promotion of some socially desired objective, which will be embodied in the legal rules being adjudicated upon. In the context of tribunal appeals from administrative decisions, these legal rules and their socially desirable objectives will concern the policy goal being pursued by government in any particular area of public administration. By adjudicating upon a dispute, the adjudicator will naturally play a role in advancing and implementing the underlying social policy goal.

The force of this point has long been recognised. Administrative law scholars such as William Robson, JAG Griffith, and JA Farmer have argued that it is impossible to draw any clear conceptual distinction between the adjudication of disputes and the administration of public policy.[11] Adjudicating disputes between individuals and a governmental agency will necessarily affect the administration and implementation of the underlying policy. This is because an adjudicator will resolve a dispute by applying the same substantive rules as the administrative

---

[11] WA Robson, *Justice and Administrative Law: A Study of the British Constitution* 3rd edn (London, Stevens, 1951) 1–39, especially at 4 ('It is very difficult to discover any method by which . . . judicial functions can be clearly distinguished from administrative functions'); JAG Griffith, 'Tribunals and Inquiries' (1959) 22 *Modern Law Review* 125, 129 ('There is no reason why the machinery of adjudication should not be part of the machinery for administration. Indeed in one sense it must be precisely that, however independent the tribunals are'); JA Farmer, *Tribunals and Government* (London, Weidenfeld and Nicolson, 1974) 4 (tribunals properly form a part of the broader administrative process). See also RE Wraith and PG Hutchesson, *Administrative Tribunals* (London, Allen and Unwin, 1973) 222–249.

agency, ⬚⬚⬚⬚⬚⬚⬚⬚ embody specific policy goals. Consequently, adjudication and adminis⬚⬚⬚⬚⬚⬚⬚ not polar opposites, but closely intermingled with each other.

A sec⬚⬚⬚⬚⬚⬚ for doubting both the sharp differentiation between administrative a⬚⬚⬚⬚⬚⬚⬚ functions, and the placing of tribunals firmly in the latter category, i⬚⬚⬚⬚⬚⬚⬚ runs against the grain of the development of the modern administrative state. In the context of the modern state, government has taken up the responsibility for making and implementing policy with regard to numerous areas of social life. As Edward Rubin has explained, the concept of the modern administrative state implies that the role and function of government has itself shifted considerably.[12] Government is no longer a passive decision-maker with limited policy goals merely focused upon the preservation of social order. In the context of a modern administrative state, government has assumed responsibility for actively solving various social and economic problems; policy making and implementation have come to define the essence of the modern state. Much of the work of modern government now involves managing large-scale administrative programmes and systems to deliver and implement an enormous number of disparate and complex public policy objectives.

This basic shift in the nature of modern government has produced numerous changes. It has, for instance, generated the intricate and highly differentiated structure of the administrative state, a structure characterised by various administrative agencies, government departments, executive agencies, regulators, inspectors, and tribunals. To implement policy programmes effectively, such bodies are often organised into delivery chains, that is, complex networks of administrative agencies and other organisations that need to work together to achieve and deliver a particular policy objective.[13] Another consequence of the change in the character of modern government has been the use of law as an instrument of social policy. For instance, the growth of the administrative state has generated an enormous increase in rules produced by governmental agencies which are made to further the achievement of policy goals. Likewise, as the scale of governmental activity has increased, adjudication processes have proliferated to enable affected individuals to appeal against initial decisions taken by an administrative agency in order to contest the application of the rules in a particular instance.

There are, of course, many techniques that government uses to implement its policy objectives. For present purposes, the important point is that the development of tribunals as a means of adjudicating upon disputes individuals have with administrative agencies has largely been a function of the development and growth of administrative power and the expansion of the range of policy objectives

---

[12] EL Rubin, *Beyond Camelot: Rethinking Politics and Law for the Modern State* (Princeton/ Oxford, Princeton University Press, 2005).

[13] See National Audit Office and Audit Commission, *Delivering Efficiently: Strengthening the Links in Public Service Delivery Chains* (2005–06 HC 940) 1; M Barber, *Instruction to Deliver* (London, Politico's, 2007) 85–87. For the argument that the development of the modern administrative state has undermined the traditional way of understanding government—that government is divided into three distinct branches, the legislature, the executive, and the judiciary—and that modern government is better understood as comprising a complex and multilevel network of interconnected units, see Rubin ibid at 39–73.

pursued by government. Modern government has assumed responsibility for a wide range of public functions and developed administrative programmes to pursue such functions. As part of this process, government has, in various contexts, established tribunals to adjudicate upon disputes that arise from the administration of those programmes. The principal advantage of adjudication, and usually the principal reason why it is deployed, is that it allows affected individuals to participate in the process by which policy is implemented. As the administrative state has developed to take on new policy objectives, the technique of tribunal adjudication has developed so that individuals affected may have a process by which they can participate in the operations of the state. Tribunals have their historical roots in the development of the administrative state in the early nineteenth century as judicial mechanisms for resolving disputes that arose from the administrative implementation of legislation.[14] With the subsequent expansion of governmental activity, tribunals have proliferated and been brought more fully within the judicial fold.

As a means of enabling individuals to participate in the implementation of policy, the operation of tribunals is usually structured in various ways by established procedures. The individual concerned must receive a negative decision from an administrative agency and then activate the adjudicatory process by lodging a notice of appeal. The adjudicator will hear the appeal to determine the issues contested by the parties. Throughout the process, both the adjudicator and the parties must act in accordance with a set of specialised procedural rules. The adjudicator will then determine the appeal by applying a set of substantive rules which embody the underlying social policy to be implemented. These operations will produce decisions which are legally binding on the parties, and the adjudicator will issue a remedy which will signal that the appeal has been either allowed or dismissed. As an aspect of the broader process for administering social policy, this adjudication procedure should also result in the implementation of policy by determining whether those individuals concerned are entitled to the relevant benefit or status. In the modern administrative state, then, adjudication is best understood not as comprising an exclusively judicial process segregated from broader governmental activities. Rather, it is one amongst many techniques by which public policy is implemented. It is often selected by policy makers when it is considered desirable to establish an institutional procedure by which individuals can directly participate in the implementation of governmental policy.[15]

If these reflections are correct, then a number of points arise. First, the use of adjudication itself requires detailed analysis. If adjudication is properly to be understood as part of the broader process of policy implementation, this invites

[14] HW Arthurs, *'Without the Law': Administrative Justice and Legal Pluralism in Nineteenth Century England* (Toronto, University of Toronto Press, 1985); C Stebbings, *Legal Foundations of Tribunals in Nineteenth Century England* (Cambridge, Cambridge University Press, 2006).
[15] There are, of course, various other non-adjudicatory mechanisms which can be used in order to secure the participation of individuals in the implementation process, such as consultation, complaint processes, and 'user-driven' public services. See House of Commons Public Administration Select Committee, *User Involvement in Public Services* (2007–08 HC 410).

examination of the reasons why it is selected over other techniques as a mechanism for implementing public policy. It also prompts detailed analysis of the effectiveness of adjudication in any particular area of government and normative prescriptions as to how its effectiveness could be enhanced.

Secondly, a more nuanced understanding of the role of administrative tribunals is required. The central rationale for having tribunals is that they provide an independent and judicial process for adjudicating upon disputes that arise in the process of administering public policy. In this way, tribunals provide affected individuals with an institutional process by which they can participate in the implementation of governmental policy. Tribunals are often created when policy makers consider such participation to be desirable. If so, then the outdated dichotomy between adjudication and administration can safely be jettisoned and seen for what it was—an attempt to legitimise the role of tribunals by seeking to assimilate them with courts—but which failed to appreciate that tribunals are not courts because their distinctiveness lies in their adjudicative task within the context of the broader administrative process. To reformulate the view of the Franks committee, adjudication is not wholly distinct and separate from administration; on the contrary, tribunal adjudication is an institutional process by which public policy can be administered.

This way of understanding tribunals has often been resisted because of the concern that it views tribunals merely as appendages of government and, in this way, implies that they are not independent of government. By contrast, a clear distinction between adjudication and administration seems a much better way of emphasising the independence of tribunals and protecting them against undesirable political and administrative influence. But locating tribunal adjudication within the broader context of policy implementation does not imply that tribunals are susceptible to undesirable political influence or that the now statutorily enshrined guarantee of the independence of the tribunal judiciary is of no consequence.[16] Tribunals are not part of the administrative institutional structure in the sense that they are independent judicial bodies which determine appeals against initial administrative decisions. There is normally a clear institutional separation between the administrative agency responsible for initial decision-making and the Tribunal which determines appeals against such decisions. Any adjudicator will need to be separate and neutral from both of the parties involved so that the procedure is fair and commands public confidence. This is often a particularly important consideration when one of the parties involved is itself an administrative agency. Nevertheless, tribunals comprise part of the broader decision-making—and therefore policy implementation—process in the sense that they are able to substitute their own decisions by applying rules which embody specific policy goals. Judicial independence guarantees the position of tribunals as neutral and impartial decision-makers, but it does not mean that tribunals operate in isolation from the underlying governmental programme. The structural independence of

---

[16] Tribunals, Courts and Enforcement Act 2007 s 1.

tribunals from administrative agencies should not, therefore, obscure their role within the wider governmental process.

Understanding tribunals in this way—as a mechanism for administering public policy in particular cases through adjudication—has a number of advantages. First, it provides a more realistic perspective from which to examine the work of tribunals. Tribunals can certainly be viewed collectively on the horizontal plane as exercising an adjudicatory function across different areas of law and administration and, from one perspective, the current restructuring of the tribunals into the First-tier and Upper Tribunals certainly encourages this perspective. Nevertheless, individual tribunals comprise a critical part of broader governmental systems designed to achieve social policy goals, whether it be collecting taxes, issuing welfare benefits, or administering immigration policy. Indeed, this understanding of tribunals comports with the concept of vertical integration which underpins and informs current reforms of the tribunal system. As the Senior President of Tribunals has explained, the idea of vertical integration means that tribunals are just one stage in a broader hierarchical process designed in the public interest to achieve fairness and finality for the individual in the most efficient way possible.[17]

From this perspective, therefore, tribunals comprise one part of the delivery chain by which public policy is implemented. This delivery chain normally commences with the administrative agency responsible for making and administering policy in a particular area. The tribunal segment will then follow by determining appeals against initial negative decisions. Given the discrete policy and administrative influences upon such delivery chains, we can expect that their particular nature and organisation will vary according to context as will the tribunal processes that operate within them.

A second advantage of this understanding of tribunals is that it provides some insight into the nature of the relationships between administrative agencies and tribunals. In general terms, for a delivery chain successfully to implement policy, the relationships between the different organisations need to be actively managed and coordinated. Various techniques or devices will often be required to link up the different agencies involved. For instance, a central government department with responsibility for policy making will usually have strong internal links with an executive agency responsible for operational front-line delivery.[18] Other types of relationships may rely upon contractual or regulatory links; for instance, a government agency may contract with a third-sector, charitable body to deliver public services on its behalf.

However, the relationship between an administrative agency and a tribunal cannot be managed by devices such as internal links or contractual or regulatory links because of the need to ensure that the tribunal remains independent of the agency. The establishment of a tribunal to adjudicate upon appeals against initial admin-

---

[17] R Carnwath, 'Tribunal Justice—A New Start' (a speech given to the Administrative Justice and Tribunals Council annual conference, November 2008) [17].

[18] Such internal links will normally comprise a framework agreement between the government department and the executive agency as well as agreed performance targets.

istrative decisions means that the government is content to allow certain decisions to be made independently of the administrative agency. The administrative agency will be prevented from implementing its decisions unless it can demonstrate to the satisfaction of an independent adjudicator that the decisions are in conformity with a general legal rule. Given the need to maintain tribunal independence, the administrative agency-tribunal relationship will then usually be managed by legal links of common purpose, that is, the two bodies will have parallel missions to work toward a common goal, namely, determining the eligibility of affected persons for the relevant benefit or status for which they have applied. Such links will often exist on a number of different levels. They will almost always include hard-law measures, such as the statutory framework governing the tribunal's jurisdiction, the substantive legal rules specifying the eligibility criteria governing decision-making, and the tribunal's specialised procedural rules. Such links may also include soft-law measures such as non-statutory performance indicators and targets agreed between the relevant government departments which may, for instance, detail the desired throughput of appeals within a given timeframe.

Finally, this way of understanding tribunals has important implications for the way to go about the task of assessing and evaluating the effectiveness and quality of the work that tribunals do. In particular, there is the issue of the values and criteria against which the functioning of tribunals should be assessed. After all, if it was realistic to understand tribunals as institutions both set apart and isolated from the broader governmental process, then the criteria for assessing them would draw exclusively upon legal values, such as fairness, impartiality, and openness. But understanding tribunals as an aspect of the broader policy implementation process means that the range of values influencing them is inevitably widened. In particular, managerial, in addition to justice considerations, will normally play a major role in both the design and operation of a particular adjudication process and therefore also in relation to its evaluation. So, which values might govern tribunals in general and the system of asylum adjudication in particular?

Considering Quality

An initial difficulty is that the search for specific criteria for evaluating the effectiveness and quality of a tribunal adjudication system is problematic because the notion of administrative justice is itself both elusive and transient. Administrative justice does not embody any fundamental or invariant principles against which decision-making systems can be evaluated; the principles and standards of administrative justice vary both with context and over time. They may also be inconsistent with each other and contingent in their nature and implementation, rather than being of universal application.[19] As Ison has observed, administrative justice

---

[19] See P Nonet, *Administrative Justice: Advocacy and Change in a Government Agency* (New York, Russell Sage, 1969); M Partington, 'Restructuring Administrative Justice? The Redress of Citizens' Grievances' (1999) 52 *Current Legal Problems* 173, 178–184.

should not be considered as a subject on its own, but rather as a body of thought informing the institutional design of a particular decision system. If so, then the values and standards of administrative justice might exist only in the context of the particular policy goals, policies, and methods of the adjudicating body.[20] As administrative-legal decision systems operate within their own particular political contexts, the values which inform them will vary accordingly.[21]

These are cogent points. Despite a renewed policy focus on the administrative justice system as a whole, that system is comprised of many different individual decision processes each of which operates within their own particular political and administrative context. What works in one system may not necessarily work elsewhere. Furthermore, the particular issues relevant to the assessment of the quality of administrative justice processes also vary. For instance, studies have investigated the reasons why unsuccessful welfare claimants are, on the whole, reluctant to challenge negative decisions.[22] There has also been much debate over the extent to which alternative dispute resolution (ADR) mechanisms, such as mediation, conciliation and early neutral evaluation, can be appropriately utilised to resolve disputes individuals have with administrative agencies.[23] While these two issues have arisen in relation to some contexts (such as homelessness, social security, and education), they are not salient concerns in the context of asylum adjudication. This is because asylum adjudication is distinguished by a high rate of challenge by individuals dissatisfied with adverse decisions. Furthermore, there is virtually no scope for the use of ADR processes to achieve a compromise solution or attempt to split the difference because of the zero-sum nature of asylum adjudication: applicants can either be returned to their country of origin safely or they cannot.

To identify criteria with which to evaluate the quality of administrative-legal decision systems, it is best to consider the experience of an individual system rather than to attempt to identify generally applicable standards; the research agenda is an inevitably wide and challenging one. Nevertheless, might it be possible to identify some core values that together define the concept of quality irrespective of context? If so, then which values are relevant? Furthermore, is it possible to derive any insights that might assist with an assessment of asylum adjudication?

At its irreducible core, the quality of an administrative-legal process is informed by four values: its propensity to produce accurate decisions; the fairness of the pro-

[20] TG Ison ' "Administrative Justice": Is It Such a Good Idea?' in M Harris and M Partington (eds), *Administrative Justice in the 21st Century* (Oxford, Hart Publishing, 1999) 33–34.

[21] Cf Wraith and Hutchesson above n 11 at 17: 'The British constitution tries to keep law and politics apart . . . but administrative tribunals inhabit a twilight world where the two intermingle'.

[22] M Adler and J Gulland, *Tribunals Users' Experiences, Perceptions and Expectations: A Literature Review* (London, Council on Tribunals, 2003) 3–15; D Cowan and S Halliday, *The Appeal of Internal Review: Law, Administrative Justice and the (Non-) emergence of Disputes* (Oxford, Hart Publishing, 2003).

[23] See Department for Constitutional Affairs above n 4 at [2.11]–[2.12]; M Supperstone, D Stilitz, and C Sheldon, 'ADR and Public Law' [2006] *Public Law* 299; C Hay, K McKenna, and T Buck, *Evaluation of Early Neutral Evaluation Alternative Dispute Resolution in the Social Security and Child Support Tribunal* (London, Ministry of Justice Research Series 2/10, 2010).

cedures by which decisions are made; the resources needed to fund the decision process; and the timeliness of decision-making. If accuracy concerns the substantive decisions, or outputs, produced, then fairness conditions the process by which the inputs are fed into the decision system. Both of these aspects have cost or resource implications and both are affected by the desired length of time to be taken to produce decisions. The quality of the decision process and its outputs are defined by the relationships between these four values.

Accuracy refers to the degree to which a decision concerning an individual's circumstances properly and correctly reflects the application of the relevant eligibility criteria with those facts. The task of making accurate decisions requires the decision-maker to collect the relevant facts concerning an individual's circumstances and then correctly apply those facts to the relevant eligibility criteria. Accuracy has been described as the primary demand of administrative justice because, irrespective of what other desirable attributes a decision-making process might embody, its decisions are unlikely to be acceptable if they are wrong.[24] It is just as much in the interests of the public as it is in the interests of affected individuals that decisions are accurate, that is, that those individuals entitled to a particular benefit or status receive it and, conversely, that those not so entitled do not. Inaccurate decisions represent not only a failure to ensure individuals are awarded the entitlements to which they are due, but also a failure to implement the underlying policy. However, despite its importance, accuracy is often a difficult value to pin down, especially when the decisions to be taken are fundamentally about facts rather than law and where there may be considerable evidential uncertainty surrounding the establishment of those facts.

The second value, fairness, concerns the procedures by which decisions are to be made. Procedural fairness is commonly understood as guaranteeing that affected individuals have a real opportunity to participate in a decision-making process carried out by a neutral decision-maker. It also conditions other aspects of a decision process such as the posture of a decision-maker when collecting facts (adversarial, inquisitorial, or enabling?) and the degree to which reasons should be given. If decisions are to be accurate, then the processes through which the facts and information are to be gathered must be fair. Fair procedures can then have an instrumental role in promoting accurate decisions and also a non-instrumental role as well in promoting the dignity and self-respect of the parties by enabling them to participate in a decision process, irrespective of the outcome. Furthermore, a fair procedure will establish and maintain public confidence in the decision system.

The cost or resource implications of an administrative-legal process is a vital consideration. Virtually every public policy decision must seek justification in terms of both the cost to the taxpayer and value for money. In this respect, the administrative justice system is just like any part of governmental administration.

---

[24] R Sainsbury, 'Administrative Justice: Discretion and Procedure in Social Security Decision-Making' in K Hawkins (ed), *The Uses of Discretion* (Oxford, Oxford University Press, 1992) 302.

Simply because it concerns the judicial segment of a broader administrative process does not mean that it is immune from scrutiny as to the levels of expenditure it receives and the value for money it provides. A quality process needs to be funded appropriately, but public resources are scarce and under pressure from competing claims. It is, therefore, necessary to secure an efficient relationship between the outputs of the adjudication process and the resources used to produce them.

Finally, there is the timeliness of decision-making. The amount of time taken to produce decisions is important for both the individuals concerned and in terms of policy implementation. Excessively long decision-making processes can mean delayed policy implementation and increased costs for government and uncertainty for the individuals concerned. On the other hand, too great an emphasis upon speed and promptness may place those individuals at a disadvantage and reduce the quality of the process and its outputs. The processing of appeals by tribunals is often measured against key performance indicators which specify that a certain proportion of their caseloads should be determined within a desired target time. But precisely how much time should be allocated to the processing of appeals? And what are the implications of timeliness in relation to other values?

The values identified here are not intended to be exhaustive. It is possible to identify various other values that inform decision-making systems. For instance, as high volume decision systems are staffed by a large number of decisional personnel, there is a risk that like cases may not be treated alike; consistency, therefore, often emerges as a desirable value. Moreover, the importance of other values may vary between the different techniques for providing administrative justice and their context. For instance, the independence of the tribunal judiciary has already been noted, but it is not a relevant value in the context of internal administrative review by superior officers of decisions already taken by their subordinates. Furthermore, the application of generally applicable standards can vary between individual systems. The obligation on virtually all decision-makers to give reasons promotes the value of rationality, but in some contexts detailed reasons are required whereas in other contexts it will only be necessary to provide summary reasons. Nevertheless, despite the existence of other principles and the variations between different decision-making systems, these four values—accuracy, fairness, cost, and timeliness—might serve as a useful starting point for considering the quality of a specific decision system.

One feature of this approach is that it recognises the importance of both justice and managerial considerations in the design and operation of administrative-legal decision systems. Justice considerations typically focus upon the need to ensure that individuals receive their entitlements and that they are subject to an open, transparent, and independent decision-making process. By contrast, managerial considerations are concerned with the collective interest in achieving policy implementation. Such an orientation will typically prioritise values such as the cost-efficiency of a process, its effectiveness, and its timeliness. The broader idea of administrative justice is necessarily informed by both sets of considerations; any concept of administrative justice that is based upon a solely individualistic premise will always risk undermining the achievement of the collective interest for which any administrative programme exists.

Another feature is that there is no necessary hierarchy or gradation as to the relative significance of these values. All of them are equally important. At the same time, there is often, if not usually, an inherent tension between them because different values frequently pull in different directions. Take a mundane example: calls to reduce the operating costs of a particular decision process and/or increase its timeliness could be accomplished by requiring decision-makers to make tick-box decisions following the most rudimentary procedure. But such changes would instil little confidence as to whether the process was fair or whether the decisions were correct. Likewise, proposals to enhance the fairness of a decision process irrespective of the additional resources required, the additional length of time imposed, or the marginal possible improvement to decisional accuracy are unlikely to find favour with policy makers. As Paul Stockton has noted, it is often assumed that the values of fairness, accuracy, and cost-effectiveness, and timeliness are essentially linear in nature; a fair process is needed to produce accurate decisions and this, in turn, needs to be adequately resourced and given sufficient time to function. But, in practice, these values tend to operate within a much more complex set of relationships in which a change to one will invariably influence other values.[25] Indeed, the values may impact upon and influence one another in such a variety of different ways that there may be no simple answers as to the proper relationships between them or to the problems that they pose.

One consequence of this is that few, if any, adjudication systems are able completely to satisfy all the demands placed upon them. It is likely that there will always be concerns that a particular decision process is deficient in one way or another, that one value or another is being accorded too high a priority at the expense of other equally important values. The design effort to attain the optimum degree of quality is, therefore, one which is likely, depending on one's perspective, to gratify and disappoint in equal measure. Nevertheless, because individuals lodge appeals to tribunals to adjudicate their disputes and because governmental policy needs to be implemented, some sort of workable decision process has to function, however compromised and difficult that may be in practice. Inevitably, competing values must be traded-off with each other as any effort to promote one value will often only be capable of being achieved by moderating the achievement of other values, but it can be difficult to say whether the right balance has been attained as it may be impossible to reach any objective judgment as to the desirability of the trade-offs reached. The question as to what the right balance between competing values is or should be may also be a highly political issue as different views may be held as to what weight ought to be accorded to one value over others. However, examining the compromises obtained may sensitise us to the complexities and difficulties raised by the task of seeking to manage an effective and high quality system of administrative justice.

---

[25] P Stockton, *Proportionate Dispute Resolution: What are the Options?* (a paper given at a Nuffield Foundation Administrative Justice Seminar, 23 January 2006).

While this approach might appear to be pessimistic, it pr￼ ￼alistic perspective from which to analyse the imperfect and messy co￼ ￼of tribunal adjudication. But what of the values that inform the partic￼ ￼al system with which this book is concerned, namely, the system of ￼ ￼eals? And how are we to evaluate this specific adjudication process? Before addressing these questions, it is necessary to have some sense of the nature, history, and process of asylum decision-making.

Asylum Adjudication

Asylum Decision-Making and Immigration Control

The right to seek asylum provides an emergency route to safety for those foreign nationals who would be at risk of persecution or serious ill-treatment on return to their country of origin. From the perspective of individuals seeking protection, a claim for asylum concerns the protection of some of their most basic and fundamental human rights—the right to be free from persecution or ill-treatment and, in some instances, the right to life itself. At the same time, this right to seek asylum cuts across one of the defining features of the modern state: its ability to control entry into its physical territory. From the governmental perspective, asylum concerns not only its legal obligations to provide protection where necessary; it also poses a threat to immigration control. Asylum adjudication raises the constant problem that the right to seek asylum is susceptible to abuse by those who do not qualify for entry under ordinary immigration procedures, but who nevertheless wish to secure entry. The inherent problem is that the state's efforts to secure immigration control may, in turn, exclude those who genuinely need asylum.

The fundamental issue posed by asylum adjudication is this: that of ensuring that those at risk on return are afforded protection whilst simultaneously ensuring that those not at risk are prevented from using asylum as a backdoor route to entry. The pervasive and intractable concern is whether the system has erected barriers so high that those in need of protection are unable to succeed or whether the system is so lax that it is susceptible to abuse by those not so in need. This tension raises particularly acute difficulties for the political, administrative, and legal systems which cannot be resolved, but managed and then only with considerable difficulty.

A further feature of asylum adjudication is the inherent tension between governmental authority and legal control. An important tool utilised by government to administer immigration control is that of authority, 'the ability to command and prohibit, commend and permit, through recognised procedures and identifying symbols'.[26] The decision-making context is, therefore, informed by a strongly

---

[26] CC Hood and HZ Margetts, *The Tools of Government in the Digital Age* (Basingstoke, Palgrave Macmillan, 2007) 50.

authority-based relationship between government and foreign nationals. At the same time, because of the rights at stake and the adverse consequences of wrong decisions, asylum adjudication now occurs within a heavily legalised environment. There is a high rate of legal challenge against negative decisions, which can both prolong the decision process and impose additional costs.

The Development of Asylum Decision-Making

Asylum decision-making has not always been conducted within a legalised framework. As a signatory state to the Refugee Convention, 1951, the UK is under a legal obligation to consider whether individuals seeking asylum qualify, but the Convention does not itself prescribe which particular procedures are to be adopted for the determination of refugee status. Before the 1970s, individualised asylum decision-making was virtually unknown in the UK. Asylum decisions were matters of high policy rather than administrative routine. They were usually taken en masse in response to specific migratory events; for instance, the UK admitted thousands of Hungarian refugees following the 1956 Hungarian uprising and Ugandan Asians following Idi Amin's expulsion order in 1972.[27] However, by the late 1980s a number of factors had coalesced to establish an individualised decision-making process: the end of the cold war, increased migratory pressures, and the continuing risk of persecution suffered by individuals in Africa, Asia, eastern Europe and elsewhere. With these pressures, decision-making was devolved from the Secretary of State and Parliament to officials within the Home Office. Claims would be initially considered by governmental officials: applicants were interviewed and then decisions produced.

Given the silence of the Refugee Convention upon the procedures for determining refugee status, it would have been perfectly possible for the UK to have left decision-making entirely in the hands of the responsible administrative agency, the Home Office, and not to establish any right of appeal against initial negative decisions. This was the position until 1993, but it was not universally accepted to be a desirable state of affairs. For years, various proposals for the establishment of a full in-country right of appeal in asylum cases had been advanced.[28] The Home Office's rejection of such proposals was based upon the concern that any appeal process would be used by unsuccessful claimants to challenge and delay unwelcome

---

[27] See T Kushner and K Knox, *Refugees in an Age of Genocide: Global, National and Local Perspectives during the Twentieth Century* (London, Frank Cass, 1999). Until the Aliens Act 1905, the UK Government did not take asylum decisions simply because it had no policy of immigration control. See B Porter, *The Refugee Question in Mid-Victorian Politics* (Cambridge, Cambridge University Press, 1979). A contemporary account of asylum decision-making by the Immigration Board, established by the 1905 Act, is to be found in MJ Landa, *The Alien Problem and its Remedy* (London, King & Son, 1911). See also E Troup, *The Home Office* (London, Putnam's, 1925) 142–155.

[28] House of Commons Home Affairs Committee, *Refugees and Asylum, with special reference to the Vietnamese* (1984–85 HC 72) [95]–[105]; M Connelly, 'Refugees and Asylum-seekers: Proposals for Policy Changes' in A Dummett (ed), *Towards a Just Immigration Policy* (London, Cobden Trust, 1986) 159, 163–164.

decisions and thereby generate an increase in unmeritorious claims.[29] In the absence of an in-country right of appeal, the only legal means of challenging decisions was by way of judicial review. The initial judicial attitude was one of restraint: asylum decisions were to be made by the Home Office without judicial oversight by the courts.[30] However, the courts subsequently changed their approach. For instance, in 1987 the House of Lords recognised that 'the most fundamental of all human rights is the individual's right to life and, when an administrative decision under challenge is said to be one which may put the applicant's life at risk, the basis of the decision must surely call for the most anxious scrutiny'.[31] The Court of Appeal subsequently noted that 'asylum decisions are of such moment that only the highest standards of fairness will suffice'.[32] Following this change of judicial attitude and an increasing number of unsuccessful asylum applicants seeking to challenge negative decisions by way of judicial review, the courts' caseload increased as did the length of the decision process.[33] A further problem with judicial review is that it is ill-equipped to resolve what is so often at issue in asylum cases—factual disputes as to whether an individual would be at risk on return. The Home Office, therefore, decided to establish a comprehensive in-country right of appeal for individuals who had been initially refused asylum. The policy rationale for this was two-fold. Establishing asylum appeals would provide procedural simplicity and finality by reducing resort to judicial review. Secondly, an appeals process would enable individuals affected to participate directly in the decision-making process and decisions would be taken by an independent and judicial body. A right of appeal to the pre-existing immigration appeals system, comprising the Immigration Appellate Authority and the Immigration Appeal Tribunal, was then created in 1993.[34]

During this period the number of asylum applications continued to rise. The 1990s are likely to be remembered, amongst other things, as the asylum decade, one of 'extraordinary human displacement' which prompted the movement of thousands of individuals to western countries to seek asylum.[35] Asylum became a

---

[29] Home Office, *A Report on the Work of the Immigration and Nationality Department* (London, Home Office, 1984) 25; Home Office, *The Government Reply to the Third Report from the Home Affairs Committee* (Cmnd 9626, 1985) 20–22.

[30] See *Ali (DM) v Immigration Appeal Tribunal* [1973] Imm AR 33, 35 (CA) (Lord Denning MR): 'the proper person to consider a claim to political asylum is the Home Secretary . . . His decision is final'; *R v Secretary of State for the Home Department, ex parte Bugdaycay* [1986] Imm AR 8, 16 (CA) (Neill LJ): the investigation of refugee status 'might involve the consideration of foreign policy and the assessment of regimes in foreign countries . . . with which a court of law would be ill-equipped to deal'. See also C Vincenzi, *Crown Powers, Subjects and Citizens* (London, Pinter, 1998) 150–151. For criticism, see GL Peiris, 'Judicial Review and Immigration Policy: Emerging Trends' [1988] *Legal Studies* 201, 226.

[31] *R v Secretary of State for the Home Department, ex parte Bugdaycay* [1987] AC 514, 531 (Lord Bridge) (HL).

[32] *Secretary of State for the Home Department v Thirukumar* [1989] Imm AR 402, 414 (Bingham LJ) (CA).

[33] R Thomas, 'The Impact of Judicial Review on Asylum' [2003] *Public Law* 479, 484–487.

[34] Asylum and Immigration Appeals Act 1993. See C Randall, 'An Asylum Policy for the UK' in S Spencer (ed), *Strangers and Citizens: A Positive Approach to Migrants and Refugees* (London, Rivers Oram Press, 1994) 220–226.

[35] AC Helton, *The Price of Indifference: Refugees and Humanitarian Action in the New Century* (Oxford, Oxford University Press, 2002) 18.

Table 1: Asylum applications and appeals 2000–2008[1]

	2000	2001	2002	2003	2004	2005	2006	2007	2008
Asylum claims lodged	80,135	71,365	84,130	49,405	33,960	25,710	23,610	23,430	25,930
Number of initial decisions	109,205	120,950	83,540	64,940	46,020	27,395	20,930	21,775	19,400
Grants of refugee status	10,375	11,450	8,270	3,865	1,565	1,940	2,170	3,545	3,725
Grants of ELR/HP/DL[2]	11,495	20,190	20,135	7,210	3,995	2,800	2,305	2,200	2,170
Refusals of refugee status and ELR/HP/DL	75,680	89,310	55,130	53,865	40,465	22,655	16,460	16,030	13,505
Appeals determined	19,395	43,415	64,405	81,725	55,975	33,440	15,955	14,935	10,720
Appeals allowed (success rate %)	3,340 (17%)	8,155 (19%)	13,875 (22%)	16,070 (20%)	10,845 (19%)	5,870 (17%)	3,540 (22%)	3,385 (23%)	2,475 (23%)
Removals	8,980	9,285	10,740	13,005	12,595	13,730	16,330	12,705	12,040

[1] Home Office, *Control of Immigration: Statistics United Kingdom 2000–2008*.
[2] ELR: Exceptional leave to remain; HP: Humanitarian Protection; DL: Discretionary Leave.

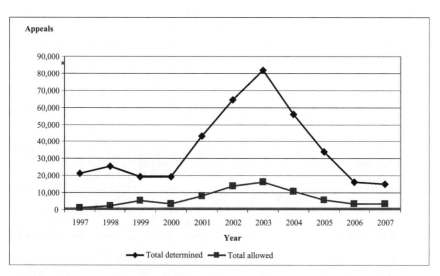

Figure 1: Asylum appeals 1997–2007

major issue of public concern and the government came under pressure to manage the system more effectively. However, the capacity of the immigration bureaucracy to process asylum claims diminished precisely because of the volume of applicants.[36] At times both initial and appellate decision processes have appeared to be virtually on the verge of collapse under the volume of claims and appeals.

This increase in applications prompted a number of responses from the Home Office. One response has been to make it more difficult for foreign nationals to enter the country to claim asylum. As asylum applicants cannot normally lawfully enter the UK to claim asylum, they are often compelled to enter unlawfully; by introducing tougher administrative enforcement of immigration control such as pre-entry checks and carriers' liability, government can seek to reduce the number of people seeking asylum. Other tactics have been to reduce the availability of social support offered to asylum claimants and attempts to increase the removal of failed asylum seekers. However, the rate of removals has rarely kept pace with the number of failed applicants, raising concerns that the lack of effective enforcement renders decision-making otiose. For instance, in 2006, it was noted that 'on current performance, it will take many years to remove failed asylum seekers, undermining the whole asylum application process'.[37] In the same year, it emerged that some 450,000 legacy cases remained within the Home Office and that, in many instances, these claimants had already been waiting several years for an initial decision.

A fourth response has been to ensure that the decision-making process operates in a sufficiently swift manner so that delay in the process will not itself encourage false applications. The asylum appeals process has itself been subject to regular legislative restructuring, more than any other tribunal system, to reduce delays, increase efficiency, and promote finality.[38] The existence of the statutory appeals process did not, however, prevent many applicants from seeking judicial review of tribunal decisions, a phenomenon often seen by the Home Office as an attempt by refused applicants to frustrate the operation of the process and by others as a necessary corrective against inadequate decision-making. Further changes to the tribunal structure occurred in 2004 when the Government made a controversial and ultimately aborted attempt to oust judicial review of tribunal decisions.[39] The result was the unification of the appeal structure in the single tier Asylum and Immigration Tribunal (AIT), which operated its own internal process for reconsidering initial appeal decisions with an onward right of appeal to the Court of Appeal.[40] In 2009,

---

[36] House of Commons Home Affairs Committee, *Asylum Applications* (2003–04 HC 218); National Audit Office, *Improving the Speed and Quality of Asylum Decisions* (2003–04 HC 535).

[37] House of Commons Public Accounts Committee, *Returning Failed Asylum Applicants* (2005–06 HC 620) 4. See also House of Commons Home Affairs Committee, *Asylum Removals* (2002–03 HC 654); National Audit Office, *Returning Failed Asylum Applicants* (2005–06 HC 76).

[38] Asylum and Immigration Act 1996; Immigration and Asylum Act 1999; Nationality, Immigration and Asylum Act 2002; Asylum and Immigration (Treatment of Claimants, etc) Act 2004; Immigration, Asylum and Nationality Act 2006; The Transfer of Functions of the Asylum and Immigration Tribunal Order SI 2010/21.

[39] R Rawlings, 'Review, Revenge and Retreat' (2005) 68 *Modern Law Review* 378.

[40] Asylum and Immigration (Treatment of Claimants, etc) Act 2004, s 26. See R Thomas, 'After the Ouster: Review and Reconsideration in a Single Tier Tribunal' [2006] *Public Law* 674.

the Home Office announced that the appeal system would undergo a further restructuring by transferring it into the two-tier appellate structure of the First-tier and Upper Tribunals in 2010.[41] Despite the reduction in the number of asylum claims, by 2009, one might be forgiven for thinking that asylum claims had colonised a substantial part of the legal system. After social security appeals, immigration and asylum appeals was the second largest tribunal system and staffed by over 700 members. Furthermore, asylum accounted for a substantial proportion of the Administrative Court's caseload while the Court of Appeal received and determined more appeals from the AIT than any other court or tribunal. The transfer of the AIT into the First-tier and Upper Tribunals (Immigration and Asylum Chamber) in 2010 was designed to reduce the burden of the high immigration and asylum caseload on the higher courts.

This, then, is the broader context in which the system of asylum adjudication has developed. There is intense political pressure on government to process claims in order to maintain immigration control. There are the difficulties of administrative organisation and the challenges posed by seeking to rectify past administrative failure. There is also the need to ensure that claims and appeals are assessed carefully. Given the importance of decisions, many unsuccessful appellants pursue onward rights of challenge. At the same time, such high rates of challenge create concerns as to the timeliness of the process and have prompted repeated attempts to modify the decision process to reduce delays, thereby creating concerns that fairness is being sacrificed to efficiency.

The Asylum Decision Process

What, then, is the process by which asylum decisions are made? While the right to seek asylum is provided for by the Refugee Convention, it is left up to each contracting state to decide upon the appropriate procedure to determine claims.[42] In 2005, the member states of the European Union agreed a directive on the minimum standards of procedures for granting and withdrawing refugee status; more recently, the European Commission has proposed to recast this directive to achieve a higher degree of harmonisation in asylum procedures across member states.[43] However, in the UK, much of the administrative and appellate processes by which claims and then appeals are handled have been devised by the Home Office. What follows is a rudimentary description of the asylum process from which its many nuances and variations have been omitted.

---

[41] Home Office, *Immigration Appeals: Response to Consultation—Fair Decisions; Faster Justice* (London, Home Office UKBA and Tribunals Service, 2009).

[42] United Nations High Commissioner for Refugees (UNHCR), *Handbook on Determining Refugee Status* (Geneva, UNHCR, 1992) [189].

[43] Council Directive 2005/85/EC on minimum standards on procedures in Member States for granting and withdrawing refugee status, OJ L 326/13 of 13 December 2005 as transposed into UK law; European Commission, *Proposal for a Directive on Minimum Standards on Procedures in Member States for Granting and Withdrawing International Protection*, COM(2009) 554.

The process of asylum decision-making is both an administrative and legal one. Claims are considered initially by the United Kingdom Border Agency of the Home Office. An asylum claim may be made at any time by a foreign national who is present in the country. Some individuals may claim asylum just after their arrival; other claimants may have been in the country for sometime. An asylum claimant may have entered the UK legally on some form of immigration status (such as a student or visitor visa). Alternatively, a claimant may have overstayed his visa or entered illegally. The process for claiming asylum will depend on when the claim was made. Someone who seeks asylum immediately on arrival will apply at the port of entry. Alternatively, someone currently present in the UK will apply to a Home Office screening unit. Either way, the asylum process will commence by an initial screening interview to establish the claimant's nationality and identity and to take fingerprints. The claimant will be interviewed by a Home Office caseworker. Claimants may be represented at their interviews at their own expense. Before 2005 asylum claimants could receive publicly funded representation for the asylum interview, but this has now been withdrawn in most cases. The courts have, however, held that asylum interviews should normally be tape-recorded.[44]

Part of the difficulty of the asylum process within the Home Office has often stemmed from the lack of coherence throughout the process: one official would interview a claimant; another would make a decision on their claim; while a third official, a Home Office presenting officer, would appear before the Tribunal. In 2005, the Home Office introduced the New Asylum Model under which a single case owner deals with every aspect of the application from beginning to end in order to strengthen the management of asylum claims. Since 2007, all new asylum applications have been managed under the New Asylum Model. If the Home Office decides to refuse an asylum claim, then it will issue a letter detailing the reasons for refusal.

Unlike some other administrative decision-making processes, there is no system of internal review of initial refusal decisions. The next stage in the process is for unsuccessful claimants to appeal. Around 70 per cent of asylum claimants refused initially lodge appeals. The appeal stage is the longest element of the broader decision process from initial application to conclusion and the Home Office's focus has long been upon speeding up the process. The Home Office has a high level Public Service Agreement target to ensure that 90 per cent of all asylum cases are finally resolved within six months.[45] As its contribution to this overarching target, the Tribunal works under a target to ensure that 75 per cent of asylum appeals are determined within six weeks and 85 per cent within 12 weeks.[46] Appeals are normally processed within the following timeframe. Two weeks after an appeal has been lodged, the Tribunal will hold a case management review

---

[44] *R (Dirshe) v Secretary of State for the Home Department* [2005] EWCA Civ 421; [2005] Imm AR 319.

[45] HM Treasury, *2007 Pre-Budget Report and Comprehensive Spending Review: Meeting the Aspirations of the British People* (Cm 7227, 2007), 'PSA Delivery Agreement 3: Ensure controlled, fair migration that protects the public and contributes to economic growth' [3.14].

[46] Tribunals Service, *Annual Report and Accounts 2008–09* (2008–09 HC 599) 118.

hearing to ensure that the appeal is ready to proceed. After another two weeks, the appeal will proceed to a substantive hearing where it will be heard by an Immigration Judge. The Tribunal has a fact-based, merits appeal jurisdiction. Appeals are determined through oral hearings which appellants normally attend. While asylum appellants may be represented, publicly funded representation is restricted. To receive such representation, an appellant must pass the 'merits test': be judged as having a 40 per cent or greater chance of success.[47] The Home Office will be represented by either a Presenting Officer or the case-owner. Appeal hearings are conducted on an adversarial basis, but this can vary depending on the presence and quality of representation. The appellant will present his own evidence and be cross-examined. Following the hearing, the Immigration Judge must produce a determination within 10 days. This will contain the reasons for the decision reached. The next stage in the process is that of onward rights of challenge; the unsuccessful party—either the appellant or the Home Office—may challenge this decision on the basis that it contains an error of law. Such reviews are undertaken by a Senior Immigration Judge. If it is concluded that there may be an error of law, then the appeal will be reconsidered within the Tribunal.

Quality and Asylum Adjudication

How is the concept of quality in asylum adjudication best approached? The range of different values that might influence the quality of a tribunal process have already been adumbrated and we need to consider whether they are applicable in relation to asylum adjudication. But before proceeding further we must note some possible objections against the whole nature of the inquiry being pursued here.

One such objection might be that it is important not to accept the use of tribunals at face-value. Tribunals may, insofar as they embody an independent and judicial process, enable individuals to participate in decision-making. But their real value, it has been argued, lies in their symbolic and expressive functions. According to this perspective, tribunals may be created to reassure both individual appellants and the public by providing a merely symbolic appearance of legality and thereby a cloak of legal respectability, but without offering much by way of legal substance. In this way, tribunals offer the appearance of participation in order to defuse political opposition to controversial policies. Tribunals are then a device by which the symbols of the judicial process can be manipulated by government in order to obtain the quiescence of individuals who have little option but to comply with that process.[48] In short, tribunal appeals are a legal ritual.

This critique has been previously applied to the immigration appeals process and, it might be argued, holds equal, if not more, weight in relation to asylum

---

[47] This test does not apply in Scotland.

[48] JL Jowell, *Law and Bureaucracy: Administrative Discretion and the Limits of Legal Action* (New York, Dunellen Publishing, 1975) 26; T Prosser, 'Poverty, Ideology and Legality: Supplementary Benefit Appeal Tribunals and their Predecessors' (1977) 4 *British Journal of Law and Society* 39.

appeals.[49] Given the intense media and political concern over asylum, government is unlikely to relinquish its control but may desire to benefit from the appearance of legitimacy that an appeal process provides. If so, then any endeavour to examine the quality of such a process is naively misguided, as it fails to appreciate that in reality this ersatz process exists to service other ulterior ends. It has, for instance, frequently been argued that the Tribunal has itself taken up the role as a subsidiary gatekeeper in the context of the policy goal of controlling migration rather than operating as an independent check against initial decisions.[50]

This is not the only objection that can be made against the inquiry being attempted here. From a different perspective, informed by public choice theory, the appeals process might be viewed as a means of maximising the self-interest of those individuals—judges, representatives, agency officials, expert witnesses, and tribunal administrators—who earn their living from it. Given their role and employment within the appeals process, it might be argued that such individuals may be motivated by their own self-interest. In this sense, the appeals process is simply another part of the asylum industry, the people and organisations whose work and employment depends upon the flows of foreign nationals seeking asylum. It is perhaps not surprising that such perspectives have often been canvassed as the asylum appeals process is itself particularly prone to generating cynical attitudes about the purposes and competence of government and the motivation of individuals.

The approach adopted is obviously contingent upon one's broader viewpoint on asylum policy and adjudication, but the difficulty is that neither of the above perspectives is able to capture the complex reality of the asylum appeals process. Can the asylum tribunal really be understood as providing only a symbolic appearance of legality when it allows approximately 20 per cent of appeals? Is it really conceivable that the individuals who work within the process do so solely for their own benefit and do not attempt to operate a system that is geared up to assessing whether appellants qualify for international protection? Decision-makers may be acutely conscious of a governmental desire that they dismiss appeals and feel under pressure to hear appeals quickly, but does that mean that they readily succumb? Are judges really likely to spin cases out intentionally in order to increase their workload? Perhaps it is more likely that they are motivated by a desire to make the best decisions that they can within the constraints within which they work. Of course, the appeals system, like most others, suffers from various problems and difficulties. The quality of the justice it dispenses, again like virtually all other systems, may be imperfect and compromised. Furthermore, the system's almost constant re-organisation might indicate that government has been motivated by ensuring that the process operates with sufficient speed, perhaps more

---

[49] See, eg, B Hepple, 'Aliens and Administrative Justice: the Dutschke Case' (1971) 34 *Modern Law Review* 501; L Bridges, 'Legality and Immigration Control' (1975) 2 *British Journal of Law and Society* 221.

[50] IA Macdonald, *Immigration Law and Practice in the United Kingdom*, 7th edn (London, LexisNexis, 2008) i.

speed than is actually necessary. But does this necessarily mean that the search for quality is simply a non-starter, that this adjudication system is necessarily a lost cause and incapable of improvement?

If the answer to all these questions is 'no', then an alternative approach is required, one which takes seriously the competing pressures under which the process operates in the attempt to assess quality. Such an approach would need to recognise explicitly the inherent ambiguities involved in assessing whether certain values are fulfilled and the inherent compromises involved in mediating conflicting values. As the above discussion indicates, the quality of tribunal adjudication is largely a function of how tensions between competing values are managed. In the context of asylum adjudication, the task of making accurate decisions, distinguishing between those deserving and those not deserving of protection, emerges at the centre of administrative justice. Accuracy assumes enormous significance because of the consequences of incorrect decisions for the individuals concerned and the public interest. Recognising the importance of accuracy is, though, the easy part; the more difficult inquiry comes in examining how, if at all, it can be assessed and secured. In light of the volume of appeals and decision-makers, consistency, the like treatment of like cases, also arises as a desirable value. However, the need to subject each case to the most anxious scrutiny rubs up against the similarly pressing managerial need to ensure that cases are considered as quickly and efficiently as possible. This tension pervades virtually all aspects of the adjudication process and can be seen, for instance, in the overriding requirement of the Tribunal's procedural rules that appeals be handled as fairly, quickly, and efficiently as possible.[51] The tension also provokes much stress and controversy with the appeals process being simultaneously admonished, from entirely different viewpoints, for both its unfairness to appellants *and* its inefficiency for not processing appeals quickly and cheaply.

Examining the ways in which competing values arise and are traded-off will provide much of the focus of the book and will require analysis of various aspects of the appeals process: the nature of the asylum decision problem; the information required to make decisions; the usual gaps in such information; the applicable standard of proof; the personnel involved in the decision process; the fact-gathering routines employed to make decisions; the reason-giving requirements; and the organisation and operation of onward rights of challenge. It is also necessary to consider the relationships between the Tribunal and other actors in the process such as the Home Office and expert witnesses.

It is unlikely that the ensuing analysis of asylum appeals will satisfy everyone who has some interest in it. Different views will be held as to the weight properly to be placed on competing values; persistent anxieties and concerns are unlikely to subside. Nevertheless, an in-depth examination of asylum adjudication will provide a better understanding with which to appreciate and understand the

---

[51] Asylum and Immigration Tribunal (Procedure) Rules SI 2005/230 r 4.

complexities and challenges posed by the task of designing and managing an effective adjudication process.

Why Asylum Adjudication?

A final issue needs to be addressed in this section: why situate a study of the quality in administrative justice in the particular context of asylum adjudication? There are various reasons for this.

First of all, there is the intrinsic importance of asylum adjudication itself. No other decision system is regularly required to produce decisions which might, if wrong, directly result in individuals suffering persecution, torture, or even death, or, alternatively, the admission into the country of people who are not entitled to enter. Asylum adjudication raises hard questions about the extent of the state's legal and moral obligations toward the nationals of other countries, the protection of their human rights, the efficacy of immigration controls, the allocation of scarce resources, and the management of decision processes. Like all other administrative justice decision systems, asylum adjudication concerns the relationship between the state and the citizen, except that the citizens involved come from other countries, unless they are stateless altogether. Most other such decision systems embody an inherent tension between managerial and justice imperatives, but it is in the asylum context that this tension finds its apogee. In short, asylum adjudication compels detailed study because of the nature of the decisions that must be taken and the context in which they are produced.

Secondly, despite its importance, asylum adjudication has been a comparatively neglected area of concern for legal scholarship. There has, of course, been much literature examining the legal rules and principles of refugee, asylum and human rights law, and their elucidation by the higher courts. But the vast majority of decisions are of necessity taken lower down the decision-making hierarchy. Further, asylum decisions do not primarily raise legal issues for determination, but factual questions as to whether claimants would be at real risk on return to their countries of origin. Comparatively little attention has been devoted to the issue as to how asylum decisions are taken in practice.

A related point is that asylum adjudication might provide a fresh perspective on human rights adjudication more generally. Since the enactment of the Human Rights Act 1998, the courts have a role in assessing whether administrative decisions and legislation are compatible with human rights law. This has prompted much discussion as to how the courts should perform this function and the deference to be afforded to government.[52] However, if we shift our focus toward substantive decision-making, then the relevant point of departure is not the constitutional issue of judicial review, but the administrative law issues of fact-finding

---

[52] See, eg, J Jowell, 'Judicial Deference and Human Rights: A Question of Competence' in P Craig and R Rawlings (eds), *Law and Administration in Europe* (Oxford, Oxford University Press, 2003); C Gearty, *Principles of Human Rights Adjudication* (Oxford, Oxford University Press, 2004).

and the organisation of adjudicative processes. As human rights are always in play in asylum adjudication, it may provide an appropriate area from which to draw some insights into human rights adjudication.

Thirdly, asylum adjudication provides an interesting context in which to situate a study of adjudicative quality precisely because there have been persistent concerns over the quality of this process. Broadly speaking, this criticism falls into two different camps. From one perspective, the asylum adjudication system operates at a level far below that of other jurisdictions in the UK. This broad critique has various strands: that decision-making is of poor or indifferent quality; that the process prioritises speed over fairness and accuracy; and that the success rate at the appeals stage is comparatively low. At the same time, from an entirely different perspective, the quality of the process has been criticised on the ground that it is susceptible to abuse by those who do not qualify for asylum, but use it as a backdoor to entry. This perspective also has a number of different strands: that the process takes too long and costs too much; that the multiple opportunities for legal challenge only create further scope for delay and are used by unmeritorious claimants to evade removal; and that the rate of successful appeals is too high. These two strongly antipathetic perspectives may be summarised by the hackneyed phrases used to describe the process; it is, depending on the perspective adopted, characterised either by 'a culture of disbelief' on the behalf of decision-makers or 'a culture of abuse' on the behalf of claimants.

These different perspectives can only be understood against the backdrop of the highly controversial political context in which the decision-making process necessarily operates.[53] However, this book does not align itself to either of these perspectives. It accepts that the system of asylum adjudication forms part of the broader process for implementing asylum policy—affording protection to those individuals who will be at risk on return. It accepts that there may be incentives for claimants to lodge claims and appeals that are without merit. It also accepts that a substantial number of claimants are in need of asylum. However, the book takes no position on the broader political dimensions of asylum adjudication; rather,

---

[53] For treatments of asylum policy debate in the UK, see N Steiner, *Arguing About Asylum: The Complexity of Refugee Debates in Europe* (New York, St Martin's Press, 2000) 97–132; LM Pirouet, *Whatever Happened to Asylum in Britain? A Tale of Two Walls* (Oxford, Berghahn, 2001); L Schuster, *The Use and Abuse of Political Asylum in Britain and Germany* (London, Frank Cass, 2003) 131–179; MJ Gibney, *The Ethics and Politics of Asylum: Liberal Democracy and the Response to Refugees* (Cambridge, Cambridge University Press, 2004) 107–131; D Stevens, *UK Asylum Law and Policy: Historical and Contemporary Perspectives* (London, Sweet & Maxwell, 2004). On UK immigration policy more generally and its administration, see A Dummett and A Nicol, *Subjects, Citizens, Aliens and Others: Nationality and Immigration Law* (London, Weidenfeld and Nicolson, 1990); IRG Spencer, *British Immigration Policy Since 1939: The Making of Multi-Racial Britain* (London, Routledge, 1997); R Hansen, *Citizenship and Immigration in Post-war Britain: The Institutional Origins of a Multicultural Nation* (Oxford, Oxford University Press, 2000); S Moxon, *The Great Immigration Scandal* (Exeter, Academic Imprint, 2004); W Somerville, *Immigration Under New Labour* (Bristol, Policy Press, 2007); House of Lords Economic Affairs Select Committee, *The Economic Impact of Immigration* (2007–08 HL 82).

its principal focus is upon examining and analysing how the system of asylum adjudication operates as against the competing values which exert influence upon it.

It remains to detail the research methods used to collect the empirical data upon which this book draws and to provide an overview of the book's structure.

Research Methods

The data presented in this book was collected during an empirical research project. Data collection and analysis was undertaken during 2007–09. The objective of the research was to collect data concerning the procedure and determination of asylum appeals in order to inform a general examination into the quality and effectiveness of the appeals process. More specifically, the purposes were to consider the procedure by which the Tribunal hears and determines appeals, how the Tribunal assesses the credibility of appellants, and how it assesses country information concerning the situation in appellant's countries of origin. The empirical research comprised three aspects: observation of appeal hearings; structured interviews with members of the immigration judiciary, representatives, Home Office presenting officers, country experts and civil servants; and analysis of the determinations from the appeals observed in addition to other reported determinations; and an examination of relevant literature.

In undertaking the research, the central focus was upon the appeals process itself. It was important to investigate the procedures by which appeals are heard, whether the parties were represented and, if so, how effectively. In exploring these issues, some 182 appeal hearings were observed at four tribunal hearing centres: Manchester (94), Bradford (12), Hatton Cross (68), and Field House (8) (the last two of which are in London). All of these hearing centres other than Field House hear and determine initial asylum appeals. By contrast with these regional hearing centres, Field House is where the senior immigration judiciary are located and where onward challenges against initial appeal decisions are heard in addition to country guidance cases. Observation of both first-stage reconsiderations and country guidance hearings were undertaken at Field House. Of the other appeal hearings observed, 84 per cent were initial appeals to the Tribunal directly against initial refusal decisions and the remainder were second-stage reconsideration cases, that is, appeals that had already been determined by an Immigration Judge, but had been found to contain an error of law and had therefore been sent back to the hearing centre to be reconsidered.

It was intended to observe a number of appeals involving appellants of different nationalities and being heard by a range of different judges. This was necessary to explore the approach of different Immigration Judges in appeal hearings, the degree of formality or informality of the hearing, and the examination of individual appeals. Which particular appeals were observed depended on which particular appeals proceeded during this observation period. It was difficult to know which particular appeals were actually going to proceed on a particular hearing day and virtually impossible to select in advance appeals to be observed because of the Tribunal's listing practices. Cases listed for hearing may not, for whatever reason, be heard. Nevertheless, it was possible to observe appeals heard by different Immigration Judges. Likewise, appeals concerning appellants from a range of different nationalities were observed to provide a cross-section of how different appeals are determined and to include both represented and unrepresented cases. Most appeal determinations are not publicly available. To acquire access, it was necessary to gain formal approval from the Tribunal and the Ministry of Justice. Reported tribunal determinations are made publicly available for broader public dissemination on the Tribunal's website.[54] In total, some 207 case files were analysed and the information categorised. Data obtained from these files was statistically processed and compared, where possible, with other statistics.

To collect qualitative data on both the procedure and determination of appeals, interviews were conducted with the main actors involved in the appeals process during the fieldwork: Immigration Judges (19) and Senior Immigration Judges (4); representatives (7); Home Office presenting officers (4); country experts (8) and medical experts (2). The purpose of the interviews was not to provide a statistically representative sample of these categories of person but to provide qualitative depth and supplement the observation of appeals; as a piece of socio-legal research, the research entailed immersion in the practice of asylum adjudication. The interviews were semi-structured and different interview questions were designed for different groups of interviewees. Interviews with Immigration Judges focused on both the procedure and determination of appeals at the initial level of the appeal process in order to understand the nature of the work and decision-making which they undertake. In addition, the Immigration Judges interviewed included a mix of salaried (full-time) judges and fee-paid (part-time) judges.

The research raised a number of ethical issues which are noted here. First, to undertake the research, it was necessary to gain the agreement of the Tribunal's senior judiciary in order to interview Immigration Judges and obtain copies of determinations. Gaining research access was undertaken through an interactive process with the Tribunal in order to clarify the scope, aims, and methods of the research project. Once access was granted, a privileged access agreement with the Ministry of Justice was signed; this is a legally binding agreement to ensure that the research fully anonymised all information collected and that certain other safeguards were met. Once the methodology for the project had been agreed with the Tribunal, its judiciary was cooperative and willing to be interviewed, subject to guarantees as to confidentiality. Secondly, the observation of appeals also raised some ethical issues. Despite the personal and sensitive nature of the issues that frequently emerge in asylum appeal hearings, every appeal hearing must, in the interests of open justice, be held in public; members of the public may be excluded only

---

[54] With the transfer of the AIT into the First-tier and Upper Tribunals in February 2010, the Tribunal's website is: www.tribunals.gov.uk/ImmigrationAsylum/.

on the basis of specific reasons such as the interests of public order or national security.[55] According to the Tribunal, it is of 'cardinal importance' that appeal hearings should be held in public, unless there is good reason to do otherwise.[56] However, in practice most appeal hearings proceed without members of the public present. It was not, therefore, necessary to obtain the consent of appellants to appeal hearings, but an appropriate degree of sensitivity was required; for instance, by not observing those appeals in which an appellant objected to the researcher's presence.

Finally, it was decided at an early stage of the research design that, for ethical and practical reasons, interviews would not be conducted with appellants. Asylum appeal hearings often involve asylum appellants giving evidence upon especially sensitive personal issues; it may involve them recounting upsetting and/or harrowing details of their personal history. Given this and the vulnerability of asylum appellants, it was considered inappropriate to undertake interviews with appellants in the context of this research project. Secondly, most appellants do not speak English and the prospect of arranging for interpreters would have been problematic.[57] This book does not, therefore, attempt to consider the views of the Tribunal's clientele—or, in the contemporary tribunal vernacular, the 'users'—of the appeals process; still less does it attempt to tell their stories.[58]

What is apparent, though, is that the position of most asylum applicants is often an unhappy and precarious one. Asylum applicants overwhelmingly originate from countries that suffer from severe problems and hardships; some may be failed states, or countries which habitually condone ill-treatment of their own citizens, and others are countries in which average living standards and the prospects for economic well-being are extremely poor. The grim reality is that conditions in such countries are sometimes so dire, that, understandably enough, people seek a better life elsewhere. Millions of people living in the poorer countries of the world suffer from the adverse effects of poverty, famine, malnutrition, disease, ill-health, and climate change in addition to various human rights abuses caused by political violence, civil war, religious intolerance, and so on. However, the legal obligation to grant asylum does not require the UK to provide protection to all of them, but only to those who fall within the legal tests governing asylum. Paradoxically, as Lord Brown has observed, those who fear of persecution or ill-treatment, are in a sense the lucky ones, provided only that they can demonstrate a good case for asylum.[59]

[55] Asylum and Immigration Tribunal (Procedure) Rules SI 2005/230 r 54.

[56] *BK v Secretary of State for the Home Department (Failed asylum seekers) Democratic Republic of Congo CG* [2007] UKAIT 00098 [2].

[57] As the research was focusing on the work of the tribunal, it would not have been satisfactory to have used the tribunal's own court appointed interpreter for research purposes.

[58] For attempts to do so, see J Harding, *The Uninvited: Refugees at the Rich Man's Gate* (London, Profile Books, 2000); C Moorhead, *Human Cargo: A Journey Among Refugees* (London, Vintage, 2006); C Bohmer and A Shuman, *Rejecting Refugees: Political Asylum in the 21st Century* (London, Routledge, 2008); DN Kenney and PG Schrag, *Asylum Denied: A Refugee's Struggle for Safety in America* (Berkeley, University of California Press, 2008).

[59] *AH (Sudan) v Secretary of State for the Home Department* [2007] UKHL 49; [2008] 1 AC 678 [32] (Lord Brown) (HL).

This is because the fear of persecution is only one of many other risks they may face; once someone at risk has been afforded asylum, they cannot be returned back to the country of origin. But, of course, such other risks may themselves motivate individuals who neither need asylum nor qualify for entry under ordinary immigration procedures to lodge false claims. This is precisely the reason why some sort of decision process is required.

The Plan of the Book

Having considered the general framework for considering quality and outlined the research methods used in this study, it is necessary to provide an overview of this book. As the principal aim of this book is to examine and assess the effectiveness and quality of asylum adjudication, the following chapters explore in detail the work and operations of the asylum tribunal, the procedures used at asylum appeal hearings, and how decision-makers go about the task of making decisions. Chapter two examines the nature of asylum decision-making by considering the legal framework of asylum decision-making, the importance of fact-finding, and the applicable standard of proof. This chapter also considers the organisation of the broader asylum decision process.

Following this, chapter three analyses an often overlooked yet critically important aspect of tribunal adjudication: the amount of resources that should be devoted to the task of making accurate decisions through fair procedures. By examining the relationship between resources, accuracy, and fairness, we might be in a better position to appreciate the compromises that must necessarily be struck when designing an adjudication process and the difficulties and uncertainties involved.

Chapters four, five and six each examine different aspects of asylum decision-making by Immigration Judges by drawing upon the empirical data. Chapter four analyses the process by which asylum appeal hearings are conducted by Immigration Judges. This chapter considers the format and mode of procedure of appeal hearings, the operation of case management review hearings, and the role of interpreters and representatives. To produce decisions, tribunal judges need to make findings of fact. Chapters five and six examine the two aspects of the fact-finding task in asylum cases. Chapter five considers how Immigration Judges decide whether or not the claim of an asylum appellant to be in need of international protection is credible, that is, whether that person's story can properly be accepted to be true. The centrality of credibility assessments to the task of making asylum decisions is perhaps matched only by the difficulty of the task and the chapter explores this complexity. Chapter six examines the other aspect of the task of making asylum decisions, that of handling and assessing country of origin information, that is, information concerning the situation in the country from which an individual is seeking refuge. Handling such information is often critical to the making of asylum decisions; however, as with the assessment of credibility, the evaluation of country information is rarely straightforward.

Having examined the procedure of initial appeals and decision-making by Immigration Judges, chapters seven and eight examine two aspects of the decision process that both influence and regulate initial appeals: country guidance and onward rights of challenge. Chapter seven examines the development and operation of the Tribunal's country guidance system: the process by which senior judges produce authoritative guidance on the situation in a particular country by identifying which particular groups of people from that country may or may not qualify for asylum. The purpose of country guidance is to ensure consistent assessments of country conditions by Immigration Judges. But consistency has to be balanced against the need for the individual consideration of the circumstances of each case. This chapter examines how the handling of this tension and whether or not country guidance assists Immigration Judges deciding individual appeals. Chapter eight examines the operation and function of onward rights of challenge against first-instance appeal determinations. Tribunal decisions are rarely the end of the process as the losing party is normally able to challenge any tribunal decision on error of law grounds. Given the exceptionally high rate of onward challenge against initial asylum appeal decisions, the design of onward systems of challenge is of critical importance in terms of managing the decision process, handling the relationship between the Tribunal and the higher courts, and assessing the quality of decision-making. This chapter examines in detail how the high rate of onward challenge has led to successive re-organisations of the tribunal system. The chapter also analyses the contribution of onward rights of challenge to quality in decision-making and the broader relationship between the asylum tribunal and the higher courts.

Chapter nine concludes this study of asylum adjudication by summarising both the concept of quality that has been developed throughout the book and the assessment made of the effectiveness and quality of asylum appeals. The chapter also considers some of the options for reforming the process so that its overall effectiveness and quality might be enhanced.

2

Asylum Decision-Making and its Organisation

I N THE PREVIOUS CHAPTER, the aims of the book were set out and placed within the broader context of considering the concept of quality in administrative justice. The purpose of this chapter is to focus the inquiry more specifically upon the nature and context of asylum decision-making and its organisation.

The chapter is divided into three parts. The first examines the asylum decision problem, that is, the challenges posed by the taking of an asylum decision. On a superficial analysis, legal decision-making is often viewed as a simple task of finding the appropriate legal rules, those criteria which guide decision-making, collecting the relevant facts, and then applying those facts to the legal rules to produce a decision. On this view, decision-making is a non-problematic, mechanical exercise of rule-application. But decision-making is rarely so straightforward.[1] The legal rules may be either unclear or leave scope for the exercise of judgment by decision-makers. Fact-finding can be highly problematic as the facts relevant to a decision will rarely be self-evident; rather, fact-finding will often involve considerable interpretative work by decision-makers to decide what weight ought to be attached to claimed facts, especially when the evidence advanced is limited or uncertain. The personal moral and ideological presuppositions of individual decision-makers may also exert influence upon decision-making and produce variations in decision outcomes. The organisational processes by which facts are found and decisions produced will also often influence decision outcomes. To examine the challenges posed by the asylum decision problem, it is therefore necessary to consider the legal rules governing eligibility for asylum, the nature of the fact-finding task, the applicable standard of proof, and the ultimate task of asylum decision-making, that of assessing risk on return.

The particular decision problem is only one part of the challenge. Another issue concerns how decision-making is to be organised; should it be organised as an administrative process, a legal adjudicatory dispute mechanism, or as the exercise of professional judgment? To explore this issue, the second part of the chapter draws upon Mashaw's well-known analysis of administrative justice under which there are often competing visions or models as to how any particular decision

---

[1] R Baldwin and K Hawkins, 'Discretionary Justice: Davis Reconsidered' [1984] *Public Law* 570, 580–581.

process ought to be organised. The problem is often how to attain an appropriate synthesis between such divergent models. The focus of this book is upon tribunal adjudication, which most clearly reflects the legal model. But to appreciate how the Tribunal operates and its relationship with other actors, it is necessary to understand the competing ways in which the decision process can be organised and the relationships between the Tribunal and other institutional actors, such as the Home Office and expert witnesses.

Having outlined the different ways of organising the asylum decision process, the third part of the chapter provides a brief overview of how the Tribunal is itself organised, in particular, its jurisdiction to determine asylum appeals, its personnel, and the training they receive.

The Asylum Decision Problem

Refugee, Asylum, and Human Rights law

The rules governing asylum are highly detailed and complex and are governed by a number of different and overlapping legal systems—national and international law in addition to European Union and European human rights law. This book does not consider this legal complexity in detail, but some consideration of the legal rules governing eligibility for asylum is necessary to understand the nature of the decision problem.[2] There are three principal legal grounds under which a foreign national may claim that removal to his country of origin would be unlawful: first, an individual may be entitled to refugee status under the Refugee Convention, 1951; secondly, he may qualify for humanitarian protection under the EC Qualification Directive; and thirdly, removal may be contrary to the European Convention on Human Rights.

The Refugee Convention defines a refugee as someone who, owing to a well-founded fear of being persecuted for reasons of race, religion, nationality, membership of a particular social group or political opinion, is outside the country of his nationality and is unable or, owing to such fear, is unwilling to avail himself of the protection of that country; or who, not having a nationality and being outside the country of his former habitual residence as a result of such events, is unable or, owing to such fear, is unwilling to return to it.[3] The purpose of the Refugee Convention is to provide surrogate protection to those in need because the claimant's own state is either unable or unwilling to protect its own nationals. The applicant must have a subjective fear of persecution for one of the five Convention

---

[2] See JC Hathaway, *The Rights of Refugees under International Law* (Cambridge, Cambridge University Press, 2005); GS Goodwin-Gill and J McAdam, *The Refugee in International Law*, 3rd edn (Oxford, Oxford University Press, 2007); J McAdam, *Complementary Protection in International Refugee Law* (Oxford, Oxford University Press, 2007).

[3] Refugee Convention 1951, Art 1A(2).

reasons, which then is objectively well-founded by reference to the assessment of conditions in the applicant's country of origin. Applicants may fear persecution from either the state authorities in the relevant country, any part or organisation of the state or any non-state actor, if the state is either unable or unwilling to provide protection.[4] Persecution must be sufficiently serious by its nature or repetition so as to constitute a severe violation of a basic human right and may take various forms, such as an act of physical or mental violence or legal, administrative, police, or judicial measures which are discriminatory or prosecution or punishment which is disproportionate or discriminatory.[5] An individual need not have left his country because of his fear of persecution; such a fear may arise on the basis of events which have taken place since his departure from that country.[6] Qualification under the Refugee Convention entitles the applicant to refugee status and to limited leave to enter or remain in the UK.[7]

Claimants who do not qualify for refugee status may qualify for humanitarian protection. This will be granted to a person if there are substantial grounds for believing that, if returned to the country of origin, he would face a real risk of suffering serious harm and that he is unable or, owing to such risk, unwilling to avail himself of the protection of that country. Serious harm consists of: (i) the death penalty or execution; (ii) unlawful killing; (iii) torture or inhuman or degrading treatment or punishment of a person in the country of return; or (iv) serious and individual threat to a civilian's life or person by reason of indiscriminate violence in situations of international or internal armed conflict.[8]

Both the rules governing refugee status and humanitarian protection admit of various exceptions and exclusions. First, there is an exception known as internal relocation. If an individual at risk in one part of his country of origin might not be at risk in another part of that country and the person could reasonably be expected to relocate internally to that part of the country, he will not be granted asylum or humanitarian protection.[9] Secondly, a person will not qualify as a refugee if he falls within one of the Refugee Convention's exclusion clauses, that is, if he has committed a crime against peace, a war crime or crime against humanity, a serious non-political crime outside the country of refugee before his admission, or is guilty of acts contrary to the purposes and principles of the United Nations.[10] Furthermore, refugee status will be denied if there are reasonable grounds for believing an individual to be a danger to the security of the UK or if, having been convicted by a final judgment of a particularly serious crime, he constitutes a danger to the community of the UK.[11]

---

[4] Refugee or Person in Need of International Protection (Qualification) Regulations SI 2006/2525 r 3.

[5] Refugee or Person in Need of International Protection (Qualification) Regulations SI 2006/2525 r 5.

[6] Immigration Rules (1994 HC 395) r 339P.

[7] Immigration Rules (1994 HC 395) r 330.

[8] Immigration Rules (1994 HC 395) r 339C.

[9] Immigration Rules (1994 HC 395) r 339O.

[10] Refuge Convention 1951, Article 1F.

[11] Refuge Convention 1951, Article 33(2); Immigration Rules (1994 HC 395) r 339; Nationality, Immigration and Asylum Act 2002 s 72.

In addition, an individual may also qualify for protection on the ground that removal would contravene his human rights under the European Convention on Human Rights. Under Article 3 ECHR, it is unlawful to remove an individual to a place where he may face a real risk of torture or inhuman or degrading treatment. Article 3 possess an 'extra-territorial effect', that is it may be invoked by a foreign national facing removal who claims that such removal will place him at a real risk of serious ill-treatment by the receiving state rather than by the UK.[12] Given the varied circumstances which may prompt individuals to seek protection, the asylum decision problem has itself become differentiated with the higher courts elucidating specific decision criteria attuned to the particular generic types of cases. So, an individual with HIV/AIDS may only succeed on the basis that removal to a country without appropriate medical care for the condition if the case is so exceptional in that there are compelling humanitarian grounds for not removing them.[13] In suicide cases—those cases in which an individual claims that he would upon removal commit suicide—removal may be contrary to Article 3 if there are substantial grounds for believing there to be a real risk of ill-treatment. However, the courts have emphasised that in order to minimise the extra-territorial effect of the ECHR, the Article 3 threshold is raised to a particularly high level.[14] As regards the applicability of other ECHR rights as a bar to removal—for instance, the right to a fair trial (Article 6)—the courts have held that removal will be unlawful only if it would result in a flagrant denial or gross violation of the right by the receiving state.[15] However, applicants may claim that the sending state, that is the UK, may breach other rights in enforcing removal. It is often contended that removal would breach the right to family life under Article 8 ECHR on the basis that a family life has been established in the UK, which the removal would violate. In such cases where the family life could not reasonably be expected to be enjoyed elsewhere, the decision-maker must determine whether the removal would prejudice the applicant's family life in a manner sufficiently serious so as to amount to a breach of the right to family life.[16]

A number of points can be distilled from this brief overview. First, the purpose of refugee, asylum, and human rights law is fundamentally a humanitarian one: to require the state to extend its protection to people to whom it generally owes no other obligation and who would otherwise not qualify to remain under immigration law. Secondly, no right to asylum as such exists; rather, there is a right to seek asylum. In practice, this means that an individual has a right to ask for a decision from the relevant authority as to whether or not he fulfils the relevant eligibility criteria.

---

[12] *Chahal v United Kingdom* (1996) 23 EHRR 413; *R v Special Adjudicator ex parte Ullah* [2004] UKHL 26; [2004] 2 AC 323.

[13] *D v United Kingdom* (1997) 24 EHRR 423; *N v Secretary of State for the Home Department* [2005] UKHL 31; [2005] 2 AC 296; *N v United Kingdom* (2008) 47 EHRR 39.

[14] *J v Secretary of State for the Home Department* [2005] Imm AR 409; [2005] EWCA Civ 629.

[15] *Devaseelan v Secretary of State for the Home Department* [2003] Imm AR 1 [111] (IAT); *Ullah* (n 12); *EM (Lebanon) v Secretary of State for the Home Department* [2008] UKHL 64.

[16] *Abdulaziz, Cabales and Balkandali v United Kingdom* (1985) 7 EHRR 471; *Huang v Secretary of State for the Home Department* [2007] UKHL 11; [2007] 2 AC 176.

Thirdly, a common feature of all the legal tests is that they are, to varying degrees, open-textured. Deciding whether treatment amounts to persecution or serious ill-treatment as opposed to mere hardship, or whether it would be reasonable to expect someone to relocate internally, or whether there are exceptional and compelling humanitarian grounds for not removing someone with HIV/AIDS, or whether there is in general a real risk on return for a whole class of person (such as failed Zimbabwean asylum applicants) all essentially involve questions of judgment, assessment, and evaluation. As Laws LJ has observed, 'there are no sharp legal tests in this area'.[17]

Fact-finding

While open-textured nature, the legal rules governing asylum provide the eligibility criteria that decision-makers must apply. However, the decision-making task does not generally turn on issues of law, but of fact. After all, the principal task of virtually all administrative and first-instance tribunal decision-making is to make findings of fact. Claimants can only succeed if they can demonstrate that their particular circumstances satisfy the applicable eligibility criteria. While there may be a general tendency to view fact-finding as a mundane or relatively low level task, the reality is that it is often a crucial and skilled task.[18] Indeed, fact-finding is of fundamental importance because it is intimately interlinked with the value of accuracy. To ensure accurate decisions, the decision-maker must ensure that the facts have been correctly found and then apply them to the relevant legal rules in order to produce a decision. The principal problem is that of seeking to make correct findings of fact.

In the asylum context, the fact-finding task is complex as it normally comprises two discrete aspects. It involves an assessment of both the *particular* circumstances of the individual's case and the *general* social and political situation in the country from which refuge is being sought in order to determine whether an individual would be at risk on return. The evidentiary needs of decision-making are then to collect the facts needed to answer two types of risk assessment questions: risk-group existence and then risk-group affiliation.[19] First, with what degree of certainty can it be concluded that various groups of people are at risk of persecution or serious ill-treatment in a particular country? For instance, are members of Somali minority clans or political opponents of the government of the Democratic Republic of Congo at risk on return? This assessment is undertaken by reference to evidence concerning the political and social conditions in the relevant country,

---

[17] *CA v Secretary of State for the Home Department* [2004] EWCA Civ 1165; [2004] Imm AR 640, 652 (Laws LJ) (CA).

[18] W Twining, 'Taking Facts Seriously' in *Rethinking Evidence: Exploratory Essays*, 2nd edn (Cambridge, Cambridge University Press, 2006) 14.

[19] H Zahle, 'Competing Patterns for Evidentiary Assessments' in G Noll (ed), *Proof, Evidentiary Assessment and Credibility in Asylum Procedures* (Leiden/Boston, Martinus Nijhoff, 2005) 21.

often referred to as country of origin information or background country materials. The second question requires an assessment of the position of the particular asylum applicant: with what degree of certainty can it concluded that an individual applicant is a member of the risk-group identified? For instance, is the applicant a member of a Somali minority clan or a political opponent of the government in the Democratic Republic of Congo? This assessment is undertaken by reference to the evidence concerning the circumstances of the individual applicant and generally involves assessing the credibility of the individual claimant's claim to be in need of international protection. Seeking answers to these deceptively simple questions—is the claimant credible? what are the conditions like in his country of origin for him?—occupies the bulk of decision-makers' time.

Fact-finders normally face considerable challenges in seeking to determine what the facts are. As it is impossible to determine objectively what the facts are, it is necessary instead to rely on representations and evidence as to what the facts might be. All fact-finding necessarily operates under some degree of evidential uncertainty. But finding facts in asylum cases is, at the best of times, a highly problematic endeavour. This is because of the higher than normal level of indeterminacy relating to the finding of 'facts' which concern the stories presented by people about what happened elsewhere in the world and the conditions that prevail in the relevant countries. There are very few asylum cases in which there are no areas of doubt and uncertainty. As the courts have noted, there are several reasons why '[t]he difficulty of the fact-finding exercise is particularly acute in asylum cases'.[20]

On a fairly basic level, the permanent challenge facing the asylum decision-maker is to make findings of fact where the evidence presented is often uncertain, limited or unsatisfactory in terms of its extent, quality, and presentation. The evidential material will normally include: the claimant's own (oral and written) evidence; documentary evidence particular to the claim; perhaps a medical report to the effect that the scarring on the claimant's body is consistent with past persecution or torture; and country information reports (from various governmental and non-governmental agencies) detailing the social and political conditions in the country from which refuge is being sought. The range of evidence will usually be of variable quality and frequently contain little that is either firm or objectively verifiable; on the contrary, most asylum cases are distinguished by the paucity, changeability, and unreliability of evidence which corroborates or contradicts the claimant's case. Most, though not all, asylum claims are made by individuals who do not possess any personal documentation, such as a passport or identity card. It can, therefore, be difficult for the decision-maker to ascertain with any degree of certainty whether the claimant is the person he claims to be and whether he is a national of the country he claims and not that of another. It will not usually be possible to verify even the most basic facts such as the individual's name, date of birth, nationality, ethnicity, and country of origin.

---

[20] *HK v Secretary of State for the Home Department* [2006] EWCA Civ 1037 [27] (Neuberger LJ). See also *Gheisari v Secretary of State for the Home Department* [2006] EWCA Civ 1854.

The decision-maker will frequently be entirely reliant on the information given by the applicant concerning the reason why he will face persecution or ill-treatment on return. The applicant's story may detail past persecution, but the veracity of these events cannot normally be confirmed one way or the other as there will not be any witness or other evidence to support or contradict the applicant. It is not usually possible for claimants to acquire other evidence; most are forced by circumstances to rely on their own statements to prove their cases. This can present difficulties for genuine claimants in seeking to substantiate their claim to be at risk; it can also mean that the process is open to exploitation and abuse by non-genuine claimants who do not feel themselves bound to tell the truth and who wish to extend their stays within the country for as long as possible. The position of the asylum claimant is very different from that of litigants engaged in, for instance, civil litigation. Rather than having to choose between two different versions of the facts, the decision-maker must assess the prospective risk of persecution or ill-treatment on the basis of the account presented by the individual claimant alone as supplemented by the relevant background information concerning the situation in the country from which refuge is being sought.

The challenges when making sustainable findings of fact are then acute, but are accentuated by other features of the process, such as: the language and cultural differences between claimants and decision-makers; the emotional and other pressures on claimants; and the decision process itself. By definition, much of the evidence will refer to societies with customs and circumstances which are very different from those familiar to decision-makers. Indeed, it is likely that the country which an asylum claimant has left will be suffering from the sort of problems and dislocations with which the overwhelming majority of residents of the decision-maker's country will be wholly unfamiliar. Decision-makers must be prepared to exercise some caution when making findings of fact because of the risk that they might be over-influenced by their own views on what is or is not plausible, and those views will have inevitably been influenced by their own background. But such caution does not require a decision-maker to accept at face value a claimant's story irrespective of how contrary to common sense and experience of human behaviour it may appear to be.

To some degree, the confused and sometimes contradictory nature of the evidence can arise from the process through which it is given. Applicants may be frightened, bewildered, perhaps even desperate, and may often not understand the process. Most will not be able to speak English; their evidence will have to be translated raising potential communication, cross-cultural and linguistic difficulties.[21] The evaluation of claims must be undertaken bearing in mind the stress to the claimant that has been generated by the making of the claim, the possible

---

[21] See W Kälin, 'Troubled Communication: Cross-cultural Misunderstandings in the Asylum Hearing' (1986) 20 *International Migration Review* 230; S. Pöllabauer, 'Interpreting in Asylum Hearings: Issues of Role, Responsibility and Power' (2004) 6 *Interpreting* 143; R Rycroft, 'Communicative Barriers in the Asylum Account' in P Shah (ed), *The Challenge of Asylum to Legal Systems* (London, Cavendish Publishing, 2005) 223.

consequences if refused, and the process of giving evidence in the formal atmosphere of an asylum interview or appeal hearing. Furthermore, as claimants will often have to present their accounts on a number of different occasions, initially to the Home Office and then before an Immigration Judge, there is always the risk that the account may not be wholly consistent throughout; errors and discrepancies may arise simply because of the way in which the story has been told on a number of different occasions.

While the fact-finder must assess the personal credibility of an applicant to be in need of international protection, this is only part of the fact-finding task. The particular situation of the applicant must also be seen within the broader situation in the relevant country. To do this, the fact-finder is normally dependant on country information produced by various governmental and non-governmental agencies. Furthermore, senior tribunal judges produce country guidance determinations which provide guidance to Immigration Judges on the general circumstances or the circumstances for a certain group of people in the relevant country and the risks, if any, they may face on return. In this respect, the demands on decision-makers are huge because of the range of different country issues raised by asylum applicants seeking protection from various countries and the amount and variable quality of country information. Country information can be incomplete, contradictory, or conditioned by the particular perspective of the agency or body which has compiled and produced it. In any event, country conditions are protean and changes in such conditions may affect the degree of risk on return. Confronted with a heterogeneous range of cases and fluctuating country scenarios, decision-makers desperately need accurate and reliable information to determine who is in need of international protection.

Despite these inherent difficulties, the fact-finding exercise is conditioned by some simple though important rules. The burden of proof is on the appellant to demonstrate their case to the requisite standard of proof. The parties must be given a fair opportunity to present the evidence that they wish to rely upon. Findings of fact can be made without it being necessary to make alternative findings. For instance, if an applicant claims that a physical injury was sustained through torture, it is not necessary for the fact-finder, if the truthfulness of this claim is rejected, then to make a finding as to how the injury was in fact occasioned. Furthermore, the decision-maker has to look at the evidence as a whole—in the round—when making findings of fact. Having been presented with evidence of various kinds and qualities, the decision-maker must assess what it all adds up to. It is not necessary for the decision-maker to deal with every piece of material evidence or even every point in making findings of fact. Furthermore, the ordinary rules of evidence do not apply. The Tribunal is entitled to consider any item of evidence, even though it would be inadmissible in a court of law.[22] The risk, of course, is that the evidence presented by an appellant may be self-serving, but an inherent safeguard is the fact-finder has to exercise his own judgment as to the

[22] Asylum and Immigration Tribunal (Procedure) Rules SI 2005/230 r 51(1).

weight to be attached to the evidence provided. As the Tribunal has explained, it is an Immigration Judge's almost invariable task 'to make an assessment of the weight that can be attached to a witness giving evidence before him by considering his age, education, experience and understanding. This consideration will rarely be voiced in a determination, far less capable of scientific evaluation'.[23]

In general terms, fact-finding is rarely a straightforward task because it often involves, indeed requires, considerable judgment and interpretation by the fact-finder.[24] On a daily basis, fact-finders are confronted with a perennial question, 'how much weight should I give to this piece of evidence?' The conventional answer is that it is all a matter of common sense and experience. But this is merely a convenient way of avoiding the issue; whose common sense and experience? The reality is that factual findings often requires the exercise of the decision-maker's judgment and inarticulate value presuppositions in order to decide how much weight ought to be attributed to the evidence so that factual findings can be made. Given the scope for judgmental assessment of the evidence, facts can be just as much created or constructed as they are found. What fact-finders make of the evidential material placed before them is ultimately a matter for their own conscientious judgment.

The Standard of Proof

Whenever a fact-finder has to make findings based upon the evidence presented, there will inevitably be some degree of uncertainty as to whether certain events actually happened. If the decision task involves the making of a judgment as to whether or not some future event is likely to occur—persecution or torture on return to the country of origin, for instance—then the level of uncertainty increases. The principal solution is to require that the facts need only be proved to some standard of proof. The value of this is that it enables decision-makers to cope with evidential uncertainty by specifying the level of confidence required before factual findings can be made. In the criminal justice context, prosecutors need to prove guilt beyond all reasonable doubt. Likewise, civil litigants need to establish the facts on the balance of probabilities. What should be the applicable standard of proof in asylum cases?

A clear concern is that if the standard of proof is set too high, then this may have the effect of disentitling those genuinely at risk because of the difficulties in proving their claims. But setting the standard at too low a level raises the prospect that individuals not genuinely at risk may secure asylum. A complicating factor is that the asylum decision-maker must make factual findings on past events (for instance, a claim by an individual that they had previously been tortured) and also prognosticate the possibility of future events (whether an individual may be at risk

---

[23] *O v Secretary of State for the Home Department (Lebanon)* [2004] UKIAT 00040 [14].

[24] J Frank, *Law and the Modern Mind* (New York, Brentano's, 1930); *Courts on Trial,* revised edn (New York, Atheneum, 1963); Twining above n 18.

on return). As the future is always uncertain, this points to a modest standard of proof; but what of the standard in relation to the proof of past events? Furthermore, how is the relevant standard to be articulated in such a way so it is generally applicable while at the same time ensuring that it is consistently applied by a large number of decision-makers?

The answer to these difficulties has been to set the standard of proof at a level below the civil standard of proof. In asylum decision-making, the burden of proof is on the asylum claimant. However, the standard to which a claimant must prove his case is not the balance of probabilities test, but the reasonable degree of likelihood test. The decision-maker must be satisfied that there is a reasonable degree of likelihood of persecution or a real risk of ill-treatment on return, that is, a real or substantial likelihood as opposed.[25] This is not a demanding, but a modest, standard of proof. Proof of a 51 per cent chance (or greater) is not required. Nevertheless, the risk of future persecution or ill-treatment must be more than a mere possibility.

There are two rationales for this. First, the lower standard of proof recognises the difficulties that claimants are likely to experience in proving future risk. It is precisely because the burden of proving what may happen may pose some difficulties for the claimant that the evidence is viewed in a more benevolent manner than in other legal proceedings. The lower standard reflects the difficulties of proving the degree of future risk or the nature of the future risk which would be run, and the difficulties of proof and disproof of the allegations which, by their nature, underlie asylum claims.[26] The civil standard of proof used to determine whether claimed past events actually happened, but is inapplicable in the context of asylum decision-making which is primarily focused on assessing the likelihood of future events, namely the degree of risk on return. Furthermore, the civil standard of proof is more appropriate in the context of proceedings in a court of law. Where facts are disputed in civil litigation conducted under common law procedures, the court has to decide where, on the balance of probabilities, the truth lies as between the evidence the parties to the litigation have thought it in their respective interests to adduce at the trial. However, the determination of an asylum claim is not an issue of litigation between two parties to be resolved by a court of law, but an essentially administrative process of examining whether an individual claimant has been able to make good his claim.

The second rationale for the lower standard stems from the consequences that may follow from incorrect decisions. If a genuine claimant is wrongly refused, then the implications—serious ill-treatment, torture, or even death—that can arise are more severe and acute than in any other context. By requiring something less than proof positive, asylum law deliberately errs on the side of caution in the

---

[25] *Sivakumaran v Secretary of State for the Home Department* [1988] AC 958 (HL); *Kacaj v Secretary of State for the Home Department (Article 3—standard of proof—non-state agents)* (Starred determination) [2002] Imm AR 213 (IAT).

[26] *Secretary of State for the Home Department v RK (Obligation to investigate) Democratic Republic of Congo* [2004] UKIAT 00129 [46].

applicant's favour. Given the notoriously difficult task of establishing the facts and that asylum decision-makers will rarely, because of the nature of the evidence, be certain as to all aspects of the evidence presented, the lower standard of proof allows 'a more positive role for uncertainty' in the claimant's favour.[27]

But what does this lower standard of proof—a reasonable degree of likelihood—itself mean? How is it to be applied? And precisely how far from the civil standard of proof must the decision-maker depart so as to avoid imposing an unduly high standard, while simultaneously requiring something more than a merely fanciful possibility that what the claimant says is true? Perhaps the lower standard of proof is something like a one in three chance or it could be one in ten, but the factual nature of asylum cases precludes this type of risk assessment. The difficulty is that the lower standard of proof is itself problematic because no-one has ever specified precisely how much proof is required to discharge it. Nor it is apparent how it could be given greater definition. Attempts to disambiguate the standard of proof have often resulted in the substitution of one set of words ('a reasonable chance', a 'serious possibility' or 'substantial grounds for believing') for another ('reasonable degree of likelihood' or 'real risk').

This fundamental ambivalence over the standard of proof is widely shared by decision-makers themselves. As one Immigration Judge has noted, the notion of the lower standard of proof is 'a pretty nebulous concept. All you can do is to keep reminding yourself that you do not have to be sure on the balance of probabilities; it is something less than that'.[28] Setting the standard of proof at the lower level may provide some assistance to asylum claimants, but it does not provide much assistance to the decision-maker who must make a decision on the basis of fragmentary and uncertain evidence.

Another alternative, that advanced by the Court of Appeal in *Karanakaran*, is for the fact-finding exercise to be approached in an holistic manner in which the decision-maker is bound to take into account all material considerations when assessing future risk. This approach does not entail the decision-maker purporting to find 'proved' facts, whether past or present on which it is not satisfied on the balance of probabilities. What it does mean is that the decision-maker must not exclude any matters from its consideration when assessing the future unless they can be safely discarded because there is no real doubt that they did not in fact occur. Similarly, it would be wrong to exclude matters totally from consideration in the balancing process simply because the decision-maker believes, on what might be fragile evidence, that a claimed occurrence probably did not occur. In the context of this balancing exercise, the decision-maker may necessarily give greater weight to some considerations rather than others depending on the degree of confidence the decision-maker may have about them or the seriousness of their effect on the applicant's safety if they should occur.[29] As the Court of Appeal

---

[27] *Kaja v Secretary of State for the Home Department* [1994] UKIAT 11038; [1995] Imm AR 1 (IAT) 8.

[28] Immigration Judge interview 3.

[29] *Karanakaran v Secretary of State for the Home Department* [2000] 3 All ER 449, 469–470 (Brooke LJ) (CA).

explained, the questions raised by an asylum claim should not be regarded 'as an assault course on which hurdles of varying heights are encountered by the asylum seeker with the decision-maker acting as an umpire, nor as a forum in which the improbable is magically endowed with the status of certainty, but as a unitary process of evaluation of material of many kinds and qualities against the Convention's criteria of eligibility for asylum'.[30]

Another difficulty is that the open-textured nature of the standard of proof inevitably opens up considerable scope for differential assessments of the evidence between different decision-makers. There is a constant risk that evidence accepted by one decision-maker as reasonably likely to be true can be rejected by another as reasonably unlikely. Indeed, one of the principal criticisms of asylum decision-making is that some decision-makers are often not sufficiently skilled in the handling of facts and in applying the lower standard of proof; some decision-makers may require claimants to prove their case to a higher standard. Another comment frequently encountered is that the whole notion of a standard of proof itself makes little sense. In the abstract, the decision-maker may proceed to apply the applicable standard, but in reality, the decision-maker will simply look at the facts and make a judgment whether or not to accept them. If so, then seeking to draw clear distinctions between differential standards of proof is very difficult.

The risk, then, is that different decision-makers may adopt differential approaches when making findings of fact. Inconsistency of decision-making is often an endemic problem in many decision processes, especially in relation to fact-finding. In the asylum context, decision-makers may themselves often candidly accept the potential for disparate decision-making as an inherent feature of a decision process operated by ordinary human beings (in any event, no-one really knows for sure what the right outcome is). Even when both the law and the facts are clear, there may still be scope for legitimate differences of opinion amongst decision-makers over whether a claimant is entitled to asylum.[31] From the perspective of some external commentators, the existence of disparities in decision-making is a predicate to the condemnation of the whole process as an arbitrary lottery in which decisions seem to turn less upon the merits of individual cases and more upon the unarticulated personal views of decision-makers.[32] However, from the perspective of decision-makers themselves, the difficulties posed are such that it can be questioned how, if at all, they are supposed to secure consistency when the applicable standard of proof is so open-textured and admits of differential approaches when handling limited and uncertain evidential materials.

A further point to note is that while the burden of proof lies on the claimant, there is (or, at least, supposed to be) a cooperative duty to ascertain and evaluate all the relevant facts which is to be shared between the claimant and the decision-maker.[33] A claimant will often be unable to support his statements by

---

[30] Ibid, 479–480 (Sedley LJ).

[31] *Saad, Diriye and Osorio v Secretary of State for the Home Department* [2001] EWCA Civ 2008; [2002] Imm AR 471, 479.

[32] See, eg, R Prasad, 'The Asylum Lottery' *The Guardian* (25 January 2002).

documentary or other proof; in most cases, an individual fleeing persecution will have arrived with only the barest of necessities and without personal documents. In some cases, it may be necessary for the decision-maker to use all available means in order to produce the necessary evidence in support of the application. Alternatively, the claimant's statements may not be susceptible of proof and the decision-maker should give the claimant the benefit of the doubt. The decision-maker is not, however, required to accept unsupported statements as true if they are at odds with the general account advanced by the claimant.

This notion of the shared duty to ascertain and collect the facts can often sit uncomfortably with both a strict legal insistence that the burden of proof remains with the claimant and an adherence to adversarial procedures. At the same time, there must be some emphasis upon the need for claimants to demonstrate their case as best they can. A burden of proof is required to resolve those cases in which the fact-finder, having examined the evidence and applying the standard of proof, simply does not know what the facts are or were and holds that the claimant has failed to discharge the burden of proof.

Assessing Future Risk

Fact-finding is, then, an essential aspect of asylum decision-making, but it is only a step toward making an asylum decision; the issues in an asylum decision 'are evaluative, not factual. The facts, so far as they can be established, are signposts on the road to a conclusion on the issues; they are not themselves conclusions'.[34] What is further required is an evaluation of whether the claimant would be at future risk on return to his country of origin. The critical decision task is for the decision-maker to assemble the factual findings into an evaluation of the degree of risk, if any, facing the individual on return.

Assessing future risk—considering the particular facts concerning the individual applicant in the context of what is generally known about conditions in the relevant country and against the standard of proof to assess whether the claimant would be at risk on return—can raise a mass of questions. Has the applicant been subjected to persecution or serious ill-treatment? If so, then what was the reason for it? Will the applicant still be at risk on return? Have country conditions improved, deteriorated, or remained the same? If the applicant would be at real risk of persecution on return, is there a place of safety in that country where he would not be at risk and, if so, would it be unduly harsh to expect him to relocate there?

The facts found by the decision-maker will inform this assessment, but are not themselves determinative. For instance, if the decision-maker has found that the

---

[33] United Nations High Commissioner for Refugees (UNHCR), *Handbook on Determining Refugee Status* (Geneva, UNHCR, 1992) [196].

[34] *Karanakaran* above n 29 at 479 (Sedley LJ).

individual's story is not accepted as reasonably likely to be true, then in most cases, this will mean that there will be no risk on return. However, despite adverse credibility findings, a claimant may still be at risk, for instance, owing to his ethnicity. At the same time, positive credibility findings are far from being conclusive of future risk. If an applicant can establish that he has suffered past persecution or serious harm, then this can be regarded as a serious indication of a well-founded fear of future persecution or serious harm, unless there are good reasons to consider otherwise.[35] But asylum is not to be granted merely to compensate for the past infliction of torture; it is the existence of future risk which is critical. An individual who has suffered past ill-treatment will not qualify for asylum if there is no future risk; conversely, someone who has entirely escaped persecution may qualify if a future risk can be established.

There will also be considerable scope for evaluative judgments as to the effects of the evidence. Consider, for instance, the case of an individual who claims that return to his country of origin to face imprisonment for a criminal offence would place him at risk of serious ill-treatment in light of prison conditions in that country. Would this amount to inhuman and degrading treatment or would it merely amount to harsh treatment? In determining which side of the line the case falls the decision-maker might seek out some benchmark to make relevant comparisons. If so, then what is the relevant yardstick—prison conditions in the decision-maker's own country or those in other countries? To put the question differently, should decision-makers in western countries seek to impose their own standards as to what is acceptable upon other countries which do not necessarily subscribe to those standards? If they did, then the risk would be that the line between prosecution and persecution would become blurred. Given the potential number of people involved, it might be considered that it is simply not possible to take in everyone who might suffer some hardship on return to their country of origin. At the same time, there may be a line below which treatment on return may be considered unacceptable. But, of course, determining precisely where to draw that line inevitably requires a value judgment as to the proper balance between immigration control and individuals' rights.[36]

Evaluating future risk is, like fact-finding, a difficult endeavour. Assessing whether the degree of risk is real as opposed to merely fanciful requires an essentially evaluative appraisal of the relevant evidence. As risk scholars have emphasised, any form of risk assessment, irrespective of context, is dependant upon the ascription of value, not just probability, to potential outcomes.[37] Furthermore, the distinctiveness of the asylum decision problem can only be understood when situated against its broader policy backdrop. While asylum decision-making is governed by the legal

---

[35] Immigration Rules (1994 HC 395) r 339K.

[36] See *Secretary of State for the Home Department v SF (Article 3—prison conditions) Iran CG* [2002] UKIAT 00973 [15].

[37] See M Douglas and A Widavsky, *Risk and Culture: An Essay on the Selection of Technological and Environmental Dangers* (Berkeley, University of California Press, 1982) 80–81; J Steele, *Risks and Legal Theory* (Oxford, Hart Publishing, 2004) 25.

tests adumbrated above, it is also implicitly concerned with the maintenance of immigration control. Indeed, the risk assessment task frequently involves an unavoidable conflict between the legal obligation to protect those at risk of persecution or ill-treatment and the public interest in maintaining legitimate immigration control. There are important policy justifications for imposing such controls: the need to discourage illegal and economic migration, people trafficking, health and welfare tourism; the prevention of the admission of a potentially unlimited volume of asylum applicants; and the protection of social cohesion. The social and economic conditions in countries producing applicants may involve considerable hardship for individuals who consequently desire a better life; the imposition of ordinary immigration controls may leave only one possibility: seeking political asylum.

Asylum decision-makers continuously have before them the risk of being either unduly lenient—and therefore risk falling into error by granting status to the undeserving—or unjustifiably mistrustful—and therefore risk committing error by refusing the truly genuine claim. Both types of error clearly involve serious adverse consequences. But the all or nothing nature of the decision task compels a decision either way: the individual is either at real risk on return or not. As the error costs of incorrect decisions are so high, the process is continually subject to systemic stress and political controversy. At the same time, an asylum decision possesses distinct and considerable social and moral importance. A positive decision on an asylum claim is an implicit recognition that the moral worth in protecting an individual outweighs the public interest in enforcing immigration control. It is also an indication that a foreign country, in some cases a country with which the UK has close relations, is either incapable or unwilling to provide basic protections to its own citizens.

Asylum decision-making then involves implicit value judgments by decision-makers not only in regard to the outcome of individual claims, but also in relation to the broader purpose of the whole decision system. Should the decision system be underpinned by a culture of protection and select as its principal focus the goal of recognising those in need of protection? Or should it be oriented toward ensuring that each claim receives close scrutiny so as to guard against abusive and unmeritorious claims? A decision-maker adopting the former purpose might be expected to approach claims or appeals generously affording each the benefit of the doubt. By contrast, a decision-maker adopting the latter purpose might be expected to scrutinise each claim closely, subject to the standard of proof, so that only those truly at risk on return are granted asylum.

The choices open to decision-makers may be understood as comprising a spectrum of different approaches.[38] At one end, there may be decision-makers who conceive of their role as gate-keepers and who assume responsibility for protecting the country's borders which are threatened by a seemingly limitless number of

---

[38] A Macklin, 'Refugee Roulette in the Canadian Casino' in J Ramji-Nogales, AI Schoenholtz and PG Schrag (eds), *Refugee Roulette: Disparities in Asylum Adjudication and Proposals for Reform* (New York, New York University Press, 2009) 135, 158.

abusive and undeserving claimants. At the other end, there may be other decision-makers who understand their role as protectors of the human rights of those who will suffer persecution. Of course, there is plenty of scope for decision-makers to situate themselves somewhere in-between these two extremes. Crucially, there is no general agreement upon this decisive issue. Nor can it be supposed that decision-makers are always internally consistent and align themselves to one approach over another. Rather, the complexity and diversity of the caseload can constantly challenge decision-makers' own assumptions, but without ever affording them the certainty of knowing whether or not their decisions were right.

Decisional Challenges

In summary, asylum decision-making is notoriously difficult, perhaps the most problematic adjudicatory function in the modern state. Its superficial simplicity conceals a mass of detailed, difficult, and very problematic factual and legal issues.[39] Determining who is in need of international protection is an essentially evaluative or interpretive appraisal of evidential material of many kinds and qualities against the eligibility criteria for asylum.[40] As Sedley LJ has observed, asylum decision-making is not a conventional lawyer's exercise of applying a litmus test to ascertained facts; 'it is a global appraisal of an individual's past and prospective situation in a particular cultural, social, political and legal milieu, judged by a test which, though it has legal and linguistic limits, has a broad humanitarian purpose'.[41]

Given the distinctiveness of the asylum decision problem, it is far from obvious exactly how the challenges it poses could even be ameliorated, let alone resolved. Other areas of immigration decision-making have experienced a major shift away from qualitative to quantitative, points-based decisional criteria in the interests of transparency and efficiency.[42] But this is simply not an option in the asylum context because the eligibility criteria are laid down primarily by international legal conventions. Other attempts to give greater definition to the key concepts of asylum law have been mixed. Consider, for instance, the 2004 EU Qualification Directive. This Directive sought to lay down minimum standards under which individuals could qualify for international protection and to ensure that EU

---

[39] CG Blake, 'Judicial Review, Second Tier Tribunals and Legality' in M Partington (ed), *The Leggatt Review of Tribunals: Academic Seminar Papers* (University of Bristol, Faculty of Law, Working Paper Series No 3, 2001) 68; C Rousseau, F Crépeau, P Foxen, and F Houle, 'The Complexity of Determining Refugeehood: A Multidisciplinary Analysis of the Decision-making Process of the Canadian Immigration and Refugee Board' (2002) 15 *Journal of Refugee Studies* 43; P Showler, *Refugee Sandwich: Stories of Exile and Asylum* (Montreal, McGill-Queen's University Press, 2006) 210; F Crépeau and D Nakache, 'Critical Spaces in the Canadian Refugee Determination System: 1989–2002' (2008) 20 *International Journal of Refugee Law* 50, 56.

[40] *Karanakaran* above n 29 at 477–480 (Sedley LJ).

[41] *R v Immigration Appeal Tribunal and Secretary of State for the Home Department, ex parte Shah* [1997] Imm AR 145, 153 (HC).

[42] Home Office, *A Points-Based System: Making Migration Work for Britain* (Cm 6741, 2006); House of Commons Home Affairs Committee, *Managing Migration: The Points Based System* (2008–09 HC 217).

member states apply common criteria when assessing asylum claims.[43] However, concerns have been raised that the vagueness and ambiguity inherent in several of the Directive's provisions have raised difficulties for decision-makers seeking to reach quick and robust decisions. The scope for interpreting legal concepts in different ways has resulted in intensive recourse to appeals and to subsequent applications, and in high rates of successful appeals against negative decisions. By 2009, proposals had been published to recast the Directive in order to simplify decision-making procedures, to enable initial decisions to be more robust, and to improve the efficiency of the asylum process.[44]

It could be argued that the intrinsic difficulties posed by asylum adjudication might not necessarily present much of a problem if decision-makers possessed limitless resources with which to make decisions. In an ideal world, the decision-maker would have unlimited resources with which to make decisions, would collect all the relevant facts and produce decisions of optimal quality. At the primary decisional level, decisions would be made by experienced, well-trained staff who could provide adequate, detailed reasons when refusing an asylum claim. At the judicial stage, judges would be assisted by competent representatives who would contribute to drawing out the relevant facts and making submissions.

But, of course, decision-making, whether at the initial, administrative level or the appellate, judicial level, is not like this at all. It is undertaken by ordinary human beings who possess limited time and resources with which to collect the facts necessary for a decision and to make such decisions. Decision-makers may operate within incentive structures which often place considerable emphasis on producing decisions quickly with limited resources. Inevitably, the knowledge of such decision-makers is limited and the information presented before them incomplete. Furthermore, decisions must be made according to organisational routines. Consequently, decision-makers cannot seek out the perfect decision, but must instead 'satisfice' by settling for a satisfactory decision.[45] In this sense, the quest for decisional quality is a search for a satisfactory as opposed to an optimal form of quality. The basic challenges posed by asylum decision-making may be compounded by the constraints under which decision-makers necessarily operate, but how should the decision-making process itself to be organised?

---

[43] Refugee Qualification Directive, EU Council Directive 2004/83/EC on minimum standards for the qualification and status of third country nationals or stateless persons as refugees or as persons who otherwise need international protection and the content of the protection granted, OJ L304/12 of 30 September 2004 as transposed into UK law. See H Storey, 'EU Refugee Qualification Directive: a Brave New World?' (2008) 20 *International Journal of Refugee Law* 1.

[44] European Commission, *Proposal for a minimum standard for the qualification and status of third country nationals or stateless persons as beneficiaries of international protection and the content of the protection granted,* COM (2009) 551.

[45] JG March and HA Simon, *Organizations,* 2nd edn (Oxford, Blackwell, 1993) 161–162.

Organising Decision-Making

Asylum decision-making may be problematic, but given that neither the abolition of immigration controls nor withdrawal from the Refugee Convention seems likely, some decision process must be designed, but how exactly? This question raises a multitude of detailed questions concerning issues such as: the appeal procedures most appropriate for finding facts in asylum cases; the appropriate time limits for challenge; the test for assessing the adequacy of reasons; the handling of expert evidence; the scope and operation of onward rights of challenge; and others. Many of these, and other, issues will provide the basis of subsequent discussion, but it is important to recognise that they comprise only part of a wider enterprise: the institutional design of an administrative process for dealing with asylum claimants. It is only by considering the broader issue—the design and organisation of an effective decision process for asylum claims—that the narrower administrative law issues can be properly placed in context.

The basic normative question is this: how should this decision process be organised? Answers to this question tend to generate at least three ways of organising a decision process, each of which possesses its own distinct, and competing, processes, cultures and legitimising values. Following Mashaw's analysis, three principal models can be identified: the administrative model; the legal model; and the professional judgment model.[46]

Under the first model, decision-making is understood as an essentially administrative process. The primary goal should be to devise an effective means by which a mass of claims can be processed accurately and efficiently in order to implement policy. According to the second model, the legal model, decision-making is understood primarily as a legal, judicial process in which disputes concerning an individual's status and rights are resolved by way of adjudication. By contrast, the third model—professional judgment—approaches decision-making from a different perspective. Under this model, professional judgment is needed in order to meet the needs of a client through, for instance, medical diagnosis and assessment. The primary goal of this model is to serve the client.

Each model reflects a different way of organising a decision-making system and is underpinned by a different set of legitimising values. As Mashaw observed, each model is coherent and attractive in its own way, but when put together they are highly competitive. The stronger the presence of any one particular model, then the weaker the other models will be. From this perspective, the degree to which any given system of decision-making is able to promote administrative justice depends

---

[46] JL Mashaw, *Bureaucratic Justice: Managing Social Security Disability Claims* (New Haven, Yale University Press, 1983) 23–31. Mashaw used somewhat different labels—bureaucratic rationality, moral judgment, and professional treatment—which have been replaced here with the administrative model, the legal model, and the professional judgment model. For a development of Mashaw's analysis and the identification of other models, which are not relevant here, see M Adler, 'A Socio-legal Approach to Administrative Justice' (2003) 25 *Law & Policy* 323; M Adler, 'Fairness in Context' (2006) 33 *Journal of Law and Society* 615.

upon the trade-offs and compromises between the competing models which are reflected in the actual functioning of the decision-making system.

This way of thinking about the organisation of administrative justice has proved to be highly influential and has become embedded within the literature.[47] This is primarily because this analysis offers a pluralistic approach to administrative justice which recognises that the notion of administrative justice is itself disputed. This is not to say that different models of decision-making do not and cannot coexist alongside each other. Rather, the tensions between different institutional actors often arise because of the different underlying values reflected in different normative models as to how decision-making should be organised. This typology provides a useful analytical framework with which to understand the organisation of asylum decision-making as each of the three models are clearly reflected in some aspect of the decision process. But while the 'models of administrative justice' approach may be illuminating, it needs to be supplemented by an analysis of the complex relationships that can arise between different institutional actors and the nature of the tensions that arise between them in the context of a particular policy-decisional context. It is this analysis to which we now turn.

Administrative Organisation

The most common way of organising those decision-making tasks for which government has assumed responsibility is through administrative organisation. The principal focus of this model is upon the effective and efficient implementation of the policy programme through an administrative agency. Such agencies are often structured by the various features of bureaucracy: formalised and standardised routine operating tasks; a proliferation of rules and regulations for officials to apply; and hierarchical organisation of the agency with an emphasis upon internal control to ensure that policy is implemented efficiently. This model has its intellectual foundations in Weber's analysis of bureaucracy and can be seen reflected in Mintzberg's concept of the machine bureaucracy.[48]

Given the centrality of the immigration control function to the modern state, the administrative model has traditionally been dominant as far as asylum has been concerned. A large-scale, heavily staffed administrative agency—the UK Border Agency—is needed to implement policy by processing claims efficiently. In turn, this requires routinisation and standardisation of decision processes. Policy is contained in the Immigration Rules, as supplemented by internal agency instructions and guidance, which are administered by various Home Office officials (such as Immigration Officers, Home Office case-owners and presenting

---

[47] See, eg, S Halliday, *Judicial Review and Compliance with Administrative Law* (Oxford, Hart Publishing, 2004) 116–124; P Cane, *Administrative Tribunals and Adjudication* (Oxford, Hart Publishing, 2009) 209–218.

[48] M Weber, *Economy and Society* (Berkeley, University of California Press, 1978) 956–1003; H Mintzberg, *The Structuring of Organizations: A Synthesis of the Research* (Englewood Cliffs NJ, Prentice-Hall, 1979) 314–347.

officers). These decision-makers form the agency's operating core and are overseen by its middle management, who in turn are overseen by its strategic apex, the agency's management board, which is answerable to ministers. Within this administrative context, asylum decision-making is organised to accomplish the government's policy objective—maintaining immigration control while also providing protection to those at risk on return—effectively and efficiently. The decision-makers involved, Home Office case-owners, are neither judges nor professional experts, but administrative officials. Their skill arises not from any particular professional knowledge, legal or otherwise, but from their ability to apply the rules. Decision-making is administrative not adjudicative; case-workers are just taking straightforward administrative decisions as to whether an individual qualifies under the rules rather than adjudicating disputes.

A particularly important factor augmenting the dominance of this model in the asylum context arises from its focus upon enforcement and removals in order to implement policy. Administering asylum policy implies not just taking decisions, but also, and crucially, implementing those decisions so that refugees are integrated and failed claimants are removed. If the policy goal is to maintain effective immigration control, then the removal of unsuccessful claimants is essential. Only the immigration bureaucracy possesses the necessary coercive legal powers, administrative personnel, financial resources, and organisational infrastructure (eg immigration detention and removal centres and escorted removals processes) to enforce that control.

The ideal type of administrative organisation is premised upon the technical superiority of bureaucracy. It provides the dominant model in the asylum decision process. However, its actual operation has long been afflicted by numerous difficulties and the Home Office's performance has rarely lived up to the ideal. An almost habitual source of criticism has been that initial decision-making is invariably of poor and inferior quality. A broader theme of administrative justice, concerns over initial decision-making are often to be found in many areas of administration, especially in high volume systems in which a mass of decisions needs to be processed quickly. Critiques of the inferior quality of initial Home Office decision-making are ubiquitous though and have often been accompanied by calls to front-load the process so as to get it right first time and thereby avoid lengthy and costly appeal proceedings.[49] In 2004, the National Audit Office found that pressure to meet processing targets, the complexity of some cases, and a lack of clear ownership within the process for decisions once a case is passed onto the next stage sometimes led to issues having to be resolved unnecessarily at the appeal stage.

---

[49] See, eg, Asylum Aid, *Still No Reason At All* (London, Asylum Aid, 1999); House of Commons Home Affairs Committee, *Asylum Applications* (2003–04 HC 218) [118]–[145]; House of Commons Constitutional Affairs Committee, *Asylum and Immigration Appeals* (2003–04 HC 211) [11]–[15]; Amnesty International, *Get It Right: How Home Office Decision-making Fails Refugees* (London, Amnesty International, 2004); Independent Asylum Commission, *Report of Interim Findings* (London, IAC, 2008); T Trueman, 'Reasons for Refusal: An Audit of 200 Refusals of Ethiopian Asylum-seekers in England' (2009) 23 *Journal of Immigration, Asylum, and Nationality Law* 281.

Consequently, significant costs were being incurred by relying upon Immigration Judges to address the weaknesses at the front-end of the process.[50] To its credit, the Home Office has instigated a number of initiatives to raise decision-making standards: quality assurance processes; a quality initiative project with the UNHCR; the new asylum model under which a single case-owner is responsible for handling the same case throughout the whole process; and the piloting of new arrangements to front-load the provision of legal advice and assistance to promote effective joint-working between representatives and the Home Office.[51] By 2009, it was concluded that while the Home Office had made progress, it still needed to do more to enhance its decision-making, for instance, by ensuring better feedback from the appeals process to case-workers to get it right first time, enhanced quality assurance, and the adoption of targets to increase the quality, as well as the speed, of initial decisions in order to improve public confidence in its decision-making process.[52] Nevertheless, there is a difficult balance to strike between the quality of decision-making and administrative performance and efficiency.[53]

However, animadversions against the immigration agency are legion and not confined to the issue of decision-making quality. Administrative backlogs and delays, poor customer service and complaint handling, and high levels of customer dissatisfaction have all been frequent criticisms.[54] The agency has sometimes been castigated as the UK's most opaque and unhelpful bureaucracy subjecting claimants to an almost Kafkaesque bureaucratic nightmare.[55] Serious accusations have been laid against the agency in relation to the use of excessive detention and force against asylum claimants.[56] At the same time, another equally strong source

[50] National Audit Office, *Improving the Speed and Quality of Asylum Decisions* (2003–04 HC 535) 7.

[51] Ibid, 41–43; United Nations High Commissioner for Refugees, *Quality Initiative Project: A UNHCR Review of the UK Home Office Refugee Status Determination Procedures* (London, UNHCR, 2005); Home Office, *Controlling Our Borders: Making Migration Work for Britain* (Cm 6472, 2005) 35–36; J Aspden, *Evaluation of the Solihull Pilot for the United Kingdom Border Agency and the Legal Services Commission* (London, UKBA, 2008).

[52] House of Commons Public Accounts Committee, *Management of Asylum Applications* (2008–09) National Audit Office, *Management of Asylum Applications by the UK Border Agency* (2008–09 HC 124); HM Treasury, *Treasury Minutes to the Twenty Eighth Report from the House of Commons Public Accounts Committee Session 2008–09* (Cm 7717, 2009).

[53] Independent Chief Inspector of the UK Border Agency, *Asylum: Getting the Balance Right? A Thematic Inspection: July—November 2009* (London, OCIUKBA, 2010).

[54] See Complaints Audit Committee, *Annual Report 2007/08* (London, UKBA, 2008); Parliamentary and Health Service Ombudsman, *'Fast and Fair?' A Report by the Parliamentary Ombudsman on the UK Border Agency* (2009–10 HC 329); United Kingdom Border Agency, *Customer Strategy 2009–2012* (London, UKBA, 2009).

[55] For judicial allusions to Kafka in the asylum context see, eg, *R v Secretary of State for the Home Department, ex parte Anufrijeva* [2003] UKHL 36; [2004] 1 AC 604 [28] (Lord Steyn); *Chikwamba v Secretary of State for the Home Department* [2008] UKHL 40; [2008] 1 WLR 1420 [4] (Lord Scott).

[56] See Northern Ireland Human Rights Commission, *Our Hidden Borders: The UK Border Agency's Powers of Detention* (NIHRC, 2008); *Outsourcing Abuse: The Use and Misuse of State-sanctioned Force During the Detention and Removal of Asylum Seekers* (A report by Birnberg Peirce & Partners, Medical Justice, and the National Coalition of Anti-Deportation Campaigns, 2008); Children's Commissioner for England, *The Arrest and Detention of Children Subject to Immigration Control* (London, Children's Commissioner for England, 2009); N O'Loan, *Report to the United Kingdom Border Agency on 'Outsourcing Abuse'* (London, UKBA, 2010).

of criticism has been the agency's apparent inability to function effectively; 'not fit for purpose' as a former Home Secretary once put it, in an unprecedented public denunciation by a government minister of his own department.[57]

In its endeavours to manage the system, the agency has encountered numerous difficulties, some of which have resulted in dysfunctional administrative outcomes, thereby generating political fall-out, and followed in turn by more restrictive legal rules. Take the large-scale failure to remove failed claimants, for instance. The problems in seeking to remove unsuccessful claimants have prompted the Home Office to process claims through expedited timeframes, which in turn have contributed to its focus upon process and on politically driven organisational imperatives rather than decisional quality. Increased timeliness generates criticism that the decisions produced are likely to be of inferior quality. However, the focus upon enforcing more asylum removals has itself produced perverse consequences as the debacle over the failure to deport foreign national prisoners illustrates.[58] Furthermore, many thousands of asylum claimants have been left to languish for years without a decision. This has resulted in several dire outcomes: the failure to recognise those genuinely entitled to asylum; the non-removal of those who do not qualify; increased costs to the taxpayer; untold misery upon those concerned; social division; and decreased public confidence in the immigration system.[59]

The underperformance of the immigration agency has, then, been substantial. It has arisen in no small part because of the sheer scale of the challenge presented by a historically high volume of asylum claims. Furthermore, the work of the immigration agency must be seen within the context of the politically hazardous nature of the Home Office's environment of balancing liberty with security and a flow of administrative work characterised by a tyranny of individual case-work and short-term crisis management. Nonetheless, the administrative model remains the dominant way of organising the asylum decision process. Despite its failings, the immigration agency continues to play the central role in the decision process. The Government's current agenda is focused upon reforming the agency and simplifying its legal framework, rather than replacing it altogether.[60] Furthermore, calls to transfer first-instance asylum decision-making from the

---

[57] See House of Commons Home Affairs Select Committee, *Immigration Control* (2005–06 HC 775) vol II Ev 155 (Dr John Reid). See also Cabinet Office, *Capability Review of the Home Office* (London, Cabinet Office, 2006); C Painter, 'A Government Department in Meltdown: Crisis at the Home Office' (2008) 28 *Public Money & Management* 275; R Ford, 'Minister Admits: We Got It Wrong On Immigration' *The Times* (3 November 2009).

[58] S Hyde, *A Review of the Failure of the Immigration and Nationality Directorate to Consider Some Foreign National Prisoners for Deportation* (London, IND, 2007). The episode resulted in the dismissal of the Home Secretary and the introduction of tougher rules governing deportation. See UK Borders Act 2007.

[59] R Ford, 'Our Asylum Failure "Has Spread Misery and Division"' *The Times* (21 October 2008) 17; L Bannerman, 'High-rise Asylum Seekers Plumb Depths of Despair' *The Times* (13 March 2010).

[60] Home Office Immigration and Nationality Directorate, *Fair, Effective, Transparent, and Trusted: Rebuilding Confidence in our Immigration System* (London, Home Office, 2006); Cabinet Office, *Security in a Global Hub: Establishing the UK's New Border Arrangements* (London, Cabinet Office, 2007); Borders, Citizenship, and Immigration Act 2009; Secretary of State for the Home Department, *Simplifying Immigration Law: The Draft Bill* (Cm 7730, 2009); Draft Immigration Bill 2009 (Cm 7666, 2009).

immigration agency to an independent body to free it from political or policy influence have habitually been resisted on the ground of ministerial responsibility. Given the high political profile of asylum, government ministers simply do not want to surrender any responsibility for it.[61] This responsibility, or control, is best achieved by retaining asylum decision-making within the immigration agency. The status of the agency itself may have changed from a directorate to an executive agency with its strategic objectives, responsibilities, and lines of accountability formally laid down in its framework agreement. Yet, it remains located within its parent government department, the Home Office, with its own minister of state to defend it before Parliament.

Tribunal Adjudication

Administrative organisation is not the only way of designing a decision process. By contrast, the introduction of a tribunal adjudicatory process represents the adoption of the legal model, and with this comes a different set of decision processes and values. Routine decision processes are still necessary, but the procedures used are primarily attuned to the adjudication of disputes. Two parties have a dispute which they cannot resolve by themselves and therefore submit it to a neutral third party whose decision is binding. In the administrative justice context, adjudication will often function as a means of implementing policy. However, unlike the administrative process, adjudication is not normally thought of in these terms; nor is it generally considered to derive its legitimacy from its role in policy implementation. Given the adjudicatory orientation, the legal model espouses certain values, principally fairness and independence. Its principal function is to enable affected parties to participate, through fair and open procedures, in the making of a decision which will resolve their dispute. To ensure the impartial application of the law, the decision-maker needs to be structurally independent of the administrative agency concerned and to act in a judicial manner.

In the asylum context, adjudication has often been viewed as a subsidiary to the dominant administrative model. One the reason for this arises from the lower number of decisions the Tribunal takes when compared with the Home Office. Even though asylum has a high appeal rate, the Tribunal only hear appeals lodged by appellants wishing to challenge initial negative decisions; initial positive and un-appealed negative decisions are outside its jurisdiction.

But the principal reason for the subsidiary role of the legal model is the influence the immigration bureaucracy exerts upon both the design and the operation of the appeals process. The Tribunal's jurisdiction is, after all, framed through legislation, which is first and foremost the legal expression of governmental policy. The appeals process is resourced by government. Furthermore, government has consistently sought—with highly varying degrees of success—to ensure that the process operates

---

[61] See House of Lords European Union Committee, *Handling EU Asylum Claims: New Approaches Examined* (2003–04 HL 74) [110].

quickly. When the Home Office's long-term opposition to creating asylum appeals eventually collapsed in 1993, a right of appeal was established to the pre-existing immigration appeal system.[62] However, by 1998, the Government was expressing concern that 'what was intended to be a simple and speedy review of immigration decisions has grown into a complex, legalistic, time consuming, and expensive process'.[63] This, in turn, prompted further efforts by the Home Office to speed up the process. So, from 1993 to 2002, the statutory appeals system operated under a certification process under which unmeritorious cases could be certified by the Home Office, with the consequence that an appellant would have limited appeal rights.[64] Other devices designed to speed up the processing of unmeritorious appeals have included the use of detained fast-track and non-suspensive appeal procedures (the process by which refused applicants from designated safe countries may only appeal from outside the UK).[65]

It has not, of course, been solely one-way traffic. The position of the Tribunal has been augmented over the years in various ways. Before 1987, Immigration Adjudicators (now Immigration Judges) were both appointed and paid by the Home Office and were not therefore structurally independent of the Home Office, though the Immigration Appeal Tribunal was always an independent judicial body.[66] Adjudicators were not legally qualified, but largely recruited from the former colonial service. However, in 1987, responsibility for appointments was transferred to (what is now) the Ministry of Justice and, over the same period, the practice of recruiting adjudicators from the ranks of legally qualified lawyers evolved.[67] The old procedure by which appellants had to lodge their appeal notices with the Home Office rather than the Tribunal—with the consequence that the speed with which an appeal progressed was entirely within the control not of the Tribunal, but of the Home Office—has ended.[68] However, this has been replaced by a curious arrange-

---

[62] The immigration appeals system has been in operation since 1970. See Home Office, *Report of the Committee on Immigration Appeals* (Cmnd 3387, 1967); Immigration Appeals Act 1969; Immigration Act 1971, pt II; D Pearl, 'Immigration and Asylum Appeals and Administrative Justice' in M Harris and M Partington (eds), *Administrative Justice in the 21st Century* (Oxford, Hart Publishing, 1999) 55.

[63] Home Office and Lord Chancellor's Department, *Review of Appeals: A Consultation Paper* (London, Home Office and LCD, 1998) [2.1].

[64] Asylum and Immigration Appeals Act 1993; Asylum and Immigration Act 1996; Immigration and Asylum Act 1999 sch 4 para 9.

[65] The Asylum and Immigration Tribunal (Fast Track Procedure) Rules SI 2005/560; Immigration Law Practitioners' Association, *The Detained Fast Track Process: A Best Practice Guide* (London, ILPA, 2008); Nationality, Immigration and Asylum Act 2002 s 94; S Woodhouse, *The Annual Report of the Certification Monitor 2005* (London, IND, 2005); Independent Chief Inspector of the UK Border Agency, *Report July 2008—September 2009* (London, OCIUKBA, 2009) 25–30.

[66] Immigration Act 1971 s 12.

[67] The Transfer of Functions (Immigration Appeals) Order SI 1987/465.

[68] CG Blake, 'Immigration Appeals—The Need for Reform' in A Dummett (ed), *Towards a Just Immigration Policy* (London, Cobden Trust, 1986) 179; Asylum and Immigration Tribunal (Procedure) Rules SI 2005/230 r 6(1). This procedure has proved particularly useful to the Home Office when it has sought to delay the determination of claims from a specific country until the conditions have improved. A specific example is provided by the Tribunal's decision to accede to a request by the Secretary of State to adjourn all Iraqi asylum appeals on the outbreak of the Iraq war in 2003. See M Quayum and M Chatwin, 'A Fair-handed Approach?' (2003) 153 *New Law Journal* 533.

ment by which the Tribunal must serve its determination on the Home Office, itself a party to the appeals process, which then serves it on the appellant.[69] Responsibility for making the Tribunal's procedure rules no longer rests with the Ministry of Justice (with substantial Home Office influence), but with the independent Tribunal Procedure Committee.[70] Statutory rules prescribing how Immigration Judges are to go about making (negative) findings of fact have largely been neutralised by the courts.[71] Furthermore, as we shall see in chapter seven, the Tribunal has developed a distinctive technique of asylum adjudication—the country guidance concept—by which it issues wide-ranging guidance upon country conditions. Finally, the courts have strongly criticised Home Office attempts to undermine the appeals process through the non-implementation of Tribunal rulings.[72]

A more frequent source of concern for the Tribunal has been at the more mundane level of daily decision-making and appeal hearings. For instance, the Tribunal has complained that the Home Office's 'lack of skilled and professional care in reaching the initial decision necessarily places extra burdens' on Immigration Judges.[73] Simple Home Office incompetence and inefficiency can pose a challenge for the Tribunal in its endeavour to operate a fair appeals process while also undermining the Home Office's own desire for efficiency. Examples of low level, amateurish Home Office bungling have been common; the law reports are replete with judicial excoriations of the Home Office: 'incapable of dealing with the appeals in the manner in which they ought to be dealt with'; 'verging on the contumacious'; 'notoriously inefficient'; 'a public disgrace'.[74] But, despite its scathing fulminations, the Tribunal has, for the most part, simply had to put up with it.

The Tribunal has, then, simultaneously rebuffed Home Office attempts to influence its approach and criticised the Home Office for its inefficiency, but the relationship between the two bodies is a complex and subtle one. To a large extent, the Tribunal is reliant upon the Home Office to give its adjudicatory function some practical meaning. Consider, for instance, the issue of removing failed claimants. As an independent judicial decision-maker, the enforcement of immigration controls is none of the Tribunal's concern; its function is to adjudicate on appeals, not to implement the outcomes reached. Nevertheless, the large-scale failure to remove unsuccessful claimants presents the Tribunal with the perennial

---

[69] Asylum and Immigration Tribunal (Procedure Rules) SI 2005/230 r 23(4).

[70] Tribunals, Courts and Enforcement Act 2007 s 22; Home Office, *Immigration Appeals: Response to Consultation—Fair Decisions; Faster Justice* (London, Home Office UKBA and Tribunals Service, 2009) 10.

[71] Asylum and Immigration (Treatment of Claimants, etc.) Act 2004 s 8; *SM v Secretary of State for the Home Department (Section 8: Judge's Process) Iran* [2005] UKAIT 00116; *JT (Cameroon) v Secretary of State for the Home Department* [2008] EWCA Civ 878; [2009] 1 WLR 1411.

[72] See, eg, *R (S) v Secretary of State for the Home Department* [2006] EWHC Admin 1111; [2006] EWCA Civ 1157.

[73] *Horvath v Secretary of State for the Home Department* [1999] Imm AR 121 (IAT) 129–130.

[74] *Tatar v Secretary of State for the Home Department* (00TH01914), date notified 27 July 2000 [3]; *Benkaddouri v Secretary of State for the Home Department* [2004] INLR 1, 3 (Sedley LJ); *M v Secretary of State for the Home Department (Chad)* [2004] UKIAT 00044 [4]; *Secretary of State for the Home Department v Akaeke* [2005] EWCA Civ 947; [2005] Imm AR 701, 704 (Carnwath LJ) (CA).

concern that its adjudication of appeals might be rendered largely hypothetical. After all, what is the point of the Tribunal administering a complex and difficult decision process from which there is a high rate of onward challenge if the Home Office rarely enforces such decisions? The structural relationship between the Tribunal and the Home Office reinforces the sense that while the legal model plays an essential role in the decision process, it is a supporting role nonetheless.

Experts

The administrative and legal models are easily recognisable in the asylum process; indeed, they are present in many decision-making systems. There is, though, a third model, that of professional judgment. Unlike the other two models, this model does not treat claimants as either the passive recipients of an administrative process or as litigants in an adjudicatory process. Rather, it treats them as individual clients whose particular needs can only be met through the application of specialised, professional knowledge, acquired through specialist training and/or membership of a professional grouping. The goal of professional judgment is to meet those needs; medical expertise is the paradigm example of reliance upon and trust in professional judgment, but other professions and experts may play some role in any given decision process.

The wider significance of the professional judgment model to governmental administration in the UK has been doubted, but its presence in the asylum context is readily discernible.[75] Indeed, the nature of the asylum decision problem may often require the exercise of specialist knowledge not only to provide assistance in the decision process, but also to meet the particular needs of people who seek protection from persecution or serious ill-treatment. If an individual has suffered torture—a serious indicator of future risk—then medical expertise may be required not just to document it, but also to enable the individual concerned to recover from the trauma of the experience. Likewise, as asylum decision-making requires an assessment of conditions in countries generating asylum claimants, then specialised knowledge of the conditions, cultures, and customs of such countries may be necessary. Neither the administrative model nor the legal model is primarily geared up to providing such specialist knowledge. Expert witnesses are often commissioned by claimants to produce their opinions on matters within their area of expertise. Medical experts are often instructed to document and interpret the physical injuries of torture survivors. Likewise, psychiatric reports diagnose whether a claimant's depressed state of mind is the result of a past traumatic experience such as torture. Both sets of professionals may also have a therapeutic role in terms of treating the claimant's (their patient's) condition.

The asylum process has also generated other specialist experts. Age assessment reports may be submitted by specialist medics to assess the age of a claimant when

---

[75] Halliday above n 47 at 119.

this has been disputed. Finally, there are country experts, those individuals with a special interest in and knowledge of a particular country generating asylum claims, who produce expert reports upon the conditions in that country, which might assist in the assessment of whether a claimant would be at risk on return. Country expertise may be relied upon to add definition and depth to the understanding of the situation in a particular country and thereby provide professional expertise that cannot be derived from other sources of country information.

Despite the range of ends for which professional judgment may be deployed in asylum decision-making, this model is, for a number of reasons, the weakest of the three that operates in this context. Experts are themselves a disparate collection of people from a variety of different disciplines. Their reports tend only to be used at the appeal stage of the decision-making process as claimants are unable to secure funding with which to instruct an expert until they lodge an appeal. There is also, as we will examine in more detail, a major source of tension between the Tribunal and experts as to the evidential value that Immigration Judges ought properly to place upon expert opinions. From the perspective of experts themselves, the Tribunal, as a legal decision-maker, is often not suitably well-qualified to substitute its own uninformed views for their professional and expert judgments; the Tribunal should therefore normally defer to an expert's professional judgment. The Tribunal's reluctance to adopt this approach has been motivated by the view that it would in effect abdicate its responsibility for deciding appeals. For instance, the Tribunal has often been unenthusiastic about accepting expert evidence predicated on the assumption that the claimant has been telling the truth when this is often precisely the issue in dispute before it. Furthermore, the Tribunal has long harboured concerns as to the quality and independence of some experts. It has, for instance, been known for some individuals to make their living by producing many expert reports, and there is a suspicion that some such people might allow their views to be influenced, even unconsciously, by the hope or prospect of receiving further instructions of a similar kind in the future. A further weakness with expert evidence is that it is routinely commissioned by claimants; the Tribunal has no power to obtain its own expert evidence. The upshot of this is that expert evidence may often be seen as party evidence rather than independent expert evidence; consequently, there may be little reason why expert evidence by itself should necessarily carry great weight.

For its part, the Home Office often tends to view expert evidence commissioned by appellants as self-serving and rarely commissions its own expert evidence. This is not to imply that the Home Office is entirely dismissive of the value of expert evidence. The Home Office has, for instance recognised the importance of medical reports in its internal guidance and instructed its case-workers to avoid making clinical judgments.[76] Nevertheless, the Home Office robustly challenges expert evidence commissioned by appellants.

---

[76] Home Office UKBA, *Asylum Process Guidance, Medical Evidence (Non-Medical Foundation Cases) and Medical Foundation Cases* www.ukba.homeoffice.gov.uk/sitecontent/documents/policyandlaw/asylumprocessguidance/consideringanddecidingtheclaim/.

Decision-Making Models and the Politics of Asylum

One would, of course, expect much tension to arise within such a politicised area. Ministers may criticise immigration lawyers for playing the system while governmental officials may view lawyers themselves as a problem and their repeated use of legal process as a means of frustrating effective administration. Many immigration lawyers are aligned with non-governmental organisations such as the Immigration Law Practitioners' Association and the Immigration Advisory Service, which have a broader campaigning role and often lobby government and Parliament. They also see their role in terms of protecting the vulnerable against the overly powerful bureaucratic machine which is the Home Office. While the Home Office formally recognises the Tribunal's independence, there is sometimes a perception that it wishes to influence the Tribunal's approach. Of course, the Tribunal is itself intimately aware of the political context, but to preserve its independence and impartiality must refrain from entering into any political controversy. Meanwhile, some experts may also have a broader campaigning role, especially if they have organised themselves as such (the Medical Foundation for the Care of Victims of Torture is the exemplar); other experts have been known to speak out to criticise both the Home Office and the Tribunal.

Putting the ongoing and pervasive political controversy of asylum decision-making to one side, it is apparent that the models of administrative justice reflect different conceptions as to how the asylum decision process should be organised. Each of the different models seems plausible in its own terms; each is rooted in some broader conception as to how decision-making can be best organised and structured. Consequently, there are competing tensions between how the different approaches operate in practice. Nevertheless, the different models are not antithetical. Because there must be some sort of decision process that, to some extent at least, actually works, different approaches must be mediated. This is not to say that the process of mediating different approaches is problem-free. On the contrary, it tends to provoke adverse reactions which in turn can fuel political controversy. If administrative justice concerns the acceptability and legitimacy of decision-making processes and institutions, then it is apparent that there is no single best way by which a decision process can be organised because each of the three models appeals to different values. Which model is desired will depend upon which underlying values are to be preferred.

The discussion in this section has focused on the issue of the overall organisation of the decision-making process, but this does exhaust our focus upon institutional design. This is because each of the different models must themselves be organised appropriately. As the focus of this book is upon the quality of asylum adjudication, that is, asylum decision-making under the legal model, it is necessary to consider some essential aspects of the Tribunal's own organisation, in particular its jurisdiction and personnel. It is these matters to which we now turn.

The Tribunal's Jurisdiction and Organisation

The Tribunal's function is to determine appeals against the refusal of asylum by the Home Office. Strictly speaking, appeals cannot be brought against the refusal of asylum; rather, individuals may appeal against an immigration decision to remove them from the UK. Appeals are brought on the ground that such removal would breach the UK's obligations under the Refugee Convention or would be incompatible with an individual's rights under the ECHR.[77] An appellant cannot normally be removed whilst an appeal is pending.[78] The Tribunal's task is either to allow an appeal if the initial decision was not made in accordance with the law or to dismiss it.[79]

In general terms, the appeals process is comprised of two parts: the initial fact-finding merits appeal stage; and then onward challenge on error of law grounds. The first stage, the hearing of initial appeals, is normally undertaken by a single Immigration Judge. The Tribunal is currently comprised of some 700 members, 591 of which are Immigration Judges. The majority of Immigration Judges (470) are fee-paid (sit on a part-time basis) while 121 are salaried (full-time). Immigration Judges hear appeals at one of the Tribunal's 15 hearing centres located throughout the UK.[80] There are also 10 Resident Senior Immigration Judges located in the hearing centres in addition to 25 Designated Immigration Judges who oversee and manage small teams of Immigration Judges. Immigration Judges must have seven years experience as a legal practitioner or have other legal experience and are appointed by the Lord Chancellor.[81] Immigration Judges are in the lowest group of the Judicial Salaries and Fees scale and equivalent to District and Employment Judges.[82] As regards their background, Immigration Judges are largely drawn from the ranks of practising lawyers; they might have practised in immigration and asylum law, but more often than not, they will not have done so. Some Immigration Judges might also hold other judicial positions whether on other tribunals (such as Mental Health Review Tribunals or the Special Educational Needs and Disability Tribunal) or as a recorder in the Crown Court.

[77] Nationality, Immigration, and Asylum Act 2002 ss 82 and 84.
[78] Nationality, Immigration, and Asylum Act 2002 s 78.
[79] Nationality, Immigration, and Asylum Act 2002 s 86(3).
[80] To illustrate the scale of the jurisdiction, the Tribunal's hearing centre in Hatton Cross (near London's Heathrow airport)—reputedly, one of Europe's largest tribunal centres—has 26 hearing rooms in addition to two of its own 'satellite' hearing centres (one of which is the Harmondsworth 'detained fast-track' appeal centre); some 120 Immigration Judges are linked to this hearing centre. As its name suggests, the Asylum and *Immigration* Tribunal also handles various types of non-asylum appeals. As regards caseload, in 2006/07 (2007/08 figures in brackets), the Tribunal determined a total number (both immigration and asylum) of 166,899 (161,517) appeals of which 14,735 (13,700) were asylum appeals; it also determined 7,284 (7,691) review applications in asylum cases and 'reconsidered' some 3,935 (3,573) asylum appeals (source: Asylum and Immigration Tribunal website, *Provisional Statistics for 2006–07 and 2007–08*).
[81] Nationality, Immigration and Asylum Act 2002 sch 4.
[82] Ministry of Justice, *Judicial Salaries and Fees 2008–09* (London, Ministry of Justice, 2008).

There are also some 52 non-legal members, a legacy of the old Immigration Appeal Tribunal, who used to sit as 'wing-members' on that tribunal and who now sit on country guidance and other types of appeals, such as deportation appeals. Since 1999, the Tribunal's President has been a High Court judge who has been supported by two Deputy Presidents—one responsible for development of the law and the other for matters of judicial administration.[83] Onward challenges against initial appeal decisions by Immigration Judges are considered by the Tribunal's 25 Senior Immigration Judges, who are located centrally in London. Onward rights of challenges have been limited to error of law grounds since 2002.[84] The senior judges also hear country guidance cases and undertake other types of appeal casework.

All newly appointed Immigration Judges receive induction training on the work of the whole jurisdiction. As regards refugee and asylum law, the training lasts for two days. It is also compulsory for judges to sit in and observe both before and after the induction course prior to hearing appeals alone. All members of the judiciary receive at least one day per year update training. In addition, under the AIT's residential continuation training programme run on a roughly three year cycle, every judge attends a course of two days. This is equivalent to the training received by Recorders of the Crown Court. Furthermore, there is a biennial conference for the salaried judges only. Immigration Judges are also subject to a formal mentoring and appraisal scheme. Designated Immigration Judges and more experienced judges act as mentors to provide support to others. In 2005, the Tribunal introduced an appraisal system to provide support and feedback to judges. This scheme focuses on the skills required of judges in order to meet high judicial standards (preparing for appeals, managing the list of appeals, conduct of the hearing and deliberation and determination preparation). There is also the informal and collegiate environment of the hearing centres.

As regards the exercise of its jurisdiction, the Tribunal performs an appellate function by producing its own decisions on the basis of the evidence; its role is not simply to evaluate the facts by another decision-maker, but to make its own findings of fact to produce determinations which replace initial Home Office decisions. An important aspect of asylum appeals concerns precisely which facts can be taken into account by the Tribunal when determining appeals. For instance, in entry clearance (visa) appeals, the Tribunal may consider only the circumstances appertaining at the time of the decision to refuse.[85] The position is, though,

---

[83] The Tribunal's Presidents since 1999 have been Collins J, Ouseley J, Hodge J, and Blake J. Both Sir Andrew Collins and Sir Duncan Ouseley were High Court judges before their appointments as IAT Presidents. Hodge was the former Chief Immigration Adjudicator until 2005 and was appointed President of the AIT in 2005. Sir Nicholas Blake was appointed as the first President of the Upper Tribunal Immigration and Asylum Chamber in February 2010, having previously been appointed as a High Court judge. Blake had many years experience as a barrister specialising in immigration, asylum, and human rights law and had published widely in the area. See N Blake and L Fransman, *Immigration, Nationality and Asylum under the Human Rights Act 1998* (London, Butterworths, 1999); N Blake and R Husain, *Immigration, Asylum and Human Rights Law* (Oxford, Oxford University Press, 2003).

[84] Nationality, Immigration and Asylum Act 2002 s 101(1).

[85] Nationality, Immigration, and Asylum Act 2002 s 85(5).

different in asylum appeals: as asylum decisions concern the prospective risk of persecution, the Tribunal is able to take account of evidence that has arisen after the date of the initial decision.[86] The Tribunal's function is to assess risk on removal on the basis of the facts in existence at the date of the appeal decision. This approach has a number of advantages. It prevents status being determined on a false basis; as new facts can come into existence after the taking of initial decisions and country conditions can change for the better or worse, appellate proceedings are focused upon current rather than historical risk. Secondly, the Tribunal builds its own knowledge of the situation in countries; the appeals process would be rendered substantially less valuable if Immigration Judges were obliged to ignore changes in country conditions of which they were aware. Finally, this approach reduces, but does not altogether eliminate, the necessity for repeat applications or fresh asylum claims made after the appeal process has concluded and as country conditions change.[87]

Given that the Tribunal may take into account facts that have arisen after the date of the initial decision, it has been noted that the appellate structure is best regarded not as a process of reviewing decisions already taken, but 'as an extension of the decision-making process.[88] This remark has been contentious insofar as it implies that the Tribunal is to be regarded as an extension of the Home Office and not therefore an independent judicial decision-maker.[89] Nevertheless, the Tribunal is part of the broader decision-making process in that it has to test the decision under appeal against facts found by it as at the date of the hearing. As the Court of Appeal has observed, 'a decision on asylum is an administrative process differing in important ways from civil litigation. It follows that an appeal which tracks the original issues will have largely the same character'.[90]

More generally, it has been recognised that while the Tribunal is independent of the Home Office, it forms a critical part of the broader decision-making process for administering immigration and asylum policy.[91] This point is well-illustrated by the close connection between the timeliness of adjudication and administrative efficiency. Since the inception of full in-country appeal rights for asylum claimants in 1993, the structure of the appellate system has been subject to constant reform. Frequent overhauls of the appeal process have been introduced in order to ensure that appeals could be handled with the desired speed. The AIT was itself introduced in order to speed up the appeals process, whilst ensuring that proceedings could continue to be handled fairly, and to reduce the proportion of appeals and onward challenges to the AIT and the higher courts by improving the quality of

---

[86] *Sandralingham and Ravichandran v Secretary of State for the Home Department* [1995] EWCA Civ 16; [1996] Imm AR 97, 112–113 (Brown LJ) (CA); Nationality, Immigration, and Asylum Act 2002 s 85(4).

[87] Immigration Rules (1994 HC 395) r 353.

[88] *Sandralingham and Ravichandran* above n 86 at 112 (Simon Brown LJ).

[89] *Secretary of State for the Home Department v SK (Return—Ethnic Serb) Croatia CG* (Starred determination) [2002] UKIAT 05613 [20].

[90] *Karanakaran* above n 29 at 477–478 (Sedley LJ).

[91] See, eg, House of Commons Home Affairs Select Committee above n 57 at [391].

decisions on applications and appeals and introducing measures to discourage unmeritorious appeals and onward challenges.

However, as we shall see in chapter eight, the operation of the AIT since its introduction in 2005 has not been without counter-productive consequences; far from reducing the rate of onward challenges, the AIT appeal structure had the effect of increasing the volume of challenges to the higher courts, thereby increasing the caseload of those courts, in addition to increasing costs and delays. The solution has been to transfer the AIT into the generic First-tier and Upper Tribunals created under the Tribunals, Courts and Enforcement Act 2007. The essential purpose behind this is to limit the scope for challenging initial appeal determinations before the higher courts by ensuring that such challenges would be handled largely within the new two-tier tribunal system. The transfer, therefore, represents a further structural fine-tuning of the appellate process rather than the establishment of an altogether different and new tribunal system. Existing judicial appointments have been mapped on to the previous appellate structure. For instance, Senior Immigration Judges have become judges of the Upper Tribunal and Immigration Judges have become First-tier Tribunal judges.[92] While the formal name of the tribunal structure has changed, its personnel has remained the same. Other aspects of the appeals process are also unaffected. The transfer has made little difference to the way first-instance appeals are heard by Immigration Judges.

This is not, however, to imply that the transfer of the AIT into the First-tier and Upper Tribunals is an insignificant reform to the appeal structure. The principal change is with regard to the handling of onward rights of challenge against initial appeal determinations, in particular the replacement of the AIT's process of reconsideration with the ability to 'opt-in' to the Administrative Court, with a right of appeal to the Upper Tribunal. The transfer was designed to reduce the burden of asylum and immigration work in the higher courts and to promote fast decisions. What this reform indicates, as will become apparent throughout this book, is that the operation of administrative justice can be just as heavily influenced by broader managerial considerations—in particular, the best allocation of limited judicial and other resources and the need for timeliness in policy implementation—as by the need to ensure justice for individuals.

At the same time, the transfer may have other consequences. For instance, by reducing the scope for onward challenge to the higher courts, the ability of the Tribunal to develop the law along its own chosen course will be enhanced. But, in turn, this may generate further conflicts. For instance, should the higher courts defer to the expertise of the Tribunal with respect to those matters within its specialist knowledge, with the risk that the law develops incorrectly? Or, alternatively, should the higher courts assert their superiority in the judicial hierarchy, with the risk that additional costs and delays will be incurred in addition to successive case-

---

[92] R Carnwath, Senior President of Tribunals, *Third Implementation Review* (London, Tribunals Service, July 2009), annex C.

law in order to clarify earlier cases? The task of designing and operating an effective adjudication process requires many subtle and value-laden choices to be made.

Conclusion

This chapter has examined the nature of the challenges posed by the asylum decision problem, the broader organisation of the asylum decision process, and the particular organisation of the Tribunal itself. Asylum decision-making is unusually difficult. The legal definition of asylum and the legal concepts of refugee status and humanitarian protection are not tight and unambiguous, but fuzzy and open-textured. By their nature, they leave much scope for the decision-maker's own individual judgment and evaluation in deciding who qualifies for asylum.

To make decisions, facts concerning both an applicant's individual circumstances and the conditions in the relevant country are needed. The evidential material from which to make such findings of fact is typically of many different kinds and qualities. While facts are needed, the principal issues for the decision-maker are evaluative: has the claimant demonstrated a good case that he will be at risk on return? Underlying such evaluations lie value judgments concerning who needs and deserves asylum and the policy considerations underpinning immigration control. There is no basic agreement over what the purpose of asylum decision-making actually is and decision-making may serve either a gate-keeping or protecting function.

Some decision process is required and there are competing models—administrative, legal, and professional judgment—as to how the process should operate. These models reflect different ideas as to both how the decision process is and ought to be organised. They also correspond to different conceptions as to what comprises an acceptable or legitimate decision process. The models assume different institutional forms: an administrative agency; a tribunal; and expert witnesses. In any particular decision system, one model might possess a predominant position over other models. In the asylum context, the administrative model dominates, but the two other models have important roles to play. In light of the different values underpinning each model, tensions inevitably arise as to how the decision process can best be organised and how to make decisions. While these strains may be inherent, a workable system needs to manage these tensions effectively so that decisions can be made.

While there are broader questions as to how the decision process ought to be organised, there are also more specific issues as to how each component of the broader decision process is itself to be organised. While the Tribunal has experienced various changes to its institutional structure, its basic structure is comprised of two sets of personnel: Immigration Judges who undertake first-instance fact-based appeals; and Senior Immigration Judges who focus upon correcting error of laws and issuing legal and other guidance.

The discussion in this chapter has only raised some of the issues as to how the decision-making function both is and should be organised. The next chapter will consider the competing values underpinning the operation of the appeals process, in particular the relationships between accuracy, procedural fairness, and efficiency. Together these two chapters will together provide the broader framework against which the rest of the book will examine the empirical reality as to how the Tribunal hears appeals and goes about the task of making decisions.

3

Costs, Accuracy and Decision Processes

T HE PREVIOUS CHAPTER considered the nature of the asylum decision task and the organisation of decision-making. The task of this chapter is to analyse two central aspects of the concept of adjudicative quality: the amount of resources that should be devoted to the task of producing good decisions and the contribution of adjudication procedures to this end.

One of the principal purposes of an adjudication process is (or should be) to reduce the number of errors that can arise. Incorrect asylum appeal decisions impose huge costs for either the individual appellants concerned or the state in terms of its desire to secure immigration control. Accurate decisions are required, but the procedures designed to reduce such errors are themselves costly. There is simply no inexhaustible supply of resources with which correct decisions are to be purchased; society is unable to allocate a limitless supply of resources to this or indeed any adjudication process.

When tribunal adjudication is viewed from the governmental standpoint, then efficiency considerations assume considerable importance.[1] In managing a decision process, government will inevitably ask itself the following questions: how much will this cost? Why should public money be spent on it? And, does it provide value for money? The governmental concern is normally to ensure that financial costs are minimised as far as possible, but how far is that to be? In principle, there is an optimal level of error reduction at which the benefits of minimising decisional errors approximates to the costs of the procedures employed. Such sentiment can be seen reflected in recent governmental policy on administrative justice through the idea that there should be a proportionate relationship between the issues at stake in a dispute and the financial cost of the procedures used.[2] But this notion merely sums up a desirable characteristic of administrative justice—the costs incurred should be proportionate to the value of decisions—it does not explain how to go about the task of finding what the proportionate or optimum balance might be.

---

[1] Given the centrality of cost to governmental administration, constitutional studies of the executive have been based on a positive theory of the constitution of the state as a set of rules for resource-allocation. See T Daintith and A Page, *The Executive in the Constitution: Structure, Autonomy, and Internal Control* (Oxford, Oxford University Press, 1999).

[2] Department for Constitutional Affairs, *Transforming Public Services: Complaints, Redress and Tribunals* (Cm 6243, 2004) ch2. See also M Adler, 'Tribunal Reform: Proportionate Dispute Resolution and the Pursuit of Administrative Justice' (2006) 69 *Modern Law Review* 958, 965–983.

Adjudicative efficiency raises a related matter: which particular procedures are most likely to produce good decisions? It is only worthwhile committing resources to those procedures which are likely to minimise decisional errors. In designing an adjudication system, there are normally a number of procedural choices concerning, for instance, the identity of the adjudicator, the procedures to be used, the presence of representation, and the organisation of onward rights of challenge. The task of designing an effective adjudicative process requires close attention to the relative advantages and disadvantages of the available procedural options. At a very basic level, the quality of an adjudication system is dependant upon the amount of resources allocated to it by which procedures can be purchased and, in turn, the ability of the procedures selected to produce good decisions.

The basic question is: how much public money should be devoted to making good decisions? This complex question raises some perplexing issues. What is a good or accurate decision? How, if at all, can one be identified? Which procedures will reduce the propensity for error? But monetary costs and the value of decisions are not the only considerations here. There is also the issue as to the amount of time that the decision process should take up and the associated costs, both direct and indirect.

Questions such as these need to be addressed when organising any justice process. For example, civil procedure is often said to be based on the premise that the parties themselves can decide how much resources to commit in order to resolve their disputes. Market forces ought to encourage litigants to think rationally about the relationship between the value they accord to a dispute and the financial resources they wish to commit to it. In practice, the vast majority of civil disputes are settled without formal court adjudication. However, the use of market forces and out of court settlements are not normally seen as viable options in the context of administrative justice disputes. After all, in the civil justice context, the adjudicator holds the ring between two private litigants. By contrast, administrative justice concerns both individual entitlement and policy implementation. There is an underlying positive interest on behalf of both government and the adjudicatory tribunal in ensuring that disputes are decided correctly so that individuals receive their due and that policy is administered; adjudication is a means of policy implementation. These considerations apply no less in the asylum context, given the underlying tension between protecting individual rights and immigration control. As the Tribunal has noted, asylum appeals are not ordinary civil proceedings, but ones in which there is a strong public interest.[3] In devising a process by which decisions are to be made, government inevitably needs to make some assessment of the value/cost ratio of adjudication decisions and processes.

---

[3] *M (Chad) v Secretary of State for the Home Department* [2004] UKIAT 00044 [16]; *LK v Secretary of State for the Home Department (Adjudicators: 'anxious scrutiny'– public interest) Democratic Republic of Congo* [2004] UKIAT 00308 [7].

Considering Costs

To examine the issues raised by the cost of good decisions, we can draw upon economic analysis of law.[4] This approach focuses upon the various costs that arise out of an adjudication process. First, there are the error costs of incorrect decisions, that is, the social costs generated when a legal procedure fails to perform its social function. In the asylum context, error costs are generated whenever an individual genuinely entitled to asylum is refused (a false negative or Type I error) or when asylum is granted to someone who is in truth ineligible (a false positive or Type II error). Secondly, there are the direct administrative costs of the adjudication process, the costs of funding the Tribunal and its administration, of representation, and of asylum seeker support, the support and accommodation provided to most claimants during the process.

From this perspective, the purpose of the legal procedure is conceived to be the minimisation of the sum of the error costs and the direct administrative costs. This should promote efficient legal procedures. However, difficulties commonly arise when attempting to allocate a monetary value to such costs. While administrative costs are often easy to calculate, error costs are normally obscure. Furthermore, there is a third type of cost, the indirect costs imposed by the timeliness of the decision process, those costs which arise because there is either excessive speed or excessive delay in the decision process.

This approach toward assessing the different types of costs involved in the asylum appeals process cannot produce an objectively correct answer as to how much public money should be devoted to funding the appeals process. It is also fraught with difficulties. For instance, how is it possible to monetise the contribution of a particular tribunal system to the broader administrative justice system, which in turn contributes to the constitutional framework of a democratic society? This approach can, however, provide a general framework for sensitising ourselves to the nature of the losses and gains and for appreciating the complexities involved. A good starting place is with the concept of error costs, but first it is necessary to consider whether it is possible to assess decisional accuracy.

Assessing Accuracy

Accuracy in decision-making requires that the correct application of the relevant legal rules to the true facts of an individual's situation. However, for a number of reasons, it is impossible to know whether asylum appeal decisions are correct in any objective sense. Since asylum decisions are fundamentally about facts rather than law and involve the process of attributing weight to the evidence presented,

---

[4] RA Posner, 'An Economic Approach to Legal Procedure and Judicial Administration' (1973) 2 *Journal of Legal Studies* 399.

there is no external, objective standard against which to assess their accuracy. The legal tests in both the Refugee Convention and Article 3 ECHR allow considerable scope for the judgment of decision-makers. In particular, the evaluation of the facts in asylum cases involves the exercise of judgment. As the decisional issues are evaluative rather than simply factual, different decision-makers may simply reach different decisions concerning prospective risk. Any attempt to assess the accuracy of decisions through second-guessing is undermined by the argument that it is simply the replacement of one person's evaluation of the facts for that of another.

Seeking to assess accuracy by looking at what happens after decisions have been taken is similarly problematic. There is not normally any tracking of cases to ascertain whether unsuccessful appellants have subsequently been subject to the persecution or ill-treatment that they claimed to be in fear of. The Home Office does not routinely monitor the safety of unsuccessful applicants on return to their country of origin; rather, it does not return those considered to be at risk.[5] It is, therefore, normally impossible to know whether a decision to refuse asylum subsequently turned out to be incorrect. But if assessing the incidence of false negatives by reference to what happens afterwards seems problematic enough, what then of false positives? The difficulty here is that it is impossible to assess the counterfactual situation as to whether an individual granted asylum would actually have been safe on return. While it is reasonable to assume that some incidence of error—everyone makes mistakes—Immigration Judges never find out whether or not their decisions were right.

The slippery nature of decisional accuracy is increased, if not exacerbated, by the intense conflict between the compassionate considerations concerning an individual appellant and the policy considerations concerning maintaining effective immigration control that arise in some types of asylum case. For instance, in HIV/AIDS cases the decision-maker must assess whether the circumstances concerning the risk of death arising from the non-availability of medical treatment are exceptional whereas in suicide cases the test is whether there are compelling humanitarian grounds or where there is a risk of suicide or other self-harm that a claimant may inflict on removal.[6] Set against the intense conflict between protecting individual rights and broader policy considerations, decision-makers have to decide whether the risk to an individual's life is sufficiently extreme, exceptional or compelling. The consequence is that the very notion of making the 'right' decision may itself be rendered almost meaningless.

---

[5] Hansard HC vol 478 col 1237W (7 July 2008). Occasionally NGOs make claims that unsuccessful asylum claimants have been subject to torture on return to their countries of origin. See, eg, Aegis Trust, *Lives We Throw Away: Darfuri Survivors Tortured in Khartoum Following Removal From the UK* (London, Aegis Trust, 2007) (presenting evidence that some Darfuri Sudanese nationals had been persecuted on return to Sudan). However, the sample size of such evidence is usually low and not subject to independent verification.

[6] *D v United Kingdom* (1997) 24 EHRR 423; *Bensaid v United Kingdom* (2001) 33 EHRR 10; *N v Secretary of State for the Home Department* [2005] UKHL 31; [2005] Imm AR 353; *J v Secretary of State for the Home Department* [2005] EWCA Civ 629; [2005] Imm AR 409.

If the outputs of the adjudication process cannot be known to be correct or incorrect, is there any proxy measure that might be used? One suggestion is to examine appeal success rates. On this basis, a success rate of approximately 20 per cent can be taken as an indication that a substantial number of initial decisions are wrong. At first glance, this way of measuring the accuracy of decision-making seems intuitively plausible because of the high rate of challenge in asylum cases. For instance, the outcomes of social security appeals may not be an effective way of measuring the quality of initial decision-making because appeals are only lodged against a very small fraction of initial decisions.[7] By contrast, the asylum appeals system is characterised by a high take-up rate; the Tribunal gets to determine a higher proportion of appeals than in other adjudication systems, which provides a wide overview of initial decision-making standards. However, despite the high appeal rate, there are a number of reasons why the proportion of successful appeals does not necessarily provide a good indicator of the quality of initial decisions.

For a start, it is not the purpose of the appeal process to identify errors in initial decisions, but to replace them with fresh appeal decisions. Appeals often succeed not because the initial decision was flawed, but because the Tribunal has arrived at a different conclusion. It might occasionally be the case that the appeal process uncovers errors in initial decisions, but this will more often that not be incidental to its primary objective of determining appeals afresh.

Secondly, as noted above, because of the borderline nature of much asylum decision-making, a Home Office case-worker and a judge may arrive at quite different conclusions as to whether an individual can properly be considered to be credible without it being able to be said that either is demonstrably wrong. Asylum decision-making raises questions of fact, judgment, and evaluation. There may be no uniquely correct outcome.

Thirdly, it is wrong to assume a simple correlation between the outcome of appeals and the correctness of initial decisions. The correctness of initial decisions may, of course, be one factor influencing appeal outcomes, but such outcomes will also be influenced by a number of other factors unrelated to the quality of the initial decision.[8] Such factors might include the passage of time between the decision and the appeal, which can mean that individual circumstances, country conditions, or case-law have changed, and so, therefore, should the outcome. Facts concerning persecutory risk can change and the decision-maker must assess the risk on the basis of facts in existence at the date of decision. As asylum appeals are *de novo*, the Tribunal does not simply review the initial decisions on the same facts as were before the initial decision-maker, rather, it is bound to take into account evidence arising after the initial decision. It is possible that an initial decision may

---

[7] House of Commons Work and Pensions Committee, *Decision Making and Appeals in the Benefits System* (2009–10 HC 313) Ev 114.

[8] Home Office, *The Government Reply to the Second Report from the Home Affairs Committee Session (2003–04 HC 218): Asylum Applications* (Cm 6166, 2004) 20; Department for Constitutional Affairs, *Government Response to the Constitutional Affairs Select Committee's Report on Asylum and Immigration Appeals* (Cm 6236, 2004) 3–4; Independent Chief Inspector of the UK Border Agency, *Asylum: Getting the Balance Right? A Thematic Inspection: July—November 2009* (London, OCIUKBA, 2010) [2.29]–[2.32].

have been correct on the basis of the facts presented, but that changes in the factual basis concerning the degree of persecutory risk at the appeal stage mean that a decision to allow the appeal was also correct. Having a short period of time between the initial decision and appeal stages may reduce the possibility of any change in country conditions having a bearing on the outcome of appeals. However, appeal outcomes can also be affected by factors arising out of the various differences between primary administrative and appellate tribunal decision-making. For instance, resource constraints, the large volume of decisions to be taken, and the differential experience of individual decision-makers may influence the outcome of initial decisions. By contrast, at the appeal stage, decision outcomes may be influenced by other factors not present at the initial decision-making stages. For instance, the process of the appeal hearing itself, whether, and, if so, how effectively, the parties were represented before the Tribunal, the questioning of the appellant, and the degree to which the Immigration Judge played an active role in the proceedings are all aspects that might influence outcomes.

Finally, it cannot be assumed that appeals are always determined correctly. The operation of an appeal process may itself introduce new errors into decision-making. In the asylum process, a substantial number of appeal decisions are themselves overturned by a senior judge on error on law grounds. Furthermore, a certain proportion of such subsequent decisions are themselves overturned by way of a further appeal to the higher courts. In short, it is often difficult to determine whether reversal on appeal is either an indication that the impugned decision was erroneous or merely the result of having an appeal process which frequently requires consideration of fresh evidence or results in a different view of existing evidence.

Another possible proxy for accuracy is inconsistency in decision-making. Significant variations in success rates between different judges or different hearing centres, may provide evidence that like cases have not been treated alike and therefore incorrect decisions were being produced (incorrect decisions in the sense of having been incorrectly allowed or incorrectly dismissed). There is certainly anecdotal evidence suggesting the existence of inconsistency in asylum appeal outcomes. However, the Tribunal does not collect statistical evidence concerning the outcome of appeals by hearing centre. Even if such statistical evidence were to be collected and published, it would not necessarily be conclusive of inaccuracy. For instance, what could be inferred from the fact that, to take a hypothetical illustration, nationals from the Democratic Republic of Congo experienced a higher success rate at one hearing centre than another? This would only invite further investigation as to the particular nature of the individual appeals determined, the credibility assessments reached, and the country materials relied upon. Few asylum cases are exactly wholly alike and many can be finely balanced. It is perfectly possible for two conscientious decision-makers to reach opposite conclusions on the same evidence without either of them being wrong.

In summary, the ongoing controversy as to who is in need of international protection as a refugee or as a person otherwise in need of asylum arises from the lack of any external, objective standard against which to assess the accuracy of decisions. Accuracy is the desired goal of substantive justice, but this ideal may often not be fully attainable. It is extremely difficult even to define what an accurate asylum appeal decision would be like, let alone to go about measuring substantive decisional accuracy. The Tribunal has not itself endeavoured to develop any working definition of what decisional accuracy might comprise. In the absence of such a definition, the nearest proximate of a 'correct' appeal decision is simply one which has not been subsequently reversed on error of law grounds. Given the significance of accuracy, this seems highly inadequate, but it is probably the nearest one is likely to get to defining accuracy. As an adjudicatory value, accuracy has the qualities of being both critically important, yet also permanently elusive.

Error Costs: The Value of Correct Decisions

Despite the difficulties in knowing whether or not decisions are accurate, it is possible to consider the costs incurred by inaccuracy. Decisions concerning the allocation of resources to a decision process inevitably require some assessment, whether expressly or implicitly, of the value to be accorded to accuracy. To analyse this, we can consider first the position of those appellants in need of asylum. Providing such people with international protection involves both a gain to them individually and socially and also a social cost. The gain to such people is obvious: they need not be compelled to return to their country of origin to face the persecution or serious ill-treatment for which they sought asylum. The social costs arise from the integration of refugees into society and in terms of the care and support such people require. However, a positive decision on an asylum claim is an implicit recognition that the moral worth in protecting an individual outweighs the public interest in enforcing immigration control. It can reasonably be assumed that there is a net gain here; if not, then government would withdraw altogether from the legal obligations to grant asylum. Equally, those granted asylum will be able to contribute to society.

Then there are the costs arising from Type I errors. Refusing protection to the genuinely entitled claimant represents a basic failure to fulfil the purpose of asylum and human rights law: the provision of surrogate protection to those in need because the claimant's own country is either unable or unwilling to protect its own nationals. It may result in considerable risk to the individual's personal safety. The costs here are, to put it mildly, quite unlike those encountered anywhere else in the legal system. Wrongful criminal convictions may result in the imposition of inappropriate penalties, such as the deprivation of liberty through imprisonment or fines, and the stigma and adverse reputational consequences that come with a criminal conviction. Incorrect determinations of civil liability will mean that one party rather than another will lose out financially. Of course, all of this must comply with human rights law. But an incorrect decision to refuse asylum may result

in exactly the breach of fundamental human rights for which the claim was originally made. It is no exaggeration to say that in many asylum cases the life of the
appellant will depend on the decision. Furthermore, public confidence in the asylum process may be undermined if genuinely entitled claimants are wrongfully
rejected.

Then there are the error costs that arise from Type II errors—granting asylum
to those individuals not at risk on return. Affording international protection to
those who do not require it, confers on them a status, such as refugee status with
the rights and privileges it entails, which they do not deserve. This clearly poses a
threat to the policy justifications for maintaining legitimate immigration control
and public confidence in the asylum process. It may also encourage other individuals without genuine cases who do not qualify for entry under ordinary immigration processes to seek asylum. Furthermore, other aspiring immigrants who have
applied under ordinary immigration procedures may feel aggrieved that others
have been able to jump the queue by using asylum as a backdoor to entry. The
error costs then include the social costs in terms of undermining the public interest in legitimate immigration control and public confidence that the integrity of
the asylum and immigration system is not susceptible to abuse.

What is the relative weight of the error costs here? While the costs and gains
attendant upon correct and incorrect decisions can be identified, the analysis here
has two principal limitations. First, it is not possible to express these costs and
gains in monetary terms. Secondly, most of the costs and gains involved here simply raise further normative questions as to the relative value they should be
assigned. Different people will hold different perceptions as to the value of both
types of error costs. Furthermore, even if it were possible to identify the error costs,
it is impossible to know the extent to which such errors in fact occur. Assessing the
overall costs of both types of errors seems equally intractable, but it is possible to
make general observations by asking whether the decision process itself has any
preference for one type of error over another. On the whole the asylum process has
a number of features which indicates its preference for false positives over false
negatives.

Consider first the critical role of the standard of proof in assigning error costs.
As was noted in the previous chapter, whenever an adjudicator hears evidence to
decide a contested factual issue, there will inevitably be some degree of factual
uncertainty; a standard of proof is required to prescribe the degree of confidence
the adjudicator must have before making factual findings. The significance of any
standard of proof lies in specifying the degree of factual uncertainty, and also the
degree of possible error, to be allowed for. The higher the applicable standard of
proof, then the greater evidential certainty required; conversely, the lower the
standard of proof, then the less evidential certainty required.[9] In the asylum context, the lower standard of proof means that claimants need only demonstrate that

---

[9] See L Kaplow, 'The Value of Accuracy in Adjudication: An Economic Analysis' (1994) 23 *Journal of Legal Studies* 307, 356–358; ML Davis, 'The Value of Truth and the Optimal Standard of Proof in Legal Disputes' (1994) 10 *Journal of Law, Economics and Organization* 343.

their future fear of harm is reasonably likely to be true. The standard of proof is set at this level because the risks of non-persuasion for genuine asylum claimants are so high. The lower standard of proof then is a means of dealing with factual uncertainty and a substantive device aimed at reducing error costs, specifically those arising from false negative decisions.

But, of course, any attempt to reduce the risk of false negatives cannot be achieved without also increasing the risk of false positives.[10] While the lower standard of proof raises the likelihood of protecting those genuinely in need of asylum, it also raises the likelihood of protecting those not so in need. To allow an asylum appeal, the judge need only be satisfied that there is a real risk of future harm; but to dismiss an appeal, the judge must be satisfied that there is no risk at all. The dismissal of an appeal, therefore, indicates a level of certainty about the effect of the evidence that may not be apparent when allowing an appeal. To illustrate the point, suppose that there was a large batch of good decisions in which the standard of proof had been applied correctly and in all of which asylum had been granted. If so, then it would be unlikely that it was right to grant asylum in all of the cases because there would be some cases in which it was unnecessary to grant asylum, but in which the standard of proof had nevertheless been correctly applied to ensure that the errors fell in claimants' favour. Such decisions would be right in the sense that the lower standard of proof had been applied, but not necessarily objectively accurate. Furthermore, by reducing the degree of factual certainty needed before granting asylum, the lower standard of proof inevitably increases the error costs arising from false positive decisions.

It is, therefore, accepted that the costs of false negative decisions outweigh those of false positive decisions. If so, then it may even be misleading to suppose that the aim of reaching accurate decisions qualifies as an important purpose of the adjudication process. Rather, the purpose of the process is not to make accurate decisions, but decisions which apply the standard of proof; whether those decisions are also accurate is a different inquiry.

But before accepting that the process prefers one kind of error over another, some qualifications are required. The way in which the standard of proof works in practice cannot easily be isolated from procedural aspects of the decision process. For instance, an unrepresented appellant may find it more difficult to discharge the standard of proof than one with representation. Furthermore, as already noted, the application of the standard of proof in asylum cases is not itself free from uncertainty. Nevertheless, the general approach is that the lower standard of proof is adopted because of the legal process recognising that false negatives incur higher error costs.

There are also other aspects of the appeals process which reinforce the focus on reducing Type I errors. Appeal rights are only generated from an initial refusal decision; initial positive decisions are outside the Tribunal's jurisdiction. The

---

[10] A Ogus, *Costs and Cautionary Tales: Economic Insights for the Law* (Oxford, Hart Publishing, 2006) 110–111.

Home Office is reliant upon the appeals process to overturn poor initial decisions where asylum has been refused, but there is no mechanism of assessing whether or not initial decisions to grant asylum were correct.[11] What is the quality of such decisions? No-one seems to know. It is difficult even to investigate this issue because administrative agencies, such as the Home Office, only give reasons when issuing refusal decisions; detailed reasons are given to justify refusals, not grants. The risk is that asylum may on occasion be granted when it need not.

Another aspect of the process which reinforces its focus upon correcting false negatives concerns the take-up of onward rights of challenge against appeal decisions. While the right of appeal only exists against initial refusal decisions, either party may challenge an appeal decision, if adverse, for any error of law. However, a major factor conditions the exercise of onward rights of challenge: such challenges are lodged overwhelmingly by claimants (89 per cent) rather than the Home Office (11 per cent).[12] As the rate of onward challenge by the Home Office against allowed appeal decisions is considerably lower than that of unsuccessful appellants against dismissed appeal decisions, errors of law in dismissed appeals stand a greater chance of being identified. In summary, key aspects of the asylum process are focused upon guarding against false negative decisions.

Direct Administrative Costs

What then of the direct costs incurred by the administration of the appeals process? By comparison with error costs, these costs are relatively easy to specify in monetary terms. The unit cost of an individual asylum appeal includes the cost to the Tribunal (judicial salaries and fees, accommodation and administration, and interpreter costs); the cost to the Home Office in preparing and presenting appeals and providing support and accommodation to asylum applicants; and the cost to the Legal Services Commission of providing publicly-funded representation for appellants and of disbursements for expert reports.[13] All appeals will already have imposed a cost in terms of the initial processing of claims and the

---

[11] The only scrutiny over initial positive decisions is the Home Office's internal quality assurance arrangements, but this focuses upon the decision-making process rather than decisional quality. See National Audit Office, *Improving the Speed and Quality of Asylum Decisions* (2003–04 HC 535) 42; National Audit Office, *Management of Asylum Applications by the UK Border Agency* (2008–09 HC 124) 18. One issue that arises here, as it does elsewhere in immigration decision-making such in the visa/entry clearance context, concerns the degree to which, if any, the requirement to give detailed reasons when refusing but not granting might itself incline decision-makers under pressure to process high caseloads to grant rather than refuse. See House of Commons Home Affairs Committee, *Monitoring of the UK Border Agency* (2008–09 HC 77) [13]–[16].

[12] Statistics supplied by the Tribunals Service.

[13] In 2008, the unit cost of an asylum appeal (excluding the costs to the Legal Services Commission of publicly-funded representation) was just under £3,400 (information supplied by the Home Office United Kingdom Border Agency (FOI 10397)). The cost will vary though depending on the characteristics of each case; for more technical detail, see National Audit Office (2008–09 HC 124) above n 11 at 35–36.

process of appealing can double the overall cost of an asylum claim. Compared with other non-asylum immigration appeals determined by the Tribunal and the average cost of other appeals handled by the Tribunals Service, the administrative cost of an asylum appeal is higher but also substantially lower than other types of judicial proceedings, such as a murder trial.[14]

The Appeal Decision Process

Significant direct costs then are incurred by having an appeals process against initial decisions. From one perspective, these costs are necessary to address weaknesses in the initial consideration of claims. As the Home Office has itself noted, '[t]here are a significant proportion of asylum claims refused at initial stage, which are subsequently overturned by an Immigration Judge. This can result in not only increased and wasted expense, but also distress and anguish for genuine claimants'.[15] There is, then, a strong argument for improving initial decision-making. It is, of course, possible that uniformly high quality initial decisions might persuade some rejected applicants that their claim has been considered properly and dissuade them from lodging appeals. At the same time, as we have seen, the fact that an initial decision to refuse an asylum claim is overturned on appeal is not necessarily an indication that the initial decision was of poor quality. Applicants who have been refused initially may pursue appeals irrespective of the quality of the initial decision. The option of an appeal gives refused applicants a second chance to present their claim. An applicant refused initially has nothing to lose by appealing, but potentially much to gain if successful. It is not, therefore, unsurprising that the appeal rate has remained relatively high; a higher quality of initial decision-making may not necessarily reduce it.

These, then, are two perspectives which commonly inform discussions of the asylum decision process. It is—depending on the standpoint adopted—characterised by either poor initial decision-making which stimulates challenges or by a reluctance of its clientele to accept adverse decisions irrespective of their quality. There is, though, a third, and less unequivocal, perspective. It is possible to view the initial consideration of claims as serving a filtering function by distinguishing between those claimants who clearly qualify for protection from those who clearly do not. By doing so, a third and much more troublesome category of borderline cases is passed onto the appeals process for more detailed consideration. If so, then

---

[14] The Home Office has previously introduced cost-recovery schemes for some types of immigration appeals, such as fees for family visitor appeals, which were subsequently withdrawn in light of concerns that they restricted access to justice on which, see R Thomas, 'Immigration Appeals for Family Visitor Refused Entry Clearance' [2004] *Public Law* 612, 623–624.

[15] Joint Committee on Human Rights, *Government Response to the Committee's Tenth Report of this Session: The Treatment of Asylum Seekers* (2006–07 HL 134 HC 790) 15.

clearly some costs need to be expended considering both appeals against clear refusals as well as the more ambiguous borderline cases.

Adjudicatory Design

Irrespective of how the relationship between primary and appeal decision-making is to be understood—and it is virtually impossible to collect sound empirical data with which test any of these perspectives—the appeals process entitles individuals refused initially to a *de novo* decision. It is only worthwhile funding this process if its procedural content is suited to minimizing the risk of incorrect decisions. There is normally a variety of procedural options available when designing an adjudication process. The suitability of procedures cannot, though, be assessed in the abstract, but only in the context of the particular subject-matter involved.[16] In the asylum context, the task is to select those procedures which provide the most appropriate means of collecting the facts with which to make correct asylum decisions, subject to the resources available, and the need for fairness. But determining which particular procedures are most appropriate and whether they are cost-effective is far from easy. If procedures are instrumental to outcomes, then how can we be certain that the procedures selected will produce good decisions, when we cannot assess decisional accuracy itself?

One approach is to consider what the participants themselves want from the process. Clearly, they want different things. Appellants will want a fair opportunity to present their case and to participate in a life changing decision. The judge will need the relevant facts collected, so far as they can be, in order that an assessment of future risk can be undertaken. The Home Office will normally want to defend its initial refusal decision. The typical features of a tribunal system, and of adjudication more generally, are: notice of the case to be met; the opportunity for an oral hearing in which both parties can present and contest the evidence; an independent and impartial decision-maker; and the production of a reasoned decision. The basic components of the asylum appeals process conform to this model. The appellant receives the Home Office's reasons for refusal letter and appeals against it; an appeal hearing is then conducted before an independent judge in which the appellant gives evidence and is cross-examined; submissions are then made as to whether the appeal should be allowed or dismissed. The judge will then go away to write a reasoned determination which either allows or dismisses the appeal. To examine whether these procedures are likely to reduce decisional errors, it is necessary to analyse the advantages and disadvantages of the procedural choices available.

---

[16] TG Ison ' "Administrative Justice": Is It Such a Good Idea?' in M Harris and M Partington (eds), *Administrative Justice in the 21st Century* (Oxford, Hart Publishing, 1999) 34.

Tribunal Composition

An initial design choice concerns the identity of the people who are to make decisions. Which attributes and qualities should decision-makers bring to the adjudication process? Independence and neutrality are provided by appointment processes free from political influence. Adjudicative competence is normally considered to require legal expertise in the form of legally qualified personnel. This expertise encompasses an ability to handle and apply legal rules as well as experience and training in judgecraft skills and techniques, such as the ability to conduct fair hearings in a neutral and impartial way, the ability to assess evidence and to make findings of fact, and to produce reasoned decisions.

But what of the particular skills and expertise suited to the nature of the specific adjudicative task? Legal expertise alone is unlikely to furnish all the knowledge required for making factual judgments. Should legal members be accompanied by non-legal members, both lay and expert? Lay membership is most likely to be of assistance in relation to fact-finding, such as determining credibility. But non-legal members need to bring some particular expertise or knowledge that judges cannot provide; otherwise, they represent an additional cost for little gain.[17] It is possible that lay members with experience of life overseas might assist in relation to credibility assessments. At the same time, such experience is intangible and can never be either comprehensive or fully reliable. It can also be just as capable of generating its own prejudices and stereotypes.

Putting lay membership to one side, what of the inclusion of experts with particular skills or professional competences as tribunal members? In general terms, tribunals have long incorporated non-legal members because of their specialist knowledge or skills in a particular area. The inclusion of greater expertise within the adjudicative body can make for more informed and better decisions. In the asylum context, experts have a recognised role. Medical experts can contribute their opinion upon the causes of an appellant's scarring, which can assist in relation to making credibility findings, while the opinions of country experts can provide further detail and insight into the nature of conditions in countries producing asylum appellants.

The role of experts in asylum adjudication is accepted; but the issue of adjudicative design is how best to secure their input into the appeals process. Should the Tribunal incorporate experts as panel members as opposed to them being available as expert witnesses? To incorporate such expertise fully into the Tribunal could bring a different perspective which compliments that of the tribunal judges. However, one difficulty is that some experts—country experts, for instance—might become well-known for holding certain views about conditions in certain countries, which might generate concerns as to their impartiality and undermine public confidence in the neutrality of the Tribunal.

---

[17] Tribunals Service, *Transforming Tribunals: Implementing Part 1 of the Tribunals, Courts and Enforcement Act 2007* (London, Ministry of Justice, 2007) 47.

A related issue concerns the process of challenging the knowledge and views of the expert tribunal member. Expert members can be used to provide expert knowledge, but how should challenges against such knowledge be dealt with? Having country experts as witnesses rather than as tribunal members avoids the situation in which a perception might arise that a tribunal panel will decide in a particular way because of the views an expert member is known to hold. It also circumvents the inevitable difficulties that can arise when the specialist knowledge of an expert tribunal member is contested by the parties and when there are clashes between the expert member and the opinions of any expert witnesses.

Another issue concerns the costs and length of the appeals process. Country and medical experts are currently used in a sizeable proportion, though still a minority, of appeals. Country experts specialise in particular countries or regions, whereas asylum appellants come from all over the world. A country expert might then be able to assist in one appeal, but not in another. Likewise, a medical report is not required in each appeal. To compel expert members to sit in every appeal, even if not needed, would only increase costs and prolong the appeals process. It is possible to circumvent such difficulties though the selective deployment of expert panel members on the basis of the needs of the individual case. But, this seems little different from having experts as witnesses. Other practical issues may pertain with medical experts: the need to undertake medical examinations may not be conducive with appeal hearings or with the doctor-patient relationship. Overall, having experts available as witnesses when required is better in terms of tribunal independence and efficiency.

Oral Hearings

A second procedural choice concerns the nature of the hearing itself. Oral hearings are a long-standing tradition in the asylum appellate jurisdiction and are recognised as an important element of an appeal process for those who challenge administrative decisions which affect their lives.[18] While the Tribunal may utilise cheaper paper-only appeals in the non-asylum context, in which appellants generally experience a lower success rate than those who opt for oral hearings, its whole organisation is geared up to determining appeals through oral *hearings* in *hearing* rooms at the Tribunal's *hearing* centres.[19] Similarly, the courts have been keen to ensure that appellants do not lose out on this opportunity especially when, as is so often the case, an appellant's personal credibility is at stake.[20] More

---

[18] *Annie Rea Sesay v Secretary of State for the Home Department* (14870), date notified 3 April 1997 (IAT).

[19] Asylum and Immigration Tribunal (Procedure) Rules SI 2005/230, r 15. On differential success rates between paper and oral appeals in the context of immigration appeals, see Thomas above n 14 at 631–639, and in the context of social security appeals, see National Audit Office, *Getting it Right, Putting it Right: Improving Decision-making and Appeals in Social Security Benefits* (2002–03 HC 1142) 44–45.

[20] *R v Immigration Appeal Tribunal, ex parte S* [1998] Imm AR 252; *FP (Iran) and MB (Libya) v Secretary of State for the Home Department* [2007] EWCA Civ 13; [2007] Imm AR 450.

generally, it has been argued that oral hearings are essential when the adjudication process concerns fundamental rights.[21] The general approach of the law then as regards asylum appeals is that procedural fairness requires factual issues to be determined on the basis of oral hearings and that this provides the best means of delineating truth from falsity. This is reflected in the deference shown by reviewing courts to the effect that factual findings on credibility issues based on oral evidence will very rarely be capable of being overturned.

What is the value of oral hearings for the participants involved? For judges, oral hearings are imperative: they can observe appellants giving evidence and being cross-examined. The value of an oral hearing lies in the opportunity for the appellant's evidence to be tested so that informed decisions can be made as to the truthfulness of the account proffered. Given the centrality of fact-finding, oral hearings with appellants in attendance enable the evidence to be available directly before the decision-maker. Making credibility assessments solely on the basis of documentary evidence would be extremely difficult especially if the appellant's written statement is incomplete or if there are inconsistencies between it and the Home Office's interview record. From the Home Office's perspective, having rejected the appellant's claim initially, it will want to defend that refusal decision and have the opportunity to cross-examine the appellant and make submissions drawing out the reasons for doubting the credibility of the appellant's account and expose its weaknesses. From the perspective of appellants, appeal hearings comprise the principal institutional process by which they can participate in the decision-making process by presenting oral evidence, which can only be achieved through hearings.

A significant feature of oral hearings is that they compel face-to-face encounters between judges and appellants. Judges directly experience the appellant and his oral testimony. By being appresented to appellants, judges are constantly reminded that they have to take decisions that directly concern appellants' lives.[22] It would be much easier for judges to dismiss appeals if appellants only ever appeared before them as names written on pieces of paper. Oral hearings also enable judges to have immediate access to a much wider range of evidence than paper only appeals. In the hearing, the judge can engage more thoroughly with an appellant's evidence and ask supplementary questions upon those issues which seem unclear, and thereby elicit additional evidence which is likely to provide a firmer basis upon which to make findings of fact, a feature lost in paper appeals.

The ability of oral hearings to uncover the truth is, though, not unmixed. One concern is that if oral hearings are the norm, then there is a risk that judges might assume that an appellant who does not attend is not pursuing his case as vigorously as he can—perhaps because its lacks merit. An appellant who does not attend may inadvertently place himself at a disadvantage; the risk is that doing an appeal on the papers may become synonymous with dismissing it. At the same time, it is equally possible that an appellant who does not attend may, perhaps on

---

[21] G Richardson and H Genn, 'Tribunals in Transition: Resolution or Adjudication' [2007] *Public Law* 116, 135–136.

[22] P Berger and T Luckman, *The Social Construction of Reality* (London, Penguin, 1991) 43–48.

advice, have taken a calculated risk: the claim on paper may have a reasonable chance of success, but may fall down if subjected to cross-examination.

A second concern relates to the utility of oral hearings in accurately collecting the facts. The hesitancy of reviewing courts and tribunals to interfere with factual findings based on live oral evidence is predicated on the assumption that the ability of the fact-finder to hear the testimony of witnesses in person necessarily confers an advantage that cannot be replicated on appeal.[23] But can it always be assumed that oral evidence necessarily possesses a superior revelatory character, especially when it is mediated by an interpreter? Truthful witnesses may, especially if traumatised, give incoherent and inarticulate evidence. Conversely, sedulous liars may be the most convincing of witnesses.[24] There is no guarantee that the fact-finder's opportunity to hear live oral evidence necessarily generates a greater ability to locate the truth. It tends to be documentary rather than oral evidence which demonstrates that an unconvincing witness has been telling the truth or a convincing one has been either deluded or lying. Checking the veracity of an appellant's story against reliable documentary evidence is likely to generate greater evidential certainty as to whether or not the story is true than the simple fact that the judge has seen the appellant in person giving evidence.

There is also the risk that the physical propinquity of an appellant to the fact-finder may be just as much capable of concealing, as it is in revealing, the truth. The potential for misinterpretation is often a particularly important consideration in the context of asylum appeals given the high degree of factual uncertainty, the decision-maker's dependence on the appellant for much of the personal testimony in support of the claim, the need for interpretation, the cultural differences separating appellants and judges, and the absence of a common background of understanding. The risk is that the judge may misinterpret the appellant's meanings by failing to appreciate the subtleties and complexities of situations, or else misinterpret the appellant's demeanour and non-verbal signals.

A related risk is that, in the relatively intimate atmosphere of the hearing room, the decision-maker's personal assessment of and visceral reaction toward the appellant may itself subconsciously or otherwise influence outcomes. The task of assessing the truthfulness of the appellant's story may become an assessment of the appellant himself, or rather the decision-maker's subjective impressions of him. The fact-finder may be just as much influenced by his own personal impression of the appellant as a witness as by the ostensible superiority of oral hearings in establishing the truth. Face-to-face encounters between an individual with decisional authority and the recipient of the decision tend to increase the scope of judgmental discretion, eliciting either sympathy or indifference. The effect of this may be either favourable or unfavourable to the individual appellant. It is possible that an appellant with an otherwise weak case may succeed simply because *the way* in which the story is recounted

---

[23] See, eg, *Montgomerie & Co Ltd v Wallace-James* [1904] AC 73, 75 (Lord Halsbury); *Subesh v Secretary of State for the Home Department* [2004] EWCA Civ 56; [2004] Imm AR 112, 131 (Laws LJ).

[24] *R v Secretary of State for the Home Department, ex parte Yousaf and Jamil* [2000] 3 All ER 649, 655 (Sedley LJ) (CA).

convinces the decision-maker that it is true. Alternatively, a judge may, having observed the appellant's appearance and demeanour, struggle to believe anything the appellant has said. This risk is an inherent aspect of the human element in the decision process.

Whatever their utility in establishing the truth, oral hearings may serve other, non-instrumental process values, such as securing respect for individual dignity irrespective of the outcomes reached. Given the critical importance of the issues at stake in asylum hearings to appellants, it is often assumed that the self-respect and dignity of appellants can only be protected through oral hearings. The symbolism of the oral hearing is also evident in the deeply-embedded notion that an appellant is entitled to his day in court, a notion which supports and underpins perceptions of the legitimacy and integrity of the legal process. Cynics might cavil at this notion and argue that scrupulously fair procedures can mask unfair substantive outcomes. Nevertheless, oral hearings can enable adjudication processes to achieve one of the principal functions, the participation of the individuals concerned. They can also assure appellants that they have been given a fair opportunity to present their case, irrespective of the outcome reached.

Oral hearings also increase transparency. The appellant is able to see that the judge is both neutral and independent of the Home Office. Openness is a long-established desideratum of tribunals, which can maintain public confidence.[25] It also supports the principle of open justice as a protection against arbitrariness, the Tribunal's position being that it is of cardinal importance that its hearings normally take place in public. At the same time, the desire for transparent and open procedures can rub up against the privacy and dignity of appellants. Asylum hearings may involve the appellant recounting traumatic events, such as torture or rape, which the appellant may wish to keep private. In practice, few hearings are attended by anyone other than those directly involved and hearings can be held *in camera* when necessary. Furthermore, most determinations are unreported and not publicly available, while those which are reported for public dissemination are anonymised.

The Mode of Appeal Procedure: Adversarial, Inquisitorial, or Enabling?

If oral hearings are generally to be used, the next issue that arises concerns the appropriate mode of the appeal procedure. Some tribunal systems—social security, for instance—are strongly inclined toward an active or investigative approach on the behalf of the tribunal panel. To ensure that correct decisions can be taken, both parties involved should cooperate and, if necessary, the Tribunal should investigate the issues. By contrast, asylum adjudication has a strong preference toward the adversary process: the appellant bears the burden of proof; it is for the

---

[25] *Report of the Committee on Administrative Tribunals and Enquiries* (Cmnd 218, 1957) (the 'Franks report') [76].

parties to present the evidence that they wish to rely upon; and, to maintain their independence, judges should refrain from descending into the arena between the parties. The adjudication process is inherently adversarial in the sense that the whole purpose is to allow an individual, whose claim has been initially rejected by an administrative agency, to contest that decision, and the findings of fact on it is based, before an independent judge. The agency's stance is usually, though not always, to defend its initial decision. Moreover, there is no middle ground in which the dispute can be mediated or settled. At the same time, the asylum juris-diction, and tribunal adjudication more generally, has been characterised by an ongoing debate as to whether appeal hearings are and should be conducted on an adversarial, inquisitorial, or an enabling basis.[26] What, then, should be the mode of appeal procedure?

An initial problem is that these labels do not possess generally accepted defini-tions. According to one definitional attempt, in adversarial proceedings, the judge is enabled to get at the truth by holding the ring while each side presents its own case and assails that of its opponent. In inquisitorial proceedings, the judge or adjudicator takes full control of the proceedings, and governs the participation of the parties. By contrast, an enabling approach requires the Tribunal to support the parties by giving them confidence in their own abilities to participate and to use its own capacity to compensate for the appellants' lack of skills or knowledge.[27] But, the dividing lines between these approaches are not necessarily clear-cut as they can merge into each other at the margins.

A second issue is that it has been questioned whether these labels are descrip-tively adequate in the context of asylum adjudication given its distinctive fea-tures—the lower standard of proof; the shared duty of cooperation between the parties; and the fact that the appellant alone will be possessed of almost all the rel-evant personal knowledge while the Home Office will be better placed to deal with general country conditions.[28] In light of these features and the overriding duty that each case be afforded the most anxious scrutiny, labels such as adversarial and inquisitorial may obscure rather than illuminate the different approaches open to asylum judges.[29] The real issue is not, therefore, which particular label best

---

[26] This debate is also evident within the higher courts. See *R v Special Adjudicator, ex parte Demeter* [2000] Imm AR 424, 430 (HC) (Moses J noting that 'the appeal should be, and is, adversarial. It is important that the special adjudicator should avoid, if possible, giving any appearance of entering into the arena by challenging the account that the applicant gives himself'); *Shirazi v Secretary of State for the Home Department* [2003] EWCA Civ 1562; [2004] 2 All ER 602, 611 (CA) (Sedley LJ noting that the asylum jurisdiction is 'as much inquisitorial as it is adversarial'); *GH (Afghanistan) v Secretary of State for the Home Department* [2005] EWCA Civ 1603 [15] (Brooke LJ noting that it is an adversarial system); *HK v Secretary of State for the Home Department* [2006] EWCA Civ 1037 [27] (Neuberger LJ noting that 'an Immigration Judge has an almost inquisitorial function, although he has none of the evidence-gathering or other investigatory powers of an inquisitorial Judge').

[27] A Leggatt, *Tribunals for Users: One System, One Service. The Report of the Review of Tribunals by Sir Andrew Leggatt* (London, The Stationery Office, 2001) [7.2]–[7.5].

[28] United Nations High Commissioner for Refugees (UNHCR), *Handbook on Determining Refugee Status* (Geneva, UNHCR, 1992) [196]; *RK v Secretary of State for the Home Department (Obligation to investigate) Democratic Republic of Congo* [2004] UKIAT 00129 [46].

[29] *Gimedhin v Secretary of State for the Home Department* (1464), date notified 23 August 1996 (IAT).

84

describes the process, but which degree of judicial intrusion—ranging from a passive to a more active posture—is necessary to resolve disputed issues.[30]

To some extent, the broader debate over the appropriate mode of tribunal procedure can be seen reflected in the differentiation between civil and administrative justice. In the civil justice context, the usual approach is to let the parties contest the issues through the adversary process. By contrast, in the administrative justice context, the underlying public interest in accuracy may often prompt the adjudicator to adopt a more interventionist approach and to assume some responsibility for collecting such evidence to ensure that decisions are taken on the best possible evidential basis. Another relevant factor will often be the presence and quality of representation before the Tribunal. When both parties are represented, then the adversary process may be the most natural to adopt. However, unrepresented appellants will naturally be at a disadvantage when disputing decisions of administrative agencies and tribunals may adopt an enabling approach designed to support the participation of appellants.

The advantages of the adversary process are, then, that it can be a good means of identifying the weaknesses, gaps, and inconsistencies in appellants' evidence. Asylum appellants can hardly be surprised if, having had their case doubted initially, the Home Office then chooses to draw out the claimed inconsistencies and ambiguities at the appeal hearing through cross-examination. To make proper findings of fact, the judge will want both sides to advance their case as fully as possible and for the appellant's account to be tested. The adversary process also augments the neutrality of the decision-maker. When evidence is being taken from a witness with representation on both sides, the judge's role is that of listening to evidence and submissions adduced. In this situation, the judge's impartiality cannot easily be questioned.

But while the adversary process may work well in principle, it may not always work so well in practice. A principal difficulty is that adversarial procedures may simply become contests in which the parties assail each other in the erroneous assumption that somehow or other the truth will come out. The adversary process may generate more heat than light and there is no guarantee that a judge will be presented with all the relevant information. By contrast, a judge trained at an inquisitorial approach may have a much better ability to get at the truth of the situation.

There is also the question as to whether the adversary process is the best means of adjudicating asylum cases. Having to make an asylum decision requires the factfinder to gather together a range of material: the individual appellant's story must be situated in the context of the available country information, which may of necessity require a more interventionist approach to plug any gaps in the evidence. While the Tribunal comprises the judicial part of the decision-making process, determining asylum claims involves an essentially administrative task of enquiring whether an individual's removal would place them at risk. In some situations this

---

[30] P Cane, *Administrative Tribunals and Adjudication* (Oxford, Hart Publishing, 2009) 239–244.

might require the judge to consider facts or arguments not raised by either party. Given the underlying public interest involved, it has sometimes been said that the task of the Tribunal, together with both of the parties, is to ascertain the true position and to that extent the proceedings are not wholly adversarial.

Another concern is that the adversary process can pose obvious risks given the power disparities between the parties. Asylum appellants are typically in a vulnerable position; they are normally unable to speak English, not legally trained, and often have to give personally sensitive evidence. The risk is that aggressive cross-examination may confuse, intimidate, or humiliate them. But it is not necessarily all one-way. Asylum appellants may also be able to benefit from the adversary process, for instance, by deliberately not disclosing evidence, such as an adverse expert report, for tactical reasons.

A further issue concerns the overall control of the hearing process. The risk with a purely adversary process is that control of the process might in effect be placed into the hands of the parties. The interest of the parties lies in contesting the evidence for the decision. By contrast, the decision-maker's interest is in adjudicating upon not only the particular appeal, but also the many other appeals waiting to be heard. Ensuring a necessary throughput of cases requires the judge to retain overall control to ensure efficiency and to focus the hearing upon the contested issues.

To compensate for these deficiencies, the alternative is for the decision-maker to take up a more active approach, but this has its own implications. One is that it requires both energy and expertise on behalf of the decision-maker. To be effective, an interventionist approach requires the judge to expend some time and demonstrate some adroitness in discerning the appropriate questions to ask and—just as importantly—the way in which to ask them. Questioning should be neither hostile nor undertaken in a manner which suggests that the judge's mind is already made up. By contrast, the typical judicial role in adversarial hearings—simply noting the evidence and arguments advanced by the parties—is safer, more conservative, and makes fewer demands on judicial energy.

But a more interventionist approach has its own costs. One risk concerns possible prejudgment, which may arise not from prejudice, but from the understandable need to bring order and coherence to a case so as to enable the relevance of the evidence to be measured. An interventionist judge may, from reading the case file prior to the hearing, form an initial view of a case. This initial diagnosis may develop into a preferred outcome, so that at the hearing the judge may give too much weight to evidence consistent with that outcome and discount evidence inconsistent with it. The temptation for a judge unconvinced by an appeal is to investigate excessively to expose its weaknesses and to make certain of the outcome. This may make the appellant feel that the judge is not merely inquiring into the circumstances of the case, but undertaking an inquisition. Nothing is to be gained by exchanging aggressive cross-examination of vulnerable witnesses for an accusatory inquisition. The only way of combating this natural human tendency to judge too quickly may be the adversary process; the two sides hold the case in suspension between two opposing interpretations of it until the judge decides in favour of one side or the other.[31]

Secondly, an interventionist approach is often seen as potentially jeopardising judicial impartiality and neutrality, which are seen somehow to be institutionally guaranteed by the adversary process. The pervasive judicial fear is that of being seen to have descended into the arena between the parties and in that way undermining the perception or the actuality of judicial independence and impartiality. There is always the risk that a judge who has interceded (too) frequently to compensate for the lack of representation on either side may be criticised by the other party for having acted as a surrogate representative. Given the political context of asylum adjudication, a high premium is understandably placed upon judicial independence. Oral hearings are the only occasion in which the Tribunal sits in public and interacts with the participants. The adversarial process may then serve a broader institutional purpose, that of preserving tribunal neutrality and independence.

There may be other implications of opting for a more explicitly interventionist approach by, for instance, allowing judges to make such inquiries as they think fit. Just how far should a judge go in making such inquiries? If judges were to be positively obliged to investigate the facts of a claim, then where would the obligation end? The risk is that an unsuccessful party could always contend that their appeal had failed not because it lacked merit, but because the judge had failed to undertake the kind of thorough investigation needed to make sustainable findings. Such an obligation could result in a de facto transfer of the burden of proof from appellants to the Tribunal. Any move toward a more inquisitorial approach may, then, have adverse consequences as regards other aspects of the process. Furthermore, there is the risk of judicial inconsistency, the extent to which different judges adopt disparate approaches when making such inquiries.

Representation

Another procedural choice concerns the presence or absence of representation. As noted above, the presence or otherwise of representation will influence the degree of judicial intervention. Good quality legal advice and representation can help parties to prepare and represent their cases. For appellants before tribunals, representation tends to increase success rates, though whether representation necessarily promotes accuracy as distinct from higher success rates is unknown. Representation can also act as an aid to good quality decision-making and underpin the adversary process.

However, formal equality might, as it often does, mask substantive inequality. If both parties are represented, then they may seem to be on a level playing field, but the equality may be more apparent than real if one side is well-represented and the other has representation which is either less able or of inferior quality. If so,

---

[31] LL Fuller, 'The Forms and Limits of Adjudication' (1978) 92 *Harvard Law Review* 353, 383.

then the rationale underpinning the adversary process is weakened. The danger is that a party with less than effective representation may end up losing not because of the particular merits of his case, but because of his representative's failings. Alternatively, the burden may fall onto the fact-finder to undertake the necessary work to collect the evidence, which weakens the rationale for having such representation in the first place.

To the extent that this potential inequality exists, it poses an obvious challenge to the effective operation of the adversary process. Furthermore, it is not necessarily only appellants who might be disadvantaged. The potential for inequality can exist just as much in relation to the Home Office as it does in relation to appellants. It would not be appropriate for an appellant to be granted asylum because, through good fortune, the Home Office's representative missed out an obvious and significant part of the case against an appellant. That some aspect of the evidence has not been challenged by the Home Office is not necessarily a good reason for accepting it. Given the consequences of incorrect decisions, judges may in such circumstances intervene more to get at the truth of the matter because they do not wish to allow an improbable account to go untested or because they want to ensure that a possibly genuine claim is drawn out as fully as possible.

Then there is the perennial issue of the extent to which representation should be publicly funded. In light of the impecuniousness of most asylum appellants, representation will normally need to be publicly funded, thereby adding to the direct costs. In 1999, the Government extended legal aid provision, but faced with a doubling of expenditure (to £174 million in 2002–03), it introduced a financial threshold of five hours for the initial decision-making process and ensured that no legal aid work was undertaken without prior approval from the Legal Services Commission in the form of the merits test. Further changes, such as graduated fees, were introduced in 2008. Government has then sought to focus its resources on providing publicly funded representation for those individuals whose cases possess merit, that is, the prospects of success are higher than 40 per cent. The result has been an increase in unrepresented appellants.

If more appellants are unrepresented, then there is an obvious inequality raising questions as to the extent to which unrepresented appellants, who might otherwise stand a reasonable prospect of success, are disadvantaged simply because they are unrepresented. The Home Office is the archetypal repeat-player; the full-time responsibility of its presenting officers is to defend refusal decisions before the Tribunal. By contrast, unrepresented asylum appellants are atypical one-shotters, who are normally unable to speak English let alone knowing how best to present their case effectively or grapple with the technicalities of asylum and human rights law.[32]

This, in turn, takes us back to the issue of the appropriate judicial posture in such cases—should judges adopt an enabling approach when hearing unrepre-

---

[32] M Galanter, 'Why the "Haves" Come Out Ahead: Speculations on the Limits of Legal Change' (1974) 9 *Law and Society Review* 95.

sented appeals? Such an approach may be used in an attempt to even out the inequality by seeking to support appellants in ways which give them confidence in their own abilities to participate in the process, and in the Tribunal's capacity to compensate for their lack of skills and knowledge. Furthermore, it may also be necessary for the judge to intervene to protect a witness or party and to prevent proceedings becoming too confrontational.

But an enabling approach is not without its own risks. Appeal hearings may take longer. Maintaining the perception of judicial independence will always remain a concern. Furthermore, there may be acute problems for judges whose intervention is motivated both by a desire to ensure appellants are able effectively to participate in the proceedings and an equally authentic desire to elicit the truth of the matter, which may involve asking those questions which the Home Office has not thought of. More broadly, the difficult conundrum is: to what extent can judicial assistance to an unrepresented appellant adequately compensate for the lack of effective representation?

Funding of representation is not, though, without its own potential costs. If representatives are not of sufficiently good quality, then the rationale underpinning publicly funding such representation is seriously weakened. After all, what is the purpose of providing publicly funded representation which may benefit neither judges nor appellants and needs to be supplemented by a more active judicial approach to ensure that appellants are not disadvantaged? The balance between error and direct costs though is unclear and not easily susceptible to empirical investigation. Are appellants better or worse off having variable quality representation than with having their evidence drawn out by a skilled judge? Does focusing publicly funded representation on those appellants whose cases are considered to possess merit disadvantage others who do not qualify for representation because the case appears to lack merit, but who might have a stronger case if represented? Would it be better to ensure representation of some kind for all appellants or, alternatively, have no representation at all and move toward a fully inquisitorial process?

Allocating publicly funded representation to some appellants and not to others certainly creates an inequality that can be difficult to justify although it may not be at all apparent to appellants themselves. For instance, it might be observed that there are substantial disparities in the amount of resources devoted to preparing some appeals compared with others. Some represented appellants may be able to amass substantial quantities of additional evidence (country and medical expert commissioned reports at public expense) which unrepresented appellants will not. To the extent that the investment behind the collection of other evidence for represented appellants is publicly funded, then it will be at the expense of unrepresented appellants. Moreover, the lack of publicly-funded representation for unrepresented appellants may not necessarily have anything to do with them having hopeless cases: this will itself be another unknown because the judge will not know their full story until the appeal hearing. It is, of course, perfectly possible that an unrepresented appellant might actually have a good case and could well have had a much better case had they been represented. However, by the time such unrepresented appellants get to the appeal hearing stage, it might be too late. Appellants themselves may be oblivious to this difference in the investment of resources throughout the process, but to judges hearing case after case and other observers of the appeals process, this feature can become quite discernible. The principal alternative to this state of affairs is to spread the public money available for representation more thinly so that all appellants get a certain level of representation.

The problems caused by the absence of representation do not, though, relate solely to appellants. The Home Office may itself, for reasons of limited manpower, be unable to field one of its own officers to attend the appeal hearing. Again, this can pose difficulties. On the one hand, the judge will want to have the appellant's evidence properly tested in order for proper findings of fact to be made; on the other hand, the judge will want to avoid the impression that he is partisan, biased, or favouring the Home Office's side. Excessive compensation for the absence of a Home Office representative might generate claims of bias or unfairness and undermine impartiality. But, in the absence of cross-examination by the Home Office, a failure by the judge to examine important issues raises the risk of not having the appellant's claim properly tested. Finally, there is the situation in which there is no representation at all. In such a situation, adversary procedure is just not an option and the judge will be required to consider all aspects of the case for and against the appellant. The problem will be that the judge will feel that he has to perform too many different roles at once.

Reason-Giving

Another procedural choice concerns the giving of reasons. Alongside appeal hearings, determination-writing accounts for the other major part of a judge's work. Written determinations are, on average, 10–15 pages long. They need to contain both the findings of fact made and the conclusions and reason for the decision reached.

There are, of course, many well-known arguments in favour of reason-giving. It can promote accurate decisions by requiring that decision-makers direct themselves to the relevant legal rules, identify the important facts or factual issues and, where these are disputed, make reasoned findings on those issues, and then state the overall conclusion drawn from those factual findings as to the outcome of the decision. It can legitimise decisions and ensure their acceptability by informing the losing party why he has lost. In the absence of reasoned decisions, the parties have to take it on faith that their participation in the process has been real and that the decision-maker has understood and conscientiously considered the evidence and addressed the arguments advanced. Reason-giving enables the parties to assess whether the decision is pregnable through the identification of any challengeable error of law; without reasons reviewing tribunals and courts will have nothing to overturn or confirm. Reason-giving also has an important role in 'developing the mental capacity and sense of fairness of the adjudicator' by enabling the adjudicator to better understand the nature of the decision problem with which they are confronted.[33] Reason-giving will also inform other parties as to how the law is likely to be applied in future cases. The giving of reasons involves the invocation of general considerations and represents a commitment to those considerations.[34] Such considerations include not only the legal rules to be applied, but also the criteria against which evidential material is to be assessed. More broadly, reason-giving can promote public confidence in the decision process. After all, it is reasonable to assume that if the public is aware that reasons must be given for decisions, then it will have confidence that decisions are being reached on a rational basis.

In the context of asylum adjudication, reason-giving possesses its own distinctive functions. In relation to credibility findings, adequately reasoned decisions are particularly important as a lack of reasoning may demonstrate a failure adequately to address the fundamental question—is the applicant telling the truth?—and a failure to distinguish between those untruths which undermine the core of the appellant's claim and those which are peripheral. Given the presence of the appellant before the judge at the hearing, it is normally necessary to give reasons for accepting or rejecting the truthfulness of the account advanced. As regards country information, it is necessary for the judge to provide reasons to demonstrate what analysis has been made of the material in establishing the degree of risk on return.

But whether reason-giving does produce better decisions is not without ambiguity. One risk is that decision-makers might think that they need to produce detailed decisions, but lapse into a 'fact-restatement' approach, that is, they might write determinations which merely regurgitate the detail of the factual evidence, but which also omit proper reasons to justify the outcome reached. Another risk is that decision-makers are able to produce decisions containing valid reasons designed to withstand onward challenge, but which notify decision outcomes reached on different grounds.

On the other hand, decision-writing is not merely a way of notifying the parties of the decision reached, but intrinsic to decision-making. Deciding an appeal involves considering all the available evidence, weighing up its value, making findings of fact, and then specifying those reasons to support the outcome reached. In asylum cases, the decision-maker must place the appellant's oral and written evidence alongside the country information, make findings, take into account relevant law and guidance, and then prognosticate future risk. If the decision-maker was not required to undertake this type of structured exercise, then the decisions reached would not be properly thought through.

Reason-giving is not, though, without its costs. These arise from the time and administrative costs that reason-giving imposes. The ratio of judicial time

---

[33] WA Robson, *Justice and Administrative Law: A Study of the British Constitution*, 3rd edn (London, Stevens, 1951) 381.

[34] F Schauer, 'Giving Reasons' (1995) 47 *Stanford Law Review* 633.

expended in appeal hearings to decision-writing is around one to two; for every hour spent hearing an appeal, it will take another two hours to write the decision.[35] Determination-writing, therefore, occupies the bulk of judicial time which comes at the cost of other appeals that could be determined. The critical question is: how detailed should the reasons be?

The established principle of administrative law is that reasons should be proper, adequate, intelligible, and deal with the substantial points raised.[36] But what degree of particularity is required to satisfy these general standards in a specific decision context? Obviously, some balance must be struck between reasons being too detailed or too brief. Too much brevity in decisions may demonstrate a failure both to engage properly with the evidence and to make reasoned conclusions. On the other hand, too much detail will increase the time required. The amount of evidence presented in asylum cases, especially country information can be voluminous and it would place an onerous burden if judges were obliged to refer to all of it. Another well-established principle of administrative law is that a decision-maker is not obliged to deal with every single point of argument or item of evidence raised; it is generally sufficient if the principal points have been addressed. It should not be assumed that the decision-maker has left a particular item of evidence out of account merely because it has not been specifically referred to in the reasoned decision. In any event, the length of a decision is not necessarily a good indication of its quality; 'conciseness in a judgment is not in itself a fault, indeed it is often a merit'.[37] Furthermore, an extensive obligation to provide reasons can provide an opportunity for the captious to challenge the absence of reasoned findings on peripheral matters, and thereby prolong the decision process, a practice often evident in onward challenges against appeal decisions and one sometimes deprecated by the higher courts.[38]

According to the Tribunal, the only guidance judges need is that their conclusions be justified, that adverse findings be based on the evidence advanced, and that a proper explanation be given to justify the conclusions reached.[39] A determination should contain four elements: a direction on the relevant law; the important factual issues and, where these are disputed, the factual findings reached; the overall conclusion drawn from the factual findings; and an explanation of the reasons why those conclusions were reached which is sufficiently detailed to enable the parties to see whether the relevant matters have been considered and why the outcome was reached. As the higher courts have explained, judges need not produce lengthy

---

[35] PA Consulting Group, *Asylum and Immigration Tribunal: Analysis of Judicial Time* (London, PA Consulting Group 2007).

[36] The classic authority is *Re Poyser and Mills' Arbitration* [1964] 2 QB 467, 478. See also *Save Britain's Heritage v Secretary of State for the Environment* [1991] 1 WLR 153 (HL); *South Bucks District Council v Porter* [2004] UKHL 33; [2004] 4 All ER 775 [36].

[37] *OD (Ivory Coast) v Secretary of State for the Home Department* [2008] EWCA Civ 1299 [13] (Toulson LJ).

[38] *R (Iran) v Secretary of State for the Home Department* [2005] EWCA Civ 982; [2005] INLR 633, 641–642 (Brooke LJ) (CA).

[39] *Slimani v Secretary of State for the Home Department (Content of Adjudicator Determination) Algeria* (Starred determination) [2001] UKIAT 00009 [10].

decisions, provided that they give proper reasons as to the principal issues in dispute.[40]

At hearing centre level, decision-writing practices can vary. Conscious that asylum decisions adverse to appellants are likely to be challenged, judges tend to produce lengthier reasons to insulate them from challenge. A move toward more summary reasons might be possible if the rate of onward challenge decreased and if it were unnecessary for the reviewing tribunal or court to scrutinise closely the reasons given, but neither course seems likely. Another alternative is for judges to make oral decisions. This might reduce the amount of time taken up by decision-writing, but would be inappropriate and impractical given the complex and sensitive issues raised in asylum cases. The other option would be for judges to notify the parties of the outcomes of appeals and then allow either party to request a full determination. However, in practice it might be likely that either party would in any event request a full determination. The alternatives to written determinations do not, therefore, present much of a way forward.

Procedural Choices

So, what of the choices as to the procedural content of the asylum appeals process? They are by no means clear-cut. There is no way of objectively determining which particular procedural choices—individual judge or multi-member panels; oral or paper appeals; represented or unrepresented appeals; passive, active, or enabling approaches; detailed or summary reasons—are better at producing good quality decisions. It cannot be guaranteed that the procedures selected will in fact secure accuracy and the choices have to be made with an awareness of this. On the other hand, any high volume decision system requires some routine process if it is to function effectively. It is not possible to re-design the process to meet the special, individual requirements of each appellant. The task of designing effective decision procedures requires the operation of routine procedures and is informed by both the need to contain administrative costs and the ability of the procedures to produce correct decisions. Whether the procedures selected achieve an acceptable balance between cost and accuracy is difficult, if not impossible, to discern.

On balance, there is perhaps much to be said for the general procedure adopted in asylum appeals. Having single legally qualified judges ensures competency in handling hearings. Oral hearings enable the parties to meet to clarify the issues and for personal testimony to be assessed. The mode of procedure can vary to such an extent that labels such as adversarial or inquisitorial do little more than merely highlight two ends of the spectrum. Focusing legal aid provision on those appeals considered to possess merit should stand to benefit those with the best cases. The adoption of an enabling approach by judges should ensure that unrepresented appellants are given assistance so that they are able to participate and that the best elements of their cases can be brought out. The task of decision-writing should

---

[40] *R (Iran)* above n 38 at 641.

ensure that losing parties know why they have lost and enable reviewing courts to either understand the reasons for the decision or else set them aside.

Of course, such procedures are not infallible and the risk of unfairness to the parties is ever-present. Furthermore, the analysis so far has only considered some of the procedural choices which arise in the design of an adjudicative process. Other procedural choices include the following: the procedures by which experts are instructed and by which expert evidence is placed before the Tribunal; whether senior tribunal judges should designate particular decisions as binding precedents and, if so, then how; the organisation of any system of onward rights of challenge against initial fact-based tribunal decisions; and the relationship between the Tribunal and the higher courts. Subsequent chapters will examine these issues and investigate the empirical reality of the adjudication process. For the present, though, it is necessary to consider another major pressure upon the appeals procedure: its timeliness.

The Timeliness of Decision-Making

In all decision-making systems, decisions have to be taken over a particular period of time. The length of time allotted to the decision process may itself have various complex ramifications as regards the types of costs arising out of the adjudication process. Delay in the legal process is often taken to be an intrinsically negative aspect of litigation. Litigants should be able to expect to receive a decision within a reasonable period of time; justice delayed is justice denied. On the other hand, too great an emphasis upon the prompt and timely dispatch of decisions may undermine one of the principal features of an adjudication process, that of enabling the affected parties to participate by affording them sufficient time with which to prepare their case and marshal relevant evidence. It may also place decision-makers under pressure to focus upon the quick disposal of appeals rather than affording each of them the careful consideration that they deserve. Some degree of delay is therefore necessary; the crucial question is: how much?

In the administrative justice context, there are two other factors which often influence the desired timeliness of decision-making. First, there is the operation of adjudication as a legal technique of policy implementation. To adopt the language of implementation theory, the requirement for a tribunal decision operates as a clearance, that is, a decision point which must be passed so that the implementation process can proceed to the next stage.[41] The greater the number of clearances or decision points and/or the longer each of them takes to complete, then the higher the probability of stoppage in the implementation process. Until the adjudication segment of the broader administrative process has been concluded, some

---

[41] JL Pressman and A Wildavsky, *Implementation*, 3rd edn (Berkeley, University of California Press, 1984) 118–120.

type of error cost will arise and policy implementation will be held up. Secondly, in some decision-making systems, delay in the adjudication process may also increase direct administrative costs.

The asylum adjudication process provides a good illustration of these points. The timeliness of the appeals system is a particularly significant aspect of the broader asylum process. From the Home Office perspective, delay risks undermining the goal of securing immigration control. To be effective, negative decisions need to be enforced through the removal of failed appellants. Given the importance of immigration control, the Home Office has a particular interest in the timeliness of both initial and appeal decision-making. The longer claims take to conclude, then the longer the period of time before unsuccessful appellants can be removed. There is also the risk that the longer the amount of time taken, then the less chance that unsuccessful appellants will be removed. The risk is that delayed decision-making may, in effect, result in positive decisions by default. Furthermore, delay can send a wider signal that the asylum process lacks integrity by providing an incentive for those without a valid claim to come to the UK and seek asylum. By contrast, a timely decision process may exert a deterrent effect on such claims. After all, if individuals tempted to evade ordinary immigration control are aware that they can do so by claiming asylum and enjoying a prolonged decision-making process, a central aspect of the decision process will be undermined. Speeding up the adjudication process will assist in removing those who have no right to remain, which in turn will help to deter future unfounded asylum claims. Indeed, indifference to delay risks undermining the underlying policy programme.

Delay will also increase direct administrative costs. Most asylum applicants are supported throughout the process by the financial and social support provided by the Home Office. The longer decision-making takes, the higher these costs will become—and this will be in addition to the lower chances of removing those claimants found ultimately not to be at risk on return. Unsurprisingly, given the policy context, the Home Office has a substantial interest in measuring the Tribunal's performance accountability against specified targets for the throughput of cases.

But it is too simplistic to assume that delay only ever works to the benefit of claimants and to the disadvantage of the Home Office. Delay can certainly impact adversely upon the clientele of the appeals process in a number of different ways. The first loss is to the successful claimants who could have received asylum during the period in which they have been awaiting an appeal decision. Secondly, delay can generate substantial stress, anxiety, and uncertainty for claimants irrespective of the merits of their claims. As the whole of the applicant's future will depend on the outcome of their asylum decision, delays in reaching that decision will obviously exert a huge impact. Thirdly, delay may also influence substantive decision-making. As risk on return must be assessed on the basis of facts in existence at the date of decision, an appellant who might initially have been at risk may, through the passage of time, no longer be at risk. Fourthly, delay can also impose social costs, not just in terms of allowing ultimately unsuccessful appellants to remain whilst they await a decision, but also in terms of the opportunity costs to society. Claimants who are eventually granted asylum could have been working and contributing to society much sooner if they had received a decision without delay.

Claimants can, of course, be disadvantaged by a process which places too great an emphasis upon speed and timeliness. The risk is always that attempts to speed-up decision-making may result in a precipitate decision system so geared up to speed and timeliness that it no longer offers appellants a fair process. An excessive focus upon the timeliness of the adjudication process will risk jeopardising the achievement of adjudicative values, namely, fair procedures and accurate outcomes.

Conversely, some claimants will benefit from delay. If an unmeritorious claimant who does not qualify to remain in the country under immigration law wishes to prolong his stay for as long as possible, then what better way to do so than by making full use of the multiple opportunities provided by the legal process for challenging adverse decisions through appeals, onward challenges, and judicial review? The adjudication process is certainly characterised by an exceptionally high volume of routine challenges against adverse decisions, without parallel elsewhere in the legal system. The strong suspicion is that this culture is motivated by the desire of unmeritorious claimants to prolong their cases for as long as possible.

The Causes of Delay

To the extent that delays arise in the decision process, they have a number of causes: initial delay by the Home Office in making an asylum decision; the appeals process itself; and the inclination of appellants to challenge adverse decisions.

Delay may often result, as the Tribunal once noted, from the Home Office's 'administrative incompetence . . . amazing as this may sometimes be'.[42] Given the increase in asylum claims over the period 1998–2006, a backlog of some 400,000–450,000 cases developed, many of which involved delays of some years. This had a number of consequences. In administrative terms, the Home Office needed to decide how best to allocate its administrative capacity in order to clear the backlog while at the same time handling new asylum claims. It therefore established its Care Resolution Directorate to resolve legacy cases while its New Asylum Model is focused on handling new claims. Allocating staff and resources was necessary to clear the backlog of cases and remove unsuccessful claimants. At the same time, the Home Office had to focus on new, in-coming claims and seek to remove failed applicants to deter future unmeritorious claimants.

Such delays can themselves have legal consequences. Asylum applicants cannot be expected to put their lives on hold pending the receipt of a decision from the Home Office and may develop a family life in the UK. The issue has been the

---

[42] *MM v Secretary of State for the Home Department (Delay—reasonable period—Akaeke—Strbać) Serbia and Montenegro* [2005] UKAIT 00163 [17].

degree to which delay may be taken into account when deciding whether or not removal would be disproportionate to the individual's right to family life under Article 8 ECHR. This has given rise to litigation on the effect of such delay on the individuals' right to family life. Without going into all the legal technicalities, it has been recognised that Home Office delay in the initial consideration of an asylum claim may be relevant in reducing the weight otherwise to be accorded to the requirements of immigration control when assessing the proportionality of removal in light of the right to family life.[43] Asylum should not be granted to compensate the appellant or punish the Home Office because of its delay. However, in some circumstances delay may render removal disproportionate, irrespective of the outcome of the asylum decision, because the appellant has developed a family life. Given the backlog of claims that amassed during the period 1998–2006, it is not at all unusual for some claimants to have waited many years before the Home Office provided them with an initial decision.

Delay is also generated by the operation of the appeals process and, as we have noted, increasing its timeliness has long been a central Home Office concern. One of the central objectives behind the introduction of the single-tier AIT in 2005 was to reduce the timescales of the appeals process. In 2003–04, the average waiting time from the receipt of an asylum appeal by the Tribunal to the promulgation of a determination by an Immigration Judge was 17 weeks; in 2007–08, it was eight weeks.[44] Set against its target to conclude 75 per cent of asylum appeals within six weeks (commencing from their receipt to the promulgation of a determination by an Immigration Judge), the Tribunal's performance in 2007–08 was 61 per cent and in 2008–09 was 68 per cent.[45]

On the other hand, some delay is necessary to ensure that the appeals process operates fairly by allowing the appellants the opportunity to collect further evidence, such as expert reports, and to enable the Tribunal to produce good decisions which can then withstand challenge. The more accelerated the appeal process is, then the greater risk of it not operating fairly or producing accurate decisions. Furthermore, too great an emphasis on timely appeal decisions first time round may be inefficient and dysfunctional if it results in decisions of inferior quality which then need to be sent back to be re-determined. The efficiency of the process will, to some extent, depend upon it being perceived as fair; unfairness, whether perceived or real, tends to generate legal challenges which increase direct costs and consume more time.

Then there are the broader institutional considerations are at play. Being overseen by the Ministry of Justice, the Tribunal is structurally independent of the Home Office, but both government departments have a joint Public Service Agreement target to grant or remove 90 per cent of asylum claimants within six

---

[43] *Huang v Secretary of State for the Home Department* [2007] UKHL 11; [2007] 2 AC 176; *EB (Kosovo) v Secretary of State for the Home Department* [2008] UKHL 41. See also *Secretary of State for the Home Department v S* [2007] EWCA Civ 346.

[44] Hansard HC vol 479 col 2264W (17 September 2008).

[45] Tribunals Service, *Annual Report and Accounts 2008–09* (2008–09 HC 599) 118.

months.[46] The timeliness of appeal decisions is critical to this target; hence the Tribunal's own target to conclude 75 per cent of asylum appeals within six weeks, itself supplemented by other internal targets as to the production of determinations within 10 days and as to the number of adjournments. Virtually all tribunal jurisdictions operate under key performance indicators as regards the timeliness of decision-making. But subjecting the judiciary to performance accountability risks intruding into the sphere of judicial independence, especially when the targets are set by the executive.[47] The targets here are more stringent than elsewhere. Furthermore, the Home Office exerts significant influence as regards the Tribunal's procedure rules. Competing models of administrative justice are obviously in play with a tension between the Home Office's emphasis on processing quickly and efficiently a large volume of cases in order to implement policy and the need to ensure the fair treatment of each individual case irrespective of broader policy concerns.

A more general point about both direct costs and the timeliness of the process arises from the political context of asylum adjudication. Asylum adjudication is not normally viewed by government as an area in which increased expenditure is likely to win political support; on the contrary. Ministers are unlikely to have much concern as to the possible adverse electoral consequences from prioritising efficiency because there are none. Unlike other tribunal users, asylum applicants do not form a constituency with much real voice and have no vote. The political imperative has been to speed up the processing of appeals and to control the amount of resources devoted to the system. At some stage, an unfavourable comparison is likely to be made with the criminal justice process. A life sentence for murder is only imposed after a full trial process in which both parties are legally represented and the evidence fully examined. By comparison, the average length of an asylum appeal hearing is approximately two hours. Is this amount of time sufficient? To the extent that the witnesses who can give live evidence are normally restricted solely to the appellant and that the appellant will have prepared a statement in advance of the hearing, then the allotted time may be taken to be sufficient. If an appellant wishes to collect further evidence, such as an expert report, then an adjournment will normally be required.

Delay may also arise from the propensity of unsuccessful appellants to pursue onward rights of challenge against initial appeal determinations. Many unsuccessful appellants seek to challenge adverse appeal decisions. However, extensive use of onward rights of challenge raises complex issues of the balance between error costs, direct cost, and timeliness. Onward rights of challenge are a necessary corrective to appeal determinations that contain an error of law. If an appellant whose appeal has been dismissed successfully challenges that decision on the ground that

---

[46] HM Treasury, *2007 Pre-Budget Report and Comprehensive Spending Review: Meeting the Aspirations of the British People* (Cm 7227, 2007), 'PSA Delivery Agreement 3: Ensure controlled, fair migration that protects the public and contributes to economic growth' [3.14].

[47] A Le Sueur, 'Developing Mechanisms for Judicial Accountability in the UK' (2004) 24 *Legal Studies* 73, 82.

it contained a material error of law and that there is a real possibility that the Tribunal would decide the appeal differently on reconsideration, the appellant still deserves a lawful determination in order to produce a good decision. As a further segment of the appeals process after the initial fact-finding appellate stage, onward rights of challenge are a further procedural requirement designed to reduce the number of errors resulting from decision-making. At the same time, they inevitably impose delay and administrative costs. It is also possible that use of onward rights of appeal may impose other types of costs (both direct and indirect). For instance, extensive use of such rights adds to the general caseload of the higher courts, thereby increasing the potential for delay in other non-asylum cases and stretching judicial resources.

Again, some balance must be attained between the timeliness of the process and the amount of time required to make decisions. In this respect, it is perhaps understandable that the governmental interest will be focused upon achieving a quick and efficient process, though there is no guarantee that either administrative or legislative action will necessarily enhance the timeliness of the decision process. As we have seen, the Home Office's administration has hardly always been conducive to this end. Home Office delay has resulted in hardship for applicants and increased the difficulties of enforcing immigration control. Nor, as we shall see in chapter eight, have legislative attempts to streamline the appeals process and onward rights of appeal always been successful. The AIT was introduced in 2005, but by 2008, the Home Office was consulting on a further reorganisation of the appeals process and, in 2010, the appeals system was transferred to the First-tier and Upper Tribunals.

Conclusion

The relationships between the resources allocated to a decision process, the fairness of that process, the accuracy of decisions, and the timeframe within which they are to be produced are a key determinant of the quality of that process. However, as the preceding discussion indicates, the problems raised by these relationships, in particular that between the cost of a decision and its value, are difficult. There is considerable force behind the observation that the 'how much money should be spent to produce good decisions?' question is the least attractive, but also the most difficult and enduring aspect of any assessment of administrative justice.[48] Questions which are hard, if not impossible, nevertheless need to be addressed. Such issues cannot be either ignored or simply brushed aside ('a price cannot be put on justice'). Furthermore, calls for additional resources are often

---

[48] P Stockton, 'Proportionate Dispute Resolution: What Are the Options' (a paper presented at a seminar on administrative justice at the Nuffield Foundation, 23 January 2006) [17].

beside the point. Most decision-making processes and virtually all public agencies desire more resources, but it is precisely because resources are scarce that efficiency is required.

There is no guarantee that government actually attempts to carry out an assessment of a similar character to that which has been considered here only in outline. Indeed, there are various reasons why government may seek to avoid undertaking this kind of calculation. Given the difficulties involved, government may simply be unwilling or unable to weigh up the cost of disputes and their value; the internal workings of government may not always be conducive to methodical and analytic policy making. Alternatively, if departmental budgets are under strain, existing spending levels may be taken as a given, but any proposed increases may be subjected to detailed scrutiny. Then there is the broader political context of asylum adjudication. Frustrated at the intractable administrative difficulties of managing an effective asylum policy, ministers may be tempted to seek a quick win by seeking to derail the 'gravy train' for lawyers by reducing legal aid entitlements. Government may also stand accused of knowing the price of everything and the value of nothing. But, at the same time, government can hardly be accused of excessive parsimony; it spends substantial sums of public money to fund a decision process, the outputs of which cannot conclusively said to be either right or wrong. Furthermore, the costs are not imposed just upon government and they are not solely financial costs either. The higher courts, concerned at the amount of time taken up with their asylum caseload and its impact on other types of litigation, may seek further re-design of onward rights of challenges in order to relieve themselves of the burden imposed by numerous and repetitive asylum cases. Nor can the desire for a timely process be questioned, given the legitimate desire to deter unmeritorious claimants.

Despite all these competing complexities, some assessment of the proportionate relationship between the costs of a dispute and its value—implicit or otherwise—must be made even though it is not possible to assess all of the precise costs involved and different views can reasonably be held as to the weight to be attributed to the value of a dispute relative to its cost. Having examined this aspect of quality, we can turn to consider the operation of the appeals process.

4

Appeal Hearings

IN THIS AND subsequent chapters, we turn to consider the empirical data
concerning how asylum appeals are heard and determined in practice. This
chapter examines appeal hearings. As a central aspect of the appeals process,
the appeal hearing affects the quality of the decision-making process and its outcomes. How appeals are conducted will also inform the perception of both appellants and the general public as to the nature of the process. We have already
identified the principal tension in the appeals process between speed and fairness.
Much of the Tribunal's organisation is geared up to achieving its target of determining 75 per cent of asylum appeals within six weeks. Targets are deemed necessary to ensure proper managerial control of the appeals process; without them
appeals might not be determined within the desired timeframe. But the appeals
system is not simply a managerial process for disposing of appeals; it is also a
judicial process for adjudicating each appeal fairly. Furthermore, a subsidiary tension arises between the need to collect the facts necessary to produce accurate decisions and the concern that an interventionist approach may undermine judicial
neutrality.

Drawing upon the empirical data, this chapter examines how these underlying
tensions are mediated in practice. More specifically, the chapter examines the
following aspects of the appeals process: the pre-hearing stage; substantive hearings; and the contribution of the participants (interpreters, representatives, and
judges) involved; the role of judges in the absence of representation; and the
impact of performance targets upon the appeals process.

The Pre-Hearing Stage

The pre-hearing stage of the process is important to ensure that appeals are prepared for substantive hearings. This section examines the following aspects of the
pre-hearing stage: pre-hearing reviews, known as case management review (CMR)
hearings; listing practices; pre-hearing preparation by judges; and adjournment
requests.

Case Management Review Hearings

CMRs are the principal stage in the appeal process before substantive appeal hearings; their purpose is to enable a judge to review the appeal file to check whether or not the appeal is ready to proceed to a substantive hearing. This review is usually undertaken by way of a short oral hearing with the parties present. All substantive asylum appeal hearings are preceded by a CMR. A related purpose of CMRs is, if possible, to narrow down the disputed issues between the parties, the idea being that the interaction between the judge and the parties may provide an opportunity to identify both contested and non-contested issues, and thereby increase the efficiency of the process.

The degree to which CMRs are successful in terms of providing a pre-hearing interaction of the parties in order to narrow down the contested issues is, however, limited. There are various reasons for this. The appellant's representative will often still be in the process of assisting the appellant in preparing the case. If the Tribunal is to achieve its target of determining 75 per cent of asylum appeals within six weeks, then a considerable proportion of appeals have to process quickly in accordance with a strict timetable. Appeals are listed for a CMR ten working days after receipt by the Tribunal and for substantive hearing after a further ten working days. These targets can create difficulties in terms of preparation of the case. Under these time constraints, a representative might have had the opportunity to prepare a written statement for the appellant, or they might not. It is likely that the best representative will not have had sufficient opportunity fully to prepare an appellant's case. The risk is that the CMR stage can often function not as a proper check to ensure that the appeal is sufficiently ready to proceed to a substantive hearing, but merely as a formal check.

Even if the case is ready to proceed to a substantive hearing, the potential to narrow down the contested issues may be limited for a number of reasons. First, the Home Office is generally unwilling to concede on any matter. Secondly, the Immigration Judge undertaking the CMR will not normally be the same judge who will hear the substantive appeal and the judge determining an appeal will not want to be bound by a previous judge.[1] Furthermore, the ability to narrow down the issues is constrained by the limited time allocated to a CMR; as one judge explained, 'there are ten CMRs in a single hearing list, which is too many in order to investigate the substance of each case. Even if you tried, the representatives on neither side are geared up for that exercise'.[2]

CMRs may, though, serve other purposes. They can be used to identify case-specific issues, for instance, the particular country issue, which can then help judges when preparing for the substantive hearing. CMRs may also have a role in identifying those issues which might require a subsequent adjournment; for instance, in cases of religious conversion, it is normally necessary for an appellant

---

[1] For instance, fee-paid Immigration Judges do not undertake CMRs but do hear substantive hearings.
[2] Immigration Judge interview 3.

to call his church pastor as a witness; by raising the issue at the CMR stage, a judge can ensure that the representatives are aware of this, and thereby prevent a subsequent adjournment request.[3] CMRs can also be useful in ensuring that the Home Office's refusal letter makes sense to the appellant and that the appellant is aware of the case to be met. CMRs also provide the opportunity for the appellant to request that the appeal be heard by an all female court or that the substantive hearing be held in private (this may happen, if, for instance, the appellant is an unaccompanied minor). Even if CMRs simply focus on the basics such as name and address checking, then this can be useful; one practical difficulty of the process is that while the Tribunal needs to keep in contact with its clientele, appellants move frequently and representatives may not inform the Tribunal; there is an ever-present risk of miscommunication with appellants.[4] CMRs may also enable the linking up of related appeals.[5] Finally, CMRs enable judges to become aware of the types of cases coming up for substantive hearings and the emerging trends within an ever-changing jurisdiction dependent on migration flows and changes within countries producing asylum applicants.

There are, however, common problems with the functioning of CMRs in practice. One is the declining level of representation for appellants. For unrepresented appellants, there is little, if any, chance that the CMR might narrow down the contested issues. Rather, the issue is whether the judge can assist the appellant to prepare adequately for the substantive hearing. The extent to which this is possible is heavily dependent on the individual judge. For instance, one judge explained that CMRs can provide an opportunity through which the unrepresented appellant can be provided with some on the spot advice as to how to prepare for the substantive hearing. 'Without the CMR unrepresented appellants might turn up at the substantive hearing without any clue as to what is going on'.[6] However, the degree to which judges provide such advice and assistance to unrepresented appellants at the CMR stage can vary.

Another problem with CMRs and the whole hearing process is the inability of the Tribunal to compel the parties to cooperate with the process. At the CMR, a judge will normally issue directions to the parties to serve certain documents with the Tribunal before the substantive hearing. An appellant may be directed to serve the following with the Tribunal: a witness statement; a bundle of documents to be relied upon; a skeleton argument; and a chronology of events. The Home Office

---

[3] *Dorodian v Secretary of State for the Home Department* (01TH01537), date notified 23 August 2001 (IAT).

[4] See, eg, *Saleem v Secretary of State for the Home Department* [2000] EWCA Civ 186; [2000] Imm AR 529 (CA) and *FP (Iran) and MB (Libya) v Secretary of State for the Home Department* [2007] EWCA Civ 13; [2007] Imm AR 450.

[5] Appeals often concern not only a single individual but also other family member(s) who may also have had their appeal(s) determined by the Tribunal. As the findings made in an earlier determination, so far as relevant and still valid, will have to be taken into account in the later appeal; the CMR may enable the judge to ensure that the previous determination is linked up. See *TK v Secretary of State for the Home Department (Consideration of Prior Determination—Directions) Georgia* [2004] UKIAT 00149.

[6] Immigration Judge interview 2.

may be directed to serve its own bundle of documents (for instance, relevant country information and a list of any authorities to be relied upon). The power to issue directions is essential to the Tribunal if it is to ensure that the parties cooperate with the process so that appeals can be determined within the desired timeframe. The problem, however, is that the parties—the appellant and his representative and the Home Office—often fail to comply with such directions. The obvious answer would be to introduce sanctions against a party for non-compliance with directions, but this is not an option. It would be wrong to punish the appellant for non-compliance, because of the need to subject each case to the most anxious scrutiny; secondly, it would be wrong to grant asylum because of the Home Office's failings. The upshot is that non-compliance with directions goes unpunished. As one judge explained:

> Every judge has experience of directing the Home Office to do a particular thing on a particular date, for instance, to file with the Tribunal the transcription of an asylum interview in two weeks' time, and then two week pass, and it has not been done. The judge then directs the Home Office to do it again and the Home Office still does not do it. So, in the end, judges just stop directing the Home Office to do things because the Tribunal has no power to issue any sanctions for non-compliance with its directions. On the other side, if the appellants' representatives do not do what they have been directed to, then there are also no sanctions to apply against them either. Judges can issue as many directions as they want, but they cannot make the parties comply with those directions.[7]

So, what of CMRs? The general view is that they have not achieved the promise of narrowing down the issues for substantive hearings. At the same time, CMRs do perform a range of important, though lesser, functions; there is a need for some system of pre-hearing reviews to ensure that appeals are ready to proceed, but the effectiveness of CMRs is limited in various ways.[8]

Listing Practices

The hearing list is the daily concern for Immigration Judges. Full-time judges work on a 'one + one' working pattern of hearing cases one day and writing determinations the next. With the introduction of the AIT in 2005, appeal lists were allocated on a 'points system', the purpose of which was to achieve the fair and speedy disposal of cases. Each hearing list has a total value of six points and cases in the list must make-up those points; points are awarded according to the category of case. Asylum cases are divided by country into three and two point cases

---

[7] Immigration Judge interview 6.

[8] In 2007, the AIT piloted two alternatives to standard CMRs: a paper-based Pre-Hearing Review (PHR) and CMRs via the telephone. The anticipated benefit of this is to free up court rooms and a reduction in costs for those representing the appellant and respondent. Whether or not CMRs should be varied along these lines remains to be seen. See A Cox, 'Asylum & Immigration Tribunal: Case Management Review (CMR) Project' in Administrative Justice and Tribunal Council, *Adjust* (December 2007) available from www.ajtc.gov.uk.

according to their supposed difficulty.[9] The advantage of this system is its simplicity. The disadvantage is that the points allocated to an appeal may not necessarily correspond with either the length or the difficulty of the individual case. For instance some two point cases may raise more complex issues. However, three point cases may turn out to be easier than expected, so some rough balance may be attained in practice.

Pre-Hearing Preparation

The asylum appeals jurisdiction is a paper heavy system. The appeal file will usually contain the following: the applicant's initial screening interview and statement of evidence form; the substantive interview record; the reasons for refusal letter; a witness statement of the evidence to be called at the hearing which will stand as evidence-in-chief at the hearing; and country information. To prepare for the substantive hearing, judges will need to examine the appeal file carefully and are expected to have read the most significant papers for the case so that they are aware of the main aspects of the claim. Most judges will examine the appeal file on the morning of the substantive appeal hearing or, if possible, the day before. Part-time paid judges are not normally able to examine appeal files until the morning of the substantive hearing. Salaried Immigration Judges can access appeal files in advance of the hearing, but this may be impracticable owing to the pressure of work. As one judge explained, when preparing appeals, he tended to focus on the 'subjective material' concerning the appellant's case—the appellant's witness statement, interview record, and Home Office refusal letter—rather than the objective country materials as he would already have some feel for this when regularly dealing with appeals from the same country. Appeal files often contain voluminous amounts of country information—for instance, some 400 page long country reports—but in practice only a small section may be directly relevant to the particular appeal. Most judges were of the view that the amount of time available to them to spend preparing for appeals was constrained. In any event, the appeal file may not always contain all relevant documents and new evidence might only be presented at the hearing itself.

Adjournments

Adjournments naturally comprise an area in which tensions between speed and fairness arise—sometimes acutely. If adjournment rates run too highly, then there

---

[9] To take a few examples, asylum appeals from Afghanistan, Chad, Democratic Republic of Congo, Iran, Iraq, Libya, Somalia and Zimbabwe, amongst other countries, are 'List One' cases that attract three points. By contrast, asylum appeals from Albania, India, Nigeria, Pakistan, Sri Lanka and Uganda, amongst others, are 'List Two' cases that attract two points. Other non-asylum cases—settlement, non-settlement, family visitor appeals—also attract differential points according to their appeal type. See Asylum and Immigration Tribunal, *Report of a Working Party* (AIT, 2005).

is a risk that appeals will not be determined within their targets. Adjourning one appeal will mean that the six week target for the case will be missed; it will also mean that other cases will be put back. At the same time, there is a risk of unfairness if an adjournment is needed to ensure that the appeal can be determined justly. The general tenor of the procedure rules does not encourage adjournments; an appeal must not be adjourned unless it cannot otherwise be justly determined.[10] A good reason is required to justify an adjournment. Adjournment requests are often made because the appellant wants to collect further evidence (such as an expert report). As one judge explained, adjournment requests at substantive hearings are sometimes the consequence of a less than complete investigation at the CMR; if more initiative was taken at the CMR to ensure that appeals were ready to proceed, then this could prevent subsequent adjournment applications. At the same time, the obligation to determine appeals justly does not imply that appellants should have a limitless amount of time to prepare their case: they need a fair opportunity; if they had not received this opportunity, then an adjournment will be justified, but not otherwise.[11] By contrast, representatives are often critical of the restrictive attitude of judges refusing requests for adjournments.

A particularly troublesome ground for requesting an adjournment is that an appellant is unrepresented. This situation can arise when the appellant has either been unable to obtain any representation at all or when the representatives have pulled out of the case because they no longer consider it to have any merit. Either of these situations can arise because of constraints on the use of publicly funded representation or because, under the legal aid regime, representatives are required to monitor the viability of their cases if they are to continue as a provider with the Legal Services Commission. Should a judge adjourn an appeal in such circumstances? According to Tribunal guidance, adjournment requests from unrepresented appellants should generally be resisted; appellants who have failed to obtain publicly funded representation with one firm of representatives are unlikely to get representation elsewhere.[12] As adjourning would not serve any useful purpose in such circumstances, it is seen very much as a last resort, unless it is impossible to dispose of the appeal justly and fairly.

For instance, in one case an unrepresented appellant requested an adjournment on the basis that a week before the hearing, her representatives decided that they would no longer represent her. The judge declined: the appellant was unrepresented because of the lack of funding and it was standard procedure for such cases to proceed without an adjournment: there was no guarantee that she would get funding if the appeal was adjourned.[13] By contrast, in another case, the appellant had recently changed representatives because her previous representatives had not been doing anything to progress with her appeal. The new representatives had

---

[10] Asylum and Immigration Tribunal (Procedure) Rules SI 2005/230 r 21(2).

[11] Immigration Judge interview 3.

[12] Immigration Appellate Authority, *Adjudicator Guidance Note No 5: Unrepresented Appellants* (IAA, 2003).

[13] Case 134.

arranged an appointment for the appellant with an expert, which would take place after the substantive hearing. The judge adjourned the hearing: it would have been unfair to have proceeded with the hearing, given that the appellant had contacted fresh representatives who were doing their best to collect further evidence which could have a decisive bearing on the outcome.[14]

Clearly, an important factor influencing judges is the institutional pressure to process appeals in accordance with the Tribunal's overall performance targets for asylum appeals. Adjournment rates are monitored within the Tribunal and the overall target to determine 75 per cent of appeals within six weeks is supported by a specific target that judges should not adjourn a certain proportion of hearings. This can itself lead to tensions within the Tribunal between its administrative staff and its judiciary. While the former may often have targets upper-most in their minds, judges naturally insistent that adjournments are a matter for judicial decision alone. As one judge noted:

> There have been times in the past in which the Tribunal's administrative staff have been told to refuse to adjourn an appeal beyond its target—that has lead to disagreement, which has been eventually resolved, almost inevitably, in favour of the judiciary. We think that is the right thing to do.[15]

Substantive Hearings

Substantive hearings are the central aspect of the process; they are the only occasion in which all the parties are assembled together specifically to present and examine the evidence on which a decision is to be based. Unlike other tribunal processes, such as social security, asylum appeals have a high rate of attendance by appellants.[16] The hearing will be conducted by a single judge with an interpreter and the appellant present; the extent to which representatives on either side are present varies. This section considers the following aspects of substantive hearings: the judge's opening statement; administrative and procedural problems in the appeal process; the degree of (in-)formality; the roles of both interpreters and representatives; and the presentation and cross-examination of evidence.

The Judge's Opening Statement

Given at the start of the appeal hearing, the judge's opening statement is of some importance. The appeal hearing will be the first occasion that the appellant has

---

[14] Case 126.

[15] Immigration Judge interview 14.

[16] On appellant non-attendance in social security appeals, see J Baldwin, N Wikeley, and R Young, *Judging Social Security: The Adjudication of Claims for Benefit in Britain* (Oxford, Clarendon Press, 1992) 103–109; National Audit Office, *Getting it Right, Putting it Right: Improving Decision-making and Appeals in Social Security Benefits* (2002–03 HC 1142) 44.

direct personal contact with the judge. In the opening statement, the judge should introduce himself and briefly explain the format of the appeal hearing.[17] The judge may also explain to the appellant his independence from the Home Office. Given the dependence on interpreters, it is also particularly important that the judge confirm whether the appellant and the interpreter understand each other. The appellant's effective participation in the hearing will usually be heavily dependant on whether the interpreter is able properly and accurately to interpret the proceedings. The judge may also remind the appellant to give truthful and accurate answers.

In practice, judges do not use a uniform opening statement. Some provide a very detailed opening statement; others may say little in their opening statement other than ensuring that the appellant and the interpreter understand each other. In unrepresented appeals, the opening statement assumes even greater importance. In such cases, judges are instructed to reassure the appellant that he will not be prejudiced by the judge proceeding to hear his case in the absence of a representative. In particular, the judge should explain at the outset of the hearing what the procedure is, and encourage the appellant to say at any point if there is something that he does not understand, or feels unhappy about.[18] From the appeals observed, judges tended to give more detailed opening introductions to unrepresented appellants.

If there is no standardised opening statement used by every judge, then what should happen? One suggestion would be that the Tribunal's guidance note ought to be more detailed to ensure consistency. Another option, that of replacing detailed opening statements with printed information, may be of limited use.[19] Furthermore, if 'from a human point of view, appearing in front of a tribunal in support of an asylum claim must be a gruelling experience at the best of times', then there is much to be said for the opening statement to be made by the judge personally in order to put the appellant at ease.[20]

What else could judges do? One suggestion is that judges explain in more detail the discrete mental operations that they undertake when making an asylum decision. In practice, judges tend to avoid specialist legal phraseology and simply inform an appellant that their job is 'to decide what is likely to happen to you if you go back to your country' and that the appeal hearing is the appellant's opportunity to tell the judge 'what your problems would be if you were to go back'. A more detailed explanation should be unnecessary for represented appellants, but should be provided to unrepresented appellants. At the same time, some sense of proportion is required. The appellant may be nervous and apprehensive and the effect of a more detailed explanation may, in some instances, be counterproductive as a long-winded statement may only increase appellants' anxiety.

---

[17] Immigration Appellate Authority, *Adjudicator Guidance Note No 3: Pre-hearing Introduction* (IAA, 2002).

[18] Ibid.

[19] This is because many asylum appellants may be illiterate.

[20] *HF (Algeria) v Secretary of State for the Home Department* [2007] EWCA Civ 445 [26] (Carnwath LJ).

While it is important, the opening statement is usually only one aspect to the commencement of proceedings. It will virtually always be necessary for the judge to discuss appropriate matters with both representatives. Despite an appeal having already gone through the CMR hearing, this housekeeping exercise is usually necessary to focus the hearing and to clarify the evidence and case-law to be relied upon and to establish time estimates of the hearing, and for the judge to undertake a document check.

Administrative and Procedural Problems

Ideally, the appeals process would operate with seamless efficiency. In reality, it is often hindered by various administrative and practical problems. Documents and files may be lost; appeal files may be incomplete; evidence may not have been submitted in accordance with directions; there may be disputes over the accuracy of the interview record; at the appeal hearing, the Home Office may be absent; representatives, appellants, and interpreters may not attend the hearing centre when they are supposed to; a representative may be double-booked for two appeals in different court rooms; and so on. Responsibility for such difficulties often lies with the parties—the Home Office and representatives—and occasionally the Tribunal and its administration. While such difficulties may be perceived to be of a relatively low level, in practical terms, they can impair the efficiency of the appeals process. Indeed, given the regularity with which such difficulties occur, it is no exaggeration to state that they are part of the culture of the jurisdiction.

The following cases, drawn from the observation of appeals, illustrate some of the difficulties that can afflict the appeals process:

- A judge had a list of 10 CMRs to hear. The Home Office should have lodged its appeal bundles with the Tribunal prior to the hearing. However, in nine of the CMRs, the Home Office had not done this, but only submitted its bundles to the judge on the day. Consequently, the judge had then been unable to examine the files in advance. In one appeal, the appellant had attended, but his representatives had not. However, the representatives had informed neither the appellant nor the Tribunal that they would not be attending the CMR; if they had, then an interpreter would have been booked by the Tribunal. In the event, the appellant was able, through some limited understanding of English, to understand the proceedings.
- An Eritrean national had sought asylum on the basis that she had been evading military service. The Home Office had rejected the appellant's credibility on the ground that, in her asylum interview, the appellant had stated that she was 'exempt' from military service. The appellant disputed that she had said this in the interview and claimed that the interview had been either incorrectly interpreted or recorded. However, the asylum interview had not, in accordance with Home Office policy, been tape-recorded in order to provide independent confirmation of what the appellant had said. This was despite the ruling of the Court

of Appeal in *Dirshe* to the effect that such asylum interviews of unrepresented claimants should be tape-recorded as it could be critical to any decision as to credibility.[21] However, the Home Office's policy had been not to tape-record interviews, unless specifically requested to do so by the applicant.[22] As the Immigration Judge noted, where an applicant is unrepresented, this policy 'rather defeats the spirit of the decision in *Dirshe* . . . If the Secretary of State is really interested in making an accurate/verbatim record of the interview, what better way to do this than by recording it'.[23]

- At a CMR hearing, the appellant had objected that the Home Office's handwritten transcription of his asylum interview was inaccurate. Adjourning the CMR, the judge had issued directions that the Home Office produce a new transcription. However, at the adjourned CMR, the Home Office had not served and filed the transcript in advance. The Home Office subsequently produced the transcript at the substantive hearing. However, the transcript provided still contained problems: some of the words and phrases were indicated in the transcription by '?????' and others were meaningless when placed in their context.[24]

Such problems are nothing new in the asylum jurisdiction, and it is important not to exaggerate their frequency, as for the most part the appeals process runs smoothly. Most Home Office presenting officers and representatives are competent. Nevertheless, administrative and practical difficulties tend to occur with an undesirable degree of regularity. The Tribunal has a long practice of subjecting both representatives and the Home Office alike to withering criticism for their failings.[25]

The Formality of Appeal Hearings

To what extent are appeal hearings conducted on a formal or informal basis? Traditionally, tribunals have been considered to be a less formal alternative to the courts. There is, though, an ongoing debate as to whether informality is desirable

---

[21] *R (Dirshe) v Secretary of State for the Home Department* [2005] EWCA Civ 421; [2005] Imm AR 319. As the Court of Appeal explained, because of problems arising from translation and inaccurate record-keeping, it was necessary in the interests of procedural fairness for such interviews to be tape-recorded when no representative or interpreter was present on behalf of the applicant; tape-recording provided the only sensible method of redressing the imbalance which results from the Home Office being able to rely on the interview record which it had created for itself without affording an adequate opportunity for the applicant to refute it.

[22] Home Office, *Asylum Process Guidance: Conducting the Asylum Interview* (Home Office, 2007).

[23] Case 38.

[24] Case 30.

[25] See, eg, *Secretary of State for the Home Department v Razi* (01TH01836), date notified 21 September 2001 (IAT) [16]–[17]: 'If we took the charitable view, that . . . [the Home Office's] . . . conduct of the case . . . was no more than institutional incompetence, then it is hard to imagine any other departments of state in this country where such incompetence would be tolerated. We often have to criticise asylum-seekers and those acting for them for at least failing to do that which they ought to have done; but in this case, they had done it, and in time . . . This begins to go beyond institutional incompetence, into the realm of an institutional culture of disregard for adjudicators, who are the primary judicial authority in this country for making sure that immigration powers are efficiently, as well as fairly exercised. That does not serve the public interest, which the Home Office are there (we think) to represent'.

and the extent to which individual tribunals systems are able to live up to this aspiration in practice. Informality is supposed to make tribunals more user-friendly and accessible. However, pretensions to informality may conceal a hidden trap for appellants: those expecting an informal hearing may be surprised that tribunal proceedings are more adversarial and legalistic than they expected. Moreover, while it has been assumed that tribunals ought to be informal because they deal with relatively trivial disputes, the reality is that not only is the law administered by tribunals complex, but also the issues at stake are often of considerable importance.[26]

What degree of informality or otherwise characterises asylum appeal hearings? From the observation of appeals, it was apparent that the degree of formality of asylum appeal hearings varies from the very formal to very informal. The degree of formality depends upon the preferences of the judge and the judge's interaction with the representatives. Some judges prefer a more informal approach:

> I think you have got to be informal because you have got difficulties. The appellant does not understand a word you say. You ask questions through an interpreter. You have got representatives on both sides, who may not necessarily be legally qualified. If I were to pull up everybody for leading or evidential points I would be here all day and would get nowhere. So you have got to leave it informal.[27]

> Overall, I am in favour of being more informal. I think that should be the role of the tribunals in the context of state-individual disputes, particularly given the nature of the work that we do. Many of the appellants that appear in front of us have problems with the state being slightly overbearing.[28]

By contrast, other judges prefer greater formality in order to recognise the seriousness of the proceedings and to provide a coherent structure to the hearing. However judges attempt to influence the formality of the hearing, it is unlikely that hearings will ever be wholly 'user-friendly' simply because their principal purpose is to test appellants' accounts. From the appeals observed it was apparent that a small minority of appellants may become upset when recounting evidence in which they claim to have suffered harrowing past torture. In response, the judge may either adjourn the hearing briefly or make sure that the appellant is able to proceed. At the same time, it is necessary that hearings proceed so that the appellant's evidence can be drawn out and tested.

Interpreters

A distinctive feature of the asylum (and immigration) appellate jurisdiction is its reliance on interpreters; all appellants are entitled to the services of an interpreter.[29] At a fairly basic level, the quality of the process is highly dependant on the quality of interpreters: correct and accurate translation by the interpreter is

---

[26] H Genn, 'Tribunals and Informal Justice' (1993) 56 *Modern Law Review* 393.
[27] Immigration Judge interview 10.
[28] Immigration Judge interview 13.
[29] Asylum and Immigration Tribunal (Procedure) Rules SI 2005/230 r 49A.

essential if the appellant's participation is to be effective and if his evidence to be understood. The ever-present risk is that the communicative, cross-cultural, and linguistic barriers between judge and applicant may not be overcome—not only will the appellant not have been able to participate in the adjudication process; the evidence presented before the judge will be incorrect. Alternatively, there is the risk that the very process of translation may itself change the meaning of the applicant's story. This is why judges are normally astute to confirm whether the appellant and interpreter can understand each other.

With respect to the quality of interpretation, it was apparent that there were some concerns. Some judges queried whether interpreters always translate word for word whereas others noted that the standards of interpreters had improved. The difficulty, of course, is that it will not normally be possible for a judge to know whether or not an interpreter is correctly interpreting the answers given by the appellant. As one judge explained, to a certain extent it is necessary to rely both on body language and the way in which the English translation is given to ascertain whether or not there may be a problem with the interpretation.[30] Otherwise, it will be for either party to challenge the interpreter's performance.

Such challenges do occur. One practice is for the appellant's representatives to employ their own interpreter to check the accuracy of the Tribunal's interpreter. The appellant's own interpreter is forbidden from translating, but may be used to challenge the Tribunal's interpreter. The difficulty with such challenges is the obvious concern as to whether they are made in the interests of fairness or motivated by more cynical considerations. Unscrupulous appellants may mount such challenges to prolong the process or for 'forum-shopping' purposes, that is if the presiding judge is considered by reputation to be 'hard-line', then such a challenge might mean that the appeal is re-listed before a different judge. At the same time, interpreters can be incompetent and fail to interpret properly with consequent risks for an appellant. If such a challenge is made, then the judge will need to resolve the disputed interpretation unambiguously before proceeding to determine the appeal.

To what extent can interpreters not only interpret the words spoken by an appellant, but also give evidence, for instance, on whether an appellant speaks with particular language or dialect? Appeals by some nationals, such as Somali nationals, often turn on whether or not the appellant is a member of either a minority or a majority clan, which might be indicated by the language or dialect they speak. There have been instances in which the Tribunal has used its interpreter to establish at the hearing whether or not the appellant can speak the language or dialect that they claim to be able to speak. However, the Tribunal has re-stated its approach that it is not part of an interpreter's function to give evidence on the language dialect used by an appellant.[31] The function and expertise of interpreters lies in their ability to comprehend and communicate, not to assess or analyse;

[30] Immigration Judge interview 11.
[31] *AA v Secretary of State for the Home Department (Language diagnosis: use of interpreters) Somalia* [2008] UKAIT 00029.

further, it is undesirable for an interpreter, as a court official and neutral party, to be asked to give evidence concerning a contested issue in an appeal.[32]

Representatives

Representation is often seen as an important contributor to the quality of tribunal procedures and decision-making.[33] However, in the asylum context, the issues are complex as the quality of representation is variable and restrictions on publicly funded legal aid have meant more unrepresented appeals. More generally, the broader debate over the desirability of representation in tribunals has become polarised. From one perspective, representation before tribunals is sometimes seen as unnecessary because of the informality, procedural simplicity, and accessibility that tribunals offer. A combination of good quality advice, effective procedures, well conducted hearings, and competent and well-trained tribunal members should go a very long way to helping the vast majority of appellants to understand and put their cases properly themselves.[34] From another perspective, the lack of representation can leave appellants at a disadvantage. Underlying both positions lie very different assumptions as to the amount of public money that should be devoted to the funding of representation.

In the context of asylum appeals, representation on behalf of the appellant is, for several reasons, seen as being important to both appellants and the Tribunal. It assists in the preparation and presentation of appeals and helps appellants understand the process. It can also assist the Tribunal by furnishing all the available information needed to reach a decision and thereby promote efficiency. It can also ensure that the disputed matters are investigated thoroughly. Given the issues at stake in asylum cases, these advantages are augmented by the consequences of erroneous decisions, the legal complexity, and the linguistic and other difficulties faced by appellants. Furthermore, as the Home Office is often represented, representation on behalf of appellants promotes equality of arms before the Tribunal. Good representation can assist the decision-making process, while bad representation may positively hinder it. Overall, an asylum claimant will be in the best position if he has access to a competent representative versed in the practice and procedure of asylum and human rights law who is able to prepare and represent an appeal before an Immigration Judge and who is also able to consider the determination and draft appropriate grounds of legal challenge. The need for competent representation is recognised by all parties to the appeals process, including the higher courts.[35]

---

[32] Ibid, [7].

[33] H Genn and Y Genn, *The Effectiveness of Representation at Tribunals: Report to the Lord Chancellor* (London, Lord Chancellor's Department, 1989). See also R Moorhead and M Sefton, *Litigants in Person: Unrepresented Litigants in First Instance Proceedings* (London, DCA Research Series 2/05, 2005).

[34] A Leggatt, *Tribunals for Users: One System, One Service. The Report of the Review of Tribunals by Sir Andrew Leggatt* (London, The Stationery Office, 2001) [4.21].

[35] See, eg, *R (Frezghi) v Secretary of State for the Home Department* [2009] EWHC Admin 335 [24] (Blake J).

Concerns over the variable quality of representation in this jurisdiction are, though, long-standing. In 1998, it was noted that there was 'considerable concern within the Immigration Appellate Authorities and many immigration advice agencies about the quality of representation at immigration appeals and, especially, asylum appeals'.[36] A particular source of anxiety has been not only the variable standard of representation, but also that some representatives have deliberately sought to exploit appellants and the legal aid budget.[37]

In 1999, Parliament established the Office of the Immigration Services Commissioner (OISC) which regulates immigration advisers by ensuring they are fit and competent and act in the best interest of their clients.[38] It is an offence to offer immigration advice and services without being registered with, or exempted by, the OISC. The only exceptions to this are those who are regulated by a Designated Professional Body (eg the Law Society). The OISC regulates immigration advisers by investigating complaints against those giving immigration advice, promoting good practice by setting standards, and prosecuting those who operate outside of the regulatory framework.[39] It also provides oversight of the regulation of those who give immigration advice and are regulated by one of the Designated Professional Bodies. These measures would appear to have had some success. In 2006, the Tribunal's President observed that the 'utterly wicked, incompetent and useless' lay advisers who used to appear in immigration had pretty much disappeared.[40] In 2009, the Home Office consulted on providing an improved regulatory framework for immigration advice and representation by improving the OISC's legislative powers and introducing new measures that will allow for greater levels of intervention against those who are incompetent or unfit, looking to abuse individuals seeking immigration advice/ services or abuse the system.[41] However, concerns as to the overall quality of representation are persistent. In 2005, the Tribunal noted that 'unfortunately, the standard of preparation and advocacy of those appearing on behalf of appellants . . . is not uniformly high . . . Sadly a small, but significant proportion of appellants . . . are poorly represented'.[42]

[36] Lord Chancellor's Advisory Committee on Legal Education and Conduct, *Improving the Quality of Immigration Advice and Representation: A Report* (London, Lord Chancellor's Department, 1998) [2.32].

[37] In *Devaseelan v Secretary of State for the Home Department* (Starred Determination) [2003] Imm AR 1, 14 the Tribunal noted that there was 'an increasing tendency to suggest that unfavourable decisions by Adjudicators are brought about by error or incompetence on the part of representatives. New representatives blame old representatives, sometimes representatives blame themselves for prolonging the litigation by their inadequacy (without, of course, offering the public any compensation for the wrong from which they have profited by fees).'

[38] See Office of the Immigration Services Commissioner, *Annual Report and Accounts 2008–09* (2008–09 HC 627). See also www.oisc.gov.uk.

[39] There are arrangements between the OSIC and the Tribunal by which an Immigration Judge may complain to the OISC about an immigration adviser.

[40] House of Commons Home Affairs Committee, *Immigration Control* (2005–06 HC 775) [376].

[41] Home Office United Kingdom Border Agency, *Oversight of the Immigration Advice Sector: Consultation Response* (London, UKBA, 2009).

[42] *IS v Secretary of State for the Home Department (Concession made by representative) Sierra Leone* [2005] UKIAT 00009 [14] and [18]. For discussion of similar concerns in the US, see MM McKeown and A McLeod, 'The Counsel Conundrum: Effective Representation in Immigration Proceedings' in

All Immigration Judges interviewed recognised the variable quality of representation; 'some representatives are absolutely brilliant; some are pretty hopeless'.[43] This was confirmed by the observation of appeals. Many representatives were able to present their client's case effectively and to its best advantage. By contrast, other representatives appeared to be less well-prepared and unable to make coherent submissions. The variable quality of representation raises a number of difficulties. At a practical level, there is usually little that the Tribunal can do in relation to a poorly represented appeal other than express its frustration that an appellant has been poorly served. Low-quality representation is seen as just another problem which Immigration Judges must put up with. Secondly, appellants who have their case handled by an incompetent representative may feel significant disempowerment and alienation from the appeals process.[44] Thirdly, appellants with good cases who are badly served by incompetent representatives might be more likely to have their appeals rejected. There will not normally be any opportunity for challenging a negative decision brought about by the failure or incompetence of a representative because the general principle is that an appellant and his legal representative are considered as a single unit; an onward challenge will only correct unfairness by the Tribunal not that resulting from poor quality representation.[45] If incompetence by a representative did provide a valid ground of challenge against an adverse Tribunal decision, then 'it would be open to every disappointed applicant to seek to re-argue his case, complaining that the advocacy in the court below had been insufficiently skilful'.[46] Such appellants may, though, lodge a fresh claim with the Home Office. Finally, the variable quality of representation raises the risk that appeal outcomes might come to depend more upon the relative merits and demerits of representation than upon the intrinsic merits of the individual appeal; the danger is that a judge may subconsciously assume that appeals represented by a law firm with a bad reputation may themselves be without merit.

The difficulties are compounded in a number of ways. Following the introduction of restrictions on legal aid in 2005, immigration representatives have to assess the merits of an individual case and have themselves become squeezed between increasing financial pressures and their ethical obligation to their clients.[47] There is also the problem of discontinuous representation. An appellant's case may be taken up by a firm of representatives only to be subsequently 'dumped' when it becomes apparent that the appellant no longer qualifies for publicly funded legal

---

J Ramji-Nogales, AI Schoenholtz and PG Schrag (eds), *Refugee Roulette: Disparities in Asylum Adjudication and Proposals for Reform* (New York, New York University Press, 2009) 286.

[43] Immigration Judge interview 11.

[44] H MacIntrye, 'Imposed Dependency: Client Perspectives of Legal Representation in Asylum Claims' (2009) 23 *Journal of Immigration, Asylum, and Nationality Law* 181.

[45] *Al-Mehdawi v Secretary of State for the Home Department* [1990] 1 AC 876; *Maqsood v the Special Adjudicator and the Secretary of State* [2001] EWHC Admin 1003; [2002] Imm AR 268. See though *Haile v Immigration Appeal Tribunal* [2001] EWCA Civ 663; [2002] INLR 283; *FP (Iran)* above n 4.

[46] *R (R) v Secretary of State for the Home Department* [2005] EWHC Admin 520 [27] (Hughes J).

[47] D James and E Killick, 'Ethical Dilemmas? UK Immigration, Legal Aid Funding Reform and Caseworkers' (2010) 26 *Anthropology Today* 13.

aid. Alternatively, an appellant may themselves decide to change representatives either because the appellant has been moved by the Home Office from one part of the country to another or because the representatives have not progressed with the appeal to the appellant's satisfaction. Either way, in view of the short timescales of the process, this can create difficulties for an appellant resulting in adjournment applications. There has also been an increase in the number of unrepresented appeals.[48] These features are viewed as part and parcel of the broader difficulties that the Tribunal has to work with. The Tribunal does not itself have any responsibility for determining the allocation of legal aid funding or the quality of representation. Its general position is that the appeals process works best when there is good quality representation on both sides. As the Tribunal's former President has explained:

> What the judiciary want is good quality representation in as many cases as we can get it. We will take reasonable quality representation, we can even put up with poor quality representation. It is much better to have representation than no representation at all. If the system reduced the ability for people to get a fair decision it may not help the wider system. We all know Government has been very interested in cutting down the money spent on immigration and asylum. We all know there has been some very poor work done by some solicitors and barristers in the system and if they are out of it then that is a very good thing.[49]

What influence does the presence or absence of a representative on behalf of an appellant exert upon the outcome of appeals? Of the 182 appeal hearings observed, appellants were represented in 82 per cent and unrepresented in the remaining 18 per cent. It was common for unrepresented appellants to have had some advice at an earlier stage and for a firm of representatives to have helped the appellant prepare a witness statement. The representative may then have pulled out of the case for funding reasons; alternatively, the appellant may have decided to change representatives. From the data collected, success rates were found to vary between represented and unrepresented cases, with represented appellants experiencing a higher degree of success (31 per cent) than unrepresented appellants (12 per cent) (see figure 1).

This might seem to confirm the finding of previous empirical studies, that representation enhances the proportion of successful outcomes for appellants. However, some caution is required in interpreting the significance of this finding. First, the empirical research was not designed in order to provide a statistically representative sample. Secondly, representation is not the only factor influencing appeal outcomes. If the merits test governing legal aid is properly applied in order to focus publicly funded representation on the most meritorious cases, then it can be expected that unrepresented appellants will experience a lower success rate because it has been decided that their cases do not possess sufficient merit in order

---

[48] It is not possible to produce statistics in this respect because the Tribunals Service of the Ministry of Justice, which provides administrative support, does not collect any reliable statistics on the proportion of unrepresented appeals.

[49] House of Commons Home Affairs Committee above n 40 at Ev 73 (Hodge J, AIT President).

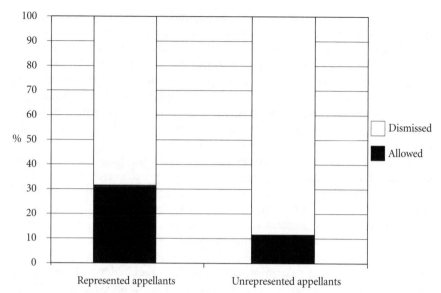

Figure 1: Outcome of appeals by presence and absence of representation on behalf of appellants

to qualify for publicly funded representation. Thirdly, the quality of representation in represented cases was of variable quality and it is not obvious what contribution low-quality representation makes to the outcome of appeals. Furthermore, in unrepresented appeals, judges tend, on the whole, to adopt a more interventionist approach. Nevertheless, at the same time, the broad implication of the finding is that representation may exert an important role in enhancing the ability of appellants to present their cases as effectively as possible.[50]

What then of representation for the Home Office? The Home Office is entitled to be represented before the Tribunal; this role is normally undertaken by either a presenting officer or the New Asylum Model (NAM) case-worker.[51] The Home Office introduced the NAM single case-worker in 2007 to ensure that a single individual would manage all aspects of an asylum claim from start of the process to its end, including the initial interview, decision-making and representation at the appeal stage, thereby increasing efficiency and personal accountability.[52] However,

[50] Other studies have demonstrated the significant influence of representation on appeal outcomes for asylum appellants. For instance, a wide-ranging empirical study of US asylum adjudication, Ramji-Nogales, Schoenholtz and Schrag above n 42 at 45 found that representation was the single most important factor affecting the outcome of the case. From a cross-tabulation analysis of a database of over 140,000 asylum appeals determined by the US Immigration Courts, the study found that 45.6% of represented asylum appellants appearing had their appeal allowed compared with only 16.3% of unrepresented appellants; even holding all other variables in the study constant, represented asylum appellants were substantially more likely to win their case than those without representation.

[51] Asylum and Immigration Tribunal (Procedure) Rules SI 2005/230 r 48(2).

[52] Home Office, *Controlling Our Borders: Making Migration Work for Britain. Five Year Strategy for Asylum and Immigration* (Cm 6472, 2005) 35–36.

by 2009, it was apparent that the NAM was not working as originally envisaged. On the one hand, by giving responsibility for concluding an application to one person without the need to pass it from one official to another, and by giving clear targets for them to work to, the Home Office had created a strong incentive for cases to be progressed and concluded. On the other hand, it became clear that not all NAM case-workers were representing cases at the appeal stage across the UK, resulting in regional inconsistency and preventing case-workers from building up their knowledge and experience of the appeals process; implementing the concept of single case ownership had proved to be exceptionally difficult.[53]

The role of the Home Office representative is to defend the initial refusal decision and to cross-examine the appellant. As with representatives, judges noted the variable quality of Home Office representatives. Part of the problem may derive from the fact that presenting officers are not normally legally qualified. Presenting officers and NAM case-workers are comparatively junior officials. Furthermore, there is regular turnover of staff within the Home Office. It has been noted that if the Home Office is serious about defending appeals, then the quality and skills of presenting officers must be improved; they should be required to meet at least the same standards as appellants' representatives.[54] Two issues concerning Home Office representatives—the quality of their cross-examination and their not infrequent absence from appeal hearings—are considered below.

Evidence-in-chief and Cross-examination

An important aspect of appeal hearings is the appellant's evidence-in-chief and cross-examination. The purpose of evidence-in-chief is to enable the appellant's representative to elicit the evidence concerning the basis of the appellant's claim for asylum. In practice, this will usually involve little more than an appellant confirming his name and the contents of his written statement. The principal focus of the appeal hearing is the appellant's cross-examination, the opportunity for the Home Office to test the appellant's evidence and to demonstrate its unreliability. However, the degree to which this occurs in practice varies. Some presenting officers subject an appellant's story to close scrutiny. Other presenting officers may become too carried away, and overstep the mark by engaging in aggressive cross-examination. By contrast, other presenting officers may not be able to undertake an effective cross-examination. Many judges noted that, in some cases, Home Office representatives are either unable or unwilling to cross-examine appellants effectively and that the overall standard of cross-examination by the Home Office was not uniformly good. As one judge noted, 'the appellant's

---

[53] National Audit Office, *Management of Asylum Applications by the UK Border Agency* (2008–09 HC 124); Independent Chief Inspector of the UK Border Agency, *Asylum: Getting the Balance Right? A Thematic Inspection: July—November 2009* (London, OCIUKBA, 2010) 18–27.

[54] House of Commons Home Affairs Select Committee above n 40 at [367].

evidence is not always tested in a hearing by the Home Office'.[55] Other judges noted that the standard of Home Office cross-examination was very mixed:

> Sometimes the Home Office will draw out good points, sometimes they are just picking up points which are not important at all. I think it could assist quite a lot if the Home Office took a much more active approach by investigating claims, but their approach almost always is simply to list what the appellant has to say and then just pick a few holes in it.[56]

When cross-examination is effective, then the appellant's account can be properly tested. However, the fact that this does not always happen can create something of a paradox as the commonest reason given by the Home Office for refusing initial claims is that they lack credibility. It also raises the issue of how, if at all, judges should question appellants.

Immigration Judge Questioning and the Absence of Representation

Questioning by Immigration Judges

The issue of whether judges should ask their own questions is one of the perennial questions in the asylum jurisdiction. On the one hand, judicial questioning raises the spectre of judges being seen to have descended into the arena and thereby undermining the perception of judicial impartiality.[57] On the other hand, there is the need to ensure that all issues are explored so that the judge can collect the necessary facts with which to make a robust decision. As the issue is unregulated by procedure rules, the Tribunal must decide for itself how to proceed.

Senior judges have produced a variety of guidance concerning the nature of questioning by judges, which is summarised here. When evidence is being taken from a witness and where there is representation on both sides, an Immigration Judge's 'role is of silent listening'.[58] It is for appellants to adduce the evidence they think appropriate and it is for the Home Office to put whatever contradictions in the evidence need to be put to the witness. Judges may ask their own questions for clarification purposes during and after evidence has been given; if so, then the parties must be given the opportunity to ask any further questions that arise out of this.[59] Judges also have obligations in relation to the general control of a case, that is, to

---

[55] Immigration Judge interview 10.

[56] Immigration Judge interview 3.

[57] Cf *Yuill v Yuill* [1945] 1 All ER 183, 189 (CA) (Lord Greene MR): a judge who 'descends into the arena . . . is liable to have his vision clouded by the dust of the conflict. Unconsciously he deprives himself of the advantage of calm and dispassionate observation'.

[58] *Oyono v Secretary of State for the Home Department* [2002] UKIAT 02034 [8].

[59] *K v Secretary of State for the Home Department (Côte d'Ivoire)* [2004] UKIAT 00061 [42]–[45]; *SA v Secretary of State for the Home Department (Clarificatory questions from IJs—best practice) Iran* [2006] UKIAT 00017.

move the hearing along if the representative's line of questioning is valueless. Questions may also be put to a witness if the answers given raise matters that trouble the judge or if such matters have not been raised or dealt with in cross-examination, especially if the judge is concerned about a point which may affect the decision. It is legitimate for judges to ask their own questions on issues of inconsistency or issues raised in the refusal letter or matters which have not been raised by the Home Office. However, judges should not develop a different case from that being presented or pursue their own theory of the case. Any questions put by the judge should not be asked in any hostile manner or in a manner which suggests that his or her mind has already been made up; the overriding principle is whether the hearing had been conducted fairly and impartially.

Putting this guidance to one side, it is apparent that there is a diversity of opinion amongst judges themselves as to the desirable degree of intervention by the judge at the hearing. Some Immigration Judges exhibit a strong predilection for an adversarial hearing with limited judicial intervention whereas others would prefer to move toward a more active, investigative approach of adjudication. The following quotations illustrate the broader themes from the interviews with Immigration Judges:

> In an ideal world, I would stick with the adversarial system, but it only works if you have good representatives on both sides who can present arguments and cross-examine so that the judge can make an informed decision. Unfortunately, in this system you do not get that. We are being asked to make written decisions on the basis of an imperfect factual basis which, in many cases, has got gaping holes in it. These decisions are then subject to close scrutiny by Senior Immigration Judges. I can see benefits in an inquisitorial system, but it would require a complete change of approach and of attitude and a great deal of thought as to precisely how it could be made to operate in practice. At the moment, we have got an imperfect system, which is neither fully adversarial nor inquisitorial. We don't have either working effectively.[60]

> There are drawbacks with the adversarial system in practice. First, there may not be representation on both sides, or the appellant's representative may be totally incompetent, so the concept behind the adversarial system breaks down to a certain extent. Secondly, because of time limits and the pressure that both parties are under, we are often sitting hearing an appeal knowing that we are not going to get at the truth. There might be things where I would like to issue directions in order to examine matters and to go where I think the truth might lie, but the system does not allow for that. With an inquisitorial system and particularly if the judge took over case management from the start, then the judge could take charge, for instance, by instructing an independent medical expert, rather than an expert who says what the appellant's representative wants. An inquisitorial approach would give us much more opportunity to get at the truth.[61]

> In this jurisdiction I certainly find myself having to behave in a much more inquisitorial way than I would use in other jurisdictions. I find that I have to guard against it—the

---

[60] Immigration Judge interview 5.
[61] Immigration Judge interview 4.

temptation when you have poor representation is to get stuck in and to start asking questions yourself, which we are rather discouraged from doing.[62]

I will ask my own questions at the hearing. Although it is an adversarial system, I want to try to get the right result. If that means asking questions which one side or the other has not asked, then I will ask those questions.[63]

If a judge just sits back (and I have colleagues who do that), takes notes, and lets the two sides argue it out, then sometimes you may miss out on a lot of important information. This is too an important an area to think 'well, the appellant didn't mention that particular issue, so I won't have a look at it'.[64]

The three general options concerning appeal procedures seem to be as follows. The first option—retention of the adversarial approach—is weakened by the absence and variable quality of representation. The second, current option has allowed judges greater scope to adopt a more active stance at appeal hearings by asking clarificatory questions. The third option is the most radical: a wholesale and decisive move toward a more fully inquisitorial approach in which judges would take over active case-management from the outset, have the ability to commission a court expert, and direct the proceedings and questioning of the appellant.

The issue is partly one of legal culture. As Allars has noted, the judicial paradigm of formal, adversarial procedure 'tends to overshadow alternative answers to procedural choices' facing tribunals.[65] But there are many other factors: caseload pressure; tribunal neutrality; the role of representation; the absence of an unequivocal statutory mandate to support a more inquisitorial approach; and the propensity of bias challenges against adverse decisions in which the judge was perceived to adopt a more active approach.

What happens at appeal hearings? In practice, the degree of judicial intervention, the nature, length, and content of judicial questioning, is highly dependent upon the personal preference and expertise of the individual judge.[66] Some judges do not ask any questions, whereas other judges may take a pro-active approach throughout the hearing. Other judges will ask questions during cross-examination to clarify a particular issue. Alternatively, the judge might raise queries with either representative about the relevance of a line of questioning or to ensure representatives focus on relevant issues. The judge may also ask questions to clarify a particular issue after both the evidence-in-chief and cross-examination on issues that were either not raised at all or not dealt with fully. On the whole, questions by judges tend to be limited to two or three key factual issues and tend not to exceed the length of time spent on cross-examination by the Home Office's representative.

---

[62] Immigration Judge interview 3.
[63] Immigration Judge interview 2.
[64] Immigration Judge interview 6.
[65] M Allars, 'Neutrality, the Judicial Paradigm, and Tribunal Procedure' (1991) 13 *Sydney Law Review* 377–378.
[66] Cf RE Wraith and PG Hutchesson, *Administrative Tribunals* (London, Allen and Unwin, 1973) 147.

There is, though, one constant anxiety for judges: whether or not their questioning will be challenged on the ground of bias. The Tribunal has accepted that while representatives may not take kindly to judicial questioning, they should not be too sensitive about it.[67] Nevertheless, challenges against the nature of questioning by judges are hardly unknown. Whether such challenges are valid will depend entirely on the reviewing court's assessment of whether the questions were, in the circumstances, fair. For instance, in one appeal, after a brief cross-examination by the Home Office, the judge asked a large number of questions of the appellant, the answers to which subsequently formed the basis of adverse credibility findings. The factual issues covered in the judge's questions had not been raised in the Home Office's refusal letter or in the course of cross-examination. On reconsideration, it was held that the impression was the judge had taken over the Home Office's task of testing the appellant's evidence. The credibility issues dealt with in the questions had not been raised previously, the appellant had not known the nature of the case she was expected to meet; there had been a sufficiently serious breach of procedural fairness so as to invalidate the hearing.[68] At the same time, whether the questioning is hostile is not to be equated with the discomfort a witness might feel or difficulties he might have in answering questions; a judge may have to ask questions which make an appellant feel uncomfortable without it being said that the judge has been hostile. A representative may feel that the questioning was hostile, but this does not necessarily mean that there was anything improper about it.[69]

Appeal Hearings Without Home Office Representation

The difficulties are accentuated in those hearings which the Home Office is absent. In general terms, the absence of an official from the respondent agency at an appeal hearing can raise difficulties for any tribunal; judges tend to feel that their impartiality is compromised because there is no-one from the agency to defend the initial decision or to cross-examine the appellant. The non-attendance of a presenting officer will also mean that the agency will lose out on a valuable source of feedback from the Tribunal as to the quality of its own decision-making.

The declining attendance of presenting officers at tribunal hearings has been a feature of large-scale adjudication systems, such as social security and immigration and asylum appeals.[70] Given its limited personnel, the Home Office is not

[67] *M (Chad) v Secretary of State for the Home Department* [2004] UKIAT 00044 [16].

[68] Case 14. See also *MK (Burma) v Secretary of State for the Home Department* [2007] EWCA Civ 187 (the Tribunal asked double the number of questions asked by the Home Office and 'the nature of those questions appears to have been very much in the nature of cross-examination').

[69] *BA v Secretary of State for the Home Department (Persistent questioning by Adjudicator) Turkey* [2004] UKAIT 00123 [27].

[70] On the decline in the attendance of presenting officers at social security appeals, see National Audit Office above n 16 at 45; President of Appeal Tribunals, *President's Report: Report by the President of Appeal Tribunals on the Standards of Decision-making by the Secretary of State 2007–2008* (Tribunals Service, 2008) 6; House of Commons Work and Pensions Committee, *Decision Making and Appeals in the Benefits System* (2009–10 HC 313) [163]–[165].

always able to provide representation at all appeal hearings.[71] The rate of Home Office non-attendance varies; in 2002–03, 28 per cent of hearings proceeded without the Home Office.[72] In 2009, the figure was 20 per cent.[73] As one judge noted, the absence of the Home Office from appeal hearings is 'depressingly familiar'.[74]

The absence of the Home Office from appeal hearings has been frequently criticised and it is not difficult to understand why.[75] The task of the Immigration Judge is to undertake a careful and thorough scrutiny of the evidence and to make clear findings as to which facts have been found and those that have not been, and then to assess future risk. The absence of a Home Office representative will increase the difficulties of this task. As the Tribunal has noted, in what is essentially an accusatorial system, Immigration Judges are all too frequently placed 'in a near impossible situation on the one hand in avoiding descending into the arena and on the other hand wishing to have the evidence properly tested in order for proper findings of fact to be made'.[76] The difficulty for the judge is that there is no-one present to cross-examine the appellant. Nevertheless, the appellant's claim should be properly tested. The risk is that appellants who are not cross-examined may win through default or alternatively that judges who do ask questions of the appellant will be criticised for bias or procedural unfairness. From the Tribunal's standpoint, the presence of Home Office representation at all appeals is essential so that judge can reach a proper assessment of the evidence and to make proper findings of fact.

How then are judges expected to handle such hearings? According to the Tribunal's *Surendran* guidelines, the appeal should be heard despite the Home Office's absence.[77] When the Immigration Judge is aware that the Home Office is

---

[71] House of Commons Constitutional Affairs Select Committee, *Asylum and Immigration Appeals* (2003–04 HC 211) [30]; Department for Constitutional Affairs, *Government Response to the Constitutional Affairs Select Committee's Report on Asylum and Immigration Appeals* (Cm 6236, 2004) 4; House of Commons Home Affairs Committee above n 40 at [364]; Home Office, *The Government Reply to the Fifth Report from the Home Affairs Committee Session 2005–06 HC 775 Immigration Control* (Cm 6910, 2006) 38.

[72] Hansard HC vol 416 col 981W (19 January 2004).

[73] C Hastings and K Dowling, 'Home Office Surrenders to Migrants' *The Sunday Times* (25 April 2010) 4.

[74] Immigration Judge interview 4.

[75] See, eg, *Surendran v Secretary of State for the Home Department* (21679) date notified 12 July 1999 (IAT) 4 (the non-attendance of presenting officers was a practice that that the Tribunal deprecated in the strongest possible terms as it placed an additional burden on judges and could call into question the fairness of the appeal procedure); *MNM v Secretary of State for the Home Department (Surendran guidelines for Adjudicators) Kenya* (starred determination) [2000] INLR 576 (IAT) 582 ('in an adversarial process . . . it is very difficult for the [Immigration Judge] if the Home Office is unrepresented. It is as if in a criminal case the Crown were unrepresented'). See also House of Commons Home Affairs Committee above n 40 at [364]; *Subesh v Secretary of State for the Home Department* [2004] EWCA Civ 56; [2004] Imm AR 112 [71]; C Hastings, A Ralph, and I Johnston, 'Asylum Seekers Win Right to Stay Because of "Shambolic" Immigration Hearings' *The Telegraph* (18 April 2009).

[76] *IA HC KD RO HG v Secretary of State for the Home Department (Risk—guidelines—separatist) Turkey CG* [2003] UKIAT 00034 [46]

[77] *Surendran* above n 75 as supplemented by subsequent guidance in *Yildizhan v Secretary of State for the Home Department* [2002] UKIAT 08325 [27]–[31] and *WN v Secretary of State for the Home Department (Surendran; credibility; new evidence) Democratic Republic of Congo* [2004] UKIAT 00213 [29]–[40].

not to be represented, then the judge should take particular care to prepare before the hearing. If credibility issues are raised in the case, then at the appeal hearing, the judge should request the appellant's representative to address these matters. Where no matters of credibility are raised in the letter of refusal but, from a reading of the papers, the judge considers that there are matters of credibility arising, then he should similarly point these out to the representative and ask that they be dealt with, either in examination of the appellant or in submissions.

According to the guidelines, it is not for the Immigration Judge to adopt an inquisitorial role in such hearings. The Home Office's argument and basis of refusal is to be taken from its refusal letter. It is not for the judge to expand upon the refusal letter or to raise matters which are not contained within it, unless these are matters which are apparent to him from a reading of the papers, in which case these matters should be drawn to the attention of the appellant's representative. After evidence and submissions, the judge may ask questions for clarification purposes. Clarification can go beyond checking whether something has been understood or for confirmation of a fact; it is legitimate for the judge to raise the questions relevant to the Home Office's refusal letter or later material to which the judge considers he needs answers if he is to deal fairly, adequately and intelligibly with the material upon which he is being asked to adjudicate. It is not for the judge to cross-examine the appellant, but to ask questions for clarification purposes subject to the necessary caveat as to their timing, length, and content. These guidelines embody a tension. For the process to be fair, an appellant must know the points on which the judge may be minded to reach conclusions adverse to him where they have not directly otherwise been raised. At the same time, the judge should not appear to be partisan by asking questions that no-one else has thought it necessary to ask.

What happens in practice? From the appeals observed, judges take one of two approaches. They can either raise with the appellant's representative the relevant issues so that they can be dealt with in the evidence-in-chief by the representative or, alternatively, raise such issues directly with the appellant. The first approach has the advantage that the judge does not directly question the appellant and is not seen to be straying from a neutral position, but this depends on the ability and willingness of the appellant's representative to deal thoroughly with the relevant issues. The second approach, in which the judge takes a more active role in questioning, runs the risk that the judge is seen to be taking on the role of a cross-examiner. For instance in one hearing, the appellant's representative raised concerns with the judge that, in the representative's opinion, the judge had gone too far in asking his own questions.[78] At the same time, this approach enables the judge to articulate the questions to which he would like the answer. The particular approach adopted will clearly depend on the preferences of the individual judge.

The operation of the *Surendran* guidelines has not been problem-free. The fairness of such hearings has often been challenged by the losing party on the basis that the judge did not follow the guidelines. The Tribunal has often taken excep-

---

[78] Case 75.

tion to challenges by the Home Office against allowed appeals on the basis that the appeal hearing was unfairly conducted because the Home Office was not represented there. Unsuccessful appellants have also frequently challenged the fairness of hearings in which the Home Office was absent on the ground that the Immigration Judge took on the role of cross-examination. The Tribunal's response has been to review those decisions in which there was unfairness, while at the same time emphasising that the *Surendran* guidelines are guidance, not rules of law.[79] Consequently, a judge's failure fully to comply with them will not necessarily invalidate the appeal hearing. The object of the guidelines is to provide guidance as to how to ensure a fair hearing and how to avoid circumstances arising in which a fair-minded and informed observer would conclude that there was a real possibility or a real danger that the judge was biased.

It is clear that appeal hearings which proceed in the absence of the Home Office can impair the effectiveness of the adjudication process. Judges need to make proper assessment of facts on which to base asylum decisions, but the absence of a Home Office representative means that the appellant's claim will not be properly tested. It would not be appropriate for the appellant to be recognised as a refugee because, through good fortune, the Home Office had been absent from the hearing. Alternatively, the judge who does ask questions of the appellant may be challenged for having descended into the arena between the parties. Moreover, the difficulties do not seem easily capable of resolution. For instance, in 2006, the Home Office noted that it was determined to improve its performance so that it is represented at all appeals, yet non-attendance at hearings remains a problem.[80] The social security appeals system has also experienced a a steady decline in the percentage of appeal hearings attended by a presenting officer, but calls to reverse this trend have had little effect. In the absence of governmental action to deal with the problem of non-attendance, the principal option would be for the appeals process to discard its adherence to the adversary process and engage in a decisive shift toward an investigative process. However, such a change would require a major change of procedure and culture.

Appeal Hearings Without Appellant Representation

What then of the situation when the appellant is without representation? In such circumstances, judges should ideally adopt an enabling approach by supporting appellants in a way which gives them confidence in their own abilities to participate in the process and compensates for their lack of skills or knowledge. As the Tribunal has noted, an Immigration Judge is obliged to give every assistance to an unrepresented appellant.[81] Judges should explain the procedures more clearly

[79] *WN* above n 78 at [29].

[80] House of Commons Home Affairs Committee above n 40 at [364]; Home Office above n 71.

[81] *Surendran* above n 75. See also Immigration Appellate Authority above n 12; Deputy Chief Adjudicator, *Guidance Note on Unrepresented Appellants Who Do Not Understand English* (IAA, 2004); Leggatt above n 34 at [7.5].

than would normally be the case, ensure that the appellant's evidence has been fully drawn out, protect the appellant against hostile cross-examination, and then ask their own questions for clarification purposes. The overriding requirement of fairness will require more judicial assistance for an unrepresented appellant and protection against any aggressive cross-examination. As one judge noted, 'a judge should not leave an unrepresented appellant completely without assistance'.[82]

How do judges handle hearings with unrepresented appellants in practice? In most of the unrepresented appeals observed, judges gave a full introduction and then took the appellant through either their interview or witness statement, if any. There were, though, some variations in how judges undertook the task. Some judges made some effort to summarise the main issues in the case and to engage in a thorough investigation of the nature of the appellant's case. The rationale for assisting the appellant is that it would be wrong to leave an unrepresented appellant completely without assistance. Moreover, the way in which judges assist unrepresented appellants is also important. As one judge explained, it is important to put questions directly to the appellant because if appellants are simply asked whether they have anything to add, then they might either reply in the negative or begin to tell the judge the whole of their personal life history, which might last for sometime. Direct questioning of appellants may identify answers to the specific issues as to their claim. By contrast, at the other end of the spectrum, other judges did not make such efforts to assist appellants; the judge would introduce the appeal as normal, but not then take the appellant through the detail of the evidence or ask questions of the appellant in order to draw out the evidence.

To illustrate the different approaches judges adopt, compare the approaches adopted by two different judges in the following hearings with unrepresented appellants. In the first hearing, the judge took the appellant through his evidence in some detail by reading out the appellant's statement, pausing frequently to ask the appellant to elaborate upon his evidence and explain in more detail the nature of his case.[83] Having gone through the appellant's evidence, the judge proceeded to summarise it, and asked the appellant to expand upon it if necessary. During cross-examination, the judge intervened frequently to ensure that the appellant understood the questions being asked. The judge then summarised the Home Office's case against the appellant, and asked the Home Office to make brief submissions to which the appellant could respond. By contrast, in another hearing, a different judge did not ask any questions of appellant, for instance, as to whether she understood the reasons for refusal. Nor did the judge take the appellant through the detail of her evidence or read out her statement. The judge did ask the appellant some brief questions concerning her entry and stay in the UK and whether there was anything else she wanted to add to her case. Other than this, the judge did little to help the appellant bring out her case as fully as possible. Following cross-examination and submissions by the Home Office, the judge

[82] Immigration Judge interview 6.
[83] Case 31.

simply asked the appellant whether or not she had anything to say in response.[84] These two cases may be at opposite ends of the spectrum; most judges handling unrepresented cases fall somewhere in the middle.

It is in relation to submissions that unrepresented appellants are in the weakest position of all. The Home Office will usually have summarised its case against the appellant; it is then for the appellant to respond. From the appeals observed, few unrepresented appellants appeared to possess much real understanding of what they were supposed to say in their submissions or what the concept meant. Indeed, most appellants appeared to possess little, if any, understanding of either the appeal process or the legal criteria governing eligibility for asylum. Familiar difficulties experienced by unrepresented appellants included the following: not appearing to appreciate which evidence was relevant to their case or where to locate country information; and not appearing to understand the nature of appeal proceedings or the difference between evidence and submissions or what to say in their submissions. Consequently, most unrepresented appellants struggled to make coherent submissions. In the appeals observed, judges tended to take one of two options in this respect.

The first approach was not to assist the appellant, but instead merely listen to what the appellant was attempting to say in their submissions. For instance, in one appeal the appellant told the Immigration Judge that he did not know what to say in response to the submissions of the Home Office Presenting Officer, who had argued that the appellant would not be of any adverse interest to the Iranian authorities on return.[85] The major drawback of this approach is that it simply represents a failure by the judge to adopt an enabling approach to provide support to the unrepresented appellant, while it leaves the appellant floundering helplessly.

The second option is for the Immigration Judge to provide assistance to the appellant by doing the following: summarise the Home Office's case that the appellant will have to meet; allow the appellant to say what they wish to say in response to the Home Office's submissions; reassure the appellant that account be will taken of the fact that he is not a practising lawyer; and inform the appellant that the usual responses to the Home Office's arguments will be taken into account.

The absence of representation for appellants is far from ideal; equally, if representation is sometimes of poor quality in any event, then it may not contribute much. To the extent that most judges adopt an enabling approach in unrepresented appeals, then they are doing what can be done to assist appellants. This can clearly be a difficult enough task. Most judges recognised that adoption of this dual role, while at times difficult, was an inevitable consequence of legal aid restrictions. As one judge noted, 'it can be difficult obviously because you are trying to help the appellant to present his case and also trying to preserve your own impartiality, knowing that you may very well decide that everything the appellant has said is a

---

[84] Case 194.
[85] Case 157.

pack of lies'.[86] At the same time, to the extent that other judges do not seek to assist appellants, then obviously this accentuates the inequalities between the parties. From the appeals observed, this was evident in a small number of cases.

What could be done to improve the handling of unrepresented appeals? The most obvious suggestion is that the Tribunal revise its guidance on unrepresented appeals. This could require that judges at both CMRs and substantive hearings ensure that appellants fully understand the reasons for refusal and provide unrepresented appellants with every possible assistance by drawing out their story as fully as possible. Another suggestion is that the agency should only be represented if the appellant is represented.[87]

Finally, there is the situation in which there is no representation at all, but just the judge, interpreter and appellant present. Judges universally acknowledged this to be the most difficult situation of all: the almost impossible task for the judge is to bring out the evidence from the appellant, then put the points raised by the Home Office in its refusal letter, while remaining impartial throughout. Of the hearings observed, only two proceeded without any representation at all. By their nature such hearings are not adversarial and rely on the judge to develop the evidence. However, because the judge undertakes the different roles, the constant danger is that the judge is not able properly to balance out their roles while retaining the perception of impartiality. Furthermore, there will not be any check over the judge's handling of the appeal hearing.

Closing the Hearing and Decision-Writing Targets

Closing the Hearing

Following submissions, the judge will typically speak directly to the appellant, almost always to say that a written determination will follow in due course. The general presumption is that judges do not announce their decision immediately. In virtually all asylum and human rights appeals, it would be impossible for the judge to have made up his mind one way or the other at this stage. Furthermore, the task of making an asylum decision is, to some extent, interconnected with the task of writing a determination.

Decision-writing Targets

The end of the hearing marks the termination of the public aspect of the appeals process, but for the judge, it only represents the end of the evidence-presentation

---

[86] Immigration Judge interview 3.

[87] JAG Griffith and H Street, *Principles of Administrative Law*, 2nd edn (London, Pitman, 1957) 196.

stage. The judge's next task—writing the determination—is heavily conditioned by the Tribunal's performance targets. As noted above, targets exert a pervasive influence upon the work of the Tribunal. Indeed, it is no exaggeration to say that legal precedents and rules compete with targets as a factor influencing the procedure and determination of appeals. The target of determining 75 per cent of asylum appeals within six weeks can certainly be far more easily summarised than the accretion of case-law governing who qualifies for asylum, a body of case-law that changes frequently and which few, if any, of the personnel involved have the time to absorb fully.

Under its procedural rules, the Tribunal is to serve its determination on the Home Office, by sending it no later than 10 days after the substantive hearing.[88] Great importance is ascribed to this target. But, of course, it is not simply the case that a judge hears an appeal, then has nothing other to do in the next 10 days other than write the determination. The determinations for all the appeals heard in the single hearing day must be written up; and then other appeals heard in the meantime. The 'one + one' hearing pattern is supposed to allow judges sufficient time in which to hear appeals on one day and then spend the next day writing up their determinations.

To what extent are judges able to comply with the targets and to what extent, if any, do such targets adversely affect the quality of decisions to be produced? From the judges interviewed, there were a number of different views concerning the utility and impact of targets on their work. One view is that targets exert a negative influence on decision-making quality:

> A determination is not going to be as good as it would be if you had more time to write it and in some cases, you need time to think about it. It is not always possible to decide all appeals straightaway. A judge may need to consult colleagues, but there is just no time to do that if you have to meet the targets. And you cannot let things carry over because otherwise you will get completely behind—if you have not written a determination on the day after hearing the appeal, then you have another sitting day and more cases to write up and you can forget which case is which. It is very easy to mix cases up, especially if they are from the same type of country. So, it is much easier to write up an appeal when it is fresh in your mind. I think the hearing lists need to be a bit lighter.[89]

A stronger variant of this theme is that the targets, imposed by government for political reasons, have the potential to undermine the proper administration of justice:

> One can understand that appellants are entitled to a decision at the earliest reasonable moment, but these targets are entirely artificial. They have no bearing whatsoever on the reality of any particular case. The problem is that the political pressure is so enormous, it can be frankly destructive and the integrity of the system is always at stake if artificial constraints are imposed upon it.[90]

---

[88] Asylum and Immigration Tribunal (Procedure) Rules SI 2005/230 r 23(4).
[89] Immigration Judge interview 8.
[90] Immigration Judge interview 14.

From another perspective targets are a managerial tool by which Immigration Judges are to be kept in line. Alternatively, targets, like rules, are there to be broken—even by judges:

> If I think that a target will get in the way of a good, reasoned determination, then I will ignore the target. I think we all will do that . . . Targets do produce difficulties, but I do not think that the integrity of the system is compromised to the extent that I have given a judgement ignoring the justice of a case simply to get a file off my desk or to comply with targets—I would not do that. The time limits would go every time.[91]

Finally, there is the spectre of dysfunctional targets: why do senior judges identify errors of law in a fair number of Immigration Judges' decisions?

> The Senior Immigration Judges, who look at our determinations, sometimes say that some of the determinations are not very good. There could be many reasons for that, but I think that one of them is that Immigration Judges are not given enough time to write determinations.[92]

At the same time, judges noted that despite the targets imposed upon them, and the occasional need to extend them, they normally had sufficient time to write their determinations. This is partly a function of the way that the Tribunal is organised in terms of targets and hearing lists. For every hour spent hearing an appeal, another two hours will be spent writing up the determination (three hours including other case activities such as preparation).[93] Immigration Judges, though, sit on the 'one + one' sitting pattern: one day hearing appeals; the next day writing up determinations. If, therefore, the ratio between hearing and determination-writing and all aspects of case activities is between one to two or one to three, then the 'one + one' sitting pattern may be insufficient. This, in turn, leads to pressure on the judges to produce determinations quickly, but can provide them with less time than is necessary. From this perspective, the solution is that judges should have more time to write up determinations commensurate with the one to two or one to three ratio. Perhaps unsurprisingly, most Immigration Judges interviewed were both sympathetic to this perspective and enthusiastic advocates of it.

One response to this is that hearing days do not always comprise six hours; the judge might conclude the appeal hearings before the end of the hearing day. Therefore, the, argument goes, this should on balance allow sufficient time for the judges to produce their determinations as the judge can use the spare time at the end of the sitting day in addition to the whole of the next day to produce their determinations. Furthermore, the nature and difficulty of individual appeals contained in hearing lists differ. A hearing list may contain some relatively simple appeals combined with more difficult and complex ones. All things being even, the relative difficulty of individual appeals should balance out so that judges have

---

[91] Immigration Judge interview 2.
[92] Immigration Judge interview 11.
[93] PA Consulting Group, *Asylum and Immigration Tribunal: Analysis of Judicial Time* (London, PA Consulting Group, 2007).

sufficient time overall to determine each appeal properly. However, one problem with this response is that it does not always work in practice. Judges, starting their hearing day at 10am, having prepared for the appeals on that day, do not always finish their hearing days at, for instance, 1pm, thereby leaving the remainder of the day to work on determinations. Not all hearing days will take a full six hours; but many will take a substantial proportion of this period of time. As judges are aware that they should produce determinations by the end of the next day, before the start of a new hearing list the day after, they will be under pressure to get their determinations written quickly. Furthermore, the tasks of hearing appeals and writing determinations are not necessarily seamless. As one judge put it, the argument that judges can use the spare time leftover in their hearing day to start writing determinations 'assumes that you are going to come out of court and start writing determinations straightaway—but often you cannot do this because you may have to think the case through'.[94]

The central problem is that of seeking an appropriate balance between the competing demands on the Tribunal to produce determinations quickly and at the same time to produce well-reasoned, good quality decisions that can withstand onward challenge. The suggestion from some judges interviewed was that the system is weighted too much toward speed at the expense of producing good quality decisions. If so, then more time ought to be allocated for determination-writing. Another suggestion has been the introduction of oral determinations in less complex types of appeals. Unsurprisingly, perspectives differ on the desirability and effects of the pressure on judges. From one viewpoint, the introduction of targets is necessary to ensure that the Tribunal performs its central task—the adjudication of appeals—in a speedy manner. From another perspective, targets inevitably rub up against the dispensation of justice. The difficulty is, though, in assessing whether or not an extension in the time for writing determinations would necessarily have a positive impact on decision quality; it is possible that it might; alternatively, judges may simply take longer to produce the same volume of decisions of much the same quality.

Conclusion

Textbook accounts of tribunal adjudication often generate the perception that it is a problem-free, leisurely activity, but such accounts rarely give us much insight into the *real* institutional and procedural influences on judicial decision-making.[95] The empirical evidence presented in this chapter strongly suggests that the reality of tribunal adjudication, certainly in the context of the asylum appellate jurisdiction, is often far from being a relaxed procedure. The principal pressure on

---

[94] Immigration Judge interview 8.
[95] JA Farmer, *Tribunals and Government* (London, Weidenfeld and Nicolson, 1974) 167.

the Tribunal is to ensure that appeals are heard and determined within their specified target times. Much of the time, the Tribunal is able to achieve these targets while also ensuring that appeals are determined fairly. However, the appeal hearing process operates under the constant prospect of being impeded by a number of problems: the limited amount of time to prepare cases fully; the variable quality or absence of representation, and the consequential difficulties for judges; administrative and procedural difficulties; the Home Office's frequent failure to engage properly with the process; concerns over interpretation; and the pressure to determine appeals quickly. The conflicting pressures are difficult to resolve satisfactorily. Better case-management throughout the process coupled with competent funded representation could perhaps enhance the quality of the process, but limited resources, the Home Office's conduct, and the emphasis on the timely handling of appeals often militate against this.

A central issue in the appeal hearing process is the appropriate degree of judicial intervention or activity. The nature of the procedure adopted can vary considerably depending upon the presence of representation and its quality, the human interaction at the appeal hearing, and the personality and expertise of the individual judge. The jurisdiction is culturally tied to an adversarial approach. However, many judges recognise the limitations and constraints of an adversarial approach and express a desire to have greater freedom to undertake an active approach. While senior judges have often been perceived as insisting upon an excessively adversarial approach, in practice many Immigration Judges are comfortable with an active approach, and some would prefer a wholesale shift toward an inquisitorial procedure in asylum cases. By contrast, other judges were observed not to provide assistance to unrepresented appellants to enable their cases to be drawn out as fully as possible. The broader picture is that the Tribunal is ambivalent as to the most appropriate mode of procedure. While many judges would welcome an explicit move to an inquisitorial jurisdiction, it has been hindered by the pressure to process appeals quickly and the unwillingness of senior tribunal judges to make a conscious shift toward a more inquisitorial approach. Furthermore, the inability of some judges to provide assistance to unrepresented appellants result in an inconsistency of approach when compared with the assistance provided by other judges; it can also undermine the effectiveness of the process for appellants.

There is a major omission in the above analysis: it has excluded consideration of the human interaction of the participants involved. Appeal hearings are not only a site of tension between competing adjudicatory values. They are also the context through which judges struggle to find reliable evidence with which to decide who may be at real risk of persecution or serious ill-treatment; how can the judge really know whether the appellant is telling the truth or has deluded himself or is deliberately seeking to mislead the Tribunal? Appeal hearings also provide the context in which people tell their stories, whether true or not. Given the diversity of individuals seeking asylum, the nature of appeal hearings can range from the tragic to the farcical, from the rational to the surreal. Some appellants may give horrific personal testimony of the suffering they have endured; others may present evidence which simply seems nonsensical and unbelievable. The performance of representatives can range from the highly professional to the incompetent. The approach of judges can also vary from those who exercise great sensitivity to others whose conduct, on occasion, exhibits impatience and frustration. This complexity has been well-described by Peter Showler, which though drawn from his experience as a former member of the Canadian Immigration and Refugee Board, is equally applicable in the UK context:

> The hearing itself is a crucible in which fact and fiction, communication and miscommunication, fear and courage, passion and indifference, logic and bias, insight and ignorance, intermingle and combine to form a story that may or may not capture the truth of the refugee's experience. Every hearing is a human drama with its players and its outcome, sometimes predictable, often surprising, and occasionally shocking. There is great emotional intensity due to the importance and uncertainty of the decision for the refugee and the subject matter of the testimony, much of it concerning persecution and its myriad forms of suffering and humiliation. There may also be a lingering sense of farce when the witness does not appear believable, words and gestures lose their power to persuade, testimony becomes performance, and the hearing a hollow drama with an unavoidable conclusion.[96]

As a means of seeking to get at the truth, the appeal hearing process may often *seem* inadequate, but this only begs the following question: what alternative is there? In the absence of any, the appeal hearing remains the best method available but, as the next chapter demonstrates, the task of finding where the truth lies is itself rarely simple or easy.

---

[96] P Showler, *Refugee Sandwich: Stories of Exile and Asylum* (Montreal, McGill-Queen's University Press, 2006) 210.

5

Credibility

T O MAKE ASYLUM decisions, the facts concerning both the individual's particular circumstances and the general situation in the country from which asylum is being sought need to be found. This chapter focuses on credibility assessments. In essence, this task involves the fact-finder determining whether it is reasonably likely that the appellant is telling the truth. Credibility assessments are the single most important determinant of asylum cases; the vast majority of appeals succeed or fail on the basis of the decision-maker's view of the claimant's credibility.[1] Indeed, despite its rarely recognised significance throughout administrative and tribunal decision-making, the role and impact of credibility far exceeds that of other adjudicatory tasks such as statutory interpretation and developing legal doctrine. It is generally recognised that the crucial task of an Immigration Judge is to decide whether or not she believes the account given by the appellant, that is, whether the appellant's claim to be in need of international protection can properly be accepted as a credible one.[2] While the ultimate focus of asylum adjudication may be on assessing risk on return, credibility provides the principal factual basis on which that assessment is undertaken. Furthermore, credibility findings reached on the basis of oral evidence can only rarely be successfully overturned on error of law grounds.[3]

The Credibility Problem

In terms of adjudicatory values, assessing credibility is closely intertwined with accuracy; correct decisions depend upon correct fact-finding. But how are fact-finders to

---

[1] D Anker, 'Determining Asylum Claims in the United States: An Empirical Case Study' (1992) *New York University Journal of Law and Social Change* 433; M Kagan, 'Is Truth in the Eye of the Beholder? Objective Credibility Assessment in Refugee Status Determination' (2003) 17 *Georgetown Immigration Law Journal* 367; R Thomas, 'Assessing the Credibility of Asylum Claims: EU and UK Approaches Examined' (2006) 8 *European Journal of Migration and Law* 79.

[2] United Nations High Commissioner for Refugees (UNHCR), *Handbook on Determining Refugee Status* (Geneva, UNHCR 1992) [41]; *SW v Secretary of State for the Home Department (Adjudicator's questions) Somalia* [2005] UKIAT 00037 [20].

[3] *Indrakumar v SSHD* [2003] EWCA Civ 1677; [2004] Imm AR 76, 84 (Hale LJ); *Subesh v Secretary of State for the Home Department* [2004] EWCA Civ 56; [2004] Imm AR 112, 131 (Laws LJ); *R (Iran) v Secretary of State for the Home Department* [2005] EWCA Civ 982; [2005] INLR 633, 640–641 (Brooke LJ) (CA).

determine whether an individual's story can properly be regarded as credible? The task is not unique to asylum adjudication, but it is problematic.[4] Even in ordinary conditions, the task of distinguishing between truth and falsity can be extremely problematic. Studies in the field of experimental psychology, for example, indicate that people habitually overrate their ability to delineate truth and falsity and are only able to do so successfully some 50 per cent of the time.[5] The inherent problem is that there is no reliable way of knowing who is telling the truth and who is not.

But, as we have already noted in chapter two, asylum adjudication presents particular difficulties which accentuate the challenges decision-makers ordinarily face. These challenges include the following: the uncertain and limited evidence presented to judges; the absence of other evidence to support or contradict the appellant's own evidence; the linguistic and cultural barriers between appellants and judges; the effect of appellants' past traumatic experiences on their ability to recall events; the stress induced by the process itself, for instance, the adversarial nature of the appeal hearing or the lack of representation; and the burdens imposed upon judges by heavy caseloads. It is rare for the asylum decision-maker ever to be completely certain as to whether or not an appellant has been telling the truth. An individual's claim might be neither wholly true nor wholly untrue. In any event, decision-makers are not looking for any absolute standard of truth or falsity; rather, the task is to determine whether an appellant has been able to demonstrate that his claim is reasonably likely to be true. The limitations of the evidence mean that the process may be easily open to exploitation. At the same time, in cases where an applicant's account is unsupported by other evidence, but appears credible, then he should, unless there are good reasons to the contrary, be given the benefit of the doubt.[6]

Determinations by Immigration Judges often contain a standard paragraph on the difficulties of assessing credibility. The following examples are typical:

> Credibility is an issue to be handled with great care and sensitivity, and that lack of credibility, on peripheral issues or even on material issues, is not to be made an easy excuse for dismissing a claim by an applicant, particularly if he comes from a state or situation in which persecution is an established fact of life.[7]

---

[4] Assessing the truthfulness of testimony is a common enough task of trial courts in the criminal and civil justices process as well as in other administrative justice decision processes such as social security adjudication.

[5] A Vrij, *Detecting Lies and Deceit: the Psychology of Lying and the Implications for Professional Practice* (Chichester, Wiley, 2000); P Ekman, *Telling Lies: Clues to Deceit in the Marketplace, Politics, and Marriage* (New York, Norton, 2001); A Memon, A Vrij, and R Bull, *Psychology and Law: Truthfulness, Accuracy and Credibility* (Chichester, Wiley, 2003).

[6] The notion of affording asylum claimants the benefit of the doubt is commonly thought to derive from the UNHCR's *Handbook on Refugee Status* above n 2 at [196], but in UK asylum adjudication, the phrase can be traced back to the 'benefit of the doubt' order issued by the Home Secretary to the Immigration Boards on 9 March 1906. This order (reproduced in MJ Landa, *The Alien Problem and its Remedy* (London, King & Son, 1911) 315–317) stated that 'while recognising the extreme difficulty of the task of determining the validity' of claims, the fact that a claimant's statements may be 'insufficient or inaccurate, yet he may be exposed to serious risk', and that 'the absence of corroborative evidence frequently makes it extremely difficult for Boards', the Secretary of States hopes that 'the benefit of the doubt, where any doubt exists, may be given in favour of any immigrants who allege that they are flying from religious or political persecution'.

[7] Case 79.

When considering the question of credibility, I use as a starting point the initial assumption that the appellant is telling the truth and seeing whether that assumption remains intact having carried out the exercise of considering the evidence in the round. Where such consideration results in matters being finely balanced, I am required to give the appellant the benefit of the doubt and resolve the issue of credibility in his favour. I believe that this is the best method of ensuring compliance with the reasonable likelihood test.[8]

I bear in mind the difficulties a genuine asylum seeker can experience in obtaining supporting evidence for a claim and I recognise the importance of assessing such a claim in the context of country conditions.[9]

However, the risk is that such standard paragraphs can often function as bromides beneath which the acute challenges of assessing the evidence remain. As judges explained:

It is extremely difficult: you have the appellant's evidence and the country information. One representative will say the appellant has been consistent throughout, the other will point out discrepancies in the appellant's story, and you will have to consider whether those discrepancies are significant.[10]

When I first started, a senior judge told me that I should walk into court hoping every time to allow the appeal. That is the mental attitude I walk into the courtroom with. You do not walk in with the assumption of 'I'm going to dismiss this appeal unless there's a miracle'. And that makes a difference as to how you approach cases. I always go in willing an appellant to show me that they deserve asylum, but regretfully sometimes being unable to do so. Sometimes stories gel, sometimes they do not—and I do not know how to explain it either. It is just that sometimes I hear an appellant's story and I think to myself: 'yes, everything in this story makes sense—this could have happened' whereas other times I think to myself 'oh, don't be ridiculous, this does not make sense at all'.[11]

How do I assess credibility? Well, that is a difficult one. I have read journal articles about this and I am none the wiser for it really. How do you assess whether someone is telling the truth? Some people are very good liars.[12]

The centrality of credibility is, then, matched by the difficulties, but also its controversy. Judges are most commonly criticised in relation to their credibility findings, for instance, for not applying the standard of proof correctly or by approaching appeals from a position of presumptive scepticism, that is, the criticism is that some judges tend to presume appellants to lack credibility and will only find in an appellant's favour if the claim is clearly and manifestly true. One response to this criticism is that the more experience judges have in assessing credibility, then the more robust their decisions become. However, experience does not necessarily provide much of a guide as Immigration Judges never find out whether their decisions were right or wrong. Another response is that judges are

[8] Case 186.
[9] Case 136.
[10] Immigration Judge interview 7.
[11] Immigration Judge interview 15.
[12] Immigration Judge interview 11.

hearing appeals in which the credibility of appellant's stories has already been doubted by the Home Office; furthermore, that some 20 per cent of appeals are allowed does not indicate that all appeals are approached sceptically.

The problems, though, run deeper. A constant risk is that different judges may reach different outcomes in essentially similar cases. A frequent criticism of the adjudication process is that it operates as a lottery; the perception is that credibility assessments often depend more upon the identity of the individual decision-maker than upon the circumstances of the individual case. Those who represent both appellants and the Home Office will relate anecdotes that they have often been able to predict the outcome of an appeal simply by knowing the identity of the individual judge who was sitting. Obviously, such disparities can, if they exist, undermine important adjudicatory norms such as consistency and equality of treatment. The degree to which such inconsistency exists within the appeals process has not, though, been the subject of detailed empirical investigation.[13]

By contrast, empirical studies of asylum decision-making systems elsewhere have uncovered dramatic and significant disparities in decision outcomes between different asylum decision-makers. For instance, a major US based study of disparities in asylum decision-making found enormous variations at all levels of the asylum decision-making structure. Such disparities existed both between different immigration courts and within them. Disparities in decision outcomes varied in accordance with factors such as appellants' nationality, the presence or absence of representation, whether or not an appellant was accompanied by a spouse of child in addition to other variables such as the backgrounds and prior work experience of the judges and the gender of judges.[14] The study's overall conclusion was that the outcomes of asylum decisions often depended just as much on the luck of the draw as on the merits of the individual case. The authors suspected that most of the disparities uncovered were related to the judgments about the credibility of an appellant and the degree of scepticism that decision-makers brought to the task.[15] Such empirical data is complimented by other evidence which is suggestive of the view that some judges may be predisposed toward a sceptical approach to assessing credibility.[16] Given the lack of

---

[13] Those who represent and campaign on behalf of asylum applicants have often discussed whether they should expend the necessary resources to collect the evidence with which to test these assumptions. One argument against this has stemmed from the concern that such an effort could be counter-productive: given the highly charged political context of asylum adjudication, the risk is that the media and a section of political opinion might use such data in order to highlight how generous some decision-makers are and therefore suggest that they ought to be reined in.

[14] J Ramji-Nogales, AI Schoenholtz and PG Schrag, (eds), *Refugee Roulette: Disparities in Asylum Adjudication and Proposals for Reform* (New York, New York University Press, 2009) 1–131. See also S Rehaag, 'Troubling Patterns in Canadian Refugee Adjudication' (2008) 39 *Ottawa Law Review* 335; United States Government Accountability Office, *US Asylum System: Significant Variation Existed in Asylum Outcomes across Immigration Courts and Judges* (GAO-08-940, September 2008).

[15] Ramji-Nogales, Schoenholtz and Schrag n 14 above at 99.

[16] For instance, in the Republic of Ireland, a legal challenge was made in 2008 to the Irish Supreme Court by three asylum applicants against having their appeals heard by an individual member of the Refugee Appeals Tribunal on the ground of that member's perceived bias. The member concerned was reported to have rejected the vast majority of the 1,000 appeals he had heard. The claim of the Tribunal's chairman that the decision record of the member concerned was not at variance with other

detailed empirical study upon the issue in the UK, it is impossible to be certain whether or not such disparate outcomes exist, and if so, how extensive they are, and to which causes they might be attributed. On the other hand, it would be both unusual and surprising if the UK system had somehow managed to attain a greater degree of consistency than asylum decision-making systems elsewhere.

Indeed, given the frequently raised concerns as to the degree of inconsistent approaches to credibility assessments and the outcomes reached between different judges, both the higher courts and the Tribunal have identified some different responses to such claims. One has been to suggest that it is difficult to say whether like cases are in practice not being treated alike because few cases can genuinely be said to be exactly the same in all respects. While the principle of equal treatment requires consistent treatment of like cases where there is no differentiating feature, it does not require the like determination of cases that merely share some similarity.[17] Indeed, the whole culture of asylum adjudication evinces a very strong sense that each case is unique in some way or other and that each case turns on its own individual facts. This is one reason why individual appeal determinations on factual issues are not treated as if they were binding precedents.[18] If so, then it is naïve to suppose that it is actually possible for judges to attain some perfect level of consistency; their role is simply to decide the individual case on the evidence presented.

Another response has been openly to acknowledge the risk of inconsistent credibility assessment as an inherent feature of the decisional task. As Carnwath LJ has noted, judging credibility 'is inevitably a difficult and imperfect exercise. Different tribunals hearing the same witnesses may reach quite different views'.[19] Likewise, Sedley LJ: 'two conscientious decision-makers can come to opposite or divergent conclusions on the same evidence'.[20] Cases of the utmost difficulty, such as asylum appeals, are inherently susceptible to more than one answer precisely because of their difficulty. As Legomsky has noted, the unavoidable abstractness, complexity, and dynamism of asylum law makes it inevitable that the human adjudicators will bring their diverse emotions and personal values to bear on their decisions.[21] Disparate outcomes are only to be expected.

Another approach has been to suggest that the potential for disparate assessments of credibility arises from the diverse nature of the immigration judiciary

members was itself contested by three other tribunal members. See *Nyembo v Refugee Appeals Tribunal* [2007] IESC 25 (Supreme Court of Ireland); 'Refugee Appeals Body' *The Irish Times* (10 March 2008); 'Minister Defends Refugee Tribunal' *The Irish Times* (12 March 2008); C Coulter, 'Call for Review of up to 1,000 Rejected Asylum Applications' *The Irish Times* (20 March 2008).

[17] *Karankaran v Secretary of State for the Home Department* (00TH03086) date notified 12 September 2000 (IAT) [23].

[18] *AO v Secretary of State for the Home Department (unreported determinations are not precedents) Japan* [2008] UKAIT 00056.

[19] *HF (Algeria) v Secretary of State for the Home Department* [2007] EWCA Civ 445 [25] (Carnwath LJ).

[20] *Otshudi v Secretary of State for the Home Department* [2004] EWCA Civ 893 [11] (Sedley LJ).

[21] SH Legomsky, 'Learning to Live with Unequal Justice: Asylum and the Limits to Consistency' in Ramji-Nogales, Schoenholtz, and Schrag (eds) above n 14 at 280.

itself. According to the Tribunal, 'a diverse judiciary such as that of this Tribunal will be diverse in its attitude and approach as well as in other characteristics. Courts and Tribunals sitting on appeal or reconsideration frequently see judgments of fact that are clearly different from those that they themselves would have made'.[22] There is also a practical argument here. Inconsistent credibility assessments cannot be allowed to support onward challenges because then the whole system could potentially descend into a series of ongoing challenges by either party on the ground that another judge might have decided the case differently. The fact that a different judge might have arrived at different credibility findings is, in law, irrelevant.

But efficiency and finality in adjudication alone do not provide wholly compelling answers to the risk of disparate decisions. If such inconsistency exists, then what, if anything, can be done about it? One suggestion commonly made is that having appeals determined by a single judge aggravates the risk of inconsistency. By contrast, greater use of panels of two or three member panels might ameliorate the risk. The overall quality of decisions might also be more robust if made by two judges rather than a single judge. For instance, elsewhere in the legal system, such as in the criminal justice process, it is the norm to have collective fact-finding through juries and panels of magistrates. In the asylum context, as Macklin has noted, deliberation between two or more judges is an 'invaluable mechanism for surfacing, challenging, and correcting the assumptions, inferences, prejudices, and intuitions that determine outcomes, yet are rarely subject to scrutiny'.[23] Panels may also minimise the risk that the idiosyncratic attitudes and behaviour of a single judge will adversely affect decision outcomes. Overall, it can be assumed that decisions produced by two judges are likely, on balance, to be of higher quality than those produced by a single judge.

However, increasing the number of decision-makers at the initial appellate stage from a single judge to a panel of two or three judges has been resisted on the ground that it would add further cost and delay to the process.[24] Furthermore, there is always the risk that a panel comprised of two judges may be unable to reach a definite decision one way or the other. As one judge explained:

> I have sat on a few appeals in which it was a panel made up of myself and another judge, but in one of them—myself and the other judge—we just could not agree on whether or not the appellant was credible. Had we been sitting separately, I would have gone in one direction and he would have gone in the other. And that has happened a few times where we became so entrenched in our views that we simply could not reach a decision. So, it does happen and that speaks for itself—you will always get different views on credibility. I am afraid that it seems a lot like a lottery when it comes to credibility because we all

---

[22] *RU v Entry Clearance Officer, Lagos (Immigration Judge: treatment of evidence)* [2008] UKAIT 00067 [10].

[23] A Macklin, 'Refugee Roulette in the Canadian Casino' in Ramji-Nogales, Schoenholtz, and Schrag (eds) above n 14 at 138.

[24] During the passage of the Asylum and Immigration (Treatment of Claimants, etc.) Act 2004, the House of Lords sought unsuccessfully to require that nearly all appeal hearings would be heard by three-member panels. See Hansard HL Debs vol 662 cols 43–51 (7 June 2004).

have such different views and different approaches. The credibility issue is just so complicated that you will always get differences of opinion.[25]

Likewise, alternative strategies to reduce the potential for disparate decision-making may threaten other adjudicatory values, such as the independence of decision-makers. For instance, requiring judges to allow or dismiss a certain proportion of appeals according to a pre-established quota would obviously have an adverse impact upon judicial independence as would any proposal to reign in those judges who deviate from an established norm.[26] In the absence of any clear solution, the prospects for inconsistency tend to generate demoralisation costs by prompting concern that the process seems so random. It can also engender displacement activities, the games and devices that go on outside the courtroom in attempts to win or, at least, to delay losing, by seeking to use procedural devices for tactical purposes. For instance, representatives with an appeal listed before a judge known by reputation not to allow many appeals may engage in forum-shopping by seeking an adjournment so that an appeal can be listed at a later date before a different judge who might be more favourably disposed.

Assessing Credibility

How then are fact-finders to go about the task of assessing credibility? In general terms, assessing credibility has three aspects: first, drawing the evidence out; secondly, attributing weight to it; and, thirdly, looking at it in the round to assess what it amounts to. There are, however, few hard rules as to how this task is to be undertaken, but rather a number of factors to be taken into account. These are: the consistency of an appellant's story throughout the decision process (internal consistency); its consistency with relevant country information (external consistency); its plausibility; the presence of corroborative evidence; and the weight to be attributed to medical evidence. There are also statutory rules governing the assessment of credibility (section 8 of the Asylum and Immigration (Treatment of Claimants, etc) Act 2004). While all these factors are important, they are not necessarily by themselves determinative. Assessing credibility requires a subjective judgment by the judge as to whether or not the appellant's account is reasonably likely to be true. This section examines how these factors are used to assess credibility.

---

[25] Immigration Judge interview 13.

[26] See R Thomas, 'Refugee Roulette: a UK Perspective' and SH Legomsky, 'Learning to Live with Unequal Justice: Asylum and the Limits to Consistency' in Ramji-Nogales, Schoenholtz, and Schrag (eds) above n 14.

Internal Consistency

Internal inconsistencies or discrepancies are raised frequently by the Home Office as a reason for disbelieving an appellant. If an appellant has given one version of events initially, and then gives a different version at a later date, the issue is whether he has been telling the truth all along. Such discrepancies might be indicative that the whole story has been made up. Inconsistencies must, though, be handled with care. That an individual's story contains some inconsistencies does not necessarily mean it is untrue. Given the fallibility of human memory, it can only be supposed that an appellant's recollection of past events may change, especially if the same story has been recounted on a number of occasions.[27] Furthermore, individuals who have suffered horrendous and traumatic experiences of past persecution are unlikely to be consistent when recounting those experiences. An illustration is the late disclosure of rape by an appellant.[28] Delay or late disclosure in claiming asylum or in revealing full details of an asylum claim will not necessarily be due to the lack of credibility of a particular asylum claim or claimant. All of these factors need to be taken into account, but there can be no hard and fast rules. It cannot be assumed that a perfectly consistent story should be accepted as a truthful one, or that the inconsistencies in a story can properly be attributed to the fallibility of human memory, or that the late disclosure of a rape claim does not mean that it has not been falsified to support an otherwise weak claim.

Tribunal guidance illustrates the difficulties. The Tribunal has accepted that it is perfectly possible for a judge to believe that a witness has not been telling the truth about some matters, has exaggerated the story to make his case better, or is simply uncertain about matters, but still to be persuaded that the centre-piece of the story stands.[29] Consistency and the truth do not necessarily go hand-in-hand. A perfectly logical and consistent account is often more likely to raise the suspicion that it is a packaged story than an account which reflects all the oddities and quirks of real life. But this does not mean that an individual who falters over peripheral matters is in all cases being truthful. A person who has fabricated their story may get the central elements right; common sense and experience are required to determine whether an account that frays at the edges is nevertheless a truthful one or alternatively whether the appellant has got himself into difficulties in unplanned departures from a pre-rehearsed and unreliable script.[30] The

---

[27] J Cohen, 'Questions of Credibility: Omissions, Discrepancies and Errors of Recall in the Testimony of Asylum Seekers' (2002) 13 *International Journal of Refugee Law* 293; L Jobson, 'Cultural Differences in Specificity of Autobiographical Memories: Implications for Asylum Decisions' (2009) 16 *Psychiatry, Psychology and Law* 453.

[28] See H Baillot, S Cowan and VE Munro, 'Seen but Not Heard? Parallels and Dissonances in the Treatment of Rape Narratives across the Asylum and Criminal Justice Contexts' (2009) 36 *Journal of Law and Society* 195, 214–215.

[29] *Chiver v Secretary of State for the Home Department* [1994] UKIAT 10758; [1997] INLR 212 (IAT) 220.

[30] *K v Secretary of State for the Home Department (Democratic Republic of Congo)* [2003] UKIAT 00014 [10].

difficulties arise in attributing weight to the inconsistencies within an appellant's account. There is simply no neat formula that could be devised; some discrepancies may be significant and others less so. It is difficult to define in a perfectly consistent way how such assessments are made. The selection of significant discrepancies is one of the tasks of the fact-finder and such decisions are informed by the sum total of their training, professional experience, life experience, and individual preconceptions.[31]

Furthermore, there is no rule that issues of credibility do not matter if they do not go to the core of the claim.[32] If a judge finds that he cannot believe an appellant on matters that can be checked, then there is no reason at all to believe the appellant on matters that cannot be checked. A judge who discovers discrepancies in an account, even if they only concern small matters, is entitled to say that he does not trust the appellant's word and as a result is minded to reject the appellant's evidence as a whole.

Immigration Judges recognise the need for caution when examining discrepancies and stressed the significance and nature of inconsistencies in the context of the evidence as a whole:

> You have to very careful with discrepancies. We often refer to them and they can be important, but you have got to be slightly cautious. If you asked me what I did last week, I could not remember. If you asked me what I was doing two or three years ago, I could be a whole year out. But then again, if you asked me about traumatic things that have made me leave my country and my family, then I might remember them more clearly—depending on the level of the trauma and how personal it was to me. That is not just everyday eventualities.[33]

> I often find that what the Home Office alleges to be a discrepancy is not really a discrepancy at all when you examine it. If I am satisfied that there is a discrepancy, then I think one has to consider whether or not it is important, whether it is actually something which causes you to have real doubt about the truth of the story you are being told. There are some discrepancies which could arise simply from the way the story is told—one time it comes out slightly different from another, but that does not really mean that it is false. Others just cannot live in the same world as each other. You have to try and sort out which kind of things you are dealing with, and whether or not it is something that really undermines the truth of the tale you have been told.[34]

A minor discrepancy between two different statements given by an appellant concerning dates may be given little weight. By comparison, a major discrepancy may be regarded as being more significant; for instance, if in one statement an appellant had stated that he had lived in a particular location for one year, whereas in a second statement, the appellant stated that he had actually lived there for five years.

---

[31] T Talbot, 'Credibility and Risk: One Adjudicator's View' (2004) 10(2) *Immigration Law Digest* 29, 30.

[32] *RS and SS v Secretary of State for the Home Department (Exclusion of appellant from hearing) Pakistan* [2008] UKAIT 00012 [7].

[33] Immigration Judge interview 13.

[34] Immigration Judge interview 3.

Significant discrepancies will, therefore, call for some explanation. For example, in one case, the appellant claimed to have been held captive in one island, to have escaped, and then to have visited a different island; at the same time, the appellant denied at any time having travelled in a boat between the two islands or to have used any other means of travel. At the hearing, the appellant was repeatedly asked to explain this discrepancy, but was unable to do so. As the judge concluded, 'despite his counsel's best efforts, and the appellant having been given every opportunity to do so, he gave no explanation for his inconsistency. The conclusion I reach is that the appellant had fabricated his abduction, detention, and escape'.[35]

A single discrepancy may not by itself be important, but the cumulative effect of a number of discrepancies may be significant. For instance, in one appeal the Immigration Judge rejected the credibility of an appellant's account in light of discrepancies in the evidence and the implausibility of several elements of her account. As the judge noted, not all of the discrepancies were individually significant, but when taken together in the context of the evidence as a whole, their cumulative effect was to lead to the conclusion that the appellant's account was not reasonably likely to be true.[36]

Given that an appellant will have had an initial screening interview, discrepancies between what was said there and subsequently may be used by the Home Office to undermine credibility. To what extent can such discrepancies be taken into account? Appellants are expected to tell the truth and answers given in screening interviews can be compared fairly with answers given later; at the same time, a screening interview is intended to establish in detail the reasons a person gives to support her claim for asylum and it may well be conducted when the asylum claimant is tired after a long journey. Such factors need to be considered when any inconsistencies between the screening interview and the later case are being evaluated.[37] Caution then is required before relying too heavily on discrepancies. For instance, in one appeal the appellant had said at her screening interview that she was a Pentecostalist and that she was seeking asylum from the Eritrean authorities in order to avoid military conscription. At the appeal hearing, the judge rejected the Home Office's argument that because the appellant's failure at the screening interview to explain that she was also seeking asylum because of her Pentecostal faith, her credibility had been damaged. As the judge explained, 'It is one thing to find a clear discrepancy between something said at a screening interview and something said later—it is quite another to attack an appellant's credibility on the basis that she did not give a full account of her claim at the screening interview' especially when the purpose of screening interviews is not to collect the full details about an individual's asylum claim.[38]

A particularly problematic area concerns those inconsistencies which may arise simply because an appellant has given his account a number of times with

---

[35] Case 37.

[36] Case 136.

[37] *YL v Secretary of State for the Home Department (Rely on SEF) China* [2004] UKIAT 00145 [19].

[38] Case 38.

different interpreters; the process of translation may itself create inconsistencies. The problem arises in deciding whether the discrepancy is properly attributable to an error of interpretation or whether the appellant has not been telling the truth and a discrepancy has arisen, which the appellant then attributes to an interpretation error. As one judge explained:

> The interpretation issue is incredibly difficult because inevitably in the vast majority of cases we are working through interpreters and it just stands to reason that if you get two, three, or four interpreters interpreting the same story at different stages of the process, then they are going to use different words and the different interpreters may make different sense of what the appellant is saying. You have to be constantly aware of that and just ask yourself this question all the time: 'is this something that could have arisen because of differences in interpreting or is it genuinely a contradiction which suggests that the appellant is not telling the truth?' This is almost a constant issue when assessing credibility.[39]

Another area for caution concerns dates. Appellants may often present a long history of their personal circumstances; for instance, when did they first come to the attention of the authorities in their home country? which student demonstrations did they take part in? on which occasions were they detained and ill-treated? when did they leave their country? To what extent should inconsistencies or vagueness concerning the dates of such events be taken into account? The problem is rendered more difficult because many countries producing asylum claimants neither use the western calendar nor attach the same cultural importance to dates as western countries do. For instance, some claimants can be very vague when it comes to dates, including their own date of birth. Furthermore, as some claimants use the Islamic rather than the western calendar, then difficulties can arise in finding the western-style year in which a particular event occurred. These difficulties can be exacerbated when an individual thinks that he is expected to provide some answer, even when he does not know the date, and then simply guesses. At the same time, if an appellant provides inconsistent dates concerning a certain event, then this may appropriately be taken as indicating that the discrepancy is indicative of a false account.

Inconsistencies may also arise because of the trauma suffered by an appellant. Individuals with a traumatic memory might have particular difficulty in recollecting their own autobiographical experiences precisely because those experiences were painfully traumatic. Rather than indicating a lack of credibility, discrepancies may be attributable to the difficulties appellants experience in recounting those events.[40] Late disclosure of a particularly traumatic event does not necessarily imply a lack of honesty as it may be explained by an individual's shame or embarrassment

---

[39] Immigration Judge interview 6.

[40] J Herlihy, P Scragg, and S Turner, 'Discrepancies in Autobiographical Memories—Implications for the Assessment of Asylum Seekers: Repeated Interviews Study' (2002) 324 *British Medical Journal* 324; J Herlihy and S Turner, 'Should Discrepant Accounts Given by Asylum Seekers be Taken as Proof of Deceit?' (2006) 16 *Torture* 81.

over the suffering or humiliation inflicted.[41] Appellants suffering from depression or post-traumatic stress disorder (PTSD) may experience a reduced ability to recall past events consistently. Emotional distress and trauma may explain either late or non-disclosure of the full details of an appellant's story rather than an intention to deceive the decision-maker.

While the Tribunal has recognised that there is a great need in asylum cases to take account of any psychological difficulties when it comes to assessing credibility, it has also cautioned that this requires examination of the particular circumstances obtaining in any individual case.[42] It would be absurd, the Tribunal has noted, if the diagnostic criteria concerning PTSD were to be read as meaning that all persons suffering from the condition have a memory loss which prevents them from giving a proper account of themselves in the context of an asylum claim. Not all inconsistencies may be a consequence of traumatic memory; late or incomplete disclosure may happen for reasons other than the experience of trauma or emotional distress. It is for the judge in the individual case to decide whether any inconsistency is the result of the fallibility of human memory, the claimant's inability to recall their story fully, a reluctance to do so in light of traumatic experiences, or because the story is untrue.

A related problem concerns the evidential weight to be attached to psychiatric reports diagnosing depression or PTSD. Such reports may conclude that an appellant has either depression or PTSD because of past persecution or torture, and therefore lend weight to the credibility of an appellant's story. But what is the evidential value of such reports? As judges are not psychiatric experts, it might thought that they are in no position to reject such reports. But what evidential weight should judges place on such reports? The difficulty is that psychiatrists are usually unable to verify objectively the causes of such depression or PTSD. Such conditions might certainly be caused by past persecution, but there may also be other obvious potential causes. Appellants may be depressed because they have sought to escape deprivation and poverty in their home country and face removal to that country. They might be desperately anxious to avoid returning to their country which may not be a pleasant place to return to. Some appellants suffer from depression or trauma because of past persecution; others because of the uncertainty facing them and the prospect of being returned to their country to live in abject poverty.

The difficulty is that it is very rare, and will usually be very difficult, for a psychiatrist to assess whether the claimant's account of the causes of the trauma is true. Furthermore, it would not normally be appropriate for a psychiatrist to attempt to assess the credibility of the appellant (or patient); their role is to treat their patient; doctor-patient relationships are not conducive to this type of exercise.[43] By

---

[41] D Bögner, J Herlihy, and CR Brewin, 'Impact of Sexual Violence on Disclosure During Home Office Interviews' (2007) 191 *British Journal of Psychiatry* 75.

[42] *A v Secretary of State for the Home Department (Turkey)* [2003] UKIAT 00061 [18].

[43] *Secretary of State for the Home Department v AE and FE* [2002] UKIAT05237; [2002] Imm AR 152, 155–156 (IAT); *HE v Secretary of State for the Home Department (DRC—credibility and psychiatric reports)* Democratic Republic of Congo [2004] UKIAT 00321; [2005] Imm AR 119, 126–127 (IAT).

contrast, it is the role of the judge to assess credibility. A psychiatric report which merely recounts a history which the judge is minded to reject, and contains nothing which does not depend upon the truthfulness of the applicant, may therefore be of negligible value when assessing credibility. As the Tribunal has noted, 'very many appellants fail in their appeals because they are not found credible, notwithstanding that they have been diagnosed by appropriate specialists as suffering from PTSD'.[44]

Unsurprisingly, this approach has been disputed by some psychiatrists who have argued that the Tribunal's approach is based upon a mistaken understanding of their role, profession, and discipline and that they are able to assess the cogency, consistency, and coherence of an individual's story. Some psychiatrists do see their role as including an assessment of their patient's credibility, if only to inform the clinical assessment required. But what is at dispute here is not so much the outcome of individual appeals—that all depends on the particular case—but the establishment of a presumption or rule that clinical assessments of depression or PTSD should automatically be accepted without more as evidence of past trauma or persecution.

This is not to imply that judges do not value such reports or habitually refuse to place any weight on such reports, but that the contribution made by any report has to be assessed in the context of the specific case. For instance, in one case, the judge noted that he could 'be assisted by the views of a skilled and experienced psychiatrist who has had the opportunity of observing the demeanour and reactions of the appellant whilst giving his account . . . By definition, if the psychiatrist's report is correct, then the appellant must have suffered some trauma in the past'.[45]

External Consistency

To what extent can the consistency or otherwise of an appellant's account with what is known about conditions in the country of origin be an indicator of its truthfulness or otherwise? Such consistency may be a useful yardstick as to whether a story is reasonably likely to be true. Determinations often contain statements to the effect that 'credibility findings can only really be made based on a complete understanding of the entire picture placing the claim into the context of the background material regarding the country of origin of the appellant'.[46] But the consistency of an appellant's story claim with known country conditions does not necessarily mean it is true. Country conditions can become reasonably well-known to people who are not at risk on return. Any individual appellant who wants to secure asylum is unlikely to present a story that is inconsistent in any significant way with known country conditions. Even if an appellant's account is

---

[44] *HH v Secretary of State for the Home Department (medical evidence; effect of Mibanga) Ethiopia* [2005] UKAIT 00164 [18].
[45] Case 162.
[46] Case 2.

consistent with the available country information, it still remains for the appellant to demonstrate that it is reasonably likely to be true. Consistency with country information may, though, lend weight to an individual's case.

A second limitation is that by its nature the country information available to judges tends to focus on general country conditions rather than the specific events or incidents which might corroborate an appellant's case. The fact that a particular incident has not been reported in the country information may simply be a consequence that the country information reports are not comprehensive; its omission may not necessarily indicate that the appellant's account lacks credibility. As one judge explained:

> Country information reports tend to be rather broad brush. Unless there is something very specific, you can only get a sort of background flavour from these reports. It is not often you can actually say, 'well, what the appellant says did or did not happen because it says so in the country report'. More often I am saying 'well, this did or did not happen because the tenor of these reports is suggesting it in one way or the other. Given that the reports are broadly consistent in saying that the police have tortured people with impunity and so forth, then it is likely or unlikely that the appellant was treated in the way that he described'. So, I think you have to take them with a little bit of care, but it is often the best that we have.[47]

Consistency between an appellant's account and available country information is not determinative, but just another factor to be weighed in the balance. For instance, in one case the judge concluded that 'the appellant's claim in outline is consistent with the objective evidence, but having regard to serious inconsistencies in the detail of his claim, I find that there is no reasonable likelihood of the appellant's claim being true'.[48]

Plausibility

Given the frequent absence of other evidence to substantiate an appellant's story, to what extent can the judge simply assess its plausibility or otherwise? Assessing credibility might often involve some judgment as to the plausibility or apparent reasonableness of the basis of a claim. But a claim that appears to be implausible is not necessarily untrue. In real life, events that appear to be implausible or improbable do sometimes occur; the question for the fact-finder is not whether the appellant's story is plausible, but whether it did in fact happen. At the same time, the ostensible plausibility of a claim does not guarantee its truthfulness. A story may be implausible and yet may properly be taken as credible; it may be plausible, but not properly believable.[49]

---

[47] Immigration Judge interview 7.

[48] Case 37.

[49] *MM v Secretary of State for the Home Department (DRC—plausibility) Democratic Republic of Congo* [2005] UKIAT 00019 [15].

A second reason for caution when using plausibility arises from the cross-cultural context. As the Tribunal has noted, 'one's judgment on plausibility is bound to be coloured or influenced by one's own values and environment. What may be plausible for a person in a western environment may be completely implausible for someone in a non-western environment'.[50] Assessing credibility by reference to the intrinsic implausibility or improbability of an appellant's story 'can be a dangerous, even a wholly inappropriate, factor to rely on in some asylum cases' because much of the evidence will have arisen from a cultural context with which the decision-maker will be wholly unfamiliar.[51] At the same time, cultural differences between the appellant and decision-maker do not necessarily mean that the judge is required to take at face value an account irrespective of how contrary to common sense and human experience it might appear; the judge is not expected to suspend disbelief and in appropriate cases is entitled to find that an account of events is so far-fetched and contrary to reason as to be incapable of belief. The judge may regard an appellant's account as incredible, but must take care not to reject the account solely because it would not seem reasonable if the events had happened in the UK.[52]

While such guidelines seem commonsensical enough, the problems lie in applying them. As one judge explained:

> It is very difficult—you have to take account of the cultural differences of appellants. We all try to do that, but there is no way getting around the fact that we can all make mistakes. It is difficult because people are going to react in different ways to different events. Not just culturally, but as individuals and yet we are conditioned to say in this situation somebody would or would not react in a particular way. Of course, it is subjective. But you need to have some common sense somewhere along the line. Otherwise the person could just say virtually anything they do is reasonably likely to be due to a culture that I know nothing about.[53]

What of the situation where an appellant's story seems just so bizarre or unusual that the judge may be reluctant, without some explanation or other evidence, to accept it as being plausible? As a judge noted in one case, the appellant had been 'evasive, truculent, and inconsistent in varying degrees. These traits permeate and taint the whole of his evidence and his overall account is one which is implausible as to be incredulous on the face of it'.[54] The danger is that in such cases, the Immigration Judges' own assessment of the plausibility or otherwise that certain events occurred in addition to their assessment of the moral worthiness of the appellant might influence their assessment of credibility. Representatives have argued that the confusion between credibility and plausibility is a major problem regarding the way Immigration Judges assess credibility. For their part, judges

---

[50] *Ibrahim Ali v Secretary of State for the Home Department* [2002] UKIAT 07001 [3].

[51] *HK v Secretary of State for the Home Department* [2006] EWCA Civ 1037 [29] (Neuberger LJ). See generally HE Cameron, 'Risk Theory and 'Subjective Fear': The Role of Risk Perception, Assessment, and Management in Refugee Status Determinations' (2008) 20 *International Journal of Refugee Law* 567.

[52] *Y v Secretary of State for the Home Department* [2006] EWCA Civ 1223 [25]–[27] (Keene LJ).

[53] Immigration Judge interview 3.

[54] Case 93.

interviewed stressed the importance of retaining an open-mind when assessing the credibility of an account that could appear to be implausible.

Demeanour

A related area of concern when assessing credibility relates to the appellant's demeanour; to what extent is the judge influenced by the way in which the appellant presents his evidence as opposed to its content? Judgments as to plausibility may have some, albeit limited, role, but 'judging demeanour across cultural divides is fraught with danger; the less it is used to disbelieve a person, the less likely is the chance of being criticised for unfair judgment'.[55] The classic example is whether or not an individual's reluctance to look at his interlocutor directly in the eye is an indication that he is not telling the truth. That assumption might be correct in some cases, but not in all: eye contact is a culturally conditioned norm. The unwillingness of an individual appellant to look at the judge in the eye may arouse suspicion that the appellant is not telling the truth, but in fact, this unwillingness on the appellant's behalf might equally signify respect or deference to a person in authority.[56] Alternatively, an individual who does look directly into the eyes of their interlocutor could potentially be taken to as behaviour indicative of a brazen desire to present a false story, but it may be because this is an accepted cultural norm. The inherent difficulty is that to rely on demeanour in such circumstances when trying to determine whether someone is telling the truth is 'in most cases to attach importance to deviations from a norm when there is in truth no norm'.[57] The non-verbal messages sent out by an individual's demeanour and by their body-language is a very imperfect indicator of whether or not they are telling the truth because those messages are themselves indeterminate and contingent upon so many different factors.

But while demeanour is not supposed to be taken into account by judges, does it play a role nonetheless? Taking a realistic perspective, judges themselves recognise the potential influence—conscious or otherwise—of an appellant's non-verbal signals:

> We are not supposed to take into account demeanour, but it does play its part—anyone who says otherwise is probably fooling themselves.[58]

> I would like to say 'no, demeanour does not count' because I really do try to avoid making decisions on demeanour: there may be cultural reasons for why an appellant may be hesitant, for instance. Demeanour should not count, but I do not think in all honesty

---

[55] *B v Secretary of State for the Home Department (Democratic Republic of Congo)* [2003] UKIAT 00012 [7]. See also *Loy Hope Luwuzi v Secretary of State for the Home Department* [2002] UKIAT 07186 [6].

[56] SL Lustig, 'Symptoms of Trauma Among Political Asylum Applicants: Don't be Fooled' (2008) 31 *Hastings International and Comparative Law Review* 725, 730.

[57] T Bingham, 'The Judge as Juror: the Judicial Determination of Factual Issues' (1985) 38 *Current Legal Problems* 1, 10–11.

[58] Immigration Judge interview 8.

I can say that it does not count. There are certain occasions when I see appellants and I find in their favour because of what I see. Sometimes you just hear a story and the way it comes out, and the way you see a person, you just know that he is telling the truth. So, it comes across as a positive credibility thing. I try not to let it interfere in terms of making negative credibility findings because I know how dangerous that is and it is probably dangerous to allow appeals that way. But you just sometimes feel . . . You know, that is just a human response and it certainly has an impact when assessing credibility.[59]

From the sample, there was only one determination in which demeanour was relied upon as a reason for rejecting credibility.[60] Of course, this does not imply that judges are not, consciously or otherwise, influenced by demeanour.

Other aspects of the judge's perception of an appellant can influence credibility. For instance, the way in which an appellant gave oral evidence, whether or not he was a good witness, or whether the appellant's evidence was marked by an absence of evasion or a sequence of changing answers, or the converse. While it has been recognised that there are aspects of the *way* in which evidence has been given that can be used to assess credibility, it is an area for real caution because it is so closely linked to demeanour and cultural differences. What is important is that it is the total content of the evidence, including consistency on essentials or major inconsistencies, omissions and details, improbabilities or reasonableness, which should provide the basis for the judge's conclusions on credibility. The way in which evidence has been given can, though, normally be reflected in the quality of the content of the evidence. So, evasiveness by an appellant may justify a conclusion well-founded in the content of the evidence, but would rarely justify a conclusion which was not sustained by the content of the evidence or its quality.[61] The risk is that an appellant who appears evasive to a judge may simply be nervous or find difficulty in answering the questions put to him: As one judge noted:

One has to be very careful when an appellant appears to be evasive because some cultures, I think, may be more adept at listening to a question and answering it. In this country we tend to have it drilled into us from school to read the question, listen to it, and then answer it. But some appellants do not do that. Some appellants find it extremely difficult to answer a direct question and you have to be very careful about implying from that that somebody is seeking to be evasive.[62]

Corroborative Evidence

For obvious reasons, it is normally impossible for asylum appellants to adduce corroborative evidence in support of their claim. If an appellant has fled his country to

---

[59] Immigration Judge interview 3.

[60] The appellant had claimed that she had not known that her destination when flying from Pakistan was the UK despite announcements during the flight because she had suffered from travel sickness; the judge was 'entirely satisfied from listening to the appellant's evidence and by observing her demeanour that that was a lie' (Case 109).

[61] *MM* above n 49 at [19].

[62] Immigration Judge interview 7.

seek asylum and then entered the UK with the aid of an agent, then he is unlikely to have considered the desirability of collecting evidence to present in support of his claim at an appeal hearing in the UK. For these reasons, corroborative evidence is not required in asylum cases.[63] Nonetheless, in many cases appellants may be able to produce some corroborative evidence—for instance, documentary evidence or oral evidence from a witness. How is such evidence, of the lack of it, to be handled?

First, although such evidence is not required, this does not mean that a judge is bound to leave out of account the absence of evidence which might reasonably be expected to have been provided. An appeal must be determined on the basis of the evidence produced, but the weight to be attached to oral evidence may be affected by a failure to produce other evidence in support.[64] It may be difficult for an asylum applicant to obtain certain documentary evidence, but, if not, then its absence may be taken into account. Secondly, appellants may call witness(es) to give evidence on their behalf to corroborate their story. If so, then their evidence needs to be assessed alongside that of the appellant. If two witnesses concur in their evidence, then both may be telling the truth or they may have colluded together to concoct an untruthful account.[65]

Thirdly, documentary evidence may be produced to support an appellant's case. Such documentary evidence is often of many different kinds. Newspaper articles or an arrest warrant in the country concerned may be submitted as evidence that the appellant is wanted by the authorities. For the Tribunal's convenience, documentary evidence should, if not written in English, be translated.[66] The principal issue often concerns the degree of weight that should be placed upon such evidence. Documents should not be viewed in isolation, but assessed in the context of the evidence as a whole.

According to the Tribunal's guidance, it is for an appellant to show that a document on which they seek to rely can be relied on.[67] It is trite asylum law that what is or is not likely to happen in other countries should not be judged by reference

---

[63] *Kasolo v Secretary of State for the Home Department* (13190), date notified 1 April 1996 (IAT). Under the EC Qualification Directive [2004] OJ L304/12 art 4(5) (transposed into UK law by the Immigration Rules (1994 HC 395), r 339L), where aspects of an asylum claimant's statements are not supported by documentary or other evidence, those aspects will not need confirmation when all of the following conditions are met: (i) the applicant has made a genuine effort to substantiate his application; (ii) all material factors at the appellant's disposal have been submitted and a satisfactory explanation regarding any lack of other relevant material has been given; (iii) the applicant's statements have been found to be coherent and plausible and do not run counter to the available specific and general information relevant to the applicant's case; (iv) the applicant has made an asylum or human rights claim at the earliest possible time, unless the applicant can demonstrate good reason for not having done so; and (v) the general credibility of the applicant has been established.

[64] *ST v Secretary of State for the Home Department (Corroboration—Kasolo) Ethiopia* [2004] UKIAT 000119 [15].

[65] *AB v Secretary of State for the Home Department (Witness corroboration in asylum appeals) Somalia* [2004] UKIAT 00125 [4].

[66] Asylum and Immigration Tribunal (Procedure) Rules SI 2005/230 r 52(3).

[67] *Tanvir Ahmed v Secretary of State for the Home Department* (Starred determination) [2002] UKIAT 00439.

to the decision-maker's perception of what is normal within the UK. It may be easy and often relatively inexpensive to obtain 'forged' documents in other countries. Some documents may be false, some may be 'genuine' in the sense that they emanate from a proper source, but the information they contain is untrue; the permutations of truth, untruth, validity, and 'genuineness' are enormous. At its simplest, it is necessary to differentiate between form and content; that is whether a document was properly issued by the purported author and whether its contents are true. It is a dangerous oversimplification merely to ask whether a document is 'forged' or even 'not genuine'.

The assessment of the reliability of documentary evidence, therefore, depends on the degree of weight that the judge is willing to place on the particular documents. This can often be a difficult task; as one judge explained:

> If there are documents, you look to see if they are reliable or unreliable. And even then, if a document is unreliable, does that mean that the appellant is lying or that he might be telling the truth, but is also trying desperately to back it up by producing a document which is actually unreliable?[68]

Even if a certain document relied on by an appellant does not attract much evidential weight, it does not necessarily mean that the appellant's story is untrue; other documents, if considered reliable, might provide the fact-finder with part of the background of the appellant's case. It all depends on the nature of the documentary evidence and its relationship to the appellant's case.

To illustrate, in one appeal, the appellant had produced a number of documents which corroborated much of his story about joining a political party in Cameroon. While the documentation did not possess much evidential weight, it did lend some support to the appellant's story. One document, for example, was written by a member of the political party and corroborated the appellant's story that he was also a member. However, the judge found that the document 'could have been produced by anyone in this day and age on a home computer. In evidential terms it is of very limited value'.[69] While the document was of limited evidential value, it did not though follow that it should be rejected out of hand. Considering other aspects of the appellant's claim, the judge concluded that it was credible. By contrast, in another appeal, the appellant had submitted a photograph of herself in support of her of claim that she had been abducted and then given military training by the Liberation Tigers of Tamil Eelam (LTTE) in Sri Lanka; the claim was one of imputed political opinion. Asked why the photograph was in immaculate condition despite the appellant having been in hiding for two years before travelling to the UK, the appellant replied that it had been kept in a book. However, the judge did not accept this sequence of events as credible; the photograph had been taken sometime after she was in the jungle in order to support an asylum claim that was already in contemplation.[70]

---

[68] Immigration Judge interview 7.
[69] Case 15.
[70] Case 41.

Assessing the reliability of a document is another factor to be taken into account when considering the evidence as a whole. By contrast, if the Home Office alleges that a document is forged, then a distinct procedure operates under which the judge must investigate the allegation in private.[71] In such circumstances, the burden of proof shifts to the Home Office to prove, on the balance of probabilities, the forgery.[72] However, more often it is simply argued that the appellant's documentary evidence is unreliable. For instance, in one appeal, the Tribunal directed the Home Office to investigate whether or not a document was forged; however, the Home Office's forgery team was unable to do so because it did not possess the necessary expertise to conduct a forgery examination of a foreign newspaper; while normal practice was for any document to be authenticated by the British High Commission or consulate abroad, this could not be undertaken as the UK does not have any High Commission or consulate in Congo Brazzaville.[73]

Medical Evidence

Many appellants may claim that they have been previously subject to torture or ill-treatment, a serious indicator that the fear of future harm is well-founded, unless there are good reasons for supposing otherwise.[74] To substantiate such claims, appellants may submit medical reports detailing physical scarring in order to corroborate and/or to lend weight to such an account by giving an opinion as to the consistency of the scarring with claimed past ill-treatment. But how is such evidence to be assessed? Judges are not medical experts; therefore, some deference to medical expertise might be expected. At the same time, it is for judges rather than medical experts to assess credibility. Furthermore, the purpose of a medical examination is not for the medical expert to determine whether the appellant has been telling the truth. It would not be right for a doctor to approach a patient whose medical condition he has been asked to diagnose in a spirit of scepticism as doctor-patient relationships are based on trust and confidence underlying which is the therapeutic purpose of medical diagnosis and treatment. By contrast, judge-appellant relationships operate in the context of a formal and legal adjudicatory process, one purpose of which is for the judicial fact-finder to assess the credibility. Judges may be reluctant to grant asylum merely because there is a medical report identifying scarring—especially if there are other adverse credibility findings. The role of medical evidence, like that of psychiatric evidence, obviously

---

[71] Nationality, Immigration and Asylum Act 2002 s 108.

[72] *OA v Entry Clearance Officer, Lagos (Alleged forgery; section 108 procedure) Nigeria* [2007] UKAIT 00096.

[73] Case 26.

[74] Immigration Rules (1994 HC 395) r 339K. The other principal situation in which medical reports will be used is in HIV/AIDS cases in which the appellant is claiming that their condition makes removal contrary to Article 3 ECHR. However, the test in such cases has been set so high that removal in such cases will only be unlawful in those rare instances where very exceptional circumstances mean that the humanitarian grounds against removal are compelling.

raises broader issues as to the respective roles of professional judgment and legal decision-making and the tensions that arise between different perspectives on the asylum decision process.[75]

Underlying such general tensions, are more specific problems with medical evidence: the inherent difficulty is that medical reports detailing scarring can normally only identify the nature of the scars, but not their precise cause. Scarring consistent with persecutory ill-treatment may also be consistent with other causes; a medical report identifying consistency between the physical scars and an appellant's account of previous torture does not mean that the scars could not have been caused through other means (or even self-inflicted). The role of such evidence is, therefore, often limited to that of not negating the appellant's case; it cannot necessarily prove that the scarring was in fact caused in the way claimed.[76] A medical report may proffer an opinion as to the degree of consistency between the scarring and the appellant's story, but the judge might, having regard to other credibility findings, decide to place little weight upon the medical report. At the same time, medical evidence can never be dismissed out of hand, but must be handled by judges as an integral part of the evidence as a whole. What a judge should not do is to assess the appellant's credibility solely by reference to his evidence and then, if that assessment is adverse, consider whether the conclusion can be shifted by the medical evidence; to do so is to separate artificially the medical evidence from the rest of the evidence.[77]

Of particular importance is the Court of Appeal's guidance on medical reports.[78] If a medical report is to have any corroborative effect and/or lend weight to the account given by the asylum applicant, then it should contain a clear statement of the doctor's opinion as to consistency, directed to the particular injuries said to have occurred as a result of the torture or other ill-treatment relied on as evidence of persecution. Where the doctor finds there to be a degree of consistency

---

[75] Another factor concerns the relative incapacity of the Home Office to subject expert medical evidence to cross-examination. Home Office presenting officers do not possess the requisite expertise with which to question either the methodology used in the preparation of a medical report or the conclusions reached. The Home Office does not commission its own medical experts to provide a rebuttal of the medical evidence commissioned by the appellant. Furthermore, a doctor who has prepared a medical report will not normally attend the appeal hearing for their evidence to be cross-examined by the Home Office or to be asked questions by the Immigration Judge.

[76] The Tribunal's approach toward medical expert reports has changed considerably over the years. Its initial view was that such reports deserved careful and specific consideration. See *Mohamed v Secretary of State for the Home Department* (12412), date notified 4 August 1995 (IAT); *Ibrahim v Secretary of State for the Home Department* [1998] INLR 511 (IAT). However, the Tribunal, in *HE* above n 43 at 125 subsequently indicated that this former approach could no longer be regarded as sound: 'The experience of the Tribunal over a number of years since then is that the quality of reports is so variable and sadly often so poor and unhelpful, that there is no necessary obligation to give them weight merely because they are medical or psychiatric reports. The consideration given to a report depends on the quality of the report and the standing and qualifications of the doctor'. See also *PT v Secretary of State for the Home Department (Medical Report, Analysis) Sri Lanka CG* [2002] UKIAT 01336 [8]; *Ademaj, Ademaj, and Urim v Secretary of State for the Home Department* [2002] UKIAT 00979 [13].

[77] *Virjon B v Special Adjudicator* [2002] EWHC Admin 1469; *Mibanga v Secretary of State for the Home Department* [2005] EWCA Civ 367.

[78] *SA (Somalia) v Secretary of State for the Home Department* [2006] EWCA Civ 1302.

between the injuries/scarring and the appellant's claimed causes which admit of there being other possible causes (whether many, few or unusually few), it is particularly important that the medical report specifically examine those to gauge how likely they are, bearing in mind what is known about the individual's life history and experiences.[79]

In response, medical experts have argued that they cannot be expected to consider explanations for which there is no context according to the evidence before them. For the Tribunal to demand that doctors consider possible alternative explanations for scarring is to raise the standard of proof beyond that of the reasonable degree of likelihood test.[80] The problem is that while medical evidence should be taken into account when assessing whether the appellant's account is reasonably likely, it comprises only one aspect of the evidence. If the judge, when surveying the evidence as a whole, makes adverse credibility findings, then the medical evidence must be assessed, but it cannot usually indicate whether or not the scars were caused in the way claimed; the next best alternative is to ask the medical expert to consider whether it is likely that they were caused in the way claimed, taking into account other possible causes consistent with the appellant's past.

As the Court of Appeal has emphasised, the Istanbul Protocol provides instructive guidance concerning medical reports.[81] This Protocol states that for each lesion and for the overall pattern of lesions, the doctor should indicate the degree of consistency between it and the attribution given by the patient.[82] Ultimately, it is the overall evaluation of all lesions and not the consistency of each lesion with a particular form of torture that is important in assessing the torture story.[83] Doctors requested to supply medical reports supporting allegations of torture by asylum claimants are expected to follow the Istanbul Protocol and to pay close attention to the requirement that medical evaluations for legal purposes should be conducted with objectivity and impartiality.[84]

What happens in practice? All judges interviewed noted the variable quality of medical reports. Some are written by doctors who specialise in detailing torture; others are written by doctors without such experience. It is also apparent that medical experts are not always provided with all the documents regarding the appellant's case. The end result may be a report at odds with the rest of the existing evidence and documentation. To some extent the problem might lie with those instructing medical experts. Representatives may not always provide medical

---

[79] *RT v Secretary of State for the Home Department (medical reports—causation of scarring) Sri Lanka* [2008] UKAIT 00009.

[80] DR Jones and SV Smith, 'Medical Evidence in Asylum and Human Rights Appeals' (2004) 16 *International Journal of Refugee Law* 381, 392–393.

[81] United Nations High Commissioner for Refugees (UNHCR), *Istanbul Protocol: Manual on the Effective Investigation and Documentation of Torture and Other Cruel, Inhuman or Degrading Treatment or Punishment* (UNHCR, 9 August 1999).

[82] Ibid, [186].

[83] Ibid, [187].

[84] *SA (Somalia)* above n 78 at [30].

experts with proper instructions.[85] As one judge noted, medical expert reports were 'very often inadequate' because 'the commissioning of these reports is done in a hurry to meet timescales and also those who commission reports do not always know exactly what it is that they are trying to achieve'.[86]

Perhaps the most important limitation of medical evidence is that it can rarely tell judges more than whether or not the scarring is consistent with past torture. Where a medical report contains diagnostic conclusions which are wholly dependant upon the history or symptoms asserted by the appellant, whose very truthfulness on such matters is at issue before the judge, but was not before the medical expert, then only limited weight may be placed on such evidence if the judge concludes that the appellant's account lacks credibility. A medical report that simply accepts the appellant's evidence concludes that what the appellant said happened because he said it happened, or accepts as truthful the appellant's own description of symptoms, may be of limited value in assessing credibility. As one judge explained:

> The appellant might say 'I was tortured so badly that my arm was broken', and the medical report will say 'on examination there is a healed fracture in the arm which is consistent with what the appellant says happened to him or her'. But all a medical expert can do is to identify the fracture. The rest of the account comes, not from the medical examination strictly, but from what the appellant has said caused the injury. So, at that point you realise that after all the paragraphs in the medical report, the valuable section is just the identification of the injury and the section which is said to corroborate the appellant's account, does not really do that.[87]

Another inherent limitation is that it is well-known that sophisticated methods of torture may leave few, if any, physical traces on an individual's body. Such techniques are used by those who inflict torture precisely because they leave no physical marks. So, the presence of scarring may not be determinative as to whether an individual has been tortured. Conversely, the absence of scarring cannot be taken as determinative as to whether an individual has not been tortured.

An appellant who produces a medical report stating that her scars are consistent with her story that she was raped may be rejected; the fact that scarring is consistent with that cause does not necessarily mean that it was caused in the way described. Even if a woman has been raped, it does not necessarily mean that it qualifies as persecution because of a convention reason such as an appellant's race or ethnicity; rape is common in all countries. But the scale of the injuries and their impression upon the decision-maker can themselves be significant. It is one thing for an individual to have an ordinary physical scar; it is quite another for an individual to have nearly 70 scars on her body consistent with her story of having been severely beaten, kicked, burnt with cigarettes, and raped and then to place this in the context of a generally credible account.

---

[85] J Gilliespie, 'Expert Evidence in Asylum Cases' (2001) 15(2) *Immigration, Asylum and Nationality Law* 88, 89–90.

[86] Immigration Judge interview 3.

[87] Immigration Judge interview 2.

The production of medical evidence could certainly be improved. It is not apparent that all medical experts are aware of the Istanbul Protocol. There may also be a need for better training of medical experts in the preparation of reports. There is almost certainly a need for better instructions of medical experts by some representatives. Another suggestion is that medical experts attend appeal hearings more to supplement their report with oral evidence. However, the value of such evidence will often be disputed not necessarily because it is inferior, but because of the nature of the issues involved.

Section 8 of the Asylum and Immigration (Treatment of Claimants, etc) Act 2004

Until 2004, Parliament had not laid down any rules governing credibility assessments. However, under the 2004 Act, asylum decision-makers must take into account, as damaging the claimant's credibility, any behaviour which the decision-maker thinks is either designed or likely to conceal information, to mislead, or to obstruct or delay the handling or resolution of a claim or the taking of a decision in relation to the claimant.[88] The policy rationale for this provision was the need to deter and reduce abusive claims and to promote consistency in decision-making. In the Government's view, by requiring such factors to be taken into account as damaging credibility, the provision would induce claimants to cooperate with the determination of their claim.

Section 8 has, though, been extensively criticised. A central concern is that the provision establishes an unreasonable evidential presumption that just because a claimant has behaved in a specified manner, then his general credibility is presumed to have been damaged. Claimants may, owing to their experiences, feel apprehensive and be afraid to speak freely and give a full and accurate account of their case and, further, untrue statements by themselves are not a reason for refusing refugee status.[89] Likewise, many asylum claimants enter the UK with false documents; it can be difficult for them to enter otherwise. The requirement that judges take into account the use of a false passport as damaging credibility may adversely affect those genuinely in need of protection. Section 8, it has been

---

[88] Asylum and Immigration (Treatment of Claimants, etc.) Act 2004 s 8. The section then details a non-exhaustive list of certain kinds of behaviour that shall be treated as designed or likely to conceal information or mislead: a failure without reasonable explanation to produce a passport; the production of a false passport; the destruction, alteration or disposal, without reasonable explanation, of a passport or travel document; a failure without reasonable explanation to answer a question asked by a decision-maker; a failure to take advantage of a reasonable opportunity to make an asylum or human rights claim while in a safe country; a failure to make a claim before being notified of an immigration decision, unless the claim relies wholly on matters arising after the notification; and a failure to make a claim before being arrested under immigration law. In relation to a failure to claim asylum *en route* to the UK, section 8 reversed previous case-law that such a failure 'cannot conceivably by itself throw doubt on whether . . . [the claimant] . . . is indeed a genuine asylum seeker' (*R (Degirmenci) v Immigration Appeal Tribunal* [2003] EWHC Admin 324 [11] (Collins J)).

[89] UNHCR above n 2 at [198]–[199].

argued, gives legislative backing to an 'agenda of disbelief' toward applicants.[90] While important, the interests of appellants is not the only issue; another is the position of the Tribunal vis-à-vis the Home Office, in particular the independence of judicial fact-finding. If, as the Court of Appeal has noted, section 8 is 'a constitutional anomaly in relation to the independence of a fact-finding judicial tribunal', then how can the Tribunal reconcile it with the obligation to apply primary legislation?[91]

The answer has been for the Tribunal to recognise that while judges must formally apply section 8, the provision is not intended to affect the general process of deriving facts from evidence.[92] The task of the fact-finder, whether official or judge, is to look at all the evidence in the round, to try and grasp it as a whole and to see how it fits together, and whether it is sufficient to discharge the burden of proof.[93] Despite the clear intention of section 8 that some behaviour counts against appellants as damaging their credibility, it is for fact-finders to make up their minds about the value of their evidence before them. Following the Tribunal's guidance, the Court of Appeal has, in effect, nullified section 8 by construing the provision so that the behaviour specified should only be taken into account by decision-makers as *potentially* damaging to an individual's credibility.[94] Such judicial legislation has the effect of protecting the independence of the fact-finding function.

In practice, section 8 appears to exert little real influence on decision-making. As judges noted, section 8 can be used to reinforce adverse credibility findings reached on other grounds or, alternatively, section 8 issues could be attributed little weight so as not to outweigh positive credibility findings. Either way, section 8 is not determinative of appeals. Consider the following case. An appellant had entered on a false passport (a behaviour caught by section 8). However, the judge held that this did not in any way undermine what was otherwise 'a highly consistent, plausible, and apparently unembellished account of events'.[95] Conscious of the Home Office's desire to influence the outcome of appeals and the importance of maintaining independent judicial fact-finding processes, judges have had to apply rules enshrined in statute, but are, in practice, able to get around them.

---

[90] J Ensor, A Shah, and M Grillo, 'Simple Myths and Complex Realities—Seeking the Truth in the Face of Section 8' (2006) 20 *Immigration, Asylum and Nationality Law* 95; JA Sweeney, 'Credibility, Proof, and Refugee Law' (2009) 21 *International Journal of Refugee Law* 700, 716–719.

[91] *NT (Togo) v Secretary of State for the Home Department* [2007] EWCA Civ 1431 [3] (Sedley LJ).

[92] *SM v Secretary of State for the Home Department (Section 8: Judge's process) Iran* [2005] UKAIT 00116.

[93] Ibid, [7]–[10].

[94] *JT (Cameroon) v Secretary of State for the Home Department* [2008] EWCA Civ 878; [2009] 1 WLR 1411 (CA).

[95] Case 127.

Hard Cases

Assessing credibility in the general run of asylum appeals is hard enough, but the difficulties are exacerbated in those especially hard cases which commonly arise in the asylum jurisdiction. To illustrate the point, we can consider three categories of such cases: age disputes; religious conversion; and disputed ethnicity or clan membership.

Age Disputes

Disputes over an appellant's age occur when the Home Office considers that the appellant is over the age of 18, but the appellant contends that he is under 18. The appellant may have no evidence to support this, or, if he does, its value may itself be disputed. Home Office's age assessments are often made on the basis of the claimant's physical appearance and demeanour; the claimant may then be referred to a local authority social services department for a second age assessment. At the appeal stage, an appellant might have a further medical expert age assessment. While the judge must make general credibility findings, this cannot often be disentangled from an assessment as to whether the claimant is of the stated age; the assumption is that if an appellant is untruthful as to his age, then it is likely that his evidence concerning other aspects of the asylum claim are also untrue.[96] The problem, though, is that there is no accepted scientific or medical process by which an individual's age can be assessed accurately; medical assessment methods usually recognise a margin of error of two years. By contrast, Home Office age assessment procedures rely simply upon an Immigration Officer's assessment of an individual's physical appearance and demeanour.[97] The concern is that individuals are not afforded the benefit of the doubt.[98]

The Tribunal's position is that it is for the appellant to demonstrate to the lower standard of proof that he is a minor. If the evidence is insufficient to demonstrate

[96] There are various reasons why age may be disputed. For instance, local authorities owe duties under the Children Act to under age asylum applicants; such authorities may argue that an appellant is over 18 years of age, in which case their support needs will be met by the Home Office. The Home Office has argued that many 'age disputed' cases arise because there are incentives for claimants to pass themselves off as being under the age of 18: asylum-seeking children are subject to more generous asylum policies and support arrangements; they will not be detained or subject to fact-track procedures; refused claimants can only be removed from the UK if there are adequate care and reception facilities in place in their country of origin; furthermore, asylum seeking children are normally granted leave to remain until their eighteenth birthday. At the same time, the incentives for an adult asylum seeker to pass himself off as a child does not diminish the possibility that an appellant may in fact be a child.

[97] H Crawley, *When Is a Child Not a Child? Asylum, Age Disputes, and the Process of Age Assessment* (London, ILPA, 2007).

[98] Joint Committee on Human Rights, *The Treatment of Asylum Seekers* (2006–07 HL 81 HC 60) [203]. For instance, in one appeal, it had been noted in a local authority age assessment report that the assessment was 'an opinion of the staff only, no-one in our organisation has had any training in this area of assessment' (Case 22).

this, then the judge is entitled simply to say so, but it would generally be inappropriate for a judge to make an assessment of a person's age merely having observed him in the formal surroundings of the tribunal hearing room.[99] The problems are then considerable because the evidence will typically be highly limited, but some assessment of credibility, and possibly of the appellant's claim to be a certain age, is required.

Religious Faith and Conversion

Claims based on religious persecution raise similarly difficult factual questions. Tribunal country guidance has recognised that certain groups of people—Eritrean Pentecostalists and Iranian Christian proselytisers, for instance—may be at risk on return because of persecution on religious grounds.[100] As country guidance has settled the existence of a risk group, the task for a judge is to establish whether a particular appellant is a member of the risk group. But how is a judge to determine whether an individual genuinely practices the religion claimed and is a genuine convert or is merely seeking to pass himself off as a follower of that faith in order to secure asylum? As one judge noted, 'there are asylum seekers who come to this country trying to pass themselves off as Eritrean Pentecostalists even though they have no allegiance to that church. It is relatively easy for an industrious asylum seeker to study and learn details of another faith'.[101] Furthermore, religious bodies in the UK may be very welcoming to religious converts, seeking them out or they might be naively unaware that they have been hoodwinked by the unscrupulous. At the same time, an appellant may be a genuine follower or converter to a religious faith and for that reason at real risk on return.

According to Tribunal guidance, no-one should be regarded as a committed Christian unless vouchsafed by a minister or pastor of some church established in the UK; it is church membership rather than mere religious belief which may create a real risk of persecution on the grounds of religion.[102] But how is a judge to know whether or not to believe the evidence presented? How possible is it that a church minister has either been deceived or colluded in the deceit? An alternative technique, sometimes practised by the Home Office, is to seek to determine the claimant's faith by asking the claimant a number of factual questions concerning the Bible. For instance, in one appeal, an Eritrean claiming to be a Pentecostalist

---

[99] *SH v Secretary of State for the Home Department (Assessment of age) Afghanistan* [2005] UKIAT 00156; [2006] Imm AR 137. See also *R (B) v London Borough of Merton* [2003] EWCA Admin 1689; *R (A) v London Borough of Croydon* [2009] UKSC 8.

[100] *YT v Secretary of State for the Home Department (Minority church members at risk) Eritrea CG* [2004] UKIAT 00218; *FS and others v Secretary of State for the Home Department (Iran—Christian Converts) Iran CG* [2004] UKIAT 00303; *SZ and JM v Secretary of State for the Home Department (Christians—FS confirmed) Iran CG* [2008] UKAIT 00082.

[101] Case 38.

[102] *Dorodian v Secretary of State for the Home Department* (01TH01537), date notified 23 August 2001 (IAT) [8].

had been asked over 50 questions about the Bible in her Home Office interview, some, though not all, of which had been correctly answered. As the judge noted:

> As a means of determining whether or not someone really is a Pentecostalist, this technique is almost a meaningless exercise. It is rarely going to distinguish someone who may be Jewish, Orthodox Christian, Pentecostalist, other form of Evangelical Christian, a theological student who may be an Atheist, or finally the individual who has had sufficient forethought or information to anticipate the format adopted by the Home Office over several years and done some homework.[103]

Ethnicity and Clan Membership

Similar problems arise in relation to disputed ethnicity and clan membership cases. Given that many of the situations producing asylum appellants involve ethnic conflicts or, as in Somalia, conflicts between different clans, the judge may have to assess whether a particular appellant is of the claimed ethnicity or clan. Country guidance often recognises some risk categories based on ethnicity or clan membership, but an appellant cannot succeed merely by asserting their ethnicity or clan membership. One approach is for the appellant to commission an expert report. This might consider the appellant's physical characteristics while clan membership reports tend to consider the appellant's knowledge of physical and geographic surroundings, family structure, passage rituals and cultural expressions; diet; language and dialects; trade, and so on. But such reports are not necessarily determinative. For instance, in one case, the appellant submitted an expert report in support of his claim to be a member of a Somali minority clan but this was rejected for a number of reasons; as the judge reasoned, 'an appellant knowing that a successful appeal rested upon the ability to establish a particular ethnicity would, it is reasonable to suppose, prepare for an interview such as this whether he was of that ethnicity or not'.[104]

Weighing it all up

Rarely will any one of the above factors by itself be determinative when assessing credibility. Real cases do not often come before the judge neatly presented and packaged with a possible internal inconsistency issue which can be considered as logically distinct from another credibility issue, such as the presence of medical evidence. Having surveyed all the evidence the judge must then assess it all as a whole and make findings of fact on the principal issues. Judges themselves differ considerably as to how they go about this task. Some will seek to identify the

[103] Case 14.
[104] Case 99.

principal contested credibility issues and then make positive or adverse findings as required, and then seek to see where the overall balance lies. This more nuanced approach contrasts with the approach adopted by judges who simply seem to go one way or the other: either the appellant is wholly credible or not. The first approach allows for a more refined and structured assessment. By contrast, the latter approach seems to over-simplify and be more outcome-based, but some judges may prefer to seek certainty in their decisions one way or the other. Yet another approach is for the judge in marginal cases to find that there is evidence pointing both for and against the appellant, and then seek to arrive at a clear conclusion one way or the other. The risk is that in such cases the appeal may be sent back to be re-heard because the reviewing judge has found that there has been a failure to make clear findings of fact, but for judges it will frequently be difficult to make wholly unambiguous findings one way or the other because of the nature of the evidence.[105] The approach adopted is obviously highly dependant on the nature of individual cases and the experience of the decision-maker.

It is because credibility is an inherently slippery notion that decision-makers can often experience difficulties in attempting to rationalise precisely why they find an individual to be credible or not. The upshot is that individual decisions can often turn upon apparently mundane issues, such as: the way in which an expert has written his expert report or his academic qualifications and experience; the apparent genuineness of a photograph or documentary evidence; or whether an individual gave slightly different accounts of the same story on different occasions. None of the various factors used to assess credibility are themselves determinative; it is all a question of the decision-maker's subjective assessment and visceral reaction toward the evidence presented. The following conclusions from appeal determinations are typical:

> In summary, it is entirely possible that the complete account provided by the appellant is a fiction provided for her by an agent or some other individual. On the other hand, the evidence that has been given by the appellant particularly in her written evidence bears no obvious signs of inconsistency, a lack of credibility, or variants with the objective material. Her responses do bear some hallmarks of being routed in the factual background. In conclusion, therefore whilst the burden remains on the appellant the standard required is a low one and in accordance with that standard I accept the evidence given by the appellant as credible and accept therefore that if returned to Eritrea she would be persecuted in respect of her beliefs as a Pentecostalist and because she would be regarded as a military deserter.[106]

> Having regard to the totality of the evidence, I find that the appellant is not a credible witness and that there is no reasonable likelihood of his claim being true. I further find

---

[105] According to one Immigration Judge, Talbot n 31 above at 30: Immigration Judges 'are always being urged by . . . [senior judges] . . . to make clear and unambiguous findings, which of course simplifies their job. We cannot always do that. I do not wish to feel pressured into making tidy findings for the administrative convenience of the appellate process. If I find evidence pointing in conflicting directions, then I think I should say so, rather than simply assemble all the evidence that points in the direction that I have decided to go'.

[106] Case 14.

that the appellant has clearly fabricated his account of the persecution to which he claims to have suffered in Somalia as the basis of what I find to be a false asylum claim. In reaching these findings I have considered carefully whether the appellant's inconsistent and discrepant evidence can properly be put down to exaggeration or embellishment. However, I find that the appellant's incorrect replies, the number and significance of the discrepancies and inconsistencies in his story which came out at the hearing, then having regard to the totality of all of these factors, I find that they go to the credibility of the very core of the appellant's claim and that they could not possibly be ignored or excused as embellishment or exaggeration, which they are clearly not.[107]

Beneath the formal reasons given by a judge in a determination, other forces and influences will be at work. Such influences may be of greater importance precisely because they are not explicitly articulated, but intangible, and not susceptible of being dissected on appeal, but only guessed at. This hinterland may be nebulous and amorphous, but influential nonetheless.

One such influence upon decision-making may arise from the repetitive nature of the adjudication process itself. The task of adjudicating requires that the judge decide each case on its own individual merits, but the judge's function is not to hear just one appeal, but many appeals day-in, day-out. While recently appointed judges may feel some diffidence initially, the experience of hearing a number of diverse appeals over time may come to augment their confidence. A judge may happen to notice broader patterns at work in the nature of the cases before him.

To cope with and handle the in-flow of cases, judges may develop a propensity, consciously or otherwise, to slot them within pre-established, generic case-profiles that over time come to provide a convenient short-hand description of a significant proportion of cases. As Macklin has perspicaciously observed, like any mass adjudication system, the asylum process 'tends to flatten out difference, demand simplicity over nuance, and compel the distillation of messy, complicated lives down to a manageable set of narrative fragments that can be inserted into the legal pigeonholes of the refugee definition'.[108] In turn, each case-profile may be underpinned by different assumptions concerning an individual's intentions. For instance, there is the unemployed and poorly educated young male claimant from Africa or Asia, the elderly claimant with health care needs, the Zimbabwean woman who only claims asylum after having overstayed for some years, the political activist who sought to advance democracy and good governance in a kleptocratic dictatorship, the African girl forced into prostitution, the Somali woman with children and so on. As the available evidence in most cases is fragmentary, judges may inevitably come to rely upon the case-profiles to fill in the gaps in the evidence and to make sense of it. Of course, those case-profiles will never be able to capture the full complexity of individual cases, especially given the cultural distances between appellants and judges. The danger is that judges might lapse into mental laziness and overlook the individual case which does not fall into the

---

[107] Case 37.
[108] Macklin above n 23 at 137.

familiar pattern. The consequences of this influence may go either for or against the appellant. There is the risk that the judge will unwittingly favour those appellants who fall within those profiles or stereotypes with which he shares an affinity. Alternatively, there is the risk of assuming that an appellants falls within a negative profile, where in fact their cases may possess much greater subtlety and complexity. The risk of rushing to rapid judgments is substantial and increased by the emphasis upon the timeliness of the appeals process.

Another feature of asylum appeals is that judges will often notice the similarities of the stories presented by nationals from certain countries. For instance, the stories presented by individuals claiming to belong to well-known categories of asylum appellants (for instance, Iranian homosexuals, political opponents in Zimbabwe, or Eritrean Pentecostalists) may share certain features. This may by itself raise suspicions as to whether the common features in such stories are just too coincidental to be true, perhaps because the appellants have been recounting well-learnt scripts given to them by the agents they have paid to facilitate their entry into the country or by other individuals. Agents can often provide claimants with a particular story, which is known to have been successful in getting asylum in the past, with the hope that it will work again in the future. The challenge, of course, is for the judge not to rush to pre-judgment, but to consider whether or not on balance the appellant's story is reasonably likely to be true, despite its resemblance with case-profiles.

Beyond this, there may be other forces at work. The longer someone hears asylum cases, then the more case-hardened and cynical they may become. Judges also have to deal with the stress and anxiety of hearing appeals, some of which contain evidence that is shocking. Judges have to become accustomed to hearing cases that feature every form of torture, suffering, and humiliation. They also have to guard against the temptation to reject a story on account of the fact that the ill-treatment it details is so extreme so that the judge does not want to consider it possible or imaginable. Another risk is that judges may allow their personal sympathies for or prejudices against an appellant to distort their judgments. It is probably too idealistic to suppose that judges who meet appellants face-to-face at oral hearings will always be able to make findings of fact with complete dispassionate detachment. On the contrary, given the pervasive human element in making such judgments, it is only realistic to suppose that judges may react directly to what they see and hear in front of them in the tribunal hearing room in a way that reviewing courts and tribunals do not.[109] And it can be easy for a judge to use the legitimate techniques of credibility assessment—internal and external consistency, for instance—to justify decisions reached on other, less legitimate, grounds. The challenge for the Immigration Judge is to recognise and guard against this. As Sir Nicholas Blake has explained:

> Immigration law is concerned with people, their families, their aspirations, their hopes, failures, and fears. However trying the caseload and however contrived the narrative

---

[109] Talbot above n 31 at 29.

appears to be, respect for human dignity must be at the heart of our processes as Immigration Judges. As an advocate I have seen over the years good and bad judicial practice in immigration and asylum hearings with respect to treatment of appellants and credibility findings . . . One task of the Tribunal is to ensure that we contribute to the development and application of the best practice even whilst we recognise that we are faced with great numbers of unsubstantiated claims based on fabricated or contrived evidence. We must be on our guard against credibility fatigue, as much as against being deceived by false claims.[110]

Conclusion

Assessing credibility is fundamental aspect to asylum adjudication. The basic problem is that no-one really knows how to decide whether or not an individual can properly be regarded as credible. Nor, in most cases, can anyone ever find out what the answer is. Assessing credibility is not just mildly difficult; it is perennially, almost impossibly, puzzling. Given the frequent absence of verifiable and objective evidence as to whether a claimant would be at risk on return, this then is the problematic nature of asylum adjudication: the great difficulty, if not impossibility, of knowing whether or not claims are being decided accurately; the elusive nature of fact-finding; and the inherent difficulty of not really being able to determine what the truth is. The risk is that some decision-makers may become case-hardened whereas others may become too credulous. Attempting to prevent Immigration Judges from straying to either extreme is difficult because there is no publicly available information on individual Immigration Judge decision-making; furthermore, appeals are heard by single Immigration Judges rather than by panels.

As credibility involves a personal assessment of the story advanced by the appellant, judges need to exercise sound judgment, but given the lack of firm, hard evidence and the cultural distances separating appellants and judges, the risk is their own presuppositions will influence their fact-finding. It is precisely because of such features that it has been argued that asylum adjudication requires a very particular conception of impartiality: that of abstention from pre-ordained or conditioned reactions to what one is being told; it means not so much knowing others as knowing oneself—perhaps the hardest form of knowledge for anyone to acquire.[111] In other words, assessing credibility requires that decision-makers not only examine the stories that appellants present, but that they also engage in much self-examination in order to interrogate the degree to which their own value

---

[110] Sir Nicholas Blake, President of UTIAC, 'The Arrival of the Upper Tribunal Immigration and Asylum Chamber' (Tribunals Service, 11 February 2010) 2.

[111] S Sedley, *Asylum: Can the Judiciary Maintain its Independence?* (a paper presented at the International Association of Refugee Law Judges World Conference, Wellington, New Zealand, April 2002).

judgments and life experiences influence their decisions.[112] There are, of course, other improvements that would assist in the assessment of credibility: enhanced selection and training for decision-makers; better quality expert reports, and more in-depth knowledge and awareness of life in other countries. But the fundamental challenges presented by assessing credibility—the limited and uncertain evidence available, the lack of any clear standards for evaluating it, and the impossibility of knowing what an accurate decision would look like—are permanent, rather than transient, problems.

---

[112] A Macklin, 'Truth and Consequences: Credibility Determination in the Refugee Context' in *The Realities of Refugee Determination on the Eve of a New Millennium: The Role of the Judiciary* (1998 Conference of the International Association of Refugee Law Judges); J Millbank ' "The Ring of Truth": A Case Study of Credibility Assessment in Particular Social Group Refugee Determinations' (2009) *International Journal of Refugee Law* 1, 29–31.

6

Country Information

CREDIBILITY MAY BE the most important determinant of asylum cases, but it is not everything. The other component of the asylum decision problem concerns the conditions in the country from which asylum is being sought. If an individual has demonstrated that his subjective fear of persecution or serious ill-treatment is credible, it must then be assessed whether that fear is objectively well-founded by reference to the conditions in the relevant country. Such conditions are commonly ascertained by reference to country information, that is, any information concerning the situation in a country generating asylum claims, in particular the prevailing political and social conditions and the country's human rights situation.[1] Country information will be used to determine the application of the legal concepts of asylum law, for example, by determining whether there is a sufficiency of protection in the country concerned or whether it would be unduly harsh for an individual at risk to relocate internally elsewhere. By itself, country information will rarely be determinative of individual cases, but it will be of crucial significance in assessing future risk.

Consider the following country issues frequently raised in asylum appeals. Will a supporter of an opposition political party in Cameroon be at risk on return? Will an Iranian Christian convert be at risk on return? What treatment would a member of the Iraqi police force receive on return? Can a Pakistani national who is a follower of the Ahmadi faith at risk in part of Pakistan find safety elsewhere in the same country? What kind of medical treatment could someone with HIV/AIDS expect to receive on return to a country in sub-Saharan Africa? In the context of a quickly changing political situation, will a former member of the Liberation Tigers of Tamil Eelam from Sri Lanka be at risk? Not only do the country issues proliferate; they constantly change. To make such assessments, judges therefore need reliable and up to date current information concerning these, and many other issues, in the countries. This chapter examines the sources of country information regularly relied upon and their treatment by the Tribunal.

---

[1] *KA v Secretary of State for the Home Department (draft-related risk categories updated) Eritrea CG* [2005] UKAIT 00165 [11]. See also Refugee Qualifications Directive, art 4(3)(a); Immigration Rule (1994 HC 395) r 339J(i).

The Problem of Country Information

The requirement for decision-makers to assess country information is a distinguishing characteristic of asylum adjudication. Each asylum case is fact-specific insofar as it concerns the individual appellant's situation; at the same time, each case is concerned, at least in part, with the situation prevailing in the particular country from which refuge is being sought. It is not for the Tribunal to pass judgment on conditions in the relevant country of origin or its human rights record.[2] Nevertheless, it must assess whether conditions in a particular country mean that an individual would be at risk if returned.[3] In the context of making assessments, the Tribunal sometimes makes general findings upon country conditions which, if designated as country guidance, will have broader significance in other appeals. Good quality country information is required if accuracy is to prosper. In this context, quality means both reliable and current.[4] Only by having reliable country information, can judges make sound judgments on country conditions. Furthermore, as country conditions are mutable and the assessment is one of future risk, the information should be current rather than historical.

These criteria may seem clear-cut, but real difficulties can arise when applying them in practice. Like credibility, the handling and evaluation of country information is often beset by a number of challenges. One such challenge is that there is no independent field of study that defines or delimits which data is entitled to be classified as country information; it is only through its use in the asylum decision process that something will become country information.[5] Moreover, merely because something has been designated as country information does not, of course, mean it should be accepted without question. The evidence presented before the judge will obviously be conditioned by the contest between the parties. Appellants will adduce information which present country conditions in a negative light; conversely, the Home Office will seek to present country conditions in the most positive light. Nonetheless, it is a widespread practice within the jurisdiction amongst representatives and Immigration Judges to refer to background country evidence as 'objective country evidence' in the sense that such information can simply be accepted as establishing objective facts concerning the country in question. But this obscures more than it illuminates because before accepting such evidence, the decision-maker needs to scrutinise it to establish whether or not it meets the standards required of country information. In other words, whether

---

[2] United Nations High Commissioner for Refugees (UNHCR), *Handbook on Determining Refugee Status* (Geneva, UNHCR, 1992) [42].

[3] Country information will also be needed in relation to decisions made under the Refugee Convention 1951, art 1C(5) to revoke refugee status on the basis that country conditions which generated the risk on return no longer exist.

[4] Immigration Rules (1994 HC 395) r 339JA; UNHCR, *Country of Origin Information: Towards Enhanced International Cooperation* (Geneva, UNHCR, 2004) 3.

[5] J Pettit, 'The Problem with Country of Origin Information (COI) in Refugee Status Determination' (2007) 13(1) *Immigration Law Digest* 13.

country information establishes objective facts is a matter of evaluation.[6] At the same time, judges themselves are not appointed because of their knowledge of country conditions and cannot be expected to possess much knowledge of country conditions other than what can be gleaned from the country information placed before them. Unlike its counterparts elsewhere, the Tribunal does not have its own research unit to compile and produce country information.[7]

A second difficulty concerns the currency of country information. By its nature, country information, even if recently published, will deal with past events and can be quickly overtaken. Country conditions can change—for better or worse—sometimes on a daily basis. The risk is that country information may age quickly and become retrospective rather than forward-looking in nature.[8] At the same time, there must be some cut-off point—otherwise, the decision process could simply become a never-ending series of decisions and challenges on the basis of ever-changing country information. Judges hearing first-instance appeals are not limited merely to a review of the information before the initial decision-maker, but can take into account fresh evidence. However, the limitation of onward challenges to error of law grounds means that fresh country information alone cannot furnish a ground for further challenge.[9]

In any event, all providers of country information operate under time and resource constraints, which in turn can limit the degree to which they are able to collect and produce comprehensive country information. Country information is only as good as what actual observers on the ground in the particular country are able to produce. However, few providers of country information are able always to present primary country information; instead, they may often rely upon secondary sources. This is known as 'round-tripping' in which secondary sources of country information begin to rely upon and cite each other in support of particular country conditions prompting inquiry into the original source of the information concerned.[10] The risk is that the validity of country information comes to rely not upon its veracity, but upon the reputation of the organisations producing it.

Another issue concerns the purpose(s) for which country information is compiled and the risks of organisational bias. A frequently voiced concern has been that the Home Office's country reports are selective and their compilation motivated by a desire to secure negative decisions. Likewise, other producers of country information, such as Amnesty International and Human Rights Watch, pursue a broader campaigning role. It may be over-simplistic simply to assume a

---

[6] *TK v Secretary of State for the Home Department (Tamils—LP updated) Sri Lanka CG* [2009] UKAIT 00049 [7].

[7] Some asylum decision-makers, such as the Canadian Immigration and Refugee Board, have their own country of origin information units which respond to focused queries or requests for information from decision-makers. See Canadian Immigration and Refugee Board (IRB) http://www.irb-cisr.gc.ca/eng/pages/index.aspx

[8] UNCHR above n 4 at 6.

[9] *CA v Secretary of State for the Home Department* [2004] EWCA Civ 1165; [2004] Imm AR 640 (CA).

[10] B Morgan, V Gelsthorpe, H Crawley, and GA Jones, *Country of Origin Information: A User and Content Evaluation* (London, Home Office Research Study 271, 2003) 14–15.

direct causal link here, but there can be a tension between the purposes for which country information is collected and its content and interpretation.

Putting these concerns to one side, there is a wider difficulty with country information: can there ever be a value-free assessment of country conditions? From one perspective, country information is objective in the sense that it merely comprises facts concerning the political and social conditions in the countries that generate asylum claimants. But from another perspective, the collection, selection, and presentation of country information can never be wholly objective because these tasks themselves inevitably involve value-judgments—conscious or otherwise—by those producing the country information concerned. Given the different purposes for which organisations produce country information, it is probably an illusion to think there can be such a thing as a single objective assessment of the situation in a country which all the parties to an asylum appeal can agree upon.

There are also difficulties arising from different sources of country information which give different impressions as to the nature of country conditions. As Laws LJ has noted, it often happens that 'the in-country evidence does not speak with an entirely single voice, and certainly does not provide an entirely unequivocal picture of the risk of future events'.[11] Different sources of country information may present different accounts of country conditions. Assessing which accounts are reasonably likely to be true may often come down to intuitive evaluation, the language used, and the reputation of the provider. Finally, different decision-makers may draw different inferences from the same country information.[12] As one judge has observed, interpreting passages from a country information report can be like 'reading the runes'; there is inevitably a substantial role for the decision-maker's own evaluative assessment when interpreting country information.[13]

So, how do judges approach and evaluate country information? In general, it is for the parties to present the country information that they seek to rely upon and for judges to assess its weight by scrutinising its independence, objectivity, and reliability, and by comparing different pieces of such evidence. According to the Tribunal:

> In all cases, we have to distil the facts from the various reports and documents. Bodies responsible for producing reports may have their own agenda and sources are not always reliable: people will sometimes believe what they want to believe and, aware of that, those with axes to grind may feed willing recipients. Many reports do their best to be objective. Often and inevitably they will recount what is said to have happened to individuals. They will select the incidents they wish to highlight. Such incidents may be wholly accurately reported, but not always. This means that there will almost always be differences of emphasis in various reports and sometimes contradictions. It is always helpful to know what sources have been used, but that may be impossible since, for obvious reasons,

---

[11] *MH (Iraq) v Secretary of State for the Home Department* [2007] EWCA Civ 852 [17] (Laws LJ).

[12] *BD v Secretary of State for the Home Department (Application of SK and DK) Croatia CG* [2004] UKIAT 00032 [49] and [56].

[13] T Talbot, 'Credibility and Risk: One Adjudicator's View' (2004) 10(2) *Immigration Law Digest* 29, 30.

sources are frequently anxious not to be identified. We are well aware of the criticisms that can be and have been levelled at some reports and are able to evaluate all the material which is put before us in this way.[14]

Elsewhere, the International Association of Refugee Law Judges, has worked out a detailed checklist for assessing country information.[15] These criteria are: the relevance of the information; whether it adequately covers the particular issue raised; its currency; its sourcing; whether it is based on publicly available and accessible sources; the soundness of the methodology employed; its impartiality and independence; whether it is balanced and not overly selective; and whether it has received judicial scrutiny elsewhere. The European Court of Human Rights has identified similar criteria for evaluating country information, which can be summarised as: accuracy; independence; reliability; objectivity; reputation; adequacy of methodology; consistency; and corroboration.[16] In general, judges should approach country information with an open and enquiring mind as to the appropriate weight to be placed upon it.[17]

Sources of Country Information

The value of country information will vary in each case, but there are different types of country information which can be segmented as follows: governmentally-produced sources (eg Home Office country reports); country information from international organisations (eg the UNHCR); non-governmental sources (eg Amnesty International and Human Rights Watch); media news stories; and country expert reports.[18] Furthermore, although they are not a direct source of country information, the Tribunal's country guidance decisions perform a major role in the adjudication process. Looking to the future, one task of the proposed European Asylum Support Office will, if established, be to organise, promote, and coordinate activities relating to country information.[19]

Different considerations apply when handling different kinds of country information. Take, for instance, the Home Office's country reports, which it produces

---

[14] *Secretary of State for the Home Department v S* (01TH00632), date notified 1 May 2001 [19] (IAT).

[15] International Association of Refugee Law Judges (IARLJ): Country of Origin Information—Country Guidance Working Party, 'Judicial Criteria for Assessing Country of Origin Information (COI): A Checklist' (2009) 21 *International Journal of Refugee Law* 149.

[16] *NA v United Kingdom* (2009) 48 EHRR 15 (ECtHR) [118]–[122]; *TK* above n 6 at [5].

[17] *LP v Secretary of State for the Home Department (LTTE area—Tamils—Colombo—risk?) Sri Lanka CG* [2007] UKAIT 00076 [45].

[18] There are a number of internet resources providing access to country information. For instance, the UNHCR's Refworld website provides 'a knowledge resource which facilitates quality, evidence-based and effective decision making in refugee status determination procedures' www.unhcr.org/cgi-bin/texis/vtx/refworld/rwmain. See also European Country of Information Network www.ecoi.net/ and the Electronic Immigration Network www.ein.org.uk.

[19] European Commission, *Proposal for a Regulation Establishing a European Asylum Support Office*, COM (2009) 66.

biannually on the top 20 asylum countries.[20] These reports figure prominently; in virtually every case, the Home Office will present its relevant country report each of which contains general background information about the issues most commonly raised in asylum claims from the particular country. The reports are compiled wholly from material from other sources and provide a convenient method of accessing a wide range of sources. The reports are intended to provide a précis of the main issues, not a comprehensive survey.

The Home Office's intention is that these reports provide accurate, objective, up to date, and sourced country information. However, the independence and quality of the reports have often been questioned. In 2004, the House of Lords EU Committee noted that while an improved asylum process should 'ensure that authoritative and credible country of origin information is available', the Home Office's country reports were not generally accepted to be 'authoritative, credible and free from political or policy bias'.[21] A second criticism has concerned the quality of such reports; it has been argued that the country information presented has been partial, inaccurate, or misleading.[22] Another concern has been that such reports have often been described as 'objective evidence' by those involved in the decision process, including the Tribunal, thereby conferring upon them the perception of being objective. However, as the reports are prepared by the Home Office, one of the parties to the appellate process, they cannot, therefore, be taken at face value.[23]

Criticisms of Home Office country reports have often been accompanied by the suggestion that the function of producing country reports be handed over to an independent documentation centre, but the Home Office has consistently refused

---

[20] These reports were initially prepared by the Home Office's Country of Information Policy Unit (CIPU) which provided case-workers with country of origin information and also developed policy on country specific issues. However, in 2004, in response to concerns over the location of this unit within the Home Office, responsibility for producing country reports was transferred to the Country of Origin Information Service (COIS), which is located within the Home Office's Research, Development and Statistics Service, which is solely concerned with providing research and statistics and not concerned with policy and operational matters. See Hansard HC vol 424 col 119WS (8 September 2004).

[21] House of Lords European Union Committee, *Handling EU Asylum Claims: New Approaches Examined* (2003–04 HL 74) [104] and [115]. Likewise, the independence of US State Department reports, occasionally relied upon in asylum appeals, has been questioned on the ground that 'there is always an element of suspicion that such reports are influenced by political expediency based on US foreign policy with reference to the situation in the country concerned and that they serve a political agenda' *Said v Netherlands* (2006) 43 EHRR 248, 262 (Judge Loucaides). See also *Gramatikov v Immigration and Nationality Service*, 128 F.3d 619, 620 (7th Circuit 1997): 'there is a perennial concern that the [State] Department softpedals human rights violations by countries which the United States wants to have good relations with'. See also LM Pirouet, 'Materials Used in Making Asylum Decisions in the UK' (2003) 93 *African Research & Documentation* 29, 32.

[22] See N Carver (ed), *Home Office Country Assessments: An Analysis* (London, Immigration Advisory Service, 2003). According to a recognised country expert on Zimbabwe, T Ranger, 'The Narratives and Counter-narratives of Zimbabwean Asylum: Female Voices' (2005) 26 *Third World Quarterly* 405, 410, the Home Office's 2001 country reports on Zimbabwe 'were grossly inadequate . . . Under criticism, however, the . . . reports on Zimbabwe have improved a great deal'. A subsequent review, N Carver (ed), *Overview of the 2004 Reports* (London, Immigration Advisory Service, 2004), found that a majority of Home Office reports had improved but that problems nevertheless remained.

[23] C Yeo, 'Country Information, the Courts, and the Truth' (2005) 11 *Immigration Law Digest* 26.

to entertain the idea; its concern perhaps being that ceding control over the provision of country information to an independent body would also involve, to some extent, handing over control of asylum policy and its administration. However, the Home Office did agree to the creation of the Advisory Panel on Country Information (APCI) to 'consider and make recommendations to the Secretary of State about the content' of the reports.[24] The APCI's detailed reviews of the reports have identified areas for improving the reports—for example in the sources used and in the level of analysis contained. On the whole, the Panel's recommendations have been accepted and incorporated in the report production process and it has been recognised to provide an independent quality control mechanism of the reports. According to a senior judge, who is also a member of the APCI, the trend has been away from partisan or policy-based information and toward more objective and accurate country information; the work of the Panel has been a major contributor to this trend.[25] Equally, the Panel's work has demonstrated some of its limitations: it can only review country information after it has been produced and has no prior input; furthermore, it can only make recommendations.

What is the Tribunal's general approach toward the Home Office's country reports? From its perspective, irrespective of the criticism they have received, the reports provide the basis through which the Home Office discharges its shared duty to cooperate with appellants.[26] As the reports emanate from one party to the process, they cannot be considered to be independent evidence. Nevertheless, the reports are generally considered by the Tribunal to 'present a cross-section of reasonably reliable information on the country in question, rather than . . . put forward a Home Office view as such'.[27] Consequently, they deserve to be taken seriously, but they also need to be considered in light of their reputation, bearing in mind that they have been criticised.[28] The Tribunal cannot itself assess the veracity of the sources used in the reports, but an appellant may always take issue with a report by presenting other country information.

[24] Nationality, Immigration and Asylum Act 2002 s 142(3). See also Advisory Panel on Country Information, *Terms of Reference* (APCI, 2005), taken from the APCI website www.apci.org.uk. This independent monitoring function was transferred to the Independent Chief Inspector of the United Kingdom Border Agency under the UK Borders Act 2007 s 48(2)(j) and, in 2009, the new Independent Advisory Group on Country Information was established. See www.ociukba.homeoffice.gov.uk/ and Independent Chief Inspector of the UK Border Agency, *Report July 2008—September 2009* (London, OCIUKBA, 2009) 20–21 and *First Annual Report of the Independent Advisory Group on Country Information* (IAGCI) (London, OCIUKBA, 2010). For an assessment of the APCI, see S Huber, J Pettitt, and E Williams, *The APCI Legacy: A Critical Assessment: Monitoring Home Office Country of Origin Information Products* (London, IAS, 2010).

[25] A Jordan, 'Country Information: The United Kingdom and the Search for Objectivity' (a paper presented at the IARLJ conference, Budapest, November 2005).

[26] *RK v Secretary of State for the Home Department (Obligation to investigate) Democratic Republic of Congo* [2004] UKIAT 00129 [46] and [49].

[27] *Dorodian v Secretary of State for the Home Department* (01TH01537) date notified 23 August 2001 [7] (IAT). See also *Devaseelan v Secretary of State for the Home Department (Second Appeals—ECHR—Extra-Territorial Effect) Sri Lanka* (Starred determination) [2002] UKIAT 000702; [2003] Imm AR 1 (IAT) 26; *AW v Secretary of State for the Home Department (Article 3—risk—general situation) Somalia* [2003] UKIAT 00111 [25].

[28] *LP* above n 17 at [43].

The main Home Office country reports are supplemented by its Operational Guidance Notes (OGNs), which provide guidance to case-workers on whether the main types of claim are likely to justify the grant of asylum or other status. Their function is to supplement the main country reports to ensure consistency of approach and in that way to bridge the gap between country information and protection policies to ensure their consistent application in individual cases. As a statement of Home Office's policy as to the risk facing appellants, OGNs must be read together with the main reports and recent information.[29] So, when an OGN stated that Sudanese prison conditions were likely to breach Article 3 ECHR, the Tribunal held that it would expect the Home Office to concede such appeals where it was accepted that the appellant had demonstrated a real risk.[30]

By contrast, consider the handling of country information produced by NGOs. Such reports are often produced to highlight human rights violations in a particular country as a part of the particular NGO's broader campaigning role, but they can be relied upon in asylum appeals. As with all sources of country information, the critical issue is how much weight can be placed on such reports. In this respect, it is possible to identify a slight difference of emphasis between the Tribunal and the higher courts concerning reports from NGOs. For instance, the Court of Appeal has noted that Amnesty International 'is recognised as a responsible, important and well-informed body'; consequently, its reports deserve due consideration.[31] However, the Tribunal has, at times, been more circumspect noting that such material can be selective and that the weight to be placed upon it depends on the reputation of the source; 'judges are aware that much of the background evidence adduced before them comes from sources with a special interest or a specific agenda'.[32] The purposes for which such reports are produced must then be borne in mind when assessing the weight to be placed upon them. However, reports by NGOs will be properly considered by the Tribunal even if they have been prepared specifically for the purpose of being relied upon in asylum appeals.[33]

Other types of country evidence raise their own particular considerations. For instance, as the guardian of the Refugee Convention, the UNHCR plays a humanitarian role in areas of deprivation and conflict and frequently publishes position papers on the treatment of asylum seekers in their countries of origin and the

---

[29] *FS v Secretary of State for the Home Department (domestic violence, SN and HM, OGN) Pakistan CG* [2006] UKAIT 00023.

[30] *MA v Secretary of State for the Home Department (Operational Guidance—prison conditions—significance) Sudan* [2005] UKAIT 00149.

[31] *R v Immigration Appeal Tribunal, ex parte K* [1999] EWCA Civ 2066 (Buxton LJ). In *SA (Syria) and IA (Syria) v Secretary of State for the Home Department* [2007] EWCA Civ 1390 [22] (Toulson LJ), the Tribunal was criticised for failing properly to engage with country information from Amnesty International.

[32] *LP* above n 17 at [44].

[33] For instance, in 2007 the Tribunal accepted a report prepared by the Parliamentary Human Rights Group compiled specifically to challenge previous country guidance. See *IA and Others v Secretary of State for the Home Department (Ahmadis: Rabwah) Pakistan CG* [2007] UKAIT 00088; *MJ and ZM v Secretary of State for the Home Department (Ahmadis—risk) Pakistan CG* [2008] UKAIT 00033.

enforcement of removals to a particular country. What weight ought to be accorded to such views if relied on in asylum appeals? On the one hand, a UNHCR position paper should be regarded as a responsible, well researched, and considered analysis if it is derived from UNHCR sources in the country concerned.[34] Nevertheless, care must be taken in assessing whether such information means that an individual is indeed a refugee in need of protection or whether the UNHCR considers that, for humanitarian reasons, the removal of failed asylum seekers to the particular country should not be enforced. For instance, the UNHCR has sought to discourage states from enforcing removals because of the over-stretched absorption capacity in a particular country. However, such considerations are irrelevant to the task of determining whether or not an individual qualifies for asylum.

Using Country Information

Country Information and Decision-Making

When assessing country issues judges have to address the country information before them. This will normally require an evaluation of competing sources of country information. In many instances, senior judges may have issued country guidance; that is, undertaken a detailed and more thorough assessment of the country information than an Immigration Judge is able to undertake.[35] But country guidance will often need to be supplemented by other sources of country information. Not all country issues have been the subject of country guidance and new issues arise as persecutory risks change.

It is axiomatic that when handling country information, judges must engage with it properly; a determination which simply notes that the judge has taken into account material country evidence is valueless as it does nothing at all to explain what is made of the country evidence.[36] For the most part, judges detail the country information relied upon in their determinations, especially those parts of it referred to by the parties. Country information is only relevant when determining an appeal insofar as it relates to the particular appellant. In most cases, judges will readily find the necessary country information from available sources and from relevant country guidance decisions. In those appeals in which judges have to assess competing sources of country information, they undertake that assessment by considering a range of different factors: the reliability of the sources of country

---

[34] *NM and Others v Secretary of State for the Home Department (Lone women—Ashraf) Somalia CG* [2005] UKIAT 00076 [108]–[115]; *GG v Secretary of State for the Home Department (political oppositionists) Ivory Coast CG* [2007] UKAIT 00086 [91].

[35] Country guidance was relevant in some 95 per cent of the appeals observed.

[36] *Secretary of State for the Home Department v T (Turkey)* [2003] UKIAT 00127 [5].

information; which of the parties' country information is more up to date; whether recent country information means that relevant country guidance is no longer applicable; and by comparing country information with other reputable sources.

While judges normally have relevant country information to hand, this is not always the case. It has been noted that 'it is remarkable how often judicial decision-makers find nothing in background country materials directly on the point about country conditions with which they have to grapple'.[37] The absence of country information might be taken to imply either that the appellant has been unable to discharge the burden of proof, even to the lower standard, that he or she is at risk on return. At the same time, the fact that the country information provides little assistance does not necessarily mean that the appellant will not be at risk on return. The fact that an event claimed to have occurred by an appellant is not detailed by the country information is not necessarily an indication that it did not happen, even when it is reasonable to expect such an event to be mentioned. Precisely how decision-makers handle this absence of relevant country information will depend largely on other factors in the particular case.

For instance, in one appeal, the country issue was whether or not it would be safe for a Pakistani woman with a young child, who might be regarded as illegitimate, to return to Pakistan.[38] Neither representative had identified any specific background information relating to the treatment of illegitimate children or the combination of a lone woman together with a perceived illegitimate child in Pakistan but had instead focused on the general position of women in Pakistan and the risk of honour killings. Having reviewed the evidence and the circumstances of the case, the panel concluded that in the absence of any material or direct evidence, there was no reason to indicate that the appellant would be at real risk on return. In another appeal, an appellant had claimed to be a member of a women's rights group in the Ivory Coast; however, there was no objective evidence as to the existence of this group (of course, that there was no evidence of the group's existence does not mean that it did not exist).[39]

Alternatively, the country information at hand may be found to give a misleading or incorrect impression of country conditions. To illustrate, in one appeal, a Cameroon appellant, a member of an opposition political party, the Southern Cameroons National Council (SCNC) who had been arrested and detained by the authorities, sought asylum on the basis of his political opinion.[40] According to Home Office and UNHCR country reports, while SCNC members had been harassed, followed, and occasionally beaten by the security forces, they had not been subject to widespread arrests, detentions, and torture. The UNHCR fact-finding mission had stated that it was unaware of any SCNC activists being detained. However, the Home Office report, which partially relied upon the

---

[37] IARLJ above n 15 at 154–155.
[38] Case 170.
[39] Case 61.
[40] Case 15.

UNHCR report, excluded any reference to this. Examining other country evidence, the judge concluded that SCNC members had indeed been imprisoned at the relevant time and that this country information lent considerable weight to the appellant's account.

By its very nature, country information is rarely fully adequate to the task, but judges have to proceed on the basis of what they are presented with. If the country information presented is less than adequate, then appeals can be determined on a very slender basis. In another appeal, a judge concluded that the appellants, who had been found to be at risk in one part of Afghanistan, could not reasonably be expected to relocate internally to Kabul as the 'general tenor of the UNHCR advice' suggested that this was not a viable option for Sikh Afghans.[41]

Judges and Country Information

What, then, do judges think of the country information presented to them? Immigration Judges are in an almost unique position: they have to assess risk on return, but without normally possessing much direct knowledge or experience of country conditions apart from what is contained in the country information adduced before them. The best way for anyone to acquire a thorough knowledge of country conditions would be to travel around the country concerned in order to experience life there. Obviously judges cannot do this in order to determine an individual appeal, though some do travel to particular countries producing asylum claimants to expand their general knowledge and awareness of country conditions.[42] Even if a judge has visited a country, he will still be largely reliant on country information presented at the appeal hearing. Nonetheless, the jurisdiction requires judges to acquire substantial knowledge of factual conditions in the countries of origin of appellants through sources of country information. Furthermore, the quantity of background material which has to be absorbed far exceeds that required in any other tribunal or court. These are the nature of the challenges.

In general terms, judges recognise the need to approach country information carefully and not to accept any source of country information uncritically. As one noted, 'every source of country information has a slant on it—the important question is: how do you weigh it up?'[43] Another view was that it is difficult for the judges themselves to assess whether the country information presented is correct:

> There is no real way of knowing how accurate the country information presented to us is. It is taken largely on trust because one of the things about the various country reports—the Home Office, the US State Department, Human Rights Watch reports and so on—is that there tends to be a circularity built into them. Each report quotes from the others and you sort of wonder: 'well, actually, where is the primary source of evidence?'[44]

---

[41] Cases 155 and 156.
[42] Some of the judges interviewed had travelled to countries producing asylum applicants. See also B Glossop, 'Immigration Judges' Visit to Ethiopia' (2008) 14(4) *Immigration Law Digest* 38.
[43] Immigration Judge interview 15.
[44] Immigration Judge interview 3.

Other judges highlighted the generic nature of country information, the speed with which country conditions can change, and the overall perception of the quality of country information:

> I usually tend to view the Home Office country reports as a kind of starting point. You have always got them and, on the whole, when you then look through other country reports, they are all broadly saying the same thing, all broadly quoting from each other. But, the country reports tend to be written in a rather broad brush way. You can only get a sort of background flavour of country conditions from these reports as opposed to the confirmation of specific events.[45]

> If you look at places like Darfur where the situation is constantly changing you are left having to make a decision on the basis of background material which does not appear to correspond at all with reality because of what you read in the newspapers and see on television screens. The reports of journalists seem to be light years away from the official stance taken by the various NGOs.[46]

> I am always frustrated that in the world in which we are living in, with the technology that we have at our disposal, that we are still not getting the standard of objective evidence materials that we should. And then we get all these expert evidence reports and I sometimes think 'who are these experts? They are only individuals having a particular opinion'. You know, what weight do you give to it? And quite a lot of the time you end up thinking, 'how biased is this person?' And it is just the same when we get the Home Office country reports.[47]

Over the years from 2002 to 2005, the quality of country information and, in particular Home Office reports, had been a major issue of concern for many of those involved in the appeals process, some judges included. The prevalent view had been that, during this period, the Home Office reports had been selective, not prepared to a uniformly high standard, and had occasionally given a misleading impression of country conditions. During the period in which the research was conducted, the consensus view was that the overall quality of country reports had improved:

> On the whole, I am reasonably trustful of the Home Office country reports. I do not really think that I have ever come across anything which I thought was blatantly inaccurate. How useful are they? The reports tend to focus on the kinds of questions to which we need answers. They have sections which tend to deal with issues arising to particular groups of people in particular countries. Generally speaking, they are useful.[48]

> There is plenty in the Home Office's reports that is useful for reference, background, and so on. The problem is if they are the only source of country evidence relied upon because they tend to be selective and there is a limited amount of resources the Home Office puts into them. They need to be supplemented by other country evidence for the appellant as well. Whether or not that happens comes back to the question whether the appellant has a decent representative. There are some representatives who do not undertake

45 Immigration Judge interview 7.
46 Immigration Judge interview 14.
47 Immigration Judge interview 11.
48 Immigration Judge interview 3.

country evidence research, but just rely on the Home Office's report, which is not normally sufficient.[49]

The Home Office reports have improved over the years. I can remember a time when I would not rely on them. You would look at these reports and it would quote something that the US reports had said. Then you look at the US report and then you see the other three sentences in that quote that were not quoted in the Home Office report. It was very one-sided, it really was. I would almost invariably never just rely on the Home Office report. The general situation has now improved, but I still like to see reports from the US State Department, Amnesty International, and Human Rights Watch—they all come from different political backgrounds, so you get a better picture.[50]

Finally, there are judges' views concerning other sources of country information produced. In this respect, the authority of such information may depend on the reputation of the particular NGO, its aims and objectives, and the standards adopted in the production of reports. In this respect, a number of judges drew a clear distinction between those NGOs with an international or global presence (eg Amnesty International) and those with a country specific focus. The concerns with the latter category are the degree to which such organisations may have a particular political agenda and the unknown rigour of their standards for assessing the country information.

Amnesty International has a vested interest in getting it right—their credibility is going to be shot pretty quickly if they start regurgitating reports that are inaccurate. They might make mistakes, but so does the US State Department. We have to be vaguely aware of that and bear that in mind. That Amnesty International has its own angle does not mean that its reports are anything other than honest.[51]

I tend to view reports by some NGOs with an increasing level of suspicion, particularly according to how partisan they look. But it is very difficult to know. These days—when things are just drawn off the internet—it is very difficult sometimes to know what kind of organisation has produced a report and also what kind of reputation it has or the standards that it adopts. You just have to do the best you can to try to form a view, but there are no real standards to go by.[52]

People do not always understand that Amnesty International writes its reports from one perspective, which is that of a wonderful campaigning organisation. The UNHCR has to work in these countries and there is a limit on how much they can upset the government. Human Rights Watch write from a slightly different perspective and so it goes on. So, although none of these organisations are deliberately lying, the way in which they express themselves inevitably means that you are going to find a difference of views about the same country conditions.[53]

---

[49] Immigration Judge interview 6.
[50] Immigration Judge interview 15.
[51] Immigration Judge interview 13.
[52] Immigration Judge interview 3.
[53] Immigration Judge interview 14.

Country Information and the Appeals Process

Country Information Research by Judges

The adversarial nature of the appeals process presupposes that the responsibility for collecting and presenting country information rests principally, if not wholly, with the parties. One issue that arises is the degree to which judges themselves should be able to seek out country information of their own initiative. Should judges undertake 'own-initiative' searches for country information? To what extent do they?

Given the short timescales and variable quality of representation, judges may be concerned that they have not been presented with comprehensive country information or may be aware that other sources of country information exist to which neither of the parties have referred. Some may be inclined occasionally to search for information after the hearing, typically through internet searches or by consulting country information in hearing centre libraries. Some degree of investigation on the behalf of the decision-maker in relation to acquiring country information can be found in other asylum decision-making systems elsewhere. For instance, some decision-makers, such as the Canadian Immigration and Refugee Board, may, unlike the UK Tribunal, have their own country of origin information units which respond to focused queries or requests for information from decision-makers.[54] Other systems may combine both approaches by informing the parties of country information within the decision-maker's knowledge and asking to consider it.

The motivation for undertaking such investigations is the need to ensure decisional accuracy, but, important as it is, accuracy is not the only relevant consideration here. Another relevant value is the timeliness of decision-making. In general terms, the search for additional information on which to base decisions is greatly affected by associated time pressures; the greater the incentive to reach decisions quickly, then the greater the disincentive to devote time searching for additional information.[55]

There is also the need for fairness to the parties. A judge must base his decision only upon the evidence that has been made available to the parties as a party will be unable to counter evidential material which it never knew would form the basis of a decision and it would be unfair to rely upon evidence which neither party has had the opportunity to test.[56] Also, decisions made on the basis of untested

---

[54] See Canadian Immigration and Refugee Board (IRB), http://www.irb-cisr.gc.ca/eng/pages/index. aspx
[55] A Downs, *Inside Bureaucracy* (Boston, Little Brown, 1967) 183.
[56] *AA (No 1) v Secretary of State for the Home Department (Involuntary returns to Zimbabwe) Zimbabwe CG* [2005] UKAIT 00144 [28]–[30]. See also Asylum and Immigration Tribunal (Procedure) Rules SI 2005/230 r 51(7); *KC v Secretary of State for the Home Department (Adjudicator wrongly obtaining post-hearing evidence) Turkey* [2005] UKIAT 00010 [10]–[12]. If the Tribunal does

evidence may be incorrect and may undermine the integrity of the process. Therefore, to allow such evidence to be scrutinised, the parties must be given the opportunity to test it. This will normally require the judge to put the parties on notice as to the information concerned and to re-convene the hearing. Of course, this will prolong the adjudication process.

The issue of own-initiative research, therefore, raises a familiar adjudicative dilemma. Should a judge undertake the search for additional evidence in order to improve the factual basis for decision-making? Or, alternatively, should they not undertake such searches and not therefore jeopardise performance targets by extending the length of the appeals process and pushing back the hearing of other appeals? The Tribunal has recognised that some circumstances, such as fast-track and unrepresented appeals, may justify, though not necessarily compel, the judge to undertake own-initiative searches for country information.[57] But the not-so-subtle message is that judges should not normally undertake this course of action as the consequent need to be fair to the parties by re-convening hearings will impose time costs.[58] Judges may also acquire the feeling that undertaking own-initiative research somehow compromises their position of neutrality. Without a clearer shift to a more inquisitorial culture in the jurisdiction, judges may sense that they are acting in a detrimental way to one party, because the information collected advances the case of the other party.

There are other reasons for the Tribunal's caution. If judges did adopt a general practice of seeking to supplement the country information presented by the parties with information they had themselves acquired, then how might representatives modify their behaviour in response? Given the problems created by the unwillingness of some representatives to engage fully with the appeals process and the high rate of onward challenge, the obvious concern is that some representatives might withdraw further from their responsibilities to represent their clients and to assist the Tribunal. Related concerns are that a practice of own-initiative searches by judges could, in effect, shift the burden of proof from appellants to the Tribunal and generate numerous challenges against adverse decisions on the ground that the judge had failed to perform his duty of anxious scrutiny because the search for additional information had not been sufficiently thorough.

---

take the initiative, then a reasonable amount of time must be given to enable the parties to examine the relevant information; so when the IAT once gave a representative 10 minutes before the hearing to read through a voluminous bundle of country information, this was procedurally unfair. See *Macharia v Secretary of State for the Home Department* [1999] EWCA Civ 3001. See generally JA Smillie, 'The Problem of "Official Notice": Reliance by Administrative Tribunals on the Personal Knowledge of Their Members' [1975] *Public Law* 64.

[57] Ibid, *AA (No 1)* at [25].

[58] See *EG v Entry Clearance Officer, Lagos (post-hearing internet research) Nigeria* [2008] UKAIT 000015 [5]: 'It is . . . most unwise for a judge to conduct post-hearing research, on the internet or otherwise, into the factual issues which have to be decided in a case . . . this determination gives absolutely no encouragement to such a process . . . [but] . . . where an immigration judge considers the research may or will affect the decision to be reached, then it will be the judge's duty to reconvene the hearing and supply copies to the parties, in order that the parties can be invited to make such submissions as they might have on it'.

In practice, the decision whether or not to undertake such searches is highly dependant upon the predilections of individual judges. On the whole, most judges are reluctant to undertake such searches. However, when judges do search out country information, then it can, on occasion, make a real difference to appeal outcomes. For instance, in one appeal, the judge had, after the hearing 'discovered a very helpful piece of research on the internet relating to blood feuds in the Yemen and therefore had the hearing re-listed for further submissions/evidence on that specific point'.[59] Placing great weight upon the research, which was 'in line with the other objective evidence produced on blood feuds in the Yemen, albeit far more detailed', the judge allowed the appeal, an outcome which would otherwise have been unlikely.

Country Specialisation by Judges

A related issue is whether judges should specialise in hearing appeals from particular countries or regions. Given the range of different countries generating asylum appellants, it may be difficult for judges to attain an up to date and reliable knowledge of all countries from which individuals seek refuge. By contrast, country specialisation may enable individual judges to build up an expertise in particular countries. Country specialist judges may also be in a better position from which to assess country information and to discern which sources of such information are reliable and which are not.

There are, though, countervailing arguments. While complicating organisational factors are not insuperable, they nevertheless present difficulties, especially given the proportion of judges who are part-time. Organising a timely appeals process so that appeals from certain countries are only heard by certain judges would create particular administrative challenges. Furthermore, country specialisation at the hearing centre level always runs the risk of promoting a more consistent approach at the individual hearing centre while increasing inconsistency between different centres. Another concern is that allocating appeals from a limited number of countries to the same judge always runs the risk of inducing a 'case-hardened' approach. In any event, any need for country specialisation has now largely been overtaken by the production of country guidance by senior judges.

Country Expert Evidence

Country information can often be accompanied by country expert evidence. Such evidence is presented by a particular individual who claims to possess an expertise in the country concerned. A country expert is typically an academic or other

---

[59] Case 186.

expert who has taken a particular interest in a country generating asylum applications.[60] Given their specialist knowledge of the country concerned, country experts can assist by giving objective, unbiased opinion on matters within his or her expertise and evidence about country conditions in particular providing comprehensive and balanced factual information relating to the particular country issues that the Tribunal must resolve.[61] However, there is a degree of ambiguity and tension in the nature and function of country expert evidence; indeed, the assessment of such evidence is, along with many other aspects of this jurisdiction, often highly contentious.

The issue of how a judicial decision-maker should handle expert evidence raises a number of questions. How can a non-expert court make findings that require specialist knowledge? If expert evidence is adduced to assist the court, then how can the court assess that evidence? And how should legal procedures be organised so as to promote accurate decision-making and other adjudicatory goals? The broader issues arising out of the proper relationship between independent judicial processes and reliance upon expert witnesses is, of course, long-running and far from unique to asylum adjudication, but the problems generated tend to arise in this jurisdiction more frequently and acutely than elsewhere.[62]

There are two reasons why the nature of country expert evidence in asylum appeals is 'rather unusual'.[63] First, there is the ambiguous nature of country expertise itself. Secondly, there are problems arising from the procedural arrangements by which country expert evidence is presented before the Tribunal.

Assessing the standing of an expert witness is not necessarily always a problem. In ordinary litigation, expert witnesses are required to demonstrate that they possess the necessary specialist knowledge with which to give an opinion which can properly be described as expert. But in asylum appeals the normal rules of evidence do not apply; an expert is merely a witness giving factual, hearsay, or opinion evidence. Country experts are not required to demonstrate any qualification to be described as such; indeed, there is no formal qualification by which someone can be identified reliably as a country expert. As the Tribunal has noted, 'a real problem arises in this jurisdiction from the use of the word "expert"'.[64] Any individual, irrespective of their lack of relevant qualifications or experience, who wishes to pass themselves off as an expert may be tempted to seek to do so. At the same time,

---

[60] Individuals who act as country experts include: academics (from the disciplines of anthropology, geography, law, and sociology); journalists; and other individuals, such as independent researchers, who may have first-hand experience of the country concerned.

[61] *MA v Secretary of State for the Home Department (Draft evaders—illegal departures—risk) Eritrea CG* [2007] UKAIT 00059 [238]; Asylum and Immigration Tribunal, *Practice Directions* (2007) [8A.4].

[62] On expert evidence generally, see M Redmayne, *Expert Evidence and Criminal Justice* (Oxford, Oxford University Press, 2001); CAG Jones, *Expert Witnesses: Science, Medicine, and the Practice of Law* (Oxford, Clarendon Press, 1994); D Dwyer, *The Judicial Assessment of Expert Evidence* (Cambridge, Cambridge University Press, 2008).

[63] *Zarour v Secretary of State for the Home Department* (01TH00078), date notified 2 August 2001 (IAT) [29].

[64] *LP* above n 17 at [38].

the Tribunal needs to take account of the views of a reputable, experienced, and well-informed individual who can properly be described as an expert. In practice, the type of people who act as country experts in asylum appeals ranges very broadly. At one extreme, there are those individuals with particular expertise in the relevant country; at the other extreme, are those who could not reasonably be said to possess any such expertise.[65]

The issue for the Tribunal when handling country expert evidence is not its admissibility, but the weight to be attributed to it and it is this which creates difficulties. Immigration Judges are not country experts. Even the claim by senior judges doing country guidance casework that they possess their own level of expertise in country conditions is disputed by some country experts.[66] On the other hand, if judges routinely accepted expert evidence without question, then this would result in the de facto delegation of decision-making to country experts and an abdication of their own responsibility to produce an independent decision. A related problem is that of objectivity. Very often, individuals who have studied a particular country will have formed their own views about its political and social circumstances. It is difficult to suppose that anyone can maintain a neutral position on issues such as torture and asylum claimants tend to come from brutal regimes. Country experts can, then, often be perceived as being associated with a particular view on a country. Whether or not this means that they are not providing the Tribunal with objective evidence is often a contested issue. The issue of country evidence, therefore, implicates the relationship between judges and country experts and their contrasting perceptions of each others' respective expertise and the objectivity of such evidence.

The use of country expert evidence is also characterised by difficulties arising from the procedural arrangements by which it comes before the Tribunal. The normal situation is that the way in which expert evidence is presented before a court in the course of litigation should enable the court to ascertain its reliability and objectivity. In civil litigation, expert evidence can be provided either by way of competing expert reports or via a single jointly instructed expert report.[67] However, experts in asylum appeals are almost always instructed solely by appellants.[68] While the Home Office could instruct its own country experts, it rarely, if ever, does so, preferring instead to focus its case on undermining the appellant's expert. The Home Office's failure to instruct its own expert will not imbue the appellant's expert evidence with any greater value than it merits when considered

---

[65] The Immigration Law Practitioners' Association (ILPA) and the Electronic Immigration Network (EIN) together maintain an online directory of country experts.

[66] *MA* above n 61 at [239].

[67] CPR 35, 'Experts and Assessors'; Lord Woolf, *Access to Justice: Final Report* (London, HMSO, 1996). See generally S Burn, *Successful Use of Expert Witnesses in Civil Disputes* (Crayford, Shaw and Sons, 2005); L Blom-Cooper (ed), *Experts in the Civil Courts* (Oxford, Oxford University Press, 2006).

[68] As regards the funding of expert reports, the cost varies with the individual expert and can range from £200 to £2,000. Unrepresented appellants will be unlikely to have an expert report, unless they can fund their own representation. In most instances, expert reports are commissioned by representatives and funded from a disbursement from the Legal Services Commission.

alongside the rest of the country information presented.[69] Nevertheless, in the Tribunal's view, it would be desirable for the Home Office to adduce its own expert evidence. Given the duty of cooperation between the parties, concerns have been raised that the Home Office does so little to contribute to the presentation of expert evidence.

A further complication is that the Tribunal itself has neither the ability nor the resources with which to commission country expert evidence or to direct that such evidence be given by a single joint expert. A principal desideratum of expert evidence is that it be both objective and unbiased. However, as country experts are largely instructed by appellants, this sometimes, if not often, generates the suspicion amongst judges that experts are simply hired guns paid to produce reports that will help appellants to succeed, rather than to assist the Tribunal to determine who will or will not be at risk on return. After all, as experts are commissioned to write reports by appellants (or rather their representatives), there is the risk that experts may be placed under pressure by representatives to write reports favourable to appellants, that is, the assumption amongst representatives may be that a country expert is paid for producing a report favourable to their appellant's case. This, in turn, can generate a degree of wariness amongst Immigration Judges when handling expert reports as it raises the concern that they are unlikely ever to see an expert report which contains anything detrimental to an appellant's case. The upshot is that expert evidence commissioned by an appellant may be seen as partisan rather than independent evidence. The basic problem is that the procedural arrangements by which country expert evidence is placed before the Tribunal are not conducive to sustaining the perception that country expert evidence is both objective and unbiased.[70]

Another procedural difficulty is that, for reasons of both cost and time, country experts rarely attend appeal hearings before Immigration Judges. Expert evidence will normally take the form of a documentary report which will simply be presented before the Immigration Judge, though it is common practice for country experts to attend hearings in country guidance cases before Senior Immigration Judges. In other jurisdictions, it might be possible to do without attendance of experts in court by narrowing down the range of contested issues prior to the hearing. However, the short timescales of the asylum appeals system normally preclude this. Furthermore, it is not unknown for an expert's report prepared in relation to one appeal to be relied upon in other, similar appeals. The upshot is that a judge presented with a country expert report will not normally have much other evidence, such as a competing expert report, against which to test it; nor will the

---

[69] *HH & Others v Secretary of State for the Home Department (Mogadishu: armed conflict: risk) Somalia CG* [2008] UKAIT 00022 [281]; *SI v Secretary of State for the Home Department (expert evidence—Kurd—SM confirmed) Iraq CG* [2008] UKAIT 00094 [56].

[70] The problem is neither unique to asylum appeals nor to the UK. Precisely the same problem exists in the United States. See BJ Einhorn, 'Consistency, Credibility, and Culture' in J Ramji-Nogales, AI Schoenholtz and PG Schrag, (eds) *Refugee Roulette: Disparities in Asylum Adjudication and Proposals for Reform* (New York, New York University Press, 2009) 187, 196.

country expert normally be cross-examined. The judge will simply have to decide whether or not to accept the expert report.

Unsurprisingly, the focus of country expert evidence tends to vary depending on the nature of the particular country issue raised in an appeal. Some expert reports will deal only with general country conditions; other reports may focus upon far more specific subjects (for instance, the treatment of young Tanzanian women forced into marriage); and other reports may take issue with the Tribunal's country guidance. Country experts may also be commissioned to report on the circumstances of the individual appellant's case, by, for instance, advancing an opinion as to whether a claimed past event in the appellant's history could have happened. Other types of expert reports may provide an opinion as to whether or not the appellant is a member of their claimed clan or ethnicity. For instance, in Somali appeals, an important issue will often be the appellant's clan membership; members of minority clans will in general be at risk on return.[71]

The Tribunal, Country Expert Evidence and Country Expertise

The Tribunal's general approach toward country expert evidence is that while such reports are entitled to respect and due consideration, they are just another item of evidence to be weighed in the balance.[72] While an expert's report can assist, this does not mean that heavy reliance should necessarily be placed upon it. Whether such evidence is independent and reliable requires careful assessment in each case.[73] Experts are in a privileged position because they are able to give evidence relying on hearsay and opinions based on expertise drawing on such hearsay evidence as well as personal knowledge. As judges rarely receive a competing expert report or see experts cross-examined, it is important, from the Tribunal's position, to assess carefully country expert evidence to determine whether it is reliable or whether the expert is merely acting as the appellant's advocate. But while judges are not bound to accept experts' opinions, they must give adequate reasons for rejecting them.[74]

One particular concern on the Tribunal's behalf is the variable quality of experts. While some are highly respected, others range from the generally reasonable to the unacceptable. Nevertheless, 'all suffer from the difficulty that very rarely are they entirely objective in their approach and the sources relied on are frequently (and no doubt sometimes with good reason) unidentified. Many have fixed opinions about

---

[71] *NM* above n 34.

[72] *MA* above n 61 at [240].

[73] *AZ v Secretary of State for the Home Department (risk on return) Ivory Coast CG* [2004] UKIAT 00170 [49]. See also *Secretary of State for the Home Department v SK (Return—Ethnic Serb) Croatia CG* (Starred determination) [2002] UKIAT 05613 [5]; *GH v Secretary of State for the Home Department (Former KAZ—country conditions—effect) Iraq CG* [2004] UKIAT 00248; [2004] Imm AR 707, 726–727 (IAT); *MA* above n 61 at [235]–[241].

[74] *K v Secretary of State for the Home Department* [2006] Imm AR 161, 165 (CA); *CM (Kenya) v Secretary of State for the Home Department* [2007] EWCA Civ 312 [13] (Moses LJ); *FS v Secretary of State for the Home Department (Treatment of Expert Evidence) Somalia* [2009] UKAIT 0004.

the regime in a particular country and will be inclined to accept anything which is detrimental to that regime'.[75] Given the comparatively small number of individuals who act as country experts, judicial experience of individual country experts, and their reputations, is likely to be influential. Some experts may be accepted by the Tribunal as reliable and others as unreliable; some might have a long track record, whereas others might have fallen out of favour. Each expert must be assessed in respect of the report presented in the particular appeal and even a generally reliable expert must be judged in the context of his individual reports.[76]

There are a number of criteria against which the Tribunal evaluates the reliability of country expert evidence. First, country experts must possess sufficient expertise in the particular country concerned and that the expert's opinion is based on current and reliable knowledge relating to conditions in that country.[77] Secondly, expert reports should be independent, balanced, and objective.[78] The expert's obligation to assist the Tribunal on matters within his own expertise is paramount and overrides any obligation to the person from whom the expert has received instructions or by whom the expert is paid.[79] For instance, a report which approaches country conditions critically and recognises that they can change is more likely to be considered as reliable as opposed to a report which evinces a tendency to exaggerate or which contains tendentious language or sweeping generalisations in the absence of a sound empirical basis.[80] One point commonly made by country experts is that the Tribunal tends to engage in a far more thorough scrutiny of their specialist evidence when compared with Home Office country reports despite the facts that the latter reports are also produced by a party to the appeals process. However, from the Tribunal's perspective, the lack of expert reports advanced by the Home Office means that the equality of arms which should characterise adjudication does not always exist.

Thirdly, an expert's report must be sufficiently well-sourced so that the facts and opinions within them can be verified.[81] This criterion needs to be qualified in

---

[75] *Slimani v Secretary of State for the Home Department (Content of Adjudicator Determination) Algeria* (Starred determination) [2001] UKIAT 00009 [17].

[76] *LP* above n 17 at [42].

[77] *LP* above n 17 at [36]; *AA v Secretary of State for the Home Department (Expert evidence, assessment) Somalia* [2004] UKIAT 00221 [8]; Asylum and Immigration Tribunal, *Practice Directions* (2007) [8A.6].

[78] *LP* above n 17 at [37] and [42]; Asylum and Immigration Tribunal, *Practice Directions* (2007) [8A.4].

[79] Asylum and Immigration Tribunal, *Practice Directions* (2007) [8A.2].

[80] *BK v Secretary of State for the Home Department (Failed asylum seekers) Democratic Republic of Congo CG* [2008] UKAIT 00098 [251]–[252], [269]. Furthermore, the fact that a particular expert has regularly produced expert reports for appellants might itself be a cause for concern. No country expert should have any interest in the outcome of an appeal. However, it may be relevant to consider whether an individual expert derives a significant level of income from producing country expert reports. See *AA v Secretary of State for the Home Department (Expert evidence, assessment) Somalia* [2004] UKIAT 00221 [9].

[81] *Zarour v Secretary of State for the Home Department* (01TH00078), date notified 2 August 2001 (IAT) [22]. As the Tribunal continued, at [23], this is not to say that a source must be quoted for each and every fact set out by the country expert; while judges 'will not expect the panoply of footnotes to be seen in academic publications, they are entitled to expect that country experts . . . have provided material in their reports or letters on which any facts about which there is likely to be any argument can be verified, and any opinions properly evaluated'.

a couple of respects. If an expert has collected facts from anonymous sources in the country concerned, then it may be impossible for the expert fully to disclose the sources of his information if those sources fear reprisals should their identity be publicly disclosed.[82] Furthermore, an expert may be entitled to form an opinion based on his experience and expertise, without necessarily supplying an array of 'objective' facts with which to back up that opinion. Nevertheless, the amount of weight to be accorded to an expert's opinion will diminish in inverse proportion to the amount of observable facts marshalled in support of the opinion advanced.[83] In other words, opinions unsupported by hard fact may be reliable, given the expertise of an expert, but the more hard facts the better.

Fourthly, the value and objectivity of country expert evidence can be evaluated by comparing it with other sources of country information.[84] If the Tribunal sees that a particular expert constantly seeks to paint a worse (sometimes rosier) picture than do other recognised sources, this may prompt the view that the expert is no longer impartial.[85] Finally, it is not for a country expert to say whether the country conditions mean that an appellant is entitled to asylum—it remains for judicial decision whether an expert's opinion evidences the existence of a real risk of persecution or of ill-treatment.[86] Country experts are not normally legally trained; their opinions, which necessarily come from a different perspective from that of the Tribunal, may be extremely informative, but assessments of risk remain for judges alone.[87] An expert who does express a view upon the risk facing an appellant is likely to be seen as having exceeded his expertise and to have trespassed upon the judicial function.

It is clear that judges can find it difficult to handle country expert evidence. Country experts often complain that their integrity and expertise are routinely denigrated by judges. Country experts may well like to have their opinions respected and tend to feel disaffected by their treatment in the context of a sometimes aggressively adversarial tribunal process. Moreover, experts' complaints are not devoid of substance. The Tribunal has occasionally been taken to task by the higher courts for not paying due regard to country expert evidence. For instance, Brooke LJ has noted that, given the extremely difficult task of assessing the credibility of asylum appellants, judges need all the help than can be given by a country

---

[82] Ibid, [28].

[83] *AN & SS v Secretary of State for the Home Department (Tamils—Colombo—risk?) Sri Lanka CG* [2008] UKAIT 00063 [102]

[84] *AZ* above n 73 at [49].

[85] As the Tribunal put it, in *AS v Secretary of State for the Home Department (Kirundi/Buyenzi—'country expert' evidence) Burundi* [2005] UKAIT 00172 [4], the fact that a country expert is an academic 'does not of course mean that anything falling from his pen is to be accepted as Gospel; but that decision-makers are entitled to accept his reasoned conclusions on general questions, without detailed sourcing, where those do not go against other information from generally accepted background sources before them, or reported decisions of the Tribunal. (On the other hand, it would in our view be a wrong approach in law not to engage in vigorous critical analysis of "country experts"' views, where those were out of line with such material)'.

[86] *NM* above n 34 at [95].

[87] *LP* above n 17 at [199].

expert. In response, the Tribunal retorted that country experts could not expect to have their opinions accepted automatically as that would be to substitute trial by expert for trial by a judge; while it is the country expert's task to put forward facts or views, it is the judge's task to assess them; 'country experts, like other expert witnesses, should not be treated as seers, whose vatic pronouncements are to be brought down from the mountain on tablets of stone, and treated with all reverence as the last word on the subject in question'.[88]

Yet there are concerns that the Tribunal's handling of country expert evidence has sometimes been unduly critical. In another instance, the Tribunal, in a country guidance case concerning the risks facing Kenyan women belonging to ethnic groups which practise female genital mutilation, observed that the country expert had gone well beyond the evidence relied upon in expressing the view that the particular appellant was unable to live safely in Kenya. However, the Court of Appeal considered this criticism unfair: the expert had been drawing upon his broader knowledge and experience in Kenya. Furthermore, the Tribunal's conclusion that the expert's report had been 'particularly partisan in its approach and lacking in objectivity' was, in the opinion of the Court of Appeal, unwarranted and could be said to said to manifest exactly the same faults—the use of wide and emotive expressions without substantive support—that the Tribunal had attributed to the country expert.[89] In another instance, a tribunal determination had strongly doubted the objectivity of a particular country expert and noted that the expert's opinions should in future be treated with caution. The Tribunal was subsequently forced into making a public apology to the country expert concerned after he had commenced libel proceedings against the Tribunal.[90]

At the same time, it is necessary to caution against any general assumption that the Tribunal has sought to minimise the role of country experts. On the contrary, the Tribunal's general view has been that it welcomes good quality expert evidence that can assist it in assessing risk on return. Furthermore, the Tribunal has rejected an attempt by the Home Office to restrict the role of country experts to that of solely presenting data concerning country conditions rather than also interpreting their significance and expressing opinions. The Home Office has, for instance,

---

[88] *R (Es Eldin) v Immigration Appeal Tribunal* (Court of Appeal, 29 November 2000, unreported) [18] (CA) (Brooke LJ); *Zarour* above n 81 at [20]–[21]. For another exchange of views between the Tribunal and the Court of Appeal over the handling of country expert evidence see *Karanakaran v Secretary of State for the Home Department* [2000] 3 All ER 449, 472 (Brooke LJ) and 473 (Sedley LJ)— it had been 'completely wrong' for the Tribunal to reject reports produced by four country experts as 'pure speculation'—but when the appeal returned to the Tribunal, *Karankaran v Secretary of State for the Home Department* (00TH03086) date notified 12 September 2000 (IAT), it concluded that the expert reports were contradictory, unsatisfactory and 'profoundly unhelpful to a Tribunal that has to make its own evaluation'.

[89] *FK v Secretary of State for the Home Department (FGM—Risk and Relocation) Kenya CG* [2007] UKIAT 00041 [96]; *FK (Kenya) v Secretary of State for the Home Department* [2008] EWCA Civ 119 [15] (Sedley LJ).

[90] *SD v Secretary of State for the Home Department (expert evidence—duties of expert) Lebanon* [2008] UKAIT00070. See also A Hirsch, 'Asylum Tribunal Apologies for Questioning Academic's Evidence' *The Guardian* (27 October 2008); M Newman, 'Tribunal Experts Fear Attacks on Integrity' *Times Higher Education* (6 November 2008) 8.

argued that the interpretation of country conditions offered by expert ought to be considered irrelevant because it is unlikely that that any specialist knowledge is required to interpret data concerning country conditions. The Home Office's concern has been that country expert might not provide a balanced picture of country conditions and so the role of country experts should be limited to the provision of the 'raw data' concerning country conditions. However, the Tribunal's response was that country experts could legitimately advance their interpretations and opinions as to the significance of country conditions.[91] The weight to be given to expert evidence and country background evidence is dependent upon the quality of the raw data from which it is drawn and the quality of the filtering process to which that data has been subjected. Sources should be given whenever possible. But country experts are not merely providers of raw data; they can also interpret its significance as well.

At the centre of the controversy then are competing claims between the Tribunal and individuals commissioned to adduce country evidence as to who possesses real country expertise. In justifying its role in assessing country conditions, the Tribunal has drawn the more familiar rationale that it is a specialist tribunal. However, expertise comes in different kinds. While legal expertise is important, it is different from expertise in the particular subject-matter or area of social life which with a particular adjudication process is concerned. While a narrow legal approach may be helpful in terms of ensuring the correct application of the law, it may leaves gaps in the decision-maker's knowledge when it comes to, for instance, assessing the conditions in countries overseas which the decision-maker may never have visited and may know little about. But, familiarity and experience with assessing country information can generate expertise. In the Tribunal's opinion, it has built up 'its own expertise in relation to the limited number of countries from which asylum seekers come'.[92] In this respect, the Tribunal has been supported by the higher courts which have been recognised that the Tribunal has its own expertise as a specialist appellate tribunal in considering and evaluating country conditions.[93] However, it is important to note that statements from the higher courts recognising the Tribunal's expertise and knowledge of country conditions have been directed more toward the Tribunal's Senior Immigration Judges than its Immigration Judges.

By contrast, country experts approach the issue from a different perspective. From their standpoint, judges do not normally possess a deep understanding of country conditions.[94] Immigration Judges may, of course, become thoroughly

---

[91] *LP* above n 17 at [18]–[42].

[92] See *SK* above n 73 at [5]. See also *Balachandran v Secretary of State for the Home Department* (20262), date notified 17 December 1999 (IAT) [9]; J Barnes, 'Expert Evidence—The Judicial Perception in Asylum and Human Rights Appeals' (2004) 16 *International Journal of Refugee Law* 349.

[93] See, eg, *Subesh v Secretary of State for the Home Department* [2004] EWCA Civ 56; [2004] Imm AR 112, 140 (Laws LJ); *AH (Sudan) v Secretary of State for the Home Department* [2007] UKHL 49; [2008] 1 AC 678, 691 (Baroness Hale) (HL).

[94] A Good, 'Expert Evidence in Asylum and Human Rights Appeals: an Expert's View' (2004) 16 *International Journal of Refugee Law* 358, 359; A Good, *Anthropology and Expertise in the Asylum Courts* (London, Routledge-Cavendish, 2007) 233.

informed at a factual level as to the political histories of countries producing asylum appellants, but it is in the assessment and interpretation of the cultural and political significance of such facts that country expertise is necessary and which judges tend to lack. Consequently, for experts, judicial claims to expertise in country conditions are, despite claims to the contrary, unreal and are used to reinforce judicial hegemony over country experts. Nevertheless, the specialisation of judges in the determination of asylum appeals is likely to generate experience and expertise in the handling, assessment, and weighing up of different sources of evidential material, such as conflicting sources of country information, and in correlating such information with the relevant legal tests governing decision-making.

A second concern for country experts is the Tribunal's presupposition that country information must be 'objective evidence'. From the perspective of country experts, it is simply mistaken to assume that it is possible to assemble objective evidence free from any prior theoretical framework.[95] The Tribunal may dismiss an expert's report on grounds of bias, but, from an expert's perspective, expecting such objectivity is itself misguided as experts necessarily operate within different explanatory paradigms in which the significance of facts are interpreted.[96] The difficulties between the Tribunal and country experts may then reflect deeply ingrained differences as to how lawyers and social scientists think and approach the same subject-matter. For some country experts the key point is that lawyers take matters which have been established to the appropriate standard of proof to be facts in an absolute sense whereas for social scientists and anthropologists 'facts' are almost always products of a particular theoretical approach. The 'truth' is more provisional, contested, and theory-laden than legal processes habitually acknowledge.[97]

The underlying tensions between the Tribunal and country experts may, then, be ascribed to different ways of organising the asylum adjudication process and of administrative justice more generally, but some compromise is required if the process is to work at all. In practice, this is achieved by the judges assessing the value of country expert evidence in each appeal and by having to give adequate reasons when rejecting it.

The Handling of Country Expert Evidence

When assessing country expert evidence judges will normally seek to assess the value of the evidence. Is it reliable and up to date? Does the expert seem to be well-informed or is he axe-grinding? Expert evidence can be helpful by filling in the

---

[95] A Good, ' "Undoubtedly an Expert"? Country Experts in the UK Asylum Courts' (2004) 10 *Journal of the Royal Anthropological Institute* 113.

[96] Cf generally TS Kuhn, *The Structure of Scientific Revolutions,* 3rd edn (Chicago, University of Chicago Press, 1996).

[97] Good traces the differential approaches between the tribunal and country experts to the basic differences in the professional training of lawyers and social scientists and suggests that this dispute is only one aspect of the continuing power struggle between the judiciary and professional experts.

gaps in other sources of country information, for instance, by confirming that a particular incident in the country concerned did actually occur. Perhaps the most problematic aspect for judges is the variable quality of country expert reports; the weight given to expert reports may vary considerably depending on the authoritative standing of the individual expert, their background, and how the reports are written. From the judicial perspective, while some experts appear to be knowledgeable and impartial, others seem to approach country conditions from a particular standpoint, that is, they seem predisposed toward a negative view of those conditions. The difficulty is in distinguishing the two.

In practice, judges tend to adopt a binary approach toward expert evidence: they either accept or reject it. The previous discussion might suggest that the Tribunal adopts a wholly sceptical approach to country experts, but the reality is not quite like this; from the sample of those appeals observed, expert reports were submitted in 28 appeals and accepted in 18 of them. Judges tend to accept expert reports when they are considered helpful and consistent with other country information. The difficulties in handling such reports can be illustrated by considering the extent to which country expert reports need to be sourced; and their role in relation to credibility issues.

Direct sourcing in expert reports will add weight to them; but its absence may be explained on the basis that the data could only have been obtained from undisclosed sources. The degree of sourcing required will, though, depend on the nature of the information disclosed. For instance, when an expert report contained a number of claims about conditions in Mauritania—that due to societal discrimination against black Mauritanian nationals, such individuals would on return be interrogated and detained by the authorities—it was rejected because of the lack of sources.[98] By contrast, un-sourced evidence may be accepted if there is a valid reason for not disclosing the source. For instance, in one appeal, the issue had been whether or not the appellant, a Sri Lankan national, would be wanted on his return as he had been previously detained by the Sri Lankan authorities for being a LTTE member. The Tribunal accepted the expert report that detailed confidential information obtained from an unidentified Sri Lankan police officer to the effect that once an individual's details had been entered onto the police's computer database, they would remain there for life.[99]

Similarly, the degree to which expert evidence may assist when assessing credibility varies. A judge might give weight to an expert report favourable to an appellant and yet disbelieve an appellant's account; the converse is also possible. Country experts have no role in concluding whether or not an appellant is credible. An expert who does express a view upon an appellant's credibility is likely to be viewed by a judge as having intruded into judicial fact-finding. At the same time, an expert report might assist in the overall appraisal of an appellant. For instance, in one appeal, an expert had stated that while he could not verify the

[98] Case 115.
[99] Case 62.

veracity of the appellant's story, there were several reasons why it was consistent with what the expert knew; the judge accepted the report and allowed the appeal.[100] By contrast, in another appeal, the expert had proffered an opinion as to the appellant's clan membership, but the judge decided that the expert, who had not met the appellant, had exceeded her expertise by seeking to explain the appellant's language preference.[101]

Reforming the Provision of Country Expert Evidence

For a number of reasons, the current procedure by which country expert evidence comes before the Tribunal seems unsatisfactory. Expert evidence is commissioned by appellants to assist the Tribunal in arriving at informed judgments about country conditions and how those conditions relate to the circumstances of the individual appellant. However, while such evidence is intended to provide objective and independence assistance, it is often suspected to be partial in some way, that it is just another piece of party evidence designed to help the appellant win rather than help the Tribunal reach a correct decision. This is problematic as valuable expert evidence might be wrongfully dismissed because it appears to lack neutrality. It is also inefficient and wasteful of resources because expert evidence still has to be paid for irrespective of whether or not the Tribunal finds it useful. The assumption that expert evidence may often not be neutral and independent arises largely, though not wholly, because of the procedure by which such evidence is assembled and placed before the Tribunal. How then might the provision of country expert evidence be improved?

One option would be to have greater self-regulation of country experts, in an attempt to assure the overall quality and impartiality of expert reports. However, this seems unlikely as experts do not comprise a professional grouping and lack the necessary resources and cohesiveness with which to self-regulate. The other obvious options focus upon the procedure by which country evidence is adduced before the Tribunal. Should there be greater use of competing expert reports or should the Tribunal have an ability to commission its own reports?

Greater use of competing expert reports might reflect better the shared duty to ascertain and evaluate all the relevant facts. The Tribunal has expressed the view on many occasions that it would be desirable for the Home Office to adduce its own expert evidence.[102] Difficulties arise, though, with regard to the cost and practicalities of having competing expert reports. It is not apparent that the Home Office has the resources with which to commission its own report to respond to an appellant's country report. Also, appeal timescales normally preclude this. Furthermore, the number of experts on a particular country issue may sometimes be so small that

---

[100] Case 17.

[101] Case 58.

[102] House of Commons Home Affairs Committee, *Immigration Control* (2005–06 HC 775) Vol II Ev 68 (Hodge J, AIT President); *SI* above n 69 at [56].

it may sometimes be difficult to see who else could be instructed by the Home Office to act as an expert in addition to the appellant's expert.

The third option—giving the Tribunal the power to commission its own expert reports—has gained some support from within the Tribunal. According to one senior judge, for country expert reports to be demonstrably impartial, the solution may be for experts to be appointed by the Tribunal at the request of the parties to an appeal so that there is a clear remit as to the area of expert testimony required in a given case.[103] The advantage of this option is that experts could be said to be genuinely objective. If experts were both selected by and responsible to the Tribunal, then judges could have greater confidence in the neutrality and independence of expert witnesses. Judges might become more at ease with the content of expert evidence reports, informed as they are by non-legal approaches, and more willing to allow such evidence to inform their decisions. Potential difficulties, though, arise in the practical operation of such a power on the Tribunal's behalf in terms of timescales and financing of expert reports. It is possible to envisage much judicial review litigation resulting when the Tribunal refused to appoint an expert despite the wishes of the parties. Furthermore, the assessment and handling of expert evidence will continue to present challenges for the Tribunal.

No option is problem-free. On balance, it might be preferable for the Tribunal to be able to commission its own expert reports; timescales could be adjusted; and the costs borne by the legal aid budget. Doing away altogether with country evidence is simply not an option, but improving the means by which such evidence is provided is possible. If the Tribunal were able to commission its own expert evidence, then the difficulties concerning the assessment of expert evidence would remain, but might be ameliorated by reducing the perception that experts are partisan and that expert reports detrimental to appellants' cases are screened out and not presented to the Tribunal. In this way, it might enhance the perception of the independence and objectivity of country expert evidence.

Conclusion

There are two general, and apparently discordant, views as to the quality of country information used in asylum appeals. One is that there has been a distinct trend away from policy-influenced information toward greater objectivity and accuracy in the provision of country information.[104] External, independent oversight of Home Office reports has come about as a result of campaigning by representative organisations and is generally recognised to have improved the quality of such reports. The other view is that asylum judges are, nevertheless, a long way away from the stage at which they can be confident that they always have to hand

---

[103] Barnes above n 92 at 354.
[104] Jordan above n 25.

country information that meets all of the standards required of it.[105] Realistically, available country information is unlikely ever to be fully comprehensive and exhaustive. But a quality adjudication process requires a higher standard of country information than is currently available. The general conclusion would appear to be shared by many involved in the appeal process: notwithstanding progress in raising the quality of country information, further improvements are clearly possible.

In considering what more could be done, it is important to appreciate that, to a large extent, the quality of country information before the Tribunal is dependant on factors that are largely outside its control. As country information reports are produced by other organisations, the quality of country information is often dependant on the resources available, the data collection processes used, the filtering and interpretation of the information collected; and the extent to which it is possible to report and investigate events in countries generating asylum appellants. Furthermore, the quality of country expert evidence depends upon which individuals are knowledgeable and qualified to give expert evidence on the particular issues raised in an appeal and the reliability of their views. The inherent problem is that country information is always likely to be subject to certain constraints and limitations; no amount of information is likely to be sufficient, but that is one reason why the standard of proof is set at the lower level.

What more then could the Tribunal itself do? One suggestion is that the Tribunal could adopt a more inquisitorial approach in respect of country information, especially in cases where the appellant is either unrepresented or has poor quality representation. At present, the pursuit of 'own-initiative' research by judges is ad hoc and heavily dependant on the individual judge. Another suggestion is that the Tribunal establish its own country of origin information unit to which judges could refer particular country issues for research by specialist staff. Of course, additional resources would be required as well as a broader shift toward a more inquisitorial judicial posture. A further suggestion is that the Tribunal should possess the ability to commission its own country expert evidence. In any event, responsibility for assessing country information has shifted within the Tribunal itself away from Immigration Judges to the Tribunal's senior judges who, through country guidance determinations, issue generic guidance on country issues. It is, therefore, the country guidance system to which we now turn.

---

[105] IARLJ above n 15 at 168.

7

Country Guidance

ORGANISING A LARGE-SCALE adjudication process requires the management of a number of different and competing values. In this milieu, consistency often emerges as an important value. The principle of equal treatment—treating like cases alike—possesses considerable intuitive appeal and resonates throughout the legal system. The possibility that the outcome of an individual's case may depend more upon the personal preferences or biases of an individual decision-maker than upon legal rules and norms of general application is seen as a particularly pernicious feature likely to generate arbitrary decision-making. However, the degree to which consistency can be secured in practice is often uncertain, especially in the context of judgmental areas of adjudication. While consistency is important, there is the countervailing risk that according it too high a priority will instigate the use of devices, such as rules or policy guidelines for instance, which introduce an undesirable degree of rigidity into decision-making, reduce individual assessment, and generate other errors. There may also, as in the asylum context, be shifting factual scenarios concerning an individual's entitlement. Efforts to promote consistency have to be mediated with the equally pressing need to take account of such factual changes. At the same time, arguments against inconsistency are insistent and difficult to resist. Consequently, an adjudication process may attempt to design some mechanism which seeks to promote consistency while also affording sufficient flexibility given the need for individual assessment against the backdrop of dynamic factual contexts.

In asylum adjudication, while each case is unique, many raise generic country issues. Consider the following. Are Eritrean draft evaders generally at risk? Do Sri Lankan Tamils comprise a distinct category of person at risk of serious harm on return from the Sri Lankan authorities? If not, then are there any factors that can be identified that increase the risk of ill-treatment in a particular case? If Immigration Judges were to be required to reach their own conclusions on these and other recurring country issues, then inconsistency would be almost guaranteed. There are other aspects of the adjudication process which can raise the risks of inconsistency: the caseload and the number of judges involved; and the variable range of country information materials relied upon. Inconsistency on important country issues would be bad enough if present at the first-tier appeal level, but even worse if present at the second-tier, that is, amongst senior judges. Inconsistency on crucial issues, such as which generic categories of asylum claimant will be at risk on return, can create uncertainty for first-tier judges, prevent the parties from predicting how their dispute is likely to be resolved, generate incentives for onward challenge, undermine public confidence, and attract censure from the courts.

The Tribunal's answer has been to develop a new technique—the country guidance system—by which senior judges produce authoritative guidance on generally recurring country issues. This system was adopted formally in 2004 and now exerts a pervasive influence throughout the appeals system and the broader asylum process. By 2010, there were 289 country guidance decisions concerning some 64 countries.[1] The purpose of this chapter is to examine the nature, development, and operation of the country guidance system and also to appraise its strengths and weaknesses.

The Country Guidance Concept

Broadly speaking, country guidance operates as follows. The Tribunal receives a number of appeals raising a particular country issue. Immigration Judges determining such appeals will consider the country information presented to them and make their own assessments concerning risk on return. However, there is the risk that different judges will either be presented with different sources of country information or reach different conclusions from the same information. In the face of such inconsistency and uncertainty, the senior tribunal judiciary may then decide to convene a country guidance hearing so that they can issue guidance on the country issue. A particular appeal will be selected; similar cases might be grouped together; and the parties will be notified that the appeal(s) are to be treated as potential country guidance.[2] At the appeal hearing, the Tribunal will consider a wider range of country information and country experts may give oral evidence. The substantive content of the guidance itself often involves the identification of a risk category (eg high level political oppositionists in a particular country will generally be at risk) or risk factors, those factors to be taken into account when assessing risk. Judges determining subsequent appeals are obliged to treat the guidance as authoritative and to apply it. In this way, country guidance becomes part of the law governing eligibility for asylum.

To illustrate both the risk of inconsistency on country issues and the development of the country guidance system, consider the issue as to whether or not the practice of religious apostasy in Iran entitles someone to asylum. While religious minorities are given constitutional protection in Iran, Sharia law prescribes the

---

[1] The Tribunal maintains a list of CG decisions on its website. The Tribunal has extended the technique outside the asylum context in order to give guidance on recurring factual situations in immigration cases (for instance, on allegedly bogus colleges). See *NA & Others v Secretary of State for the Home Department (Cambridge College of Learning) Pakistan* [2009] UKAIT 00031.

[2] Appeals listed as potential country guidance tend to have a longer 'lead in' time than ordinary asylum appeals with the Tribunal panel holding a 'For Mention Only' hearing prior to the substantive hearing in order to clarify the issues and evidence to be relied upon. Some substantive hearings are concluded in a day while others have been conducted over several days.

death penalty for a Muslim man who becomes an apostate by conversion; there is, though, little evidence as to the frequency with which the penalty is either imposed or carried out; will an Iranian asylum applicant who has converted to Christianity be at risk on return? In 2001–02, one tribunal panel decided that a Christian convert would not be at risk whereas another accepted that converts actively involved in church life might be at risk of persecution.[3] Presented with such disparate decisions, the Court of Appeal expressed 'concern that the same political and legal situation, attested by much the same in-country data from case to case, is being evaluated differently by different tribunals'.[4] To remedy the situation, the Tribunal had to adopt 'in any one period a judicial policy (with the flexibility that the word implies) . . . on the effect of the in-country data in recurrent classes of case'.[5] This the Tribunal did when it issued country guidance that an ordinary Christian convert would not be at risk of persecution or ill-treatment on return to Iran. However, the more active convert, Pastor, church leader, proselytiser or evangelist could be regarded as being at a real risk; their higher profile and role would be more likely to attract the malevolence of the licensed zealot and the serious adverse attention of the Iranian theocratic state when it sought to repress conversions from Islam which it sees as a menace and an affront to the state and God. Furthermore, where an ordinary individual convert has additional risk factors, he too could be at risk.[6]

A number of rationales underpin the country guidance system. First, consistency: it would, the Tribunal has observed, be self-evidently unjust for a judicial Tribunal to treat similar cases differently where there was no differentiating feature.[7] Country guidance does not concern individual personal facts, but the general circumstances, or the circumstances for a certain group of people, in the relevant country. Its purpose is to promote consistency in relation to the treatment of general country conditions. Secondly, country guidance is the means by which senior judges issue detailed and authoritative guidance for Immigration Judges on generally recurring country issues.[8] A third rationale is adjudicative efficiency. By issuing country guidance, the Tribunal can avoid 'the necessity for fresh decisions on the same material in situations of common application in a particular country'.[9] Rather than reinventing the wheel on each occasion, country guidance allows for in-depth consideration only when it is considered necessary, for instance,

[3] *Dorodian v Secretary of State for the Home Department* (01TH01537), date notified 23 August 2001 (IAT); *Ahmadi v Secretary of State for the Home Department* [2002] UKIAT 05079.

[4] *Shirazi v Secretary of State for the Home Department* [2003] EWCA Civ 1562; [2004] 2 All ER 602, 611 (Sedley LJ) (CA).

[5] Ibid.

[6] *FS and others v Secretary of State for the Home Department (Iran—Christian converts) Iran CG* [2004] UKIAT 00303. See also *SZ and JM v Secretary of State for the Home Department (Christians—FS confirmed) Iran CG* [2008] UKAIT 00082.

[7] *NM v Secretary of State for the Home Department (Lone women—Ashraf) Somalia CG* [2005] UKIAT 00076 [136].

[8] *KA v Secretary of State for the Home Department (Draft-related risk categories updated) Eritrea CG* [2005] UKAIT 00165 [10].

[9] *SL and Others v Secretary of State for the Home Department (Returning Sikhs and Hindus) Afghanistan CG* [2005] UKIAT 00137 [26].

when country conditions have changed or fresh country information warrants re-examination of existing guidance.

Securing these values is, though, not without its own difficulties. Consistency needs to be mediated with the need to give consideration to the specific circumstances of an individual case. The constant risk is that an Immigration Judge might try to fit the facts of an individual appeal into the context of generic guidance. Another concern is that as country guidance is developed in the context of fluctuating country conditions, it may be quickly overtaken by events. Judges may end up applying out of date country guidance. Furthermore, the time and resources taken to produce such guidance might have been unnecessarily expended.

The country guidance system came into being, in large part, as a response to the concerns of the higher courts as to disparate assessments of country conditions by different tribunal panels. In 1997, the Court of Appeal had observed that it would 'be beneficial to the general administration of asylum appeals for special adjudicators to have the benefit of the views of a Tribunal in other cases on the general situation in a particular part of the world, as long as that situation has not changed in the meantime'.[10] The Tribunal subsequently experimented with country guidance.[11] In 2002, the Court of Appeal endorsed the nascent technique. As Laws LJ explained, asylum claims from a particular country are inevitably made against the political backdrop in that country which over a period of time, however long or short, may be identifiable, if not constant. The impact of those country conditions can vary between one claimant and another, and it is always the Tribunal's duty to examine the facts of individual cases. Nonetheless, there was, Laws LJ noted, no public interest, nor any legitimate individual interest, in multiple examinations of country conditions at any particular time. Such revisits would give rise to the risk, perhaps the likelihood, of inconsistent results; and the likelihood, perhaps the certainty, of repeated and, therefore, wasted expenditure of judicial and financial resources upon the same issues and the same evidence. However, Laws LJ cautioned that if a factual determination, as opposed to a legal one, were to be authoritative in subsequent appeals, then certain safeguards had to apply. A principal requirement would be the 'application of the duty to give reasons with particular rigour'.[12] The Tribunal would have to 'take special care to see that its decision is effectively comprehensive' by ensuring that it addressed all the real issues and by explaining what it made of the relevant country information.[13] A subsidiary safeguard would be the need to pay particular attention to relevant country expert evidence.

[10] *Manzeke v Secretary of State for the Home Department* [1997] EWCA Civ 1888; [1997] Imm AR 524, 529 (Lord Woolf MR).

[11] Initial CG decisions appeared in 2001 on the situation concerning Czech Roma and ethnic Serbs in Croatia, which were intended to be definitive assuming no material change in country conditions. See *OP & Others v Secretary of State for the Home Department (Roma—ethnicity) Czech Republic CG* [2001] UKIAT 00001; *Secretary of State for the Home Department v S* (01TH00632), date notified 1 May 2001 (IAT).

[12] *S & Others v Secretary of State for the Home Department* [2002] EWCA Civ 539; [2002] INLR 416, 436 (Laws LJ) (CA).

[13] Ibid.

Following this, the status of country guidance was enhanced in a number of ways. Country guidance was given a statutory basis in 2004.[14] Secondly, the higher courts held that the restriction of onward challenges to error of law grounds alone did not impair the Tribunal's ability to issue country guidance on the basis of up to date evidence, even though it is concerned with issues of fact not law.[15] Given its importance in achieving consistency in decision-making, it would take very clear statutory language to end the practice of giving country guidance.[16]

Thirdly, other actors within the asylum process have come to recognise the importance of the Tribunal's function in issuing country guidance and to modify their behaviour accordingly. For instance, the Home Office usually incorporates country guidance into its Operational Guidance Notes. A theme well-recognised in the administrative law literature is that if the external forms of legal account-ability provided by courts and tribunals are to exert influence upon the operation of administrative organisations, then the messages they contain often need to be incorporated within the internal forms of administrative accountability, such as soft-law and internal guidance issued by higher-level agency officials, which are normally the most powerful means of influencing the work of subordinate officials.[17] Through this process, country guidance tends to filter down into initial Home Office decision-making.

Country guidance has also come to play a central role in relation to the suspension or resumption of returns to a particular country. For instance, in 2007 some Members of Parliament called for a deferral of, and then the High Court issued an injunction against, the removal of failed asylum seekers to the Democratic Republic of Congo until the Tribunal had issued country guidance on whether or not this category of person would be at risk on return.[18]

[14] Under the Nationality, Immigration and Asylum Act 2002 Act, s 107(3) (as inserted by the Asylum and Immigration (Treatment of Claimants, etc.) Act 2004, schedule 2, para 22(1)(c)), the Tribunal's practice directions 'may, in particular, require the Tribunal to treat a specified decision of the Tribunal as authoritative in respect of a particular matter'. The AIT's *Practice Directions* (2007) [18.2] state that a reported Tribunal decision 'bearing the letters "CG" shall be treated as an authoritative finding on the country guidance issue identified in the determination, based upon the evidence before the members of the Tribunal' that determined the appeal. See also *HGMO v Secretary of State for the Home Department (Relocation to Khartoum) Sudan CG* [2006] UKAIT 00062 [141]–[142].

[15] When the scope of onward challenge against initial appeal determination had been confined to errors of law alone, there had been some uncertainty as to whether this restriction also limited the Tribunal's jurisdiction to issue country guidance. See *Miftari v Secretary of State for the Home Department* [2005] EWCA Civ 481 [32]–[33] (Buxton LJ).

[16] *R (Iran) v Secretary of State for the Home Department* [2005] EWCA Civ 982; [2005] INLR 633, 661 (Brooke LJ) (CA).

[17] See generally S Halliday, *Judicial Review and Compliance with Administrative Law* (Oxford, Hart Publishing, 2003).

[18] See House of Commons Early Day Motion 1729, 'Country Guidance Tribunal on the Democratic Republic of Congo', 19 June 2007; *R (Lutete and Others) v Secretary of State for the Home Department* [2007] EWHC Admin 2331; 'Judge Halts Democratic Republic of Congo Deportations', BBC News website, 23 August 2007. The Tribunal's subsequent country guidance was provided in *BK v Secretary of State for the Home Department (Failed asylum seekers) Democratic Republic of Congo CG* [2007] UKAIT 00098. In July 2008, the Home Office announced that it would defer enforcing returns of non-Arab Darfuri asylum seekers to Sudan until the Tribunal had issued country guidance on the safety of return to Khartoum. See Hansard HL Deb vol 703 col WA263 (22 July 2008).

Country guidance is then a distinctive type of asylum adjudication and can be distinguished from ordinary appeals in the following ways. First, with regard to decision outcomes, the unusually high error costs of ordinary asylum adjudications are raised higher still in the country guidance context because the guidance is designed to influence other appeals. While accurate country guidance can promote consistently accurate decisions, inaccurate guidance can promote consistently inaccurate decisions. While the system's unifying and prospective guidance function is desirable, it is essential that the guidance issued be of high quality.

Secondly, given the importance accorded to country guidance, ordinary appeal procedures are modified. Normal time limits do not apply. Good quality representation becomes essential. The range of country information relied upon will be considerably expanded and experts will often attend hearings to be cross-examined. The Tribunal may adopt a more inquisitorial approach and the Home Office may submit more country information than would normally be the case. The length of time required to produce the country guidance determination will be much longer than in the case of ordinary appeal determinations.

Thirdly, country guidance has an enhanced status. Ordinary determinations by Immigration Judges are merely individual decisions and not binding in subsequent cases, but country guidance is intended to be binding in future cases. An important consideration is that as country guidance concerns the assessment of country conditions, it raises issues of fact not law. Furthermore, the nature of those factual issues—country conditions—is inherently susceptible to frequent change. While the legal process recognises precedents of the higher courts on points of law, decisions binding on issues of fact are, in general terms, unknown. Consequently, it is important to examine carefully the precedential nature of country guidance.

A more general point is that guidance function of tribunals illustrates their developing policy making function. In the modern state, adjudication is best understood as a means of implementing public policy. However, if there is no clear distinction between adjudication and administration, it is important to recognise that there is no absolute or categorical division between the making of policy and its administration.[19] On the contrary, the need to apply generally stated policies in particular instances and the variety of different and fluctuating situations will, in practice, means that policy making is often a pervasive and inextricable feature of the administrative process. If so, then tribunals will, on occasion, engage in policy making though adjudication.

In the country guidance context, the Tribunal's policy making function becomes evident because the whole purpose is to identify those general categories of claimant who may or may not be at risk in return. Furthermore, country guidance is to be treated as authoritative in subsequent appeals. No-one doubts that when the Tribunal issues country guidance that it is developing asylum policy by

---

[19] A Dunsire, *Administration: the Word and the Science* (London, Martin Robertson, 1973) 98–100; HA Simon, *Administrative Behavior*, 4th edn (New York, Free Press, 1997) 61–67.

indicating which general groups of people will and will not be at risk on return. The nature of this policy role will be conditioned by the adjudicative nature of the Tribunal process and will involve assessment of the factual evidence and application of the legal rules; by issuing country guidance, the Tribunal will, nevertheless, in effect exercise a policy making function. If so, then it is important to consider the appropriateness of adjudication of a means of making and implementing asylum policy when compared with other techniques such as administrative rule-making.

But first: how does the country guidance system operate in practice? What range of country information does the Tribunal draw upon when seeking to establish such wide-ranging guidance? And which particular techniques has the Tribunal utilised in order to issue country guidance?

Managing Country Guidance

Responsibility for managing country guidance rests principally with the Tribunal's senior judges. Overall management of the country guidance system rests with a Senior Immigration Judge and the senior judiciary is organised into three 'country groups' which oversee a number of different refugee producing countries and monitor the country issues that arise in relation to each country. To issue guidance, it is necessary to identify the particular country issue and an appeal(s) to act as the appropriate vehicle. As a judicial decision-maker, the Tribunal can only to issue guidance in the context of a particular appeal.

In terms of tribunal composition, a country guidance panel will normally comprise either three Senior Immigration Judges or two and a non-legal member. Senior judges specialise in country guidance, thereby building up their experience, while, in the hearing centres, Immigration Judges hear individual appeals and apply the guidance provided. Given the short timescales of ordinary asylum appeals, it is not realistic to expect judges to consider and analyse the copious amounts of country information which characterise country guidance hearings. Country guidance is the means by which senior judges provide a lead to Immigration Judges, or, alternatively, the means by which a centralised corps of senior judges can seek to constrain decision-making by the decentralised Immigration Judges.

These organisational arrangements are buttressed by greater interaction between senior judges and Immigration Judges. Until the AIT's introduction in 2005, it could take up to a year before the senior judges became aware of particular country issues frequently raised at the first-tier. However, a distinctive feature introduced with the AIT was the practice of senior judges going out on circuit to the regional hearing centres. This peripatetic working practice enables Immigration Judges to benefit from the assistance of senior judges and allows senior judges to come into contact with the types of cases coming up at first-instance with a view to identifying potential country guidance issues. In the hearing centres, Designated Immigration

Judges, who oversee and manage small teams of Immigration Judges, also notify senior judges of those country issues coming up for decision.

In terms of selecting particular appeals as appropriate vehicles for country guidance purposes, the Tribunal has indicated that it is a matter for its own decision, and not for the parties concerned, whether a particular appeal is to be selected for country guidance purposes. The fact that conditions in a particular country are unstable or fluid does not necessarily preclude country guidance.[20] While unusually unstable or fluid country conditions might sometimes justify the Tribunal not proceeding with giving guidance in relation to claims made by asylum seekers from that country, much depends on the particular context and the extent to which it is possible, notwithstanding such fluidity, to draw conclusions about risk categories. After all, many asylum seekers tend to come from countries in which conditions are unstable and fluid.

Various practical challenges can arise here. The appeal selected must be appropriate to the task of issuing country guidance.[21] One practical difficulty concerns the Tribunal's ability to identify appropriate cases coming up on sufficiently regular intervals as potential vehicles by which country guidance can be issued. To illustrate the point, consider the case of Bidoon asylum applicants seeking protection from persecution in Kuwait. In 2004, the Tribunal issued country guidance to the effect that, because of the widespread and systematic nature of the discriminatory measures they experience, the majority of, though not all, Bidoon in Kuwait would face a real risk of persecution.[22] In 2006, subsequent country guidance found no material change.[23] However, following these cases, the Tribunal has simply not been presented with the opportunity to issue subsequent guidance taking into account any change in country conditions. This was because of a reduction in the number of such asylum applicants; furthermore, as the country guidance was favourable to applicants, there were few onward challenges against adverse determinations by Immigration Judges. It might be that the situation for Bidoon and their treatment had since improved—it might not; in any event, the Tribunal has been unable to revisit the issue. The consequence of this is that country guidance is always at the risk of becoming—or appearing to become—out of date.

The Tribunal's practice is only to select appeals for country guidance purposes if the appellant is in receipt of publicly funded representation. But while the Home Office is often represented in country guidance cases by experienced counsel, concerns have been raised that this may militate against an equality of arms if appellants are represented by less competent representatives. Moreover, representatives

---

[20] *KG v Secretary of State for the Home Department (Review of current situation) Nepal CG* [2006] UKAIT 00076 [43].

[21] Individual appeals selected for country guidance purposes are almost always cases that have already been within the appeal system for a period of time, that is an Immigration Judge has dismissed the appeal and reconsideration has been ordered, rather than being cases in which there has been no previous judicial decision by the Tribunal.

[22] *BA and Others v Secretary of State for the Home Department (Bedoon—statelessness—risk of persecution) Kuwait CG* [2004] UKIAT 00256.

[23] *HE v Secretary of State for the Home Department (Bidoon—statelessness—risk of persecution) Kuwait CG* [2006] UKAIT 00051.

themselves may be undecided as to whether or not they should assist the Tribunal in establishing wide-ranging country guidance and where their duties lie (to their individual client or to a wider class of asylum applicant?).

There may be difficulties on the other side also. Given the Tribunal's policy role in country guidance cases, there are bound to instances when the Home Office does not wish the Tribunal to issue wide-ranging guidance which may potentially open the door to a large number of applicants. A recurrent problem has then been the last-minute concession or reconsideration by the Home Office of appeals selected for country guidance purposes.[24] While it is always open to the Home Office to withdraw an initial refusal decision and to grant status to an individual appellant, for it to do so in the knowledge that individual's appeal has been listed as potential country guidance risks both undermining the system and generating the perception that of seeking to evade a judicial decision.[25] The potential for such tactics illustrates the way in which an administrative agency is able, to some degree, to control which cases and issues proceed for the creation of broader guidance. From one perspective, this is all part of the cynical game that is the asylum process, but it is deeply troubling on both constitutional and efficiency grounds. Constitutionally, it is anomalous as it enables the executive to undermine the ability of the senior level of the asylum judiciary to issue guidance to its lower level; in practical terms, it is wasteful of time and resources. However, with the transfer of asylum appeals to the Upper Tribunal (Immigration and Asylum Chamber), this ability of the Home Office has been significantly reduced as appeals can only be withdrawn with the Tribunal's consent.[26]

In arranging potential country guidance, it might be necessary for the Tribunal to link some appeals together so that they may be heard together; this obviously requires effective case-management within the Tribunal. Then the appeal must be then heard and determined. Here other difficulties can arise. At the appeal hearing it may turn out that a particular appeal is not, despite early indications, suited to the task. For instance, if an appeal, which has been listed as potential country guidance, can be determined without too much examination of the broader country issue, then it will not be reported as such. In determining appeals, the Tribunal's primary focus is on the resolution of the individual case; broader country guidance is viewed by the Tribunal as an extra, value-added component. As a senior judge has explained, country guidance is a feature not of individual cases, but of written Tribunal determinations.[27]

---

[24] For instance, in 2009, a country guidance case was arranged to consider the situation in Somalia. The representatives undertook substantial preparatory work, including a visit to Kenya to obtain eye-witness accounts, but when the country information was served on the Home Office, it granted asylum, and the case collapsed, noted by R McKee (2010) 13(1) *Immigration Law Update* 14.

[25] *MA v Secretary of State for the Home Department (Operational guidance—prison conditions—significance) Sudan* [2005] UKAIT 00149 [27]–[28].

[26] Tribunal Procedure (Upper Tribunal) Rules SI 2008/2698 r 17(2); *CS v Secretary of State for the Home Department (Tier 1—home regulator) USA* [2010] UKUT 163 (IAC) [7].

[27] Interview with a Senior Immigration Judge.

Once a determination has been produced, the Tribunal's reporting committee will then decide whether it should receive the special cachet of the 'CG' designation. The reporting committee's practice is only to designate an appeal as 'CG' if it provides a comprehensive overview of the country situation. A determination will not be reported as country guidance if, although dealing with a fair amount of country information, it does not seem to have considered all the country material that it could have. The criteria for being designated as country guidance is that it not just adequately determine the particular appeal, but also provide a balanced, impartial, and authoritative assessment of available country information drawing out guidance relevant in subsequent appeals.

The production of country guidance is, of course, not the end of the story. If its purpose is to promote consistency, then country guidance will need to be applied in similar, subsequent appeals. Immigration Judges are expected to apply country guidance decisions in other appeals to which it is relevant; it will normally be an error of law to do otherwise. However, as country conditions are protean, there needs to be some built-in mechanism by which factual changes in country conditions can be taken account of and by which representatives can argue that the country guidance has been superseded. The precise precedential value of country guidance is therefore an important issue, which is considered in detail below. Country guidance decisions can themselves be challenged before the higher courts. Such oversight clearly performs an important function in assessing whether the Tribunal made any error of law in its guidance. At the same time, there can be a cost here in terms of the length of time such challenges take and the consequent uncertainty in the meantime. Unsurprisingly, given the nature of the country issues (is it unduly harsh to expect non-Arab Sudanese nationals at risk in Darfur to relocate internally to Khartoum? will failed Zimbabwean asylum applicants be at risk on return?) a number of country guidance cases have generated onward challenges to the higher courts which then either endorse the decision or remit it to the Tribunal for reconsideration. This, of course, raises concerns about the finality of the country guidance process.

But onward challenges against country guidance to the higher courts are not the only or principal mechanism for managing the system. After country guidance has been issued, the Tribunal will endeavour to keep the situation in the particular country under review and also monitor the types of issues arising in initial appeals with a view to convening another country guidance case, if and when necessary. The broader picture is that country guidance is an incremental, ongoing process by which the Tribunal seeks to decide on whether any reassessment of risk categories or factors is needed in the light of changing country conditions. It enables the Tribunal to seek consistency and efficiency in the adjudication process and also to refine its own understanding of country conditions when those conditions change, whether for better or worse, or when new country information comes to light.

Assessing Country Information and Producing Guidance

How then does the Tribunal go about the task of issuing country guidance? There are normally two interrelated components. First, the relevant country information must be assembled and assessed. The Tribunal will then need to decide what, if any, guidance it is able to distil from this information about the existence and degree of risk on return that will be of use in subsequent appeals. We can, therefore, examine how country information comes before the Tribunal and the techniques used.

Country Information and Country Guidance

Good country guidance presupposes good quality country information. It can only be disadvantageous to all concerned if an ostensibly comprehensive country guidance appraisal, upon which other decision-makers thereafter rely upon, has been produced in ignorance of relevant country information and therefore has to be undone.[28] Early country guidance decisions were criticised because of the paucity of country information to which they referred.[29] In subsequent country guidance cases, the Tribunal sought to improve the quality of guidance by relying upon a wider array of country information. The Tribunal normally lists the country information relied upon in an appendix to the determination so that representatives can know what was in the Tribunal's factual 'database'. Indeed, some decisions are very lengthy because of the volume of country information considered and the detailed assessment it receives from the Tribunal.[30] Some concerns have been raised over the length of some decisions: given the pressures on judges and representatives, who has the time to read them? Furthermore, the longer country guidance determinations are, then the greater the scope for any onward challenge. However, issuing country guidance imposes special demands: that the range of country information is effectively comprehensive and that the Tribunal give detailed reasons. To meet these requirements, the Tribunal will provide a comprehensive evaluation of the relevant country information. By so doing, the Tribunal will identify those sources of country information that are accepted and those that are not, thereby enabling the parties in subsequent appeals to know which sources of country information they can rely upon without having to reproduce them on each occasion.

[28] *Batayav v Secretary of State for the Home Department* [2003] EWCA Civ 1489 [35] (Munby J) [40] (Sedley LJ).

[29] C Yeo (ed), *Country Guideline Cases: Benign and Practical?* (London, Immigration Advisory Service, 2005) 3.

[30] For instance, two country guidance determinations were each some 144 pages long. See *BK* above n 18 and *HH & Others v Secretary of State for the Home Department (Mogadishu: armed conflict: risk) Somalia CG* [2008] UKAIT 00022 (AIT). In *BK*, the appendix listing the background country materials considered by the Tribunal was nine pages long.

The issue of where country information comes from and who has responsibility for producing it goes to the centre of the utility of adjudication for country guidance purposes. In particular, there is the question of the appropriate adjudicative procedure; to what extent does country guidance require modification of normal adversarial procedures? And what input can be expected from the parties?

To a large extent, the range of country information depends on the willingness of appellants' representatives to undertake country information research. For those representatives who pursue a broader campaigning agenda, positive country guidance potentially offers the opportunity to increase the chances of asylum being granted to a wide-ranging group of appellants. Conversely, other representatives may resist the Tribunal's desire to use their particular client's appeal as a country guidance vehicle. Furthermore, having less able representatives may reduce the quality of country guidance. On a practical level, it may be possible to overcome this potential problem if the Tribunal ensures that appeals selected for country guidance purposes are taken up by experienced representatives.[31]

What of the Home Office's contribution? Given the wider significance of country guidance, the Home Office's usual approach toward presenting country information—just submitting its relevant country report—is unlikely to suffice. The relevant sections of a Home Office country report may, when placed under the microscope, be found to be wanting. Consequently, it might be argued that, given the resources at its disposal and the duty of cooperation between the parties, the Home Office should assume a greater responsibility for presenting more country information in country guidance hearings. Actual Home Office practice varies. In some instances, it has made efforts to present a wide range of country information and undertaken fact-finding missions specifically for the purpose of informing country guidance cases.[32] But, in other cases, the Home Office has often adopted a passive stance. The Court of Appeal has noted that as the Home Office is likely to have a more comprehensive knowledge of conditions in foreign countries, not least through diplomatic and consular channels, and it would therefore be appropriate for that information to be presented in country guidance cases to ensure that they are effectively comprehensive.[33] The Home Office has subsequently presented such information in a small number of country guidance cases.[34] From the Tribunal's perspective such sources of information are to be welcomed as much as

---

[31] In particular country guidance issues, such as Zimbabwe, there may be continuity of representation, even though the individual appeal(s) selected as the country guidance vehicle changes. See *HS v Secretary of State for the Home Department (returning asylum seekers) Zimbabwe CG* [2007] UKAIT 00094 [38].

[32] See, eg, the range of country information adduced by the Home Office on the issue of Russian prison conditions in *ZB v Secretary of State for the Home Department (Russian prison conditions) Russian Federation CG* [2004] UKIAT 00239. For an example of a Home Office fact-finding mission (and strong criticism of it by the Tribunal), see *AA v Secretary of State for the Home Department (Involuntary returns to Zimbabwe) Zimbabwe CG* [2005] UKAIT 00144.

[33] *AH (Sudan), IG (Sudan) and NM (Sudan) v Secretary of State for the Home Department* [2007] Imm AR 584, 601 (Buxton LJ) (CA).

[34] See, eg, *LP v Secretary of State for the Home Department (LTTE area—Tamils—Colombo—risk?) Sri Lanka CG* [2007] UKAIT 00076 and *BK* above n 18.

country expert reports in furtherance of both producing balanced decisions and obtaining the highest quality of country guidance determinations.[35] Such sources of country information are, though, not without their own difficulty: they emanate from a different branch of the executive; the sources relied upon may not be disclosed; and little is known about the information-gathering process. On the other hand, such information is produced by a diplomatic post with a permanent presence in the country concerned as opposed to the temporary presence of a country expert and should normally be accorded an equivalent weight.[36]

Country expert evidence often assumes particular importance in country guidance cases and this is partially reflected in the different procedures used; experts will often give live evidence in country guidance cases and a number of expert opinions may be obtained. The advantage of this is that a selection of different experts can be drawn upon and tested. The nature of the expert evidence will also normally be much wider going to general country conditions and the Tribunal will often engage in a more detailed assessment of that evidence. However, expert evidence is almost invariably still adduced solely by appellants. The Home Office rarely commissions its own expert evidence in country guidance cases, preferring instead to rely upon country information that has been corroborated in order to ensure its reliability. The general concern that the Home Office should make more of an effort to present its own country expert evidence is heightened in the country guidance context because of its broader influence upon subsequent appeals. While it has not been unknown for the Home Office to instruct its own country expert, it would appear that there is still some way for the Home Office to go in order fully to fulfil the shared duty of cooperation in country guidance cases.[37] As regards the assessment of country expert evidence, the Tribunal has maintained an approach of not implicitly accepting such evidence, but subjecting it to close examination.[38]

To what extent does country guidance presuppose a more active approach from the Tribunal itself? For country guidance to work, it is essential that the Tribunal have before it all material information irrespective of whether it has been presented to it by the parties. The enterprise may assume 'something of an inquisitorial quality, although the adversarial structure of the appeal procedure of course remains'.[39] In an early country guidance case on a recurrent issue—are Congolese

---

[35] *LP* above n 34 at [204].

[36] Ibid, [45] and [205].

[37] For a case in which the Home Office did instruct its own expert, see *JC v Secretary of State for the Home Department (Double jeopardy: Art 10 CL) China CG* [2008] UKAIT 00036.

[38] So, when in *S and Others* above n 12 at 436 Laws LJ stated that 'the fact-finding tribunal is bound to place heavy reliance on the views of experts and specialists', the Tribunal, in *Secretary of State for the Home Department v SK (Return—Ethnic Serb) Croatia CG* (Starred determination) [2002] UKIAT 05613 [5], responded by rejecting this view: 'an expert's report can assist, but we do not accept that heavy reliance is or should be placed upon such reports. All will depend on the nature of the report and the particular expert'. On a further appeal back to the Court of Appeal, *SK v Secretary of State for the Home Department* [2003] EWCA Civ 841 [18] Laws LJ noted that while 'one might baulk at the Tribunal's apparently stark departure' from the Court of Appeal's view of the importance of expert evidence, there was no great difference of view. The Tribunal was not bound to accept expert evidence, but such reports, as a class of evidence, had an important role to play in compiling country guidance.

[39] *S & Others* above n 12 at 431 (Laws LJ).

nationals at risk on return solely because they have sought asylum in the UK?—the Tribunal made use of country information that was known to it but which had not been presented by either party.[40] Its justification being that it was in the interest of all concerned that the Tribunal had before it all known country materials relevant to the disputed issue. It would defeat the object of the exercise if the Tribunal were to be confined to the body of evidence adduced by the parties when it was aware of other material evidence.

Nevertheless, the degree to which the Tribunal adopts a more active approach appears to be limited. The Tribunal does not have its own country documentation unit specifically to undertake country information research in such cases. In practice, it may be able to accommodate a more active approach through a combination of ensuring that appeals selected for country guidance purposes are well-represented with advance preparation such as pre-hearing reviews in which the Tribunal clarifies the relevant country issues and raises any important pieces of country information with the parties. The degree of activism on the Tribunal's behalf is clearly connected with the degree of country specialisation amongst senior judges. As the senior judges undertaking country guidance work are organised into country groups, they may be better informed as to sources of relevant country information and recent developments. Furthermore, there is also the safeguard that a decision which does not engage in a comprehensive examination of country information will not be designated as country guidance.

One proposal has been to introduce a system of assisting counsel in which a third representative would present evidence as to the wider country situation perhaps with support from a country information unit within the Tribunal.[41] An alternative option would be for a new non-governmental organisation to have a specific remit to assist representatives in country guidance cases. Of course, a basic stumbling block with both of these is the additional resources required. Nevertheless, it cannot be assumed that senior judges are always presented with all available information. Additional mechanisms to inform the Tribunal as to the wider country situation could enhance the operation of country guidance and serve as an additional quality control mechanism. In any event, the application of country guidance requires Immigration Judges to take account of any fresh country information. More generally, it has been argued that country guidance decisions exemplify an endemic problem with regard to the Tribunal's expectations of available country information, namely, the supposition that some sort of proof or evidence will be forthcoming. The consequent inference is that if such evidence is not forthcoming, then it is because it does not exist at all—as opposed to there being no evidence available to that particular claimant—and that without some

---

[40] *VL v Secretary of State for the Home Department (Risk—failed Asylum Seekers) Democratic Republic of Congo CG* [2004] UKIAT 00007. The same country issue was the subject of a subsequent country guidance case, see *BK* above n 18.

[41] Yeo above n 28 at 131. The closest analogy here is with special advocates before the Special Immigration Appeals Commission, but the analogy is inexact as a special advocate is appointed to assist those individuals to whom evidence cannot be disclosed for national security reasons.

specific evidence, the asylum appeal must fail.[42] At the same time, while the burden of proof is on the appellant, it is set at the lower standard.

Country Guidance Techniques

Having assembled the relevant country information, the task is then one of attributing weight to the sources of country information when assessing risk and issuing country guidance. How then does the Tribunal actually issue country guidance? If we examine country guidance decisions, do any distinctive country guidance techniques emerge? If so, then what advantages and disadvantages do they possess?

Surveying current country guidance determinations, it is apparent that the manner or technique through which guidance is provided is highly dependant on the nature of the particular country issue. Given the range of country issues covered, a number of different country guidance techniques have been utilised. In an effort to identify some general trends the following, non-exhaustive taxonomy is suggested. First, country guidance may be closely linked to the application of a particular concept of refugee, asylum, or human rights law. Secondly, the Tribunal may identify a risk category, that is, a particular category of person who may be at risk on return. Thirdly, the Tribunal may enumerate a number of risk factors, that is, those factors which are likely to be relevant when determining the degree of risk on return in any individual case.

Country guidance and the concepts of asylum law As the adjudication of asylum appeals involves the application of the legal concepts of asylum, refugee, and human rights law to the application of individual facts and country conditions, a clear means of issuing guidance has been for the Tribunal to link up its consideration of country information with particular concepts of asylum law. The specific nature of the country guidance will depend largely on the particular nature of the country issue and the relevant legal rule.

To illustrate, consider the following guidance. For some years, Pakistan Ahmadis have sought asylum on the basis that they will be at risk of persecution because of their religion on return, Ahmadis being subject to various restrictions on the public practice of their faith. In one country guidance, the Tribunal had accepted that such individuals may, if found to be at risk on return, internally relocate to Rabwah. However, in 2007 the Tribunal accepted evidence prepared on behalf of the Parliamentary Human Rights Group that Rabwah could no longer be considered to be an appropriate place of internal relocation.[43] Elsewhere, country guidance has been linked to other concepts of asylum law. For instance, the

---

[42] C Yeo, 'Country Information, the Courts and Truth' (2005) 11(2) *Immigration Law Digest* 26, 27.
[43] *IA and Others v Secretary of State for the Home Department (Ahmadis: Rabwah) Pakistan CG* [2007] UKAIT 00088. See also *MJ and ZM v Secretary of State for the Home Department (Ahmadis—risk) Pakistan CG* [2008] UKAIT 00033.

Tribunal has issued guidance that a Moldovan woman, who has been trafficked for the purposes of sexual exploitation, is a member of a particular social group; whether an individual is at risk of persecution because of their membership of this particular social group must be decided on the individual facts of the case.[44] Furthermore, country guidance may be suited to dealing with certain rules of asylum law. Under article 15(c) of the EC Qualification Directive, a person who does not qualify for refugee status may nevertheless be eligible for subsidiary protection on the basis that he is at risk of serious harm consisting of a serious and individual threat by reason of indiscriminate violence in situations of international or internal armed conflict. The assessment of whether or not a particular country (Iraq, for instance) or a region/city (Mogadishu, for example) is in a situation of internal armed conflict, almost presupposes a country guidance system by which such assessments are to be made.[45] The advantage of this technique, as with country guidance more generally, is that it promotes consistency in the application of the concepts of asylum law in the context of particular country issues.

Risk categories A second technique has been for the Tribunal to identify a distinct risk category, that is, a class of people who, because they share certain characteristics, will be at real risk on return. Risk categories tend to be recognised when the evidence strongly suggests that a particular group of people will be at risk on return. For instance, Congolese nationals who possess an ethnic, political or military profile in opposition to the Congolese government, Eritrean nationals who have left that country illegally and are of draft age, and Zimbabwean nationals who are unable to demonstrate support for or loyalty to the Mugabe/Zanu PF regime.[46] The identification of such risk categories does not determine the outcomes of subsequent appeals; that still depends on the individual assessment of the particular case. Risk categories do, though, provide a clear guide and focus for such appeals thereby promoting a consistent approach by recognising the existence of a generic category of people who will be at risk on return.

The advantage of this technique is its flexibility. Risk categories may be drawn by the Tribunal more or less widely depending on the degree to which available country information enables the Tribunal to make relevant conclusions. The widest possible risk category is that of failed asylum seekers, that is, those claimants who claim to be at risk on return by having sought asylum. Alternatively, the width of risk categories may be more circumscribed through the identification of a narrow group of people who will be at risk on return (for instance, members of a particular tribe or

---

[44] *SB v Secretary of State for the Home Department (PSG—protection regulations—Reg 6) Moldova CG* [2008] UKAIT 00002.

[45] See *HH & Others* above n 29; *KH v Secretary of State for the Home Department (Article 15 (c) Qualification Directive) Iraq CG* [2008] UKAIT 00023; *AM & AM v Secretary of State for the Home Department (armed conflict: risk categories) Somalia CG* [2008] UKAIT 00091.

[46] *AB and DM v Secretary of State for the Home Department (Risk categories reviewed—Tutsis added) DRC CG* [2005] UKIAT 00118; *MA v Secretary of State for the Home Department (Draft evaders—illegal departures—risk) Eritrea CG* [2007] UKAIT 00059; *RN v Secretary of State for the Home Department (Returnees) Zimbabwe CG* [2008] UKAIT 00083.

certain high-level members of an opposition political party). Risk categories can also be reaffirmed, refined, supplemented, or amended as new country information emerges. In this way, the country guidance process allows the Tribunal to revisit particular risk categories in subsequent cases as it evolves its understanding of country conditions and as new country information comes to light. Furthermore, techniques can be combined. So, for instance, when the Tribunal held that it would not be unduly harsh to expect a non-Arab Sudanese national at risk in Darfur to relocate internally from there to Khartoum, it also identified limited risk categories of Darfuri returnees who would be at risk in Khartoum. These limited risk categories included *inter alia* persons from Darfuri 'hotspots' or 'rebel strongholds' from which rebel leaders are known to originate and female returnees if they are associated with a man of adverse interest to the authorities or have no alternative but to become the female head of a household in a squatter camp around Khartoum.[47]

The identification of risk categories is, though, not without its possible disadvantages. There is always the possibility that appellants may seek to fit their case within existing risk categories. The use of risk categories creates a risk of judges stereotyping appellants and failing to take into account individual circumstances.[48] However, in recognising risk categories, the Tribunal is issuing guidance that all members of a particular class of person are at risk; membership of that class will entitle an individual to succeed. At the same time, if an individual is not a member of an identified risk category, then, to qualify, he will need to demonstrate additional characteristics that place him at risk.

Risk factors The third technique is for the Tribunal to identify those risk factors appertaining in particular country contexts that are to be considered by Immigration Judges when assessing risk in an individual appeal. By itemising risk factors, the Tribunal is seeking to select those criteria which, on a proper view of the country information, are likely to be regarded as relevant in determining the degree of risk in any particular case. The particular risk factors identified will be drawn from the assessment of the relevant country information. As with risk categories, risk factors can be modified over time through subsequent country guidance either as the Tribunal develops it own thinking about a particular country issue or as the higher courts indicate to the Tribunal which risk factors they think that the Tribunal should consider.[49]

To illustrate, consider the development of country guidance concerning Sri Lankan Tamils. While the Tribunal has concluded that Tamils are not *per se* at risk

---

[47] *HGMO* above n 14. The Home Office subsequently accepted that all non-Arab Darfuris were at risk of persecution in Darfur and could not reasonably be expected to relocate elsewhere in Sudan. See *AA v Secretary of State for the Home Department (Non-Arab Darfuris—relocation) Sudan CG* [2009] UKAIT 00056.

[48] See *NABD v Minister for Immigration and Multicultural and Indigenous Affairs* (2005) 216 ALR 1 [27] (McHugh J) (Australian High Court).

[49] Some of the impetus to identify risk factors has on occasion emanated from the higher courts; for instance, on the country issue of Albanian blood feuds, see *Koci v Secretary of State for the Home Department* [2003] EWCA Civ 1507; *TB v Secretary of State for the Home Department (Blood Feuds—Relevant Risk Factors) Albania CG* [2004] UKIAT 00158.

on return, it has recognised 12 risk factors that might increase the risk in a particular case.[50] In its guidance, the Tribunal explained that its assessment of the various risk factors had highlighted the need to determine each case on its own facts. In some individual cases, it might be that the fulfilment of one individual risk factor would be sufficient for an appellant to be at risk. In other cases, appellants with a lower profile would need to have their own specific profiles assessed in their own individual situation and placed against the non-exhaustive and non-conclusive, set of risk factors and the volatile country situation. Some factors were identified by the Tribunal as indicating a much higher level of propensity to risk than various other factors.[51] Overall, the Tribunal explained that, given the volatile and worsening situation in Sri Lanka, the assessment of risk in any individual case by an Immigration Judge would require serious consideration of all of the risk factors together with a review of up to date country of origin information set against the very carefully assessed profile of the appellant.[52]

The High Court subsequently delineated the 12 risk factors into those 'background factors' which would not in themselves, either singly or cumulatively, create a real risk on return, though in conjunction with other factors would exacerbate the degree of risk on return, and other risk factors *per se* which were likely to make a person of adverse interest to the Sri Lankan authorities.[53] So, therefore, an individual exhibiting any 'background factor' (for instance, being of Tamil ethnicity, having departed illegally from Sri Lanka or having made an asylum claim abroad) would not for that reason alone be reasonably likely to fear ill-treatment. However, if that individual also possessed other risk factors *per se* (for instance, a previous record as a suspected actual member of the LTTE, a previous criminal record and/or outstanding arrest warrant), then this would signify to the Sri Lankan authorities that the claimant had been significantly involved with the LTTE and generate a risk of warrant detention or interrogation sufficient to amount to serious ill-treatment. The European Court of Human Rights subsequently indicated that, in its view, it was in principle legitimate, when assessing the individual risk to Sri Lankan Tamil returnees, to carry out that assessment on the basis of these risk factors.[54]

---

[50] *LP* above n 34 at [207]–[222]. The risk factors were: Tamil ethnicity; a previous record as a suspected or actual member or supporter of the Liberation Tigers of Tamil Eelam (LTTE); a previous criminal record and/or outstanding arrest warrant; bail jumping and/or escaping from custody; having signed a confession or similar document; having been asked by the security forces to become an informer; the presence of scarring; having returned from London or other centre of LTTE activity or fund-raising; illegal departure from Sri Lanka; the lack of ID card or other documentation; having made an asylum claim abroad; and having relatives in the LTTE.

[51] For instance, being subject to an outstanding arrest warrant, or being a proven bail jumper from a formal bail hearing.

[52] *LP* above n 34 at [227].

[53] *R (Thangeswarajah) v Secretary of State for the Home Department* [2007] EWHC Admin 3288 [10]; *AN & SS v Secretary of State for the Home Department (Tamils—Colombo—risk?) Sri Lanka CG* [2008] UKAIT 00063 [109]–[110]; *TK v Secretary of State for the Home Department (Tamils—LP updated) Sri Lanka CG* [2009] UKAIT 00049.

[54] *NA v United Kingdom* (2009) 48 EHRR 15 [129] (ECtHR).

The clear intention is that by identifying risk factors, generic guidance can assist in the assessment of risk, while also allowing sufficient consideration of the circumstances of an individual case. Risk factors are not intended to be exhaustive, but to require the consideration of characteristics that are likely to be relevant in deciding whether an appellant will face a real risk of persecution in the circumstances of his own case. Immigration Judges also need to pay due regard to the possibility that a number of individual risk factors may not, when considered separately, result in a real risk, but when taken cumulatively and considered in the context of general country conditions, those factors may give rise to a real risk.

The advantage is that while the evidence does not support a distinct risk category, it is still possible to issue generic guidance on those factors indicative of risk. The potential drawback is that judges may approach the assessment of individual appeals by applying the relevant risk factors by rote and not attune them to the particular circumstances of the case. Put simply, a list of risk factors may be used by judges as a checklist, rather than as a series of factors to be considered in the round in the assessment of an individual case. Furthermore, there is always the risk that appellants might be tempted to tailor their stories to the risk factors identified.

Binding Factual Precedent or Authoritative Guidance?

For country guidance to promote consistency it needs to possess some degree of binding effect, but precisely how much? Factual country guidance is not analogous with legally binding precedent. Country conditions are mutable and the application of the guidance needs to be sensitive to changes in such conditions. On the other hand, if country guidance could be disregarded, then it would not secure consistency. The ability of senior judges to designate certain decisions as authoritative guidance to be applied in future appeals must, to some extent, constrain the ability of decentralised adjudicators if the guidance is to function as a unifying force. At the same time, it is always for the decentralised adjudicators to consider individual cases. The task, then, is to pinpoint the optimum degree of binding effect—neither too strong nor too weak—necessary to promote consistency and to avoid rigidity.[55]

Country guidance is to be treated as authoritative in any subsequent appeal, so far as that appeal relates to the country guidance issue in question and depends upon the same or similar evidence, unless it has been expressly superseded or replaced by any later 'CG' determination, or is inconsistent with other authority

---

[55] KC Davis, *Discretionary Justice: A Preliminary Inquiry* (Urbana and Chicago, University of Illinois Press, 1969) 107. On the general issue of the use of precedent or guidance by tribunals, see HJ Elcock, *Administrative Justice* (London, Longmans, 1969) 78–83; T Buck, D Bonner, and R Sainsbury, *Making Social Security Law: The Role and Work of the Social Security and Child Support Commissioners* (Aldershot, Ashgate, 2005) 137–166; T Buck, 'Precedent in Tribunals and the Development of Principles' (2006) 25 *Civil Justice Quarterly* 458; R Carnwath, 'Tribunal Justice—A New Start' [2009] *Public Law* 48, 58–60.

that is binding on the Tribunal (eg a decision of the higher courts).[56] Any failure by an Immigration Judge to follow a clear, apparently applicable country guidance case or to provide reasons why it is inapplicable may be an error of law.[57] The requirement to apply country guidance is rather different from that of legally binding precedent; country guidance should be applied except where it does not apply to the particular facts in an appeal. It is always possible for either party to adduce fresh country evidence to show that an original country guidance decision was wrong or to expose other country issues which require authoritative examination. Such fresh country information must be new evidence—either in the sense of only having come into existence after the country guidance or in the sense of having been newly ascertained—which changes the assessment of future risk.[58] Country guidance may then be authoritative, but it can never be regarded as being definitive for all time.[59] The system does not possess the 'rigidity of legally binding precedent, but has instead the flexibility to accommodate individual cases, changes, fresh evidence and . . . other circumstances'.[60] Country guidance decisions are not 'factual precedents'.[61] However, any attempt to argue that established country guidance should not apply does require new country information which changes the degree of risk posed by country conditions; backdoor attempts to re-litigate country guidance in the absence of such evidence are likely to receive short shrift.[62]

There are other features of the system that militate against inflexible application of country guidance in subsequent appeals. First, an established technique is for guidance to which contain sufficient built-in flexibility so that its application can take into account individual cases.[63] Some cases exemplify the point. When the Tribunal enumerates a list of risk factors, it will normally do so subject to the proviso that the list is neither a checklist nor intended to be exhaustive. The assessment of a claim should be undertaken in the round taking into account any risk factors identified in country guidance alongside the careful scrutiny and assessment of the

---

[56] Asylum and Immigration Tribunal, *Practice Directions* (2007) [18.2].

[57] Ibid, [18.4].

[58] *IA v Secretary of State for the Home Department (Somalia)* [2007] EWCA Civ 323; [2007] Imm AR 685, 690–691 (Keene LJ) (CA); *KH (Sudan) v Secretary of State for the Home Department* [2008] EWCA Civ 887 [4] (Sedley LJ).

[59] In *LT v Secretary of State for the Home Department (Internal flight—registration system) Turkey* [2004] UKIAT 000175 [3] the Tribunal explained that '[n]o judicial decision has the power of crystallising the facts of the real world to an extent where not reality, but what has been said about it is the guide. What "country guidance" cases are intended to do is to lay down an approach to a settled factual situation, not to decree that that situation is to be treated as if it were the same for ever'. See also *OM v Secretary of State for the Home Department (AA(1) wrong in law) Zimbabwe CG* [2006] UKAIT 00077 [12].

[60] *NM* above n 7 at [140].

[61] Ibid, [141].

[62] *MY v Secretary of State for the Home Department (Country guidance cases—no fresh evidence) Eritrea* [2005] UKAIT 00158; *Ariaya v Secretary of State for the Home Department* [2006] EWCA Civ 48; [2006] Imm AR 347, 364 (Richards LJ) (CA).

[63] JA Farmer, *Tribunals and Government* (London, Weidenfeld and Nicolson, 1974) 174–175.

evidence in an individual appeal.[64] Likewise, when giving guidance concerning the existence or otherwise of 'risk categories', the Tribunal will often subject this to the need to assess each appeal carefully. So, for instance, despite the societal discrimination they may experience, Afghan Sikhs and Hindus have not been recognised as a distinct risk category, but an individual's status as a Sikh or Hindu is a factor to be taken into account in assessing individual cases.[65] Similarly, country guidance may state that mere membership of a political party is unlikely to give rise to a real risk of persecution, but the degree of risk may increase with an individual's profile within that party.[66]

A second feature concerns the temporal dimension of country guidance. Country guidance remains valid until it is replaced by subsequent guidance. However, its temporal validity may vary depending on the nature of the country issue dealt with. For instance, in 2005, the Tribunal noted that 'Iraq is a country where change occurs at a faster rate than most other countries of the world. Country Guidance cases on Iraq are unlikely to have a very long shelf life'.[67] By contrast, country guidance concerning deeply rooted moral, social and religious causes of persecution or ill-treatment—for example, female genital mutilation, the treatment of ethnic minorities or religious apostasy—may by its nature possess greater longevity.

More generally, the Tribunal has explained that the passage of time after a country guidance decision may itself warrant a re-examination of the country situation even though the outcome may be unchanged.[68] Judges applying country guidance are aware that the age of individual country guidance decisions may mean that they have been overtaken by changes in country conditions and should therefore be treated with a corresponding degree of caution. In any event, fresh country information will still need to be taken into account when applying country guidance. In this way, country guidance may provide the parameters for decision-making by establishing a benchmark against which subsequent country developments are to be assessed. In summary, country guidance is to be considered as authoritative until fresh evidence demonstrates a change in country conditions; it is intended as authoritative, though flexible, guidance, but not legally binding precedent.

---

[64] See *IA HC KD RO HG v Secretary of State for the Home Department (Risk—guidelines—separatist) Turkey CG* [2003] UKIAT 00034 [46]; *IK v Secretary of State for the Home Department (Returnees—records—IFA) Turkey CG* [2004] UKIAT 00312 [133].

[65] *SL* above n 9.

[66] See *GG v Secretary of State for the Home Department (political oppositionists) Ivory Coast CG* [2007] UKAIT 00086.

[67] *RA v Secretary of State for the Home Department (Christians) Iraq CG* [2005] UKIAT 00091 [74].

[68] *NM* above n 7 at [140].

Using Country Guidance

Applying Country Guidance

After country guidance has been issued, it then needs to be applied. The decision produced in an individual case should be a composite one which blends together the individual facts, the guidance, and other relevant considerations. Country guidance does not absolve Immigration Judges from undertaking their own reasoning. An Immigration Judge cannot simply conclude that 'this country guidance case means that this particular appeal is either allowed or dismissed'; it will also be necessary to explain and justify the application of that guidance in the context of the particular appeal.[69] The courts have, for instance, stressed that while authoritative, a country guidance decision should not be interpreted as if it was a statute. The Immigration Judge's task is not a simple tick box exercise, but should involve making an assessment of risk on the full evidence. The weight to be attached to any particular factor, such as a risk factor, is a matter of judgment.[70] In this respect, the senior judges who compile country guidance have little control over its application. At the same time, any party who considers that country guidance has been inappropriately applied may challenge that decision on the basis that it contains a legal error.

But applying country guidance is not necessarily problem-free. There is always the risk that a judge—by reason of a lack of either proper consideration or sufficient effort and care—will not tailor country guidance to the particular circumstances of an individual appeal. In other words, country guidance may be used as a checklist rather than as a guide which informs the assessment of risk. In this respect, it is important to bear in mind the time pressures on judges to produce determinations. As one judge explained:

> There is a risk with country guidance cases that you try to fit an appellant's circumstances into a box represented by that guidance and you turn the particular appeal into a sort of check list and you try to see how many features of the appellant's case match those of the appellant in the country guidance case and you say appeal dismissed or appeal allowed. And that is to be avoided. There is sometimes a temptation to do that, but the focus should be on the individual case at hand.[71]

The alternate risk is that some Immigration Judges may have reservations about the content of individual country guidance decisions and be reluctant to apply them. But the position is that country guidance should be applied, unless an individual appeal is distinguishable on its facts or if cogent reasons can be given for the non-application of country guidance.

---

[69] Interview with a Senior Immigration Judge.

[70] *OD (Ivory Coast) v Secretary of State for the Home Department* [2008] EWCA Civ 1299 [11] (Touslon LJ).

[71] Immigration Judge interview 2.

Country guidance has other implications for Immigration Judges. It reduces their role in handling primary country information and focuses their attention more exclusively upon credibility; if country guidance identifies risk categories or risk factors, then what is the position of the appellant in this context?

To illustrate, consider the country guidance concerning Eritrean draft evaders who have left that country illegally. In a number of decisions, the Tribunal has recognised that a person who is reasonably likely to have left Eritrea illegally will in general be at real risk on return if he is of draft age, even if he has completed active national service, because he is reasonably likely to be regarded by the Eritrean authorities as a deserter and subjected to ill-treatment on return.[72] However, while many Eritrean nationals do leave their country illegally, it cannot simply be assumed that this was always the case; a finding as to whether an Eritrean appellant has shown that it is reasonably likely he left the country illegally is therefore likely to be of crucial importance in deciding risk on return to that country.[73] In applying this guidance, an Immigration Judge will then have to assess the credibility of the individual claim: is an individual appellant who claims to have left Eritrea illegally credible? If so, then he may well be at risk on return.

While country guidance means that judges do not have to grapple with copious amounts of country information, they still have to supplement the guidance with recent country information. If a judge simply follows country guidance without also considering any subsequent changes in country conditions, then this may comprise an error of law. If it is argued at a subsequent appeal that there is fresh country information requiring a departure from country guidance, then the Immigration Judge must assess whether the information relied upon does in fact justify such a departure.

By way of an example, consider the following appeal concerning a Somali woman, who had been found by the Immigration Judge to be a member of a majority clan.[74] In *NM* the Tribunal had issued country guidance to the effect that it is likely that such an individual will be able to find protection of a majority clan in southern Somalia and will not therefore be at risk.[75] At the same time, lone females will be at a greater risk than males, but they will not be able to show that, simply as lone female returnees from the United Kingdom, that they have no place of clan majority safety. In considering the appellant's argument that fresh country information demonstrated that conditions in Somalia had changed, the judge noted that when deciding whether country guidance remained generally applicable, 'it is not just a question of deciding whether some pieces of the jigsaw have

---

[72] *MA* above n 46. Before this decision, the Tribunal had produced a number of other country guidance decisions on the same country issue. See *IN v Secretary of State for the Home Department (Draft evaders—evidence of risk) Eritrea CG* [2005] UKIAT 00106, *KA* above n 8; *AH v Secretary of State for the Home Department (Failed asylum seekers—involuntary returns) Eritrea CG* [2006] UKAIT00078; *WA v Secretary of State for the Home Department (Draft-related risks updated—Muslim Women) Eritrea CG* [2006] UKAIT 00079.

[73] *MA* above n 46 at [234] and [449].

[74] Case 80.

[75] *NM* above n 7 at [119].

changed. It is almost inevitable that they will have done. The real issue is whether there is fresh evidence to show that the overall picture in the jigsaw has changed'. Having examined recent developments in Somalia—the return of Somalis to Mogadishu after the end of fighting; patrols by African Union peacekeepers; and serious clan fighting in Kismayo—the Immigration Judge concluded that the situation in Somalia remained precarious. Nonetheless, 'the picture so far as majority clans and the security position are concerned is essentially unchanged since the Tribunal reached its decision in *NM*. It follows that this country guidance case should be applied'.

Immigration Judges themselves generally welcome the assistance provided by country guidance, while recognising some of its limitations. The following comments reflect the general view of those judges interviewed:

> If country guidance is done properly it should be a very good system. Some of my colleagues do not agree with some of the cases, but you need some continuity of decision-making. When I started as an Immigration Judge, I tried to learn about country conditions by speaking with other judges, but they would come up with completely different views on the objective situation in relation to certain countries. So, country guidance has brought something of a level playing field with people knowing what the consensus view is on a particular country issue. The only trouble is that time marches on and often you get to the hearing and then you have to take on board additional country information that representatives put in front of you by way of updated material that was not considered in the relevant country guidance case.[76]

> Country guidance is not a perfect system. It is in danger of getting out of date. Nevertheless, it is a useful way of trying to clarify country issues which come up repeatedly, and to provide some kind of consistency across the jurisdiction. Without country guidance, the system would, I think, quickly descend into chaos. You still have to have your eye open for the possibility that the individual case should be distinguished from general country guidance. But, with those sorts of qualifications aside, it is a helpful system and gives us some kind of benchmark to work with. We have got to have some landmarks with which to navigate country issues.[77]

Disapplying Country Guidance

In what circumstances can a judge legitimately not apply country guidance? The critical issue here is the adequacy of a judge's reasons given to justify non-application of country guidance. If a judge departs from wide-ranging and authoritative country guidance concerning a broadly defined risk category, then the obligation to give adequate reasons justifying departure may be heightened. The content of those reasons will normally focus upon the fresh country evidence that has come into existence after the country guidance case. Judges are not normally required to refer specifically in their determinations to every piece of

---

[76] Immigration Judge interview 11.
[77] Immigration Judge interview 3.

country information relied upon in an appeal, but they should refer to such evidence in sufficient detail so as to justify why relevant country guidance is not being followed.

For instance, in an appeal, an Immigration Judge found that country guidance to the effect that Sikhs were not generally at risk in Afghanistan was no longer applicable because that guidance was two years old and there were frequent reports of fighting. However, a senior judge subsequently held that the judge had erred because of the lack of proper reasons and reference to specific country information to justify departure from country guidance.[78] Another appeal concerned the status of country guidance concerning whether Congolese nationals were at risk on return because of their status as failed asylum claimants. A tribunal panel had previously issued country guidance to the effect that failed Congolese asylum claimants were not, as a general category of person, at risk on return. But in a subsequent appeal, an Immigration Judge departed from the guidance in light of the existence of a country report which supported the claimed practice that the Congolese authorities both detained and ill-treated returnees. Again, the judge was found to have erred: the mere existence of a recent country report was insufficient; what was required was an assessment of why that report should be accepted. A further consideration in this instance was the breadth of the risk category involved; as the Tribunal explained, '[t]he wider the risk category posited, the greater the duty on an Immigration Judge to give careful reasons based on an adequate body of evidence'.[79]

Those judges interviewed recognised that departing from country guidance required them to provide valid reasons. They also recognised that both fresh country reports and changes in country conditions can also be used to distinguish a specific appeal from apparently applicable country guidance. As one judge noted, 'country guidance is only binding if nothing has changed. And that is very rare because more often than not things have changed or there are more reports available or something more up to date'.[80] However, from the sample of appeals examined, a number of features were apparent: country guidance is frequently relied upon by all parties; representatives rarely contest country guidance; and judges overwhelmingly apply country guidance to individual appeals.

Appraising Country Guidance

What then is to be made of country guidance? What value does the system have? What of the requisite expertise to produce country guidance? To what extent does country guidance promote quality in asylum adjudication? Finally, is adjudication

[78] Case 11.

[79] *MK v Secretary of State for the Home Department (AB and DM confirmed) Democratic Republic of Congo CG* [2006] UKAIT 00001 [18].

[80] Immigration Judge interview 8.

an appropriate and effective legal mechanism by which to issue broad-ranging country guidance when compared with the alternatives?

The Benefits and Criticisms of Country Guidance

On the benefits of country guidance, the Tribunal has had this to say:

> The system enables the parties and the judiciary to know where to look for what the Tribunal sees as the relevant guidance, the parties to know what they have to deal with, and, if they wish to take issue with it, what it is that has to be the target of their evidence or argument. It enables parties to rely on the material which others have had accepted without reproducing or repeating it every time, or if it has been rejected, to know that there is no point in repeating it. Consistency and the justice which that brings can be provided for, even though differing and perhaps reasonable views can be taken of a wide variety of material. It also has the advantage of enabling the understanding of country conditions to be refined as successive decisions may lead to the identification of consequential issues to be grappled with which had hitherto been unrecognised ... parties can focus their evidence and arguments upon the aspect with which they take issue.[81]

At the same time, the system inevitably suffers from some drawbacks. First, country guidance tends only to be issued after claims raising a particular country issue have been within the appeal process for sometime. This is not necessarily always a problem; some countries generate continuing flows of applicants. But, in relation to other countries, it may mean that the Tribunal has spent its time and resources unnecessarily. This can lead to country guidance decisions of marginal use remaining on the CG list because the Tribunal's view is that as country guidance is a judicial function it can only be generated and replaced by subsequent judicial decisions.[82]

A second difficulty concerns the types of country issues selected for country guidance purposes. The value of country guidance is that country issues of general application can be considered in particular depth by examining a wide range of country information sources. But devoting resources to producing wide-ranging guidance can though come at a cost as country issues affecting smaller numbers of appellants may not receive the same kind of assessment.

A further practical difficulty concerns the amount of time it takes to produce country guidance. The word may get around that country guidance on a particular

---

[81] *NM* above n 7 at [142].

[82] Other asylum decision-makers elsewhere, such as the Canadian Immigration and Refugee Board, are statutorily empowered to issue policy guidelines as a function separate from and in addition to adjudication. See F Houle and L Sossin, 'Tribunals and Guidelines: Exploring the Relationship Between Fairness and Legitimacy in Administrative Decision-making' (2006) 49 *Canadian Public Administration* 282; A Macklin, 'Refugee Roulette in the Canadian Casino' in J Ramji-Nogales, AI Schoenholtz and PG Schrag (eds), *Refugee Roulette: Disparities in Asylum Adjudication and Proposals for Reform* (New York, New York University Press, 2009) 135, 151–157. Putting to one side the Tribunal's unhappy experience with the *Asylum Gender Guidelines* (IAA, 2000)—which were issued in 2000 only to be subsequently withdrawn—its position is that it only has the legal power to issue country guidance through adjudication; to do otherwise would be to in an administrative, rather than a judicial, capacity.

issue is imminent, but it is not always certain that an appeal listed as potential country guidance will in fact be reported as such. Then there is the balance to be drawn by the Tribunal panel hearing a country guidance case between ensuring that its guidance is effectively comprehensive by taking into account recent country information, which can always be updated, and finality in decision-making.[83] Furthermore, a potential country guidance decision will have to proceed through the Tribunal's own quality assurance processes, the internal review of that decision by other senior judges, and its reporting committee will have to decide whether to assign the CG designation. In the meantime, other ordinary asylum appeals will still need to be heard and determined. In this respect, the Tribunal's position is that an individual appeal should not be adjourned pending the promulgation of a forthcoming country guidance decision. The administration of justice 'does not dictate that the Tribunal should routinely adjourn appeals on the off chance that, at some future point, the Tribunal will be in a position to consider an issue in greater detail or on the off chance that the law or views of the Tribunal might change'.[84] If it did, then the whole adjudication process would simply grind to a halt.

A fourth difficulty is that country guidance decisions are always susceptible to becoming out of date and overtaken by changes in country conditions; there is no necessary reason to suppose that country guidance issued in 2010 will be adequate in relation to appeals heard in 2011. As we have already seen, Immigration Judges applying country guidance will need to supplement it with up to date country information. But is this sufficient when country conditions can change rapidly? In 2007, the Tribunal produced country guidance on the situation in Zimbabwe on the basis of evidence about conditions in that country largely concerning the previous two years or so before then.[85] Conditions in Zimbabwe subsequently deteriorated swiftly. The consequence is that there may be an air of unreality in handling country guidance dealing with past events when it is apparent that country conditions have changed; effective country guidance presumes active management by the Tribunal to guard against its own guidance becoming obsolete.

Another difficulty is that while it is possible for appellants in subsequent appeals to adduce fresh country information, there is no guarantee that they will always be in a position to do, especially if unrepresented. One remedy may be for country guidance decisions to be subject to a sunset clause, a technique familiar enough from its deployment in the legislative process to ensure that a provision or statute will lapse unless specifically renewed.[86] Given the importance of country guidance, it might well be preferable if such cases had a limited lifespan—say one year—after

---

[83] For instance, representatives may wish to submit further evidence after the hearing has finished, a course which the Tribunal has indicated will only be allowed in exceptional circumstances. See *AN & SS* above n 53 at [95]: 'Country guidance cases take long enough as it is to be written and promulgated. The hearing should normally be the cut-off point. If the Tribunal is bombarded with further evidence and arguments after the hearing, but before the determination has been written up, it may be an unconscionably long time before the determination is complete'.

[84] Case 59.

[85] *HS* above n 30.

[86] See, eg, the Prevention of Terrorism Act 2005, s 13.

which time they would automatically cease to have an authoritative status, though they could still be drawn upon by judges, as supplemented by fresh country information. If so, then this would require the Tribunal to consider, on a regular basis, whether fresh country information and changes in country conditions necessitated modification of its guidance. But the problem is that one size does not fit all; old country guidance may be perfectly serviceable.

Two particular concerns with country guidance have been raised by representatives. The first is that overall country guidance tends to be negative toward appellants, that is, country guidance limits rather than extends the range of people who qualify for asylum. On a factual level, this criticism may be misplaced since a fair amount of country guidance concerning major asylum generating countries—the Democratic Republic of Congo, Somalia and Zimbabwe—recognises particular risk categories. At the same time, an explanatory factor for the perception that country guidance seems negative toward asylum applicants arises from the dynamics of reason-giving and decision-writing itself. The trend within the Tribunal is that detailed reasons are given when dismissing appeals because of the importance of informing an appellant why he has lost; when allowing an appeal, it is not usually necessary for the Tribunal to give such detailed reasons. When on examination at the hearing an individual appellant, whose case has been selected for potential country guidance purposes, succeeds on an issue particular to his own appeal, the resulting determination is unlikely to generate the long discourse that is necessary for comprehensive country guidance.

A second ground of criticism has been the opacity of the criteria by which senior judges select potential country guidance issues and cases; how do senior judges decide which issues and cases are to be used for country guidance purposes? Representatives have also complained of preparing for a country guidance case only to be informed at the hearing that the appeal will no longer be a country guidance vehicle. As noted above, the country guidance function is centralised within the Tribunal. Senior judges have been wary about formally stating the criteria by which certain country issues and cases have been selected, perhaps out of a fear of challenge as to why one particular country issue was chosen but not another. Furthermore, the task of managing the system is at times beset with practical difficulties. The obvious implication is that, as the Tribunal has been developing its country guidance system, it has been cautiously feeling its way as well as undergoing its own learning process: to understand the nature of the endeavour upon which it has embarked. Nonetheless, a more formal statement as to the Tribunal's policy concerning the selection and management of country guidance would be welcome.

Other concerns with the country guidance process have concerned the amount of time that particular country issues take to get finally resolved and the actual effectiveness of such guidance once issued. Country guidance issues can often be challenged in the higher courts and then sent back and forth between them and the Tribunal. The classic example is provided by the extraordinary country guidance litigation over returns to Zimbabwe. Over a four year period, the Tribunal issued four country guidance decisions on the safety of returnees to Zimbabwe after successive remittals by the Court of Appeal.[87] Given the factual complexity of the country issues involved and their dynamic nature, the litigation illustrates how the system ensures anxious scrutiny of issues affecting a large number of people with life or death consequences. At the same time, the protracted nature of the litigation over essentially the same country issue induced delays which were disadvantageous to all concerned and may have undermined public confidence in the system. In the Court of Appeal, hundreds of Zimbabwean appeals were stacked up at different points to await definitive tribunal country guidance. In any event, the cost and time taken up by the litigation were soon overtaken by events. In late 2008, the Tribunal had recognised that those Zimbabweans at risk on return included not only members of the opposition party, but also those unable to demonstrate support for the ruling party (Mugabe's Zanu PF). However, in 2009, the Home Office issued its own guidance that the Tribunal's view had been undermined by political developments in Zimbabwe and ought not therefore to be followed.[88] The rather incongruous consequence of this was that one party to the adjudication process was in effect seeking to undermine a judicial decision by administrative guidance rather than seeking to challenge it through subsequent litigation.

Country Guidance, Adjudication, and Polycentricity

Practicalities and criticism of individual decisions aside, a more fundamental critique has developed.[89] Country guidance, it has been argued, prioritises certainty and consistency over individual justice. The system subverts the rule that obiter comments in a judicial decision are not binding in subsequent cases as they were not determinative. Furthermore, the system undermines the principle that precedents are generally binding on points of law, not fact. A party to the adjudication process should be free to invite the adjudicator to make factual findings on the basis of the evidence presented there and should not be bound by factual findings reached in the adjudication of a previous dispute to which he was not party to. In short, country guidance is too blunt a tool with which to perform a sensitive and complex adjudicative task.

---

[87] See *AA (No 1) v Secretary of State for the Home Department (Involuntary returns to Zimbabwe) Zimbabwe CG* [2005] UKAIT 00144; *AA and LK v Secretary of State for the Home Department* [2007] 2 All ER 160 (CA); *AA (No 2) v Secretary of State for the Home Department (Risk for involuntary returnees) Zimbabwe CG* [2006] UKAIT 00061; *AA (Zimbabwe) v Secretary of State for the Home Department* [2007] EWCA Civ 149 (CA); *HS* above n 30; *HS (Zimbabwe) v Secretary of State for the Home Department* [2008] EWCA Civ 915 (CA); *RN v Secretary of State for the Home Department (Returnees) Zimbabwe CG* [2008] UKAIT 00083.

[88] Home Office United Kingdom Border Agency, *Zimbabwe: Operational Guidance Note* (London, Home Office, 2009) [3.6.14]–[3.6.16]. See G Clayton, 'Home Office Guidance and Zimbabwe' (2009) 15(2) *Immigration Law Digest* 21.

[89] See, eg, C Yeo, 'Certainty, Consistency, and Justice' in Yeo (ed) above n 28; J Ensor, 'Country Guideline Cases: Can they be Challenged?' (2005) 11 *Immigration Law Digest* 19.

While not framed in such terms, this critique is redolent of Fuller's analysis of the limits to adjudication posed by polycentric tasks.[90] A polycentric decision can be described as one which possesses and exerts an effect beyond the resolution of the particular dispute between the two parties involved; its ramifications may affect others who were not party to the dispute. While Fuller recognised that polycentric issues should not be excluded altogether from adjudication and that the matter is often one of degree, he emphasised that such issues tended to highlight the limits of adjudication. This is because the adjudication of disputes arising out of a polycentric situation can affect those individuals who have been unable to participate. In relation to country guidance, the concerns may be said to be heightened because the (country) issues involved are factual and evidential, not legal, and prone to frequent change. The determination of a *lis inter partes* may not be the most appropriate means of producing generic country guidance designed to be applied in relation to many other individuals.

There are a number of responses to be made here. First, country guidance necessarily restricts the ability of other potentially affected individuals to become parties to the litigation; were it otherwise, the whole process would be rendered unmanageable. But this restriction is not absolute; affected individuals can always participate in their own appeals to contest the applicability and validity of country guidance. Secondly, country guidance has a built-in remedy by which fresh evidence can be presented. Indeed, Fuller's own description of the desirable degree of flexibility of precedent in such situations is an appropriate enough description of the authoritative, though not binding, status of country guidance cases: '[i]f judicial precedents are liberally interpreted and are subject to reformulation and clarification as problems not originally foreseen arise, the judicial process is enabled to absorb . . . polycentric elements'.[91] As Fuller recognised, if adjudication is understood as a collaborative enterprise projected through time, then an accommodation of legal doctrine—or, in this context, country guidance—to the complex aspects of a problem can be made as these aspects reveal themselves in successive cases. An incremental approach can ameliorate the challenges posed for adjudication by polycentric issues.[92] Thirdly, judges have to assess risk on the basis of evidence in existence at the date of decision.

More generally, it has been argued that Fuller's analysis of the limits to adjudication posed by polycentric issues is itself deficient in that it is premised upon too strict an adherence to the adversary process and that it marginalises the role of the decision-maker's expert investigation of the issues.[93] If adjudication is understood not just as a forum by which affected parties participate in the making of a

[90] LL Fuller, 'The Forms and Limits of Adjudication' (1978) 92 *Harvard Law Review* 353, 393–404. Fuller's concept of polycentricity is derived from M Polyani, *The Logic of Liberty: Reflections and Rejoinders* [1951] (Indianapolis, Liberty Fund, 1998).

[91] Fuller n 90 above at 398.

[92] See MM Feeley and EL Rubin, *Judicial Policy Making and the Modern State: How the Courts Reformed America's Prisons* (Cambridge, Cambridge University Press, 1999) 320–321.

[93] JWF Allison, 'Fuller's Analysis of Polycentric Disputes and the Limits of Adjudication' (1994) 53 *Cambridge Law Journal* 367.

decision, but also as an organisation by collaborative expert investigation, then the challenges posed by polycentric issues may, to a large extent, be overcome. In other words, if the legitimacy of adjudication is not solely predicated upon the participation of affected parties, but also upon the expertise of the adjudicator and the adoption of an inquisitorial approach toward investigating the issues, then the problems for adjudication by polycentric issues may be ameliorated. However, this begs the question whether the adjudicatory body is properly entitled to be considered as expert in the relevant subject-matter. The question of tribunal expertise in country conditions is, of course, precisely the issue that has been contested by the Tribunal and country experts, and the tensions are, if anything, accentuated as regards country guidance.

Country Guidance and Country Expertise

In undertaking the country guidance function, much will inevitably depend on the Tribunal's own expertise, but what kind of expertise is required and how is it to be attained? As a former Tribunal judge has noted, there is little or no training for decision-makers on either fact-finding in general or, more specifically, on how to evaluate country of origin information.[94] The justification of senior judges is that they build up their own expertise in country conditions.[95] In practice, this expertise is built up by having a select group of senior judges who undertake the country guidance work.

As discussed in the previous chapter, these views have been challenged by country experts. For Good, country guidance 'presupposes that tribunals are indeed able to carry out comprehensive, effective analyses of all available country material'.[96] Even if the country information presented to the Tribunal is comprehensive, the country guidance system 'takes for granted the ability of the asylum judiciary alone, bereft of independent expert advice, to assess for itself bodies of evidence . . . regarding countries for which it lacks first-hand knowledge or experience, and contexts whose cultural nuances call for specialised hermeneutic elucidation'.[97] From this perspective, country guidance cannot be accepted without reservation.

For their part, the higher courts have recognised that the Tribunal's senior judges possess 'a background of experience, not least experience in assessing evidence about country conditions' unavailable to the higher courts.[98] While the

---

[94] G Care, 'The Judiciary, the State and the Refugee: the Evolution of Judicial Protection in Asylum—A UK Perspective' (2005) 28 *Fordham International Law Journal* 1421, 1455.

[95] *SK* above n 37 at [5]; J Barnes, 'Expert Evidence—The Judicial Perspective in Asylum and Human Rights Appeals' (2004) 16 *International Journal of Refugee Law* 349.

[96] A Good, *Anthropology and Expertise in the Asylum Courts* (London, Routledge-Cavendish, 2007) 234.

[97] Ibid, 235.

[98] *R (Madan and Kapoor) v Secretary of State for the Home Department* [2007] EWCA Civ 770; [2008] 1 All ER 973, 978 (CA). See also *Subesh v Secretary of State for the Home Department* [2004] EWCA Civ 56; [2004] Imm AR 112, 140 (Laws LJ) noting that the Tribunal 'is a specialist appellate

higher courts oversee and supervise the country guidance system, responsibility for fact-finding and guidance on country conditions rests principally with the Tribunal, which is recognised by the higher courts as the specialist body to deal with such matters. This is not to imply that the higher courts have been excessively deferential to the country guidance decisions and have not entertained challenges against such determinations seriously. The only evidence that the Tribunal has been able to deploy its specialised knowledge in assessing country information lies in the adequacy of its reasons.[99] While the higher courts have adopted a generally deferential approach, this has not deterred them from allowing some challenges to country guidance cases on the grounds that the Tribunal's guidance was deficient in some way.[100] At the same time, other challenges have been rejected on the basis that the assessment of risk reached by the Tribunal was properly open to it.[101]

From the Tribunal's perspective, recognition by the higher courts of its expert and specialist nature is likely to fortify both its position and standing. By comparison, for country experts, such recognition is itself just as deluded as the Tribunal's own espousal of its expertise; the higher courts, like the Tribunal, are composed of judges not experts, who possess no greater knowledge of country conditions than the Tribunal.[102] To point out the obvious: the views espoused by country experts and the Tribunal depend greatly upon the different presuppositions of those involved. Country experts may take exception to legal decision-makers who closely scrutinise their professional judgment; declarations of expertise by the Tribunal in country conditions may be viewed by country experts as unjustifiably self-reinforcing judicial hegemony. By contrast, Tribunal members may be

---

tribunal. An important part of its work has been to identify current trends and problems and, where appropriate, to give general guidance on in-country conditions on the basis of its expert consideration of the latest material'. See also *AH (Sudan) v Secretary of State for the Home Department* [2007] UKHL 49; [2008] 1 AC 678, 691 (Baroness Hale) (HL).

[99] Cf the Tribunal's comments, in *TK* above n 53 at [6] on the approval of the European Court of Human Rights in *NA* above n 54) of the AIT's country guidance in *LP* above n 34: '. . . it is clear that the European Court of Human Right's endorsement of the validity of a system of country guidance such as is applied in the UK was not unconditional. It was given only because the Court was satisfied that the UK AIT had conducted a careful and comprehensive assessment weighing different sources according to their objective merit. The Court also fully recognised that country guidance is not inflexible; it must be applied by reference to new evidence as it emerges; otherwise it would fall foul of the principle of *ex nunc* assessment of risk. Our country guidance system can only expect to have authority domestically and command respect abroad, therefore, if it maintains these standards'.

[100] For successful challenges against country guidance cases, see *S & Others* above n 12 (the Tribunal failed to explain what it had made of a special rapporteur's reports); *AA (Zimbabwe) v Secretary of State for the Home Department* [2008] EWCA Civ 149 (the Tribunal failed to take account of witness evidence that failed asylum seekers were at risk); *FK (Kenya) v Secretary of State for the Home Department* [2008] EWCA Civ 119 (the Tribunal failed properly to determine the reasonableness of internal relocation).

[101] For unsuccessful challenges against country guidance, see *AH (Sudan)* above n 98 (despite some lack of clarity in the Tribunal's drafting of its determination, there was no error of law); *BK (Democratic Republic of Congo) v Secretary of State for the Home Department* [2008] EWCA Civ 1322 (grounds of challenge amounted to no more than a complaint that the facts should have been decided differently); *JC (China) v Secretary of State for the Home Department* [2009] EWCA Civ 81 (it was a matter of judgment whether the risk had reached the level where the human rights framework was engaged).

[102] A Good, 'Expert Evidence in Asylum and Human Rights Appeals: an Expert's View' (2004) 16 *International Journal of Refugee Law* 358, 359.

similarly sceptical of self-proclaimed experts, some of whom may be seen to wish to confer upon themselves the sole ability to pronounce on country conditions.

Some synthesis of these two approaches is required. In practice, this is attained in the following ways. First, country experts are fully entitled to present their own views and readings of country conditions but these will not automatically be accepted by the Tribunal. While judges scrutinise such evidence, they take seriously the views of experts accepted to be knowledgeable on the country concerned. Secondly, while the Tribunal will draw upon country information, the task of assessing whether or not there is a risk on return remains one for legal decision by the Tribunal itself. Much of the skill of judicial decision-making when dealing with country information consists in correlating what it says about risk and dangers for particular categories with the concepts of asylum law.[103] As country experts are neither legally qualified nor use the same legal vocabulary as judicial decision-makers, their assessment of risk cannot be taken to be determinative of the ultimate question of risk on return.

The Effectiveness of Adjudication Relative to Other Legal Mechanisms

A further issue concerns whether adjudication is an effective legal instrument for country guidance purposes. Adjudication may be an appropriate means for securing fairness in the context of a dispute that an individual has with an administrative agency as it will prevent the agency from acting unless its decision can be upheld. However, different considerations can arise when the adjudicative process has fashioned a new technique which not only determines individual cases, but also creates and develops policy by laying down broad-ranging guidance as to how the cases of general categories of person are to be handled. Adjudication is, of course, not the only legal technique which can be utilised in order to formulate such policies. To assess the appropriateness and effectiveness of adjudication as a means of policy making, it is, therefore, instructive to compare it with another legal technique: administrative rule-making.

How, then, does adjudication compare with administrative rule-making as a legal tool for developing policy? It has been noted that appeal procedures are best suited to resolving issues of adjudicative fact that concern the parties involved (ie who did what, where, and when?), while questions of legislative fact (those general facts which help the Tribunal decide broader issues of law and policy) are best resolved through administrative rule-making.[104] But this distinction merely begs the question whether a particular factual/policy issue ought to be resolved through

---

[103] International Association of Refugee Law Judges (IARLJ): Country of Origin Information—Country Guidance Working Party, 'Judicial Criteria for Assessing Country of Origin Information (COI): A Checklist' (2009) 21 *International Journal of Refugee Law* 149, 166.

[104] KC Davis, *Administrative Law Treatise Vol 2* (California, KC Davis Publishing, 1979) 409–415.

either adjudication or rule-making policy. Both adjudication and administrative rule-making have their pros and cons, which, in turn, influence whether a particular issue ought to be classified as one of adjudicative or legislative fact.[105] Assessments of the relative advantages and disadvantages can only be made by taking account of the particular policy-administrative context.[106] It is, therefore, appropriate to compare the production of country guidance through adjudication with the Home Office's exercise of its administrative rule-making power to designate certain states (or a part of a state) which generate asylum claimants as being generally safe.[107]

This rule-making power affects the consideration of initial claims by the Home Office, and the operation of the appeals process, in cases where the claimant is from a designated safe country. Under this power, the Home Office is able to designate certain states as being generally safe. Claims from designated states are initially considered on their merits; if rejected, then a claim must be certified as clearly unfounded—'so clearly without substance that it is bound to fail'—unless the claim is not clearly unfounded.[108] Certified claims only attract an out of country appeal.[109] The Home Office can by order designate states as generally safe if there is no serious risk of persecution in that state or in part of it and removal

---

[105] See generally DL Shapiro, 'The Choice of Rulemaking or Adjudication in the Development of Administrative Policy' (1965) 78 *Harvard Law Review* 921; GO Robinson, 'The Making of Administrative Policy: Another Look at Rulemaking and Adjudication and Administrative Procedure Reform' (1970) 118 *University of Pennsylvania Law Review* 485; JL Jowell, *Law and Bureaucracy: Administrative Discretion and the Limits of Legal Action* (New York, Dunellen Publishing, 1975) 11–38.

[106] Ibid, Jowell at 30–31; R Baldwin, *Rules and Government* (Oxford, Oxford University Press, 1995) 299.

[107] Nationality, Immigration and Asylum Act 2002 s 94. Another option used in the past has been for the Home Office to adopt blanket exceptional leave to remain policies in relation to particular countries under which it would not enforce the removal of claimants to the particular country. However, such policies were largely withdrawn by the Home Office in 2002 and since its general policy has been to consider removal on the circumstances of the individual case. See Hansard HC Debs vol 426 cols 2050–2051WA (18 November 2004).

[108] Nationality, Immigration and Asylum Act 2002 s 94(3); *R v Secretary of State for the Home Department ex parte Thangarasa and Yogathas* [2002] UKHL 36; [2003] 1 AC 920. Certification decisions are challengeable by way of judicial review. See *ZL and VL v Secretary of State for the Home Department* [2003] EWCA Civ 25; [2003] Imm AR 330.

[109] Nationality, Immigration and Asylum Act 2002 s 94(9). For a similar, earlier process, see Asylum and Immigration Act 1996 s 2 under which claimants from designated countries in which there was in general no serious risk of persecution could appeal to an adjudicator inside the UK, but had no onward right of appeal to the Immigration Appeal Tribunal; the Asylum (Designated Countries of Destination and Designated Safe Third Countries) Order SI 1996/2671 designated the following countries: Bulgaria, Cyprus, Ghana, India, Pakistan, Poland, and Romania. According to the Immigration Appeal Tribunal, in *Zenovics v Secretary of State for the Home Department (Right of Appeal—certification) Latvia (Starred determination)* [2001] UKIAT 00013 [12], 'the ability to certify in relation to a country so designated was always anomalous . . . It was hardly fair that an asylum seeker who had a reasonable although ultimately unsuccessful claim should have no appeal to the IAT simply because the country he was fleeing was regarded as generally safe'. Nonetheless, in 2002, the Home Office extended the policy so that certification precluded an in-country right of appeal; its justification being that this process was a useful tool in deterring unmeritorious claims. The concern with non-suspensive appeals is the procedure used, the out of country nature of the appeal process, may deter individuals from lodging appeals, significantly reduce the fairness of the process, and adversely affect the substance of the tribunal process and decision-making, because the appellant cannot attend the appeal hearing.

would not contravene human rights obligations.[110] In deciding whether to desig-nate, regard is to be had to all the circumstances of the state concerned and to country information from any source.[111] Designation orders are subject to the affirmative resolution procedure and do not come into effect unless approved by Parliament.[112] They are also supplemented by Home Office Operational Guidance Notes. Furthermore, the operation of the non-suspensive appeals process is subject to independent oversight.[113]

Both mechanisms—country guidance and designation orders—operate in different ways, but the common thread is that both seek to identify general cat-egories of asylum claimant who may have a stronger or weaker case for asylum, while seeking to balance this up with individual consideration. Both mechanisms are different legal techniques for the development of asylum policy, for explicat-ing the general policy goal (granting asylum to those who qualify) through sup-plementary policy making (identify general categories of claimant) to promote decisional efficiency and consistency. But which legal tool is best suited to the task?

Rule-making has various attractions. While adjudication may be independent, the primary responsibility for administering asylum policy rests with the Home Office and it has delegated legislative power to make designation orders; such orders have a clear legislative mandate. Rule-making is also a more flexible process for designating particular countries when compared with adjudication. It is not dependant upon the vagaries of litigation. Rule-making is also quicker. To issue country guidance, the Tribunal has to go through all the difficulties of trying to set up a country guidance case for hearing and so on. Furthermore, the rate of onward challenge against country guidance can increase the uncertainty whilst the issue is being resolved. Rule-making avoids the time and administrative costs of country guidance and of dealing with onward challenges.

A related advantage is that the Home Office can amend the list of designated safe countries so as to remove states entirely or to retain a state or part of a state in respect of a description of person as its assessment of country conditions

---

[110] Nationality, Immigration and Asylum Act 2002 s 94(5). Under ss 94(5A)–(5C), the Home Office can designate a state or part of a state as generally safe in relation to a particular category of person (eg men only). Ten states were originally designed by the 2002 Act s 94(4) (Cyprus, Czech Republic, Estonia, Hungary, Latvia, Lithuania, Malta, Poland, Slovakia, and Slovenia). For subsequent Asylum (Designated States) Orders (and the countries designated) see SI 2003/970 (Albania, Bulgaria, Serbia and Montenegro, Jamaica, Macedonia, Moldova, and Romania); SI 2003/1919 (Bangladesh, Bolivia, Brazil, Ecuador, Sri Lanka, South Africa, and Ukraine); SI 2005/330 (India), SI 2005/3306 (Mongolia and, for men only, Ghana and Nigeria), SI 2007/2221 (Bosnia Herzegovina, Mauritius, Montenegro, Peru and, for men only, Gambia, Kenya, Liberia, Malawi, Mali, and Sierra Leone); and SI 2010/561 (South Korea and Kosovo).

[111] Nationality, Immigration and Asylum Act 2002 s 94(5D) as inserted by the Asylum (Procedures) Regulations SI 2007/3187 in order to comply with the Council Directive 2005/85/EC on minimum standards on procedures in Member States for granting and withdrawing refugee status.

[112] Nationality, Immigration and Asylum Act 2002 s 112(4).

[113] See S Woodhouse, *The Annual Report of the Certification Monitor 2005* (London, IND, 2005); Independent Chief Inspector of the UK Border Agency, *Report July 2008—September 2009* (London, OCIUKBA, 2009) 25–30.

changes.[114] However, there is no guarantee that such changes in country conditions will in fact be rapidly reflected in an amended designation order. Consider,
for instance, the handling of asylum claims from Jamaica. In 2003, Jamaica was
designated as a safe country.[115] But, in 2005, the Tribunal guidance held that
homosexual men were at risk.[116] The Home Office conceded that, as a general rule,
the Jamaican authorities did not provide homosexual men with sufficient protection against persecution. Nevertheless, there was no subsequent rule-change to the
designation order, though country guidance is taken into account in the Home
Office's Operational Guidance Note.[117]

A related point is that the Home Office has often introduced wider designations
than are necessary without considering whether to make exceptions in the case of
certain categories of person in light of well-recognised persecutory risks for certain
groups. Specific groups of people may be at risk in generally safe countries. To be
useful, the rule-making power will often have to identify which categories of person will be at risk and to make necessary exemptions from the general designation
of a country as safe; the example of Jamaican homosexuals is a good illustration.
One possible advantage of rule-making is that the power could be exercised in
such a manner so as to identify specific categories of asylum claimant, but most
designation orders are blanket designations. The Home Office is able to make
specific designations in respect of a description of person (for instance, by reference, to characteristics such as: gender, language, race, religion, nationality, membership of a social or other group, political opinion, or any other attribute or
circumstance thought appropriate).[118] But it has only made limited use of this;
certain African countries have been designated as generally safe for men only in
light of concerns as to the persecutory risk for women (eg female genital mutilation, trafficking, domestic violence, and forced marriage). Despite calls for more
specific designations, the Home Office has declined to use its powers to do so.[119]
By contrast, in country guidance, the Tribunal has provided a more nuanced
approach by identifying risk categories as appropriate.

Rule-making has other advantages. Unlike country guidance, it is subject to some
degree of political scrutiny.[120] Furthermore, rules have prospective application

---

[114] Nationality, Immigration and Asylum Act 2002 s 94(6). For Asylum (Designated States) Orders
removing states from the list, see SI 2006/3275 (Sri Lanka) and SI 2006/3215 (Bulgaria and Romania).

[115] The Asylum (Designated States) Order SI 2003/970.

[116] *DW v Secretary of State for the Home Department (Homosexual Men—persecution—sufficiency
of protection) Jamaica CG* [2005] UKAIT 00168. See also Hansard HL Deb vol 717 cols 149–150GC
10 February 2010 (Lord Avebury).

[117] Home Office United Kingdom Border Agency, *Jamaica: Operational Guidance Note* (London,
UKBA, 2009). On the general issue of post-implementation review of secondary legislation, see House
of Lords Merits Committee, *What Happened Next? A Study of Post-Implementation Reviews of
Secondary Legislation* (2008–09 HL 180).

[118] Nationality, Immigration and Asylum Act 2002 ss 94(5A)–(5C) (as inserted by the Asylum and
Immigration (Treatment of Claimants etc) Act 2004 s 27(5)).

[119] See Hansard HL Deb vol 717 cols 149–150GC 10 February 2010 (Lord Avebury).

[120] See, eg, Hansard HL Deb vol 693 cols 208–215GC (10 July 2007); Hansard HL Deb vol 717 cols
147–152GC (10 February 2010).

whereas country guidance has retrospective application. While country guidance is designed in part to enhance legal certainty, there can be little certainty for the individual appellant whose appeal is selected as the country guidance vehicle; on the other hand, this absence of certainty is to be expected as all asylum appeals must be determined on the basis of up to date facts.

A critical area of comparison concerns the procedures by which country guidance and designation orders are made and, in particular, the nature of country information relied upon and its assessment. An initial point of contrast concerns the possibilities for consultation; 'whereas adjudication allows consultation of the litigating parties alone, rule-making allows notice and opportunity for comment to all affected parties'.[121] However, the Home Office is not, as with most immigration rule-making, obliged to consult.[122] It has, though, been the Home Office's practice to consult the Independent Advisory Group on Country Information (IAGCI) on the country information considered in arriving at the decision to designate. The IAGCI may commission and consider expert reviews of the relevant country information, but it only reviews relevant country information. Furthermore, the views of the IAGCI are not binding and it cannot comment upon the decision to designate. Both rule-making and adjudication, therefore, allow for some expert input, but without allowing experts to have the final decision.

A second procedural difference concerns the process of assessing country information. In this respect, a particular weakness of the designation order-making process is that, unlike country guidance, there is no formal, open procedure by which the country information relied upon can be disputed and assessed or by which additional evidence can be advanced. Designation orders are not subject to a comprehensive, independent fact-based assessment, though they are subject to judicial review.[123] They are accompanied by bland and uninformative reasons ('the country information used looked at the circumstances of the State'), which compare unfavourably with the detailed evaluation produced by the Tribunal.[124] Country guidance may be immune from political accountability, but the reasons given are open to scrutiny and onward challenge. By contrast, it can be difficult to know which particular items of country information were taken into account in

---

[121] Jowell above n 105 at 18.

[122] See *R (BAPIO Action Ltd) v Secretary of State for the Home Department* [2007] EWCA Civ 1139.

[123] See *R (Javed) v Secretary of State for the Home Department* [2001] EWCA Civ 789; [2001] Imm AR 529 (designation of Pakistan unlawful); *R (Husan) v Secretary of State for the Home Department* [2005] EWHC Admin 189 (designation of Bangladesh irrational). See also the Asylum (Designated States) (Amendment) Order SI 2005/1016.

[124] See, eg, Explanatory Memorandum to the Asylum (Designated States) Order SI 2007/2221 which details neither the country information relied upon nor the assessment reached, but merely notes that the IAGCI found the country information used 'to be generally balanced, accurate, and comprehensive'. According to Explanatory Memorandum to the Asylum (Designated States) Order SI 2010/561 [7.5] the country information considered included information available from the UNHCR, human rights organisations, inter-governmental organisations, NGOs, news media, and the Foreign and Commonwealth Office.

the making of a designation order and what weight was placed upon such information, unless the order is challenged by way of judicial review.

Another advantage of adjudication is that it can operate not just as a process for resolving individual disputes, but also as an ongoing, collaborative enterprise in which the parties concerned seek to cooperate together in the broader interest of ensuring consistency and quality in the asylum process.[125] From this perspective, the adjudication process can accommodate its guidance to the complex aspects of a problem as they reveal themselves in successive cases; a particular advantage of adjudication is that it allows for the incremental elaboration of the issues on a case-by-case basis. Country guidance, like precedents more generally, not only steers judges makers towards certain answers to the questions before them; it frequently helps them to understand both what the questions are and what the answers might be.[126]

As both adjudication and rule-making have their pros and cons, the question is: what is the best mix of strategy and legal technique which achieves the highest rating against legitimising values, such as adherence to legislative mandate, accountability, fairness, expertise, and efficiency?[127] In this respect, it is important to note that both mechanisms are viewed differently by their respective authors. For the Home Office, the success of designation orders is to be evaluated in administrative-policy terms; that is, their contribution to discouraging unfounded claims, preventing the use of the appeals process to frustrate removal, minimising administrative costs, and enhancing public confidence in the broader process.[128] Such designation orders are 'negative' in the sense that they are entirely geared up to designating certain types of claim as clearly unfounded; the Home Office's choice of legal instrument is itself clearly a product of policy considerations. By contrast, country guidance recognises categories of claimant who both will and will not be at risk and there does not appear to be any underlying policy agenda, other than for the Tribunal to augment its own role and status.

On balance, it seems preferable for the decision process to utilise adjudication as the principal means of identifying general categories of asylum claimant. Designation orders may have their place by identifying general categories of claimant which clearly do not in general possess valid claims, but there is much scope for improvement: the Home Office could consult more widely, produce more specific designations by identifying discrete categories, and give far detailed assessments of the country information used. However, adjudication possesses certain features—independence, open procedures, and detailed reason-giving—which raise it above rule-making. The general trend is then that the Tribunal has come to assume responsibility for developing specific country guidance; in the

---

[125] Jowell above n 105 at 28.

[126] N Duxbury, *The Nature and Authority of Precedent* (Cambridge, Cambridge University Press, 2008) 182.

[127] Baldwin above n 106 at 299.

[128] See Explanatory Memorandum to the Asylum (Designated States) Order SI 2007/2221 [7.3]–[7.4]; Explanatory Memorandum to the Asylum (Designated States) Order SI 2010/561 [12.2].

absence of legislative intervention or some major difficulty with the country guidance system, this trend is likely to continue as the Tribunal refines the system.

Conclusion

Tribunals often have to be procedurally innovative in order to handle a heavy caseload effectively and to make efficient use of scarce adjudicative resources. Country guidance is a good illustration of a novel adjudicative technique designed to promote the consistent, authoritative, and efficient handling of appeals. As Laws LJ has noted, the notion of a judicial decision binding on factual issues may be 'foreign to the common law' and 'exotic', but is 'benign and practical' in the asylum context.[129] Criticisms arising from the inconsistency of asylum decisions prompted the Tribunal to establish and develop its country guidance system which is now an established input into the decision process. Further criticisms as to the range and quality of initial country guidance decisions have likewise prompted the Tribunal to improve the standard of its guidance.

Country guidance is also of broader significance outside the context of asylum adjudication. First, it demonstrates that tribunal procedures can develop pragmatically in order to issue guidance not just on legal issues but also factual issues. Second, country guidance also exemplifies the advantages and risks of seeking to issue factual guidance and balance the competing demands of uniformity and flexibility. Finally, country guidance provides both a precedent for the Upper Tribunal to develop expansive guidance function in other adjudicative contexts.[130]

This is, though, not to imply that country guidance is or should be a necessary feature of any asylum process. After all, the Tribunal could continue without the country guidance system; refugee determination processes in many other countries do not operate a comparable system. Even if the need for such guidance is accepted, then adjudication is not the only means of issuing broad-ranging guidance; rule-making could be utilised instead. However, that the country guidance system has been developed in the interests of consistency and efficiency means that those values have been considered sufficiently important for the Tribunal to establish and develop the country guidance system as a means of securing those values. Furthermore, in the context of the asylum process, adjudication possesses various advantages over rule-making as a means of issuing broad-ranging guidance.

The realistic future project is, therefore, not whether country guidance remains a component of the asylum adjudication process, but how it may be refined and improved. In this regard, the following suggestions for the improvement of the country guidance system are advanced. The Tribunal should continue to ensure that it receives a wide range of country information needed for country guidance

---

[129] *S and Others* above n 12 at 435 (Laws LJ).
[130] Carnwath above n 55 at 60.

purposes. The Home Office should continue and also deepen its reliance on information drawn from overseas consular and diplomatic posts. A more rigorous methodology could be employed in this respect to ensure that such information can be evaluated against the same robust criteria as that expected and applied to country expert reports. Furthermore, consideration might also be given as to whether the Tribunal should itself be able to commission country expert evidence; alternatively, the Home Office should be far more willing to instruct its own country experts in country guidance cases. Immigration Judges may need further training on the application of country guidance. Finally, regular re-visits of country issues may ensure that country guidance remains reasonably up to date and also enhance the depth of the Tribunal's understanding of those issues.

It is important to recognise that, by itself, country guidance can only do so much to reduce the risk of the asylum lottery. The application of country guidance is still heavily dependant on the decision-maker's assessment of the credibility of the individual appellant's account. The notion of treating like cases alike is important, but an equally pervasive adage throughout the jurisdiction is that each case must be decided on its own individual facts. While country guidance establishes some parameters in which the assessment of credibility is to be undertaken, it cannot, and is not intended to, eliminate the risks of inconsistency in credibility assessments. Promoting greater consistency as regards the assessment of credibility is likely to be a far more elusive endeavour, one that may not even be possible.

Since the introduction of the country guidance system, the Tribunal has, with support from the higher courts, made substantial efforts to improve the quality of the guidance issued and to broaden the range of country information relied upon. Recent country guidance determinations have been of a demonstrably higher quality than earlier ones. Properly performed and applied, country guidance can assist those deciding asylum claims and thereby contribute to the promotion of a quality asylum decision process.

8

Onward Rights of Challenge

S O FAR THIS book has analysed initial asylum appeals and the issuing of country guidance, but the adjudication process does not terminate here. The losing party is always able to challenge a tribunal decision on error of law grounds. Such challenges come in two types. First, there are a small number of challenges which exert a broader impact on the development of the law ('policy' judicial review); these are to be found amidst a much larger number of fact-specific challenges which do not have any wider importance ('bureaucratic' or 'retail' judicial review).[1] The number of these challenges can be substantial and, to cope with the volume, ordinary judicial review procedures have been modified by the use of paper-only consideration and short time limits to ensure efficient processing of challenges. In any event, onward challenges against tribunal decisions are not the exclusive preserve of judicial review procedure as it is commonly referred to, but encompass any onward challenges whether by senior tribunal judges or the higher courts. A principal issue is to ensure that the right cases are decided at the right level; cases of wider public importance should be dealt with by a suitably higher court, and the mass of fact-specific cases can be dealt with by the second-tier tribunal.

Another problem is how to handle onward challenges in the majority of the cases. The identification of any error of law in an impugned tribunal decision is itself very far from the end of the process. Once an error of law has been detected, it must then be corrected and a new, lawful, decision substituted. This may often require fresh findings of fact. Appeals may, then, have to be remitted, that is, sent from the reviewing court or tribunal back to the lower tribunal for necessary findings of fact to be made in order to conclude the case. How should such processes be handled? There is also the issue of onward challenges against these remitted or reconsideration decisions. To which judicial body should such challenges lie—a senior tribunal judge, the Administrative Court, or the Court of Appeal? And how many times should an individual appeal be capable of being remitted from a higher court or tribunal to a lower one?

A further complicating feature is that legal challenges may not necessarily be confined to the operation of the appellate process. There may be scope for indi-

---

[1] P Cane, 'Understanding Judicial Review and Its Impact' in M Hertogh and S Halliday (eds), *Judicial Review and Bureaucratic Impact: International and Interdisciplinary Perspectives* (Cambridge, Cambridge University Press, 2004) 18–19.

viduals to access ordinary judicial review procedure before the commencement of the appellate process, throughout it, or after its completion. While such challenges lie outside the appeals system, they are nevertheless intimately connected with the broader decision process. Given the tension between the competing background adjudicatory values—access to administrative justice and efficiency—both the procedural design of any system of onward challenge and the issue of tribunal organisation are central to adjudicative quality.

Set against this background, this chapter seeks to do the following. First, it examines the benefits and costs of onward challenges, and their organisation in the asylum appellate context. The system of onward challenges against asylum appeal decisions has been subject to almost perpetual redesign since the creation of asylum appeals in 1993. The latest set of changes has involved the relocation of the jurisdiction from the single-tier AIT to the new two-tier tribunal system, the First-tier and Upper Tribunals, and the transfer of one particular category of immigration and asylum judicial reviews—fresh claim asylum judicial reviews—from the Administrative Court to the Upper Tribunal. The chapter presents a detailed analysis of these changes. Secondly, the chapter assesses the extent to which systems of onward challenge provide an effective technique for promoting and assessing the quality of appeal decision-making. Thirdly, the chapter picks up a topic of wider significance throughout the tribunals world: the relationship between specialist tribunals and generalist higher courts. By considering this topic and the re-positioning of tribunals within the judicial hierarchy, we can shed additional light upon the decisional quality expected from tribunals.

The Benefits and Costs of Onward Challenges

Benefits

The benefits of onward challenges correspond with their functions of which there are at least four. First, onward challenges serve a retrospective error-correction function. Put simply, systems of onward challenge enable unsuccessful parties to contest tribunal decisions on the ground that they contain an error of law. Tribunal decisions are binding on both parties, unless they can be set aside through onward challenges.[2] If accuracy and quality are to prosper, then errors of law have to be detected and corrected. Secondly, onward challenges have a deterrent function. If first-instance judges are aware that their decisions may be challenged, then they might adopt a more careful and considered approach when making their decisions.

---

[2] *R (Boafo) v Secretary of State for the Home Department* [2002] EWCA Civ 44; [2002] 1 WLR 1919 [25]–[26] (Auld LJ); *R (Saribal) v Secretary of State for the Home Department* [2002] EWHC 1542 (Admin); [2002] INLR 596, [17] (Moses J).

Thirdly, onward challenges can serve a prospective guidance function. By considering such challenges, senior tribunal judges acquire an extensive overview of the trends and issues arising in first-tier decisions. In turn, this can enable senior judges and the higher courts to identify those issues on which guidance would be helpful to promote uniformity and certainty on difficult and important points of law and practice.

Beyond the confines of the particular adjudicative context, onward challenges have a fourth function: enhancing the legitimacy of the tribunal process. The fact that all parties concerned are aware that a tribunal decision is not final, but always open to further challenge is likely to promote public confidence in the decision process. While the particular tribunal system will need to operate in accordance with its own rules, procedures, and relevant guidance, oversight by the higher courts can also enhance compliance with general legal principles. By being subject to onward challenge, tribunal decisions benefit from the same degree of support and legitimacy that administrative decisions do when they are susceptible to challenge by way of judicial review.

Costs

The costs of onward challenges can be segmented into two types: administrative and delay costs. The administrative costs involved—the costs of litigating review applications to the parties involved and the administrative processing of such applications—may be fairly modest, but must nevertheless be borne by the system. The principal cost is delay. In 2008, a review application against an initial appeal decision to a senior judge typically took two weeks to be decided while any subsequent renewal to the Administrative Court typically took a further eight weeks.[3] If an appellant choose to exercise their full onward appeal rights, then the whole process would take four and a half months.[4]

Such delays might not necessarily present much of a problem if they were confined to a small number of cases. Throughout the broader tribunal system, onward challenges against initial appeals typically run at a low level. From one perspective, this might be a cause of concern; 'the total volume of injustice is likely to be much greater among those who accept initial decisions than among those who complain or appeal'.[5] From another perspective, the low rate of onward challenge could be taken as an indication that the tribunals are doing their job well. But the asylum process is the conspicuous exception to this because of its high rate of onward challenge. Between 2005 and 2008, the rate of onward challenge against initial appeal decisions ranged from 67 per cent in 2005–06 to 56 per cent in

---

[3] Home Office United Kingdom Border Agency, *Consultation: Immigration Appeals—Fair Decisions; Faster Justice* (London, Home Office UKBA, 2008) 2.

[4] Ibid, 4.

[5] TG Ison ' "Administrative Justice": Is It Such a Good Idea?' in M Harris and M Partington (eds), *Administrative Justice in the 21st Century* (Oxford, Hart Publishing, 1999) 23.

2007–08; 89 per cent of such challenges were lodged by appellants.[6] Indeed, the asylum process is often singled out as the exemplary case of an adjudication system characterised by a high rate of challenges with seemingly innumerable cases that proceed round and round the system, delaying finality and undermining public confidence.

The delay costs are increased in two ways. First, there are the delays imposed by remittals or reconsiderations of appeals. Such processes are often necessary to make fresh findings of fact with which to conclude an appeal, but can considerably lengthen the time taken to conclude an appeal and require the use of judicial resources that could be devoted to hearing other first-instance appeals. There are additional delays incurred by the handling of onward challenges against reconsidered decisions to the higher courts. Secondly, because of the volume, the delays can overflow to other areas. The general concern is that the pressure on the courts from asylum cases will exacerbate delays elsewhere in the judicial system, weaken judicial scrutiny of other administrative agencies and tribunals, and undermine public confidence. While caseload is of concern throughout the judicial system, it has found its apotheosis in the asylum context; the policy challenge is how to manage it.

For the Home Office, the high rate of challenge is fuelled more by the intention of many appellants to postpone their removal from the country for as long as possible, than by quality concerns.[7] There is little disincentive for unsuccessful asylum appellants not to pursue onward challenges as they cannot be removed before their appeal rights have been exhausted and it would be difficult to impose any form of cost sanctions against unmeritorious challenges. From a different perspective, appellants can hardly be criticised for using their statutory rights of challenge against life or death decisions. Furthermore, it might be argued that there is a direct correlation between caseload and decisional quality; a high number of challenges will reflect concerns over decisional quality. The messy complex reality is that there is some element of truth in both of these positions. But the general point is that the high rate of onward challenge should enable individuals dissatisfied with initial decisions to secure justice.

---

[6] Figures supplied by the Tribunal Service, Ministry of Justice. This phenomenon has not been confined to the UK. In the US, since 2002 there has been a dramatic increase in the number of court challenges against immigration and asylum decisions. See JRB Palmer, SW Yale-Loehr and E Cronin, 'Why Are So Many People Challenging Board of Immigration Appeal Decisions in Federal Court? An Empirical Analysis of the Recent Surge in Petitions for Review' (2005) 20 *Georgetown Immigration Law Journal* 1; SB Alexander, 'A Political Response to the Crisis in the Immigration Courts' (2006) 21 *Georgetown Immigration Law Journal* 1.

[7] The courts have themselves sometimes voiced similar concerns. See, eg, *R (Benda) v Secretary of State for the Home Department* [2002] Imm AR 314, 316 (Maurice Kay J): 'I say this with some hesitation, but in this field one can sometimes gain the impression that there is a culture in which no decision of the Secretary of State and no decision at first-instance or even on appeal is thought not to warrant further challenge'. See also *R (Pharis) v Secretary of State for the Home Department* [2004] EWCA Civ 654; [2004] 3 All ER 310 [17] (Brooke LJ): 'Experience has shown that the practice of pursuing a further appeal to this court in a judicial review matter in the immigration and asylum field has given rise to very serious abuse, with appellants pursuing wholly unmeritorious appeals simply to delay the time when they are to be deported'.

Organising Onward Challenges: An Excursus

Given this backdrop, the design and operation of onward challenges emerges as a fundamental aspect of the organisation and functioning of the adjudication system. Since the inception of asylum appeals in 1993, onward challenges have been organised along different models: a specialist second-tier tribunal determining onward appeals (the IAT); a single-tier tribunal with internal review and reconsiderations system (AIT); and, from 2010, a reversion back to a specialist second-tier tribunal through the AIT's transfer into the First-tier Tribunal Immigration and Asylum Chamber (FTTIAC) and the Upper Tribunal Immigration and Asylum Chamber (UTIAC).[8]

An examination of the evolution of the successive systems of onward challenge may possess its own inherent interest; after all, there is something both distinctive and unprecedented about how this appeal structure has been continually altered. An examination of the largely procedural nature of onward challenges might also illuminate broader issues of tribunal organisation. Losing parties to appeal decisions must have some means of challenging them, but how? Should a second-tier tribunal regularly remit appeals back to the first-tier? How should a lower tribunal deal with remitted appeals? How many times should an appeal be capable of being remitted? What should be the relationship between generalist appellate courts and the specialist tribunal? What role should there be for judicial review after the appeals process has been exhausted and how should such judicial reviews be handled? More generally, the critical issue is this: what is the optimal balance to be struck between the demands of legality, fairness to the parties, efficient policy implementation, the preservation of higher court oversight of tribunals, and the best use of scarce judicial resources? As the ensuing discussion demonstrates, reaching a definitive answer has proved to be difficult.

Specialist Appeal Tribunal: The IAT

Before 2003, onward challenges against Immigration Judge (then Adjudicator) determinations lay to the Immigration Appeal Tribunal (IAT), which could either substantively determine appeals or remit them back. Refusals of permission to appeal could be challenged by way of ordinary judicial review. Various problems afflicted these arrangements. IAT decisions were inconsistent and frequently overturned by the higher courts. Furthermore, the IAT remitted a high number of

---

[8] Tribunals, Courts and Enforcement Act 2007; Tribunals Service, *Transforming Tribunals: Implementing Part 1 of the Tribunals, Courts and Enforcement Act 2007* (London, Ministry of Justice, CP 20/07, 2007), ch8; Home Office United Kingdom Border Agency, *Immigration Appeals: Response to Consultation—Fair Decisions; Faster Justice* (London, Home Office, 2009); Hansard HC Debs vol 294 col 20ws 8 May 2009 (Minister of State for Borders and Immigration); The Transfer of Functions of the Asylum and Immigration Tribunal Order SI 2010/21.

appeals back to the first-tier level, thereby prolonging the process.[9] There were other delays in the process. The IAT could take up to a year to hear substantive appeals and successive backlogs of cases built up. These delays were exacerbated by numerous judicial review challenges against the IAT's refusal of permission to appeal. Such challenges were primarily against adverse reasons given by the Adjudicator, but the IAT did not assist itself by adopting a formulaic approach when refusing permission to appeal.[10] Between 2003 and 2005, ordinary judicial review procedure was replaced with a paper-only statutory review process with short-time limits which was undertaken by the Administrative Court.[11] A further distinctive feature was that until 2002, the IAT's jurisdiction was not limited to error of law grounds, but extended to issues of both fact and law.[12] Confining onward challenges to error of law grounds was intended to control the proliferation of challenges against adverse factual findings.

Nevertheless, the high rate of challenge continued. Ministers took umbrage and, in a fit of pique in 2003, decided upon the nuclear option: simultaneously to replace the two-tier appeal structure with a single-tier tribunal and to oust the ability to seek judicial review of its decisions. While appeal decisions were to be capable of being reviewed internally within the new tribunal structure, the Government did not want the courts to have any supervisory jurisdiction.[13] Predictably, the Government was trenchantly criticised for seeking to undermine the basic notion that tribunal decisions should be subject to legal oversight.[14] The Government's

---

[9] Home Office and Lord Chancellor's Department, *Review of Appeals: A Consultation Paper* (London, Home Office and LCD, 1998) [5.3]; C Blake and M Sunkin, 'Immigration: Appeals and Judicial Review' [1998] *Public Law* 583, 588–590.

[10] *Slimani v Secretary of State for the Home Department (Content of Adjudicator Determination) Algeria* (Starred determination) [2001] UKIAT 00009 [8].

[11] Nationality, Immigration and Asylum Act 2002 s 101(2). See R Thomas, 'Asylum Appeals Overhauled Again' [2003] *Public Law* 260.

[12] Immigration and Asylum Act 1999 sch 4 para 22; *Indrakumar v Secretary of State for the Home Department* [2004] Imm AR 76 (CA); *Subesh, Suthan, Nagulananthan and Vanniyaingam v Secretary of State for the Home Department* [2004] EWCA Civ 56; [2004] Imm AR 112 (CA); Nationality, Immigration and Asylum Act 2002 s 101(1). Furthermore, the IAT was occasionally criticised by the courts for adopting a more benign approach when considering Home Office challenges against allowed appeals than in relation to challenges by appellants. See, eg, *Arshad v Secretary of State for the Home Department* [2001] EWCA Civ 587 [20] (Laws LJ): 'this case portrays a (no doubt unconscious) lack of even-handedness on the part of the IAT as between an immigrant's appeal and a Home Office appeal'. See also *P and M v Secretary of State for the Home Department* [2004] EWCA Civ 1640; [2005] Imm AR 84, 93–95 (Lord Woolf LCJ) (CA) (it is important that the IAT confine itself to its proper reviewing role and not undertake the primary fact-finding role).

[13] Home Office Immigration and Nationality Directorate and Department for Constitutional Affairs, *New Legislative Proposals on Asylum Reform* (London, Home Office, 2003); Asylum and Immigration (Treatment of Claimants, etc.) HC Bill (2003–04) [53] cl 11 (as originally introduced into Parliament).

[14] House of Commons Constitutional Affairs Committee, *Asylum and Immigration Appeals* (2003–04 HC 211); House of Commons Home Affairs Committee, *Asylum and Immigration (Treatment of Claimants, etc) Bill* (2003–04 HC 109); Joint Committee on Human Rights, *Asylum and Immigration (Treatment of Claimants, etc) Bill* (2003–04 HL 35 HC 304); M Fordham, 'Common Law Illegality of Ousting Judicial Review' (2004) 9 *Judicial Review* 86; Lord Woolf, 'The Rule of Law and a Change in the Constitution' (2004) 63 *Cambridge Law Journal* 317, 327–329. See also R Rawlings, 'Review, Revenge and Retreat' (2005) 68 *Modern Law Review* 378.

subsequent change of mind produced the AIT and its internal review and reconsideration process.[15]

Single-tier Tribunal: The AIT

The objectives of the AIT were to speed up the processing of appeals and to reduce the proportion of onward appeals (see figure 1). Onward challenges were considered initially by a Senior Immigration Judge through a quick paper-based perusal—the AIT 'filter' mechanism.[16] Reconsideration could be ordered only if there might have been an error of law and there was a real possibility that the appeal would be decided differently on reconsideration.[17] If rejected, then the party could renew the application—the Administrative Court 'opt-in'.[18] If reconsideration was ordered, then the Tribunal had to determine whether there was a material error of law in the original decision.[19] If so, then the error had to be corrected and substituted with a fresh decision.

To discourage unmeritorious challenges, the process was subject to short time limits and retrospective legal aid funding. Appellants had five days to lodge an application, a period considered to be 'too short'; but some of the stringency could be ameliorated if the application 'could not reasonably practicably have been made within' the time limit.[20] As regards legal aid, a scheme of retrospective funding operated so that representatives would only know at the end of reconsideration process whether their work would be funded.[21] The concern was that this could inhibit representatives from taking on meritorious cases if funding was not

---

[15] Asylum and Immigration (Treatment of Claimants, etc) Act 2004 s 26. Incidental effects of the ouster clause debacle were that it damaged executive-judiciary relations and, at least in part, prompted some judges to posit the possibility that the courts might, in certain circumstances, review the constitutionality of legislation. See *R (Jackson) v Attorney-General* [2006] 1 AC 262; J Jowell, 'Parliamentary Sovereignty under the New Constitutional Hypothesis' [2006] *Public Law* 562; T Mullen, 'Reflections on *Jackson v Attorney-General*: Questioning Sovereignty' (2007) 27 *Legal Studies* 1.

[16] Asylum and Immigration (Treatment of Claimants, etc.) Act 2004 sch 2 para 30.

[17] Asylum and Immigration Tribunal (Procedure) Rules SI 2005/230 r 26(6).

[18] Asylum and Immigration (Treatment of Claimants, etc.) Act 2004 sch 2 para 30(5).

[19] Asylum and Immigration Tribunal (Procedure) Rules SI 2005/230 r 31(2).

[20] Nationality, Immigration and Asylum Act 2002 s 103A(3)(a) (as inserted by the Asylum and Immigration (Treatment of Claimants, etc) Act 2004 s 26); Asylum and Immigration (Fast Track Time Limits) Order SI 2005/561; Asylum and Immigration (Treatment of Claimants, etc) Act 2004 sch 2 para 30(5); Council on Tribunals, *Annual Report 2004/2005* (2004–05 HC 472) 15. See also S Craig, M Fletcher, and K Goodall, *Challenging Asylum and Immigration Tribunal Decisions in Scotland: An Evaluation of Onward Appeals and Reconsiderations* (Glasgow, University of Glasgow, 2009) 111. Nationality, Immigration and Asylum Act 2002 s 103A(4)(b) (as inserted by the Asylum and Immigration (Treatment of Claimants, etc.) Act 2004 s 26). Of some 4,719 'out of time' review applications made between April 2005 and January 2006, only 690 (14.6 per cent) were refused solely on the basis that they were lodged out of time. See Tribunals Service, *The AIT Review Report April 2006* (London, DCA, 2006) 72.

[21] Nationality, Immigration and Asylum Act 2002 s 103D (as inserted by the Asylum and Immigration (Treatment of Claimants, etc.) Act 2004 s 26); Department for Constitutional Affairs, *The Asylum and Immigration Tribunal—The Legal Aid Arrangements for Onward Appeals* (London, DCA, CP 30/04, 2004); The Community Legal Service (Asylum and Immigration Appeals) Regulations SI 2005/966; Immigration, Asylum and Nationality Act 2006 s 8.

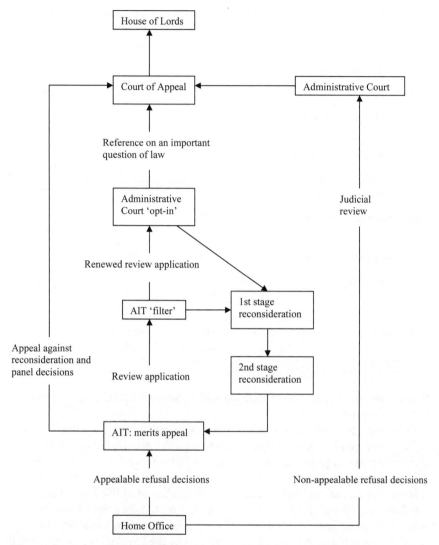

Figure 1: Asylum appeals and judicial reviews in the Asylum and Immigration Tribunal (2005–2010)

guaranteed.[22] In practice, if an error of law had been identified, then funding would follow.[23] However, one consequence has been increasing numbers of unrepresented appellants.[24] One of the most difficult tasks for reviewing judges is

[22] House of Commons Constitutional Affairs Committee, *Legal Aid: Asylum Appeals* (2004–05 HC 276).

[23] *RS v Secretary of State for the Home Department (Funding—meaning of 'significant prospect') Iran* [2005] UKAIT 00138; [2005] Imm AR 726.

[24] *AIT Review* above n 20 at 82–85.

Table 1: Asylum Appeals, Review Applications, and Reconsiderations 2005–2008[1]

	2005–06	2006–07	2007–08
Asylum appeals decided	27,253	14,735	13,700
Review applications decided	18,487	7,284	7,691
Review applications granted	4,023 (22%)	2,202 (30%)	1,967 (26%)
Review applications refused	14,448 (78%)	5,076 (70%)	5,720 (74%)
Reconsideration appeals decided	5,863	3,935	3,573
Reconsiderations allowed	1,540 (26%)	1,231 (31%)	1,381 (39%)
Reconsiderations dismissed	3,859 (66%)	2,467 (63%)	1,938 (54%)
Remitted	104 (2%)	0	0
Withdrawn	360 (6%)	237 (6%)	254 (7%)

[1] Source: Tribunals Service, Ministry of Justice.

that of assisting unrepresented appellants when the jurisdiction is limited to error of law grounds.[25]

Other aspects of the process included the time-pressures: senior judges were initially given a list of 24 review applications to consider in a single day; this was subsequently reduced to 18. Another distinctive feature was that, conceptually, the process was one of reconsideration rather than appeal. One consequence of this was that any factual findings and conclusions unaffected by the error of law identified would, if possible, be preserved.[26] For instance, if the original Immigration Judge had failed to apply relevant country guidance, then credibility findings could be preserved as they would be unaffected by the error of law. By contrast, if either party had been deprived of a fair hearing because of an unfair hearing or biased judge, then it would not be possible to preserve any of the previous findings; rather, the appeal would have to be heard *de novo*. By preserving unaffected findings, the intention was that the reconsideration would be able to promote both

---

[25] As one Senior Immigration Judge noted in interview, 'one's heart sinks when an unrepresented appellant comes into the hearing room with her carrier bags and I think "oh dear, we are in for a long day"—you obviously have to do your best to assist an appellant in person without being unfair to the Home Office'.

[26] *Murkarkar v Secretary of State for the Home Department* [2006] EWCA Civ 1045 [44] (Sedley LJ); *DK (Serbia) v Secretary of State for the Home Department* [2006] EWCA Civ 1747; [2007] Imm AR 411 [22] (Latham LJ).

efficiency and fairness. There would be no need to re-determine issues that had been lawfully concluded. Equally, this process would be fairer because an appellant did not need to be subjected to the stress and uncertainty of a new appeal hearing on an issue which he had already succeeded.[27] However, in practice, the system generated a number of problems.

The first problem was the high number of Administrative Court opt-in applications. Notwithstanding the senior judge 'filter' mechanism, the volume of 'opt-ins' was substantial; 2,640 in 2006, 3,570 in 2007, and 4,201 in 2008.[28] The view from within the Administrative Court was that the opt-ins were placing a disproportionate burden on its caseload generating 'unacceptable delays'.[29] In 2008, the Administrative Court had 'been in a continuing state of crisis for three years' and the volume of asylum and immigration casework was perceived to be the principal cause.[30] Caseload pressure prompted well-publicised delays in other areas of the court's caseload and concerns that the court was unable to deliver effective justice.[31] Yet, 'opt-in' success rates—11 per cent in 2006, 8.9 per cent in 2007, and 11 per cent in 2008—did not paint an unequivocal picture of abuse. As regards the adequacy of the expedited process, the courts held that it afforded a satisfactory safeguard but also carved out some limited exceptions to allow access to ordinary judicial review procedure.[32]

---

[27] *HF (Algeria) v Secretary of State for the Home Department* [2007] EWCA Civ 445 [11]–[18] and [26] (Carnwath LJ).

[28] Ministry of Justice, *Judicial and Court Statistics 2006* (Cm 7273, 2007) 27; Ministry of Justice, *Judicial and Court Statistics 2007* (Cm 7467, 2008) 28; Ministry of Justice, *Judicial and Court Statistics 2008* (Cm 7697, 2009) 28. While not all of these renewed review applications concerned asylum appeals, it is reasonably safe to assume that many did. To put this in perspective, in 2007, the Administrative Court substantively determined some 336 judicial review claims across the whole range of administrative and appellate decision-making.

[29] Judicial Working Group, *Justice Outside London* (London, Judiciary of England and Wales, 2007) [46]; Lord Philips LCJ, *The Lord Chief Justice's Review of the Administration of Justice in the Courts* (2007–08 HC 448) 36; President of the Queen's Bench Division, *Response of the President of the Queen's Bench Division to the UK Border Agency Consultation on Immigration Appeals* (London, RCJ, 2008).

[30] H Brooke, *Should the Civil Courts be Unified? A Report by Sir Henry Brooke* (London, Judicial Office, 2008) 54 and 126.

[31] In 2008, the Public Law Project launched judicial review proceedings against the Ministry of Justice concerning delays in the Administrative Court to which the Ministry of Justice and the Administrative Court settled out of court by implementing some remedial changes. See HM Courts Service, *Delays in the Administrative Court* (London, HMCS, November 2007); Public Law Project, *Action on Administrative Court Delays* (London, Public Law Project, April 2008); Statement by Collins J, Lead Judge of the Administrative Court, *Administrative Court List* (London, Administrative Court, April 2008); HM Courts Service, *Overview of Current Position in the Administrative Court* (London, HMCS, July 2008); F Gibb, 'Extra judges drafted in to hear immigration appeals: Asylum Backlog Delays Other Cases "For A Year"' *The Times* (15 December 2008) 5. See also *R (Casey) v Restormel Borough Council* [2007] EWHC Admin 2554 [29] and [33] (Munby J): '[i]t is no secret that the Administrative Court is having great difficulty coping with its present workload. . . . Hard pressed local and other public authorities should not be prejudiced . . . tax payers and rate-payers should not be financially disadvantaged, other more deserving claimants seeking recourse to over-stretched public resources should not be prejudiced, because of delays in the Royal Courts of Justice'.

[32] *R (G and M) v Immigration Appeal Tribunal* [2004] EWCA Civ 1731; [2005] 1 WLR 1445 (CA); *R ((F) (Mongolia)) v Asylum and Immigration Tribunal* [2007] EWCA Civ 769; [2007] 1 WLR 2523 (CA); *R ((AM) (Cameroon)) v Asylum and Immigration Tribunal and the Secretary of State for the Home Department* [2008] EWCA Civ 100.

A second difficulty was the actual operation of the reconsideration process itself. To ensure the timely disposal of cases, the Government had initially wanted all reconsiderations to be concluded in a single hearing, but the Tribunal considered this impracticable and introduced the split first-stage and second-stage reconsideration process.[33] The whole process could then include three distinct aspects: (i) a paper-based review by a senior judge that the original judge *may have* made an error of law, which led to an order for reconsideration; (ii) an oral first-stage reconsideration by a senior judge to determine whether there *has* been an error of law; and, if necessary, (iii) a second-stage reconsideration by an ordinary judge to re-determine the appeal by making fresh findings of fact, second-stage reconsiderations were essentially remittals by a different name. The reason for this split reconsideration process was that it would normally be impracticable for the senior judge undertaking the first-stage reconsideration to proceed to determine the appeal and make necessary findings of facts straightaway; if fresh findings of fact were needed, then the appeal would have to be sent back to the regional hearing centre to be re-heard.[34] Between April 2005 and January 2006, 58 per cent of reconsideration hearings were concluded in a single hearing while 42 per cent were adjourned for a second-stage reconsideration.[35]

In practice, a number of problems arose with this system. One was the difficulties in individual cases of assessing the materiality of an error of law and the degree to which previous findings could be preserved. There was often scope for the parties to dispute the degree to which an error of law infected other findings. Appellants would naturally seek to expand the materiality of an identified error of law, perhaps so that no previous findings could be preserved, while the Home Office would normally wish to confine closely the extent to which an error of law had infected other findings adverse to the appellant. The scope for argument was sometimes increased if the senior judge merely identified an error of law, but did not specify the degree to which unaffected findings could be preserved.

Another problem concerned the evidence that could be admitted at a reconsideration hearing. Appeals must be determined on the basis of the facts in existence at the date of the hearing, there needs to be scope for fresh evidence to be submitted and this was subject to rules that the party indicate the nature of the evidence and explain why it was not submitted on any previous occasion.[36] At the same time, there is always the risk that either party might seek to adduce evidence that

---

[33] *R (Wani) v Secretary of State for the Home Department and the Asylum and Immigration Tribunal* [2005] EWHC 2815 (Admin); [2005] Imm AR 125 (HC); *AH v Secretary of State for the Home Department (Scope of s 103A reconsideration) Sudan* [2006] UKAIT 00038; Asylum and Immigration Tribunal, *Practice Directions* (2007) [14.1]–[14.14].

[34] First-stage reconsiderations were conducted by senior judges in London. Given that the first-stage reconsideration hearing would definitely conclude whether or not there was an error of law, it would be inefficient to assemble all the evidence, witnesses, expert reports, and so on the off-chance that they would be required at the first-stage reconsideration. Concluding all challenges in a single hearing would also impose an undue burden throughout such cases on senior tribunal judges.

[35] *AIT Review* above n 20 at 76.

[36] Asylum and Immigration Tribunal (Procedure) Rules SI 2005/230 r 32(2).

could reasonably have been submitted at the previous appeal hearing. The risk was that the reconsideration process could descend into a re-run of the initial appeal process.

The third problem with the AIT appeals system concerned onward challenges against reconsidered appeals. Before the AIT's introduction, challenges against remitted and re-determined appeals by first-tier judges lay direct to the specialist second-tier tribunal, the IAT. While the IAT was an appropriate venue for identifying errors within such decisions, the disadvantage was that remittals could escalate with appeals bouncing back and forth between the first and second-tier appeal levels; it was not unknown for some cases to have gone round the appeals process on multiple occasions. To eliminate this, a direct right of appeal to the Court of Appeal against reconsideration appeals was created with the introduction of the AIT.[37] But this only had the consequence of shifting the caseload onto the Court of Appeal. In 2006, a quarter (300 appeals) of the Court of Appeal's caseload came from the AIT and nearly a third in both 2007 (358 appeals) and in 2008 (395 appeals).[38] Given the position of the Court of Appeal as a generalist appellate court wanting to resolve difficult issues of law of general application, the pressures placed upon it by having a considerable amount of its caseload taken up by asylum cases was unsustainable. According to the Lord Chief Justice, the appeal structure had placed 'enormous burden on the resources of the Court . . . judges of the highest calibre are devoting over 25 per cent of their time to appeals from a single immigration judge, the majority of which raise no point of general importance'.[39] The tension here was between the Home Office and the Court of Appeal, the former not wanting to have multiple remittals from a second-tier tribunal back to the first-tier, while the latter not wanting to be overloaded by numerous appeals, which could be adequately dealt with by a second-tier tribunal.

Other difficulties also became apparent., The multiple and repetitive nature of the process meant that a case could only reach the Court of Appeal if it had already been considered on at least some five previous occasions—possibly even seven occasions—with many cases before the Court of Appeal raising fact-specific issues. Furthermore, there were administrative inefficiencies in the handling of appeals before the Court of Appeal. The Home Office's practice was to concede a substantial

---

[37] Nationality, Immigration and Asylum Act 2002 s 103B (as inserted by the Asylum and Immigration (Treatment of Claimants, etc) Act 2004 s 26).

[38] Ministry of Justice 2006 above n 28 at 23; Ministry of Justice 2007 above n 28 at 24; Ministry of Justice 2008 above n 28 at 24. These figures might appear high for a court in the position of the Court of Appeal, which in most forms of litigation, operates as the final appellate court. Nevertheless, the figures do not accurately reflect the actual amount of asylum caseload as they do not include the number of permission to appeal applications. In 2008, the AIT was given the power, when determining whether permission to appeal to the Court of Appeal should be granted, to set aside the Tribunal's determination and direct that the proceedings be re-heard. See Asylum and Immigration Tribunal (Procedure) (Amendment) Rules 2008/1088 r 8. But this provision was insufficient to stem the number of appeals before the Court of Appeal. Asylum has accounted for a substantial proportion of the Court of Appeal's general casework since at least 1998.

[39] Lord Philips LCJ above n 29 at 44–45. See also H Brooke, 'A Last Word' in *Court of Appeal Civil Division—Review of the Legal Year 2005–2006* (London, Court of Appeal, 2006) 6.

number of cases going to the Court of Appeal, but only at a very late stage of proceedings. This, in turn, prevented the court from putting other appeals in place to maximise the use of court time.[40] Predictably, Court of Appeal deprecated such delay because of its 'serious problems for the proper administration of justice'.[41] The broader difficulty was that the reconsideration of appeals within the AIT did not function, nor was it perceived to function, as a second-tier appeal process.

In summary, the 2005 appeals system was designed to reduce the caseload of the higher courts, but only resulted in an increase in such caseload. The design of the appeals process was flawed, principally because of the failure to ensure that most appeals would end at the second-tier tribunal level. The introduction of the AIT had collapsed the previous two-tier structure into a single tier of appeal, but the senior judges in the *de facto* second-tier did not have sufficient authority with which to deal with and resolve the majority of onward challenges without leakage to the higher courts. Given the burden of asylum cases upon those courts and the wider impact upon the administration of justice, the need for restructuring of the appeals process came to be recognised. In 2007, a high level appeals working group was established to examine the operation of the system and to make recommendations.[42]

Transfer to the First-tier and Upper Tribunals

The principal recommendation of this group was to transfer the AIT into the new two-tier tribunal structure—the First-tier and Upper Tribunals.[43] This generic appeal structure had been established in 2008 to rationalise the broader tribunal system and to make it more coherent by bringing together existing tribunal jurisdictions and providing a structure for new tribunal jurisdictions and new appeal rights. It had long been recognised that, across the whole tribunal 'system', onward challenges against initial appeal decisions were confused and in need of rationalisation.[44] The new, two-tier system has been designed to provide a more coherent structure. In general terms, initial appeals in a particular appeal context are determined by the First-tier Tribunal, which is organised into distinct chambers. Onward appeals lie to the Upper Tribunal, which is a superior court of record.[45] Senior judicial leadership is provided by the Senior President of Tribunals.[46]

---

[40] Lord Justice Waller, 'A First Word' in *Court of Appeal Civil Division—Review of the Legal Year 2006–2007* (London, Court of Appeal, 2007) 6.

[41] *Ghebru v Secretary of State for the Home Department* [2006] EWCA Civ 1043 [12] (Brooke LJ).

[42] This working group was chaired by Lin Homer, the chief executive of the United Kingdom Border Agency and Sir Stephen Richards, a Lord Justice of Appeal.

[43] Home Office above n 3. See also Senior President of Tribunals, *The Senior President of Tribunals' Annual Report: Tribunals Transformed* (London, Tribunals Service, 2010) 23. The AIT was transferred on 15 February 2010. See the First-tier Tribunal and Upper Tribunal (Chambers) (Amendment) Order SI 2010/40.

[44] See, eg, H Woolf, 'A Hotchpotch of Appeals—the Need for a Blender?' (1988) 7 *Civil Justice Quarterly* 44.

[45] Tribunals, Courts and Enforcement Act 2007 s 3(5).

[46] The first Senior President of Tribunals is Carnwath LJ.

In the transferred immigration and asylum appeals system, first-instance appeals are heard in the FTTIAC and onward appeals in the UTIAC (see figure 2). There is little change as regards the hearing of initial appeals; the key structural difference arises in relation to onward challenges; without the Administrative Court opt-in, the Upper Tribunal is the only destination for onward challenges. By placing the ultimate responsibility for permission to appeal applications with the Upper Tribunal rather than the Administrative Court, the creation of a two-tier system has the advantage of enabling legally erroneous decisions to be remade in the Upper Tribunal, thereby reducing the higher courts' caseload. The Home Office will also benefit from a further truncation of the process. As some commentators noted, the proposals would seem to achieve, by the back-door, the same objective of reducing access to the higher courts which motivated the aborted ouster clause.[47] However, the essential idea is that the Upper Tribunal be the principal body for dealing with legal issues, country guidance, and more generic guidance. As the Upper Tribunal is equivalent in status to the Administrative Court, this should limit the number of onward appeals. There are three issues which the new appellate system has sought to restructure: the volume of appeals remitted back to Immigration Judges for reconsideration; recourse to the Administrative Court by way of judicial review; and onward challenges to the Court of Appeal from reconsidered tribunal appeals.

In the new system, the clear intention is to reduce drastically the volume of reconsideration cases being sent back to the First-tier tribunal.[48] If there is an error of law, then the Upper Tribunal is likely to re-make the decision, instead of remitting it, unless a party has been deprived of a fair hearing before the FTTIAC or if there are other highly compelling reasons why the decision should not be re-made by the UTIAC (such reasons are likely to be rare).[49] If new evidence is required, the Upper Tribunal can adjourn the case, hear the evidence, and then complete the appeal itself. A more stringent approach is also envisaged in relation to the submission of evidence in second-tier appeals by the Upper Tribunal having regard to whether there has been unreasonable delay in producing that evidence. Overall, the clear intention is to do away with a high level of remittals by ensuring that the UTIAC deals with appeals rather than by sending them back to the first-tier. According to Sir Nicholas Blake, the UTIAC's overriding objective is to determine the case itself rather than remit it to the First-tier Tribunal; 'apart from a limited class of complete nullity cases, we should not be circulating cases, but deciding them, even if that means either the error of law involves a partial *de novo* hearing, or at least supplementary evidence on issues that have developed since the last hearing'.[50]

---

[47] Constitutional and Administrative Law Bar Association, *Response to UK Border Agency Consultation: Immigration Appeals, Fair Decisions, Faster Justice* (London, ALBA, 2008).

[48] Tribunal Procedure Committee, *The Tribunal Procedure (Upper Tribunal) Rules 2008—Consultation on Rule Amendments for Asylum and Immigration Upper Tribunal Chamber* (London, Tribunals Service, July 2009).

[49] Senior President of Tribunals, *Practice Statement: Immigration and Asylum Chambers of the First-tier Tribunal and Upper Tribunal* (Tribunal Service, 2010) [7.2].

[50] Sir Nicholas Blake, President of UTIAC, 'The Arrival of the Upper Tribunal Immigration and Asylum Chamber' (Tribunals Service, 11 February 2010) 5.

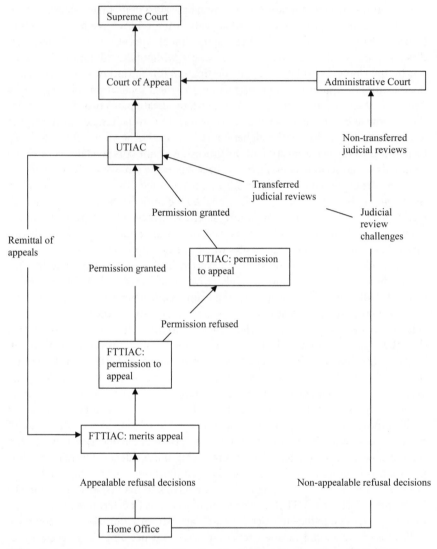

Figure 2: Asylum appeals and judicial reviews in the First-tier and Upper Tribunals structure (2010–)

While this is designed to prevent multiple remittals, it does, though, pose some potential managerial challenges; not remitting an appeal back to the first-tier will shift the burden to the second-tier. The inevitable future challenge for the UTIAC will be in the handling of the volume of paper-only permissions to appeal alongside concluding those cases in which an error of law has been found and also producing guidance. The key issue will be whether the judicial resources available are sufficient for the Tribunal to handle the caseload; the constant risk is that if a high number of appeals accumulate, then backlogs will develop.[51] Furthermore, if senior tribunal judges have to resolve more factual disputes in routine cases that would otherwise have been previously remitted to the first-tier, then the risk is that this may jeopardise the role of the Upper Tribunal in developing immigration and asylum jurisprudence and country guidance.

A second issue concerns the scope for judicial review of the refusal of permission to appeal by the UTIAC decisions. If it were possible for the Upper Tribunal to be subject to extensive judicial review challenges, then the whole purpose of transferring to the new tribunal system would be undermined. At the same time, the question as to whether the status of the Upper Tribunal as a superior court of record excludes judicial review challenges has remained uncertain. And, of course, the whole issue has been overshadowed by the episode of the ouster clause battle. Acutely conscious of the possibility of successive judicial review challenges against the Upper Tribunal, the Home Office had initially proposed to legislate to clarify that the Upper Tribunal should not routinely be subject to judicial review. But, the Home Office preferred instead to leave it to the courts to deal with.[52]

This judicial clarification came in *Cart*.[53] Here, the Court of Appeal held that the new tribunal structure was designed to be a self-sufficient structure, dealing internally with errors of law. Nevertheless, judicial review of the Upper Tribunal to the Administrative Court would remain on exceptional grounds, such as a substantial denial of a fair hearing or an exceptional procedural error so as to amount to actual bias of the behalf of the Upper Tribunal. *Cart*, therefore, confirms the position to be what the Home Office wanted: the Upper Tribunal cannot be routinely subject to judicial review. It is important to note the symbiosis here between higher court oversight and the adequacy of tribunal reason-giving. If the reasons are inadequate, then this generates a demand for closer scrutiny and vice versa. The essential tension is between case-processing and quality: senior judges must give adequate reasons, but have a high caseload. The IAT had been criticised for giving formulaic reasons when refusing permission. The challenge for the UTIAC is for its decisions to command respect and confidence from practitioners, the general public, and the higher courts. For this to be achieved, the UTIAC will have to give proper and adequate reasons on permission to appeal decisions. Such reasons need not be extensive, but must be sufficient in order to explain the decision reached and to manage the case efficiently.[54]

The third issue concerns routes of challenge against substantive reconsidered appeal decisions and, in particular, the role of the Court of Appeal. Under the 2005 appeals system, the volume of cases reaching the Court of Appeal had increased.

---

[51] When the UTIAC came into operation in February 2010, it envisaged receiving a substantial number of renewed permission to appeal applications from the FTTIAC—240 per week. See Blake ibid. Depending on the proportion of those applications that need to be reconsidered substantively, fluctuations in flow cases, and the availability of judicial resources, it is possible that delays can easily accrue.

[52] Home Office above n 8 at 5.

[53] *R (Cart) v Upper Tribunal* [2010] EWCA Civ 859.

[54] Blake above n 50 at 5–6.

This was partly because of the generous test governing permission to appeal; permission would be granted if there was an arguable error of law which had real prospects of success. However, under the Tribunals, Courts and Enforcement Act 2007, onward appeals are subject to the more restrictive test that permission should only be granted if there is an important point of principle or practice or if there is some other compelling reason why the appeal should be heard.[55] The restrictive test is designed to limit second appeals, that is, a further appeal on the same point against a decision which was itself an appeal from the original tribunal decision, unless there is a wider public interest. Its extension to asylum appeals has been controversial on the ground that may prevent the Court of Appeal from hearing those cases in which there is a real prospect that the Upper Tribunal may have misinterpreted or misapplied human rights law, but which do not raise an important point of principle or practice.[56] In response, the Home Office noted that those cases that might arise in which the Upper Tribunal made a decision in breach of the UK's human rights obligations are precisely the sort of cases that would meet the more restrictive test. Furthermore, the majority of appeals to the Court of Appeal under the 2005 appeals system raised no point of general importance; it was therefore deemed disproportionate to continue with an automatic right for such cases to be substantively considered by the Court of Appeal.[57]

Whatever the legal provisions governing the appeals process, attempts to avoid a high volume of remittals and an overburdening of the higher courts will largely depend upon the authority and leadership of the Upper Tribunal itself. The clear intention is that the Upper Tribunal will have a high status as an expert appellate body.[58] In this respect, it is important to highlight what has been the most successful feature of the AIT: the close interaction between the different levels of the tribunal judiciary. The previous lack of interaction had a number of disadvantages in terms of senior judges not being aware of the types of issues coming up for decision at the initial appeal stage and Immigration Judges not being made sufficiently aware of the thinking of the senior judges. In the AIT, the working practices of senior judges became more peripatetic, with those judges regularly travelling from their own collegial centre in London to the regional hearing centres to learn of issues coming up in initial appeals and to assist Immigration Judges. In the First-tier and Upper Tribunals, the intention is to extend this closer working and collaboration to the Court of Appeal and the Supreme Court and beyond to the European Court of Justice and the European Court of Human

---

[55] Tribunals, Courts and Enforcement Act 2007 s 13(6); The Appeals from the Upper Tribunal to the Court of Appeal Order SI 2008/2834. For a similar restriction on second appeals in relation to civil appeals, see Access to Justice Act 1999 s 55(1); CPR 52.13.

[56] Joint Committee on Human Rights, *Legislative Scrutiny: Borders, Citizenship and Immigration Bill* (2008–09 HL 62 HC 375) [1.30]–[1.32]; R Buxton, 'Application of Section 13(6) of the Tribunals, Courts, and Enforcement Act 2007 to Immigration Appeals from the Proposed Upper Tribunal' (2009) 14 *Judicial Review* 225.

[57] Joint Committee on Human Rights, *Government Replies to the Second, Fourth, Eighth, Ninth and Twelfth Reports of Session 2008–09* (2008–09 HL 104 HC 592) 6.

[58] Tribunals Service above n 8 at ch8.

Rights to ensure that lead cases are decided appropriately at the right level without backlogs building up.

Whether the new appeal structure will provide the solution remains to be seen. For Sir Robert Carnwath, the Senior President of Tribunals, the transfer provides a 'stronger and more logical structure' for immigration and asylum appeals as opposed to remaining a separate pillar outside the new system.[59] For instance, responsibility for the tribunal procedural rules has been transferred from the Ministry of Justice (with substantial Home Office input) to the Tribunal Procedure Committee.[60] The transfer's success will depend heavily upon the success of the Upper Tribunal in handling onward appeals and its caseload. As the scope for judicial review will, following *Cart*, be extremely limited, the refusal of permission to appeal by the UTIAC will normally mark the end of the road for the losing party. Setting limits on the process at this stage places a formidable responsibility with the UTIAC. Restructuring of the appeals process has not, though, been the only area of reform.

Tribunalising Judicial Review

In an inherently litigious area of administration such as immigration and asylum, appeal rights are not the sole avenue of legal challenge; there is often scope to invoke ordinary judicial review procedure. Immigration and asylum judicial reviews have comprised the bulk of the Administrative Court's caseload for the last two decades.[61] In 2008, of the 7,169 judicial review claims that were lodged with the Administrative Court, 4,643 (64 per cent) concerned immigration and asylum decisions.[62] In general terms, the establishment or withdrawal of immigration and asylum appeal rights exerts a major influence upon the caseload of the Administrative Court. One reason for creating appeal rights has typically been the need to reduce the burden on that court, but there are many categories of immigration decisions that are challengeable only through judicial review. Much of the litigation is not, therefore, directly concerned with the substantive asylum determination or with the appeals process, but concerns collateral aspects of the asylum process, such as challenges against asylum support decisions, certification of asylum claims as clearly unfounded; third country removal; and detention decisions.[63]

---

[59] R Carnwath, Senior President of Tribunals, *Third Implementation Review* (London, Tribunals Service, July 2009) [19].

[60] Tribunals, Courts and Enforcement Act 2007 s 22; Hansard HL Debs vol 708 col 802 4 March 2009.

[61] See M Sunkin, 'What is Happening to Applications for Judicial Review?' (1987) 50 *Modern Law Review* 432, 443–447; L Bridges, G Mészáros, and M Sunkin, *Judicial Review in Perspective*, 2nd edn (London, Cavendish, 1995) 19–26; S Sterett, *Creating Constitutionalism? The Politics of Legal Expertise and Administrative Law in England and Wales* (Ann Arbor, University of Michigan Press, 1997) 151–181; J Bowman, *Review of the Crown Office List: A Report to the Lord Chancellor* (London, Lord Chancellor's Department, 2000) 29–43; R Thomas, 'The Impact of Judicial Review on Asylum' [2003] *Public Law* 479.

[62] Ministry of Justice 2008 above n 28 at 27.

[63] Nationality, Immigration and Asylum Act 2002 s 94; *R (Martin) v Secretary of State for the Home Department* [2006] EWHC Admin 799; *R (Yogachandran) v Secretary of State for the Home Department* [2006] EWHC Admin 392; Nationality, Immigration and Asylum Act 2002 s 93; *R (Katshunga) v*

Two principal types of asylum judicial reviews that have featured prominently over recent years have been challenges arising in the post-appeal stage of the asylum process: challenges against Home Office decisions to set removal directions and challenges against Home Office decisions not to treat an unsuccessful asylum claimant's submissions as a fresh claim for asylum. The former class of case arises as follows: the Home Office is required to set removal directions before it can effectuate the removal of a failed claimant from the country; the decision to set such removals is susceptible to challenge by way of judicial review. The latter class of case—fresh asylum claim judicial reviews—concerns the situation in which a failed asylum claimant, having exhausted his appeal rights, then makes submissions to the Home Office to lodge a fresh claim for asylum. The Home Office is only obliged to consider such submissions as a fresh asylum claim if they are significantly different from those previously considered in that they have not previously been considered and that, when taken together with previously considered material, create a realistic prospect of success, notwithstanding its rejection.[64] Claimants awaiting a fresh claim decision cannot be removed.[65] If the submissions are not accepted as a fresh claim, then this decision is challengeable by way of judicial review.

In both types of challenges—removal action and fresh claims—judicial review may well be necessary to ensure that individuals are not subjected to risk of persecution or ill-treatment if removed. There may, for instance, be some period of time between the dismissal of an individual's appeal and removal action by the Home Office or the lodging of a fresh asylum claim, during which country conditions might have deteriorated. However, the volume of such challenges has been substantial. In 2008, there were, on average 230 applications for judicial review each month against removal action, of which less than 10 per cent were granted permission to proceed; a very small number of substantive judicial reviews were then successful (only one during the period January 2008–April 2008) and the majority of substantive decisions took more than six months to complete.[66] The number of fresh claim judicial reviews has been approximately 900 a year, thereby comprising the largest single class of judicial review applications.[67] When added all together with the Administrative Court 'opt-ins', asylum and immigration

---

Secretary of State for the Home Department [2006] EWHC Admin 1208; *R (Karas and Miladinovic) v Secretary of State for the Home Department* [2006] EWHC Admin 747.

[64] Immigration Rules (1994 HC 395) r 353. Much judicial review litigation has focused upon the precise test to be applied in such challenges. See *R v Secretary of State for the Home Department, ex parte Onibiyo* [1996] QB 768 (CA); *WM (DRC) v Secretary of State for the Home Department; Secretary of State for the Home Department v AR (Afghanistan)* [2006] EWCA Civ 1495; [2007] Imm AR 337; *ZT (Kosovo) v Secretary of State for the Home Department* [2009] UKHL 6; [2009] 1 WLR 348; *R (AK (Sri Lanka) v Secretary of State for the Home Department* [2009] EWCA Civ 447; *BA (Nigeria) v Secretary of State for the Home Department* [2009] UKSC 7; *R (YH) v Secretary of State for the Home Department* [2010] EWCA Civ 116.

[65] Immigration Rules (1994 HC 395) r 353A.

[66] National Audit Office, *Management of Asylum Applications by the UK Border Agency* (2008–09 HC 124) [2.20].

[67] Hansard HC Debs vol 496 col 209 14 July 2009 (Minister of State for Borders and Immigration).

accounted for nearly three-quarters of the court's caseload in 2007–08, which have meant unacceptable delays for the court.[68]

For the Home Office, this is all evidence of abuse and of hopeless challenges, but the litigation dynamics are more complex than this. Relatively few challenges proceed to a substantive hearing.[69] The individual may withdraw the claim, the Home Office may produce a new decision to avoid further delay and costs, or it may concede to prevent the setting of an adverse precedent. Furthermore, the Home Office has on occasion failed to comply with court rulings. The general expectation is, of course, that the executive will comply without delay with judicial decisions holding its (in-)actions to be illegal but, in the asylum context, this expectation has, at times, been pushed beyond straining point. For instance, the Home Office has on occasion removed individuals from the UK despite court injunctions prohibiting such removal.[70] The cause of such non-compliance appears to be systemic failure within the Home Office itself and the apparent inability of its different units to communicate properly with each other. Despite internal administrative guidance emphasising that it is the responsibility of individual officials to take all reasonable steps to verify whether an injunction exists, the Home Office has, in at least one instance, made an illegal return.[71] Then there has been administrative delay in giving effect to positive decisions, including in one instance, deliberate delay in giving effect to a politically unpalatable decision.[72] The courts have frequently affirmed that tribunal decisions are binding on the Home Office and cannot be circumvented through administrative action or

---

[68] Lord Philips LCJ above n 28 at 36. Or, as R Rawlings, 'Modelling Judicial Review' (2008) 61 *Current Legal Problems* 95, 111 has put it: 'It is today hard to avoid the impression of the Administrative Court as a specialist asylum and immigration court with knobs on'.

[69] In 2007, of the 4,344 immigration and asylum judicial reviews, 310 were granted permission to proceed to a substantive hearing, and of them only 58 were determined substantively, while 2,306 were refused—leaving 1,737 claims unaccounted for. See Ministry of Justice 2007 above n 28 at 27. In 2006, 831 asylum judicial reviews were withdrawn; in 2007, the figure was 997. The High Court does not record the reasons why judicial reviews are withdrawn (Hansard HL Deb vol 711 col 5WA 1 June 2009). According to the Immigration Law Practitioners' Association, *ILPA Briefing House on the Borders, Citizenship and Immigration Bill: Transfer of Judicial Reviews & Appeals to the Court of Appeal* (London, ILPA, 2009) 2, it is commonplace for the Home Office either to concede a challenge and/or to make a fresh decision and in that way the case will not be heard in court. See generally M Sunkin, 'Withdrawing: A Problem in Judicial Review?' in P Leyland and T Woods (eds), *Administrative Law Facing the Future: Old Constraints and New Horizons* (London, Blackstone, 1997) ch10.

[70] See, eg, R Ford, 'Home Office Ignored Judge Over Deportation' *The Times* (27 August 2004); A Travis, 'Home Office Ignored Court Injunction on Deportation' *The Guardian* (16 August 2006); R Ford, 'Mother of Three Was Deported After Court Ruled She Could Stay' *The Times* (16 August 2006) 20.

[71] Home Office Immigration and Nationality Directorate, *Process Communication: Revised Instructions for Handling Injunctions Against Removal* (London, IND, 16 August 2006); *R (N) v Secretary of State for the Home Department* [2009] EWHC Admin 873; 'Government to Face Legal Action by Returned Asylum-seeker' *The Independent* (31 May 2009).

[72] *R v Secretary of State for the Home Department, ex parte Deniz Mersin* [2000] INLR 511 (QB); *R (S) v Secretary of State for the Home Department* [2006] EWHC Admin 1111; [2006] EWCA Civ 1157; [2006] INLR 575. See also the earlier immigration case *R v Secretary of State for the Home Department, ex parte Phansopkar* [1976] QB 606.

inaction.[73] On occasion, the courts have castigated the Home Office's disregard for legality.[74] In these instances, such misfeasance would not appear to be caused simply by substandard or incompetent administration, but by darker motivations deliberately to ignore court rulings. Then there are the litigation games played by Home Office officials, such as operating a secret policy of detaining foreign national prisoners even though the policy was recognised internally within the Home Office to be legally vulnerable.[75]

This is not to imply that the problems have been unreal. The Home Office has been particularly concerned that 'judicial review is often used purely as a tactic to disrupt the removal process when the underlying claim has no merit'.[76] When a claimant lodges judicial reviews against removal, the Home Office will be unable to continue with the removal, and the claimant may then abscond. 'Making a successful enforced removal of a failed asylum applicant is challenging as it requires the Department to coordinate documentation, transport and escorts against the backdrop of legal challenges and international relations'.[77] Claims for judicial review typically come at the end of the process before removal. The concern is that judicial review is being used deliberately to delay removal.[78]

In response, the Home Office has sought (improperly) to warn the courts against allowing judicial review against removals and has modified its policy of automatically suspending removals when subject to judicial review.[79] But, the longer-term

---

[73] See *Boafo* above n 2; *Saribal* above n 2; *Secretary of State for the Home Department v TB (Jamaica)* [2008] EWCA Civ 977 [32]–[33] (Stanley Burton LJ); *R (Jenner) v Secretary of State for the Home Department* [2010] EWHC Admin 132 [30].

[74] See, eg, *R (SK) v Secretary of State for the Home Department* [2008] EWHC Admin 98 [2] (Munby J): 'the melancholy facts that have been exposed as a result of these proceedings are both shocking and scandalous. They are shocking even to those who still live in the shadow of the damning admission by a former Secretary of State that a great Department of State is "unfit for purpose". They are scandalous for what they expose as the seeming inability of that Department to comply not merely with the law but with the very rule of law itself'. See also *R (Karas and Miladinovic) v Secretary of State for the Home Department* [2006] EWHC Admin 747 [87]; R Ford, 'Home Office "Disregarded Law"' *The Times* (8 April 2006) 8; *Muuse v Secretary of State for the Home Department* [2010] EWCA Civ 453.

[75] *Abdi, Ashori, Madani, Mighty and Lumba v Secretary of State for the Home Department* [2008] EWHC Admin 3166.

[76] Home Office Immigration and Nationality Directorate, *Background Note to Revised IND Policy on Handling JR Challenges to Removal Decisions* (London, Home Office, 2006).

[77] House of Commons Public Accounts Committee, *Management of Asylum Applications* (2008–09 HC 325) 6. The average cost of an enforced removal was £11,000 in 2005. See National Audit Office, *Returning Failed Asylum Applicants* (2005–06 HC 76) [19].

[78] According to the National Audit Office, above n 66 at [2.20]: 'the low level of success and impact on removals suggests that judicial review is used to block' the Home Office from removing failed claimants. In *R (FH; K; A; V; H; SW; HH; AM; SI & ZW) v Secretary of State for the Home Department* [2007] EWHC Admin 1571 [25], Collins J has observed that 'any judge sitting in the Administrative Court cannot fail to be aware that many allegedly fresh claims are brought when removal is at last attempted and that the majority of such claims are unarguable, being attempts to delay a justifiable removal. But some, albeit a small minority, are genuine'.

[79] A Travis, 'Reid Warns Judges Not to Block Iraqis' Deportation' *The Guardian* (5 September 2006); Home Office Immigration and Nationality Directorate, *Change of Policy Relating to the Circumstances in Which Removal Will be Deferred Following Challenge by Judicial Review* (London, IND, 2007); CPR Practice Direction 54.18; *R (Madan and Kapoor) v Secretary of State for the Home Department* [2007] EWCA Civ 770; [2008] 1 All ER 973, 979–980 (CA); Home Office United Kingdom Border Agency, *New Policy on Judicial Reviews that Challenge Removals* (London, UKBA, 9 January

solution has been to transfer some of the work to the Upper Tribunal. The purpose of the Upper Tribunal's judicial review jurisdiction is to allow parties to benefit from it specialist expertise in cases similar to those with which the Tribunal routinely deals in the exercise of its statutory appellate jurisdiction; a subsidiary effect being to reduce the Administrative Court's caseload.[80] In 2009, the Home Office had proposed to remove this statutory bar against the transfer of immigration and asylum judicial reviews.[81] This was not without controversy; the ouster clause had cast a long shadow and the cases are 'at the most sensitive end of judicial review'.[82] Select Committees recognised the problem of overburdening the higher courts and saw no reason why routine judicial reviews could not be handled in the Upper Tribunal, but expressed concern that cases of sufficient significance and complexity should be heard by an Administrative Court judge.[83] By contrast, the Administrative Court itself has warmly endorsed the transfer. To deal with its increased caseload, the Administrative Court has, over recent years, drafted in many deputy-judges, many with little immigration experience. According to the President of the Queen's Bench Division, while some immigration and asylum judicial reviews are plainly suited to the Administrative Court, a 'substantial number could be dealt with appropriately in the Upper Tribunal' by senior tribunal judges with immigration law expertise; the transfer 'would provide a further means of relieving the pressure on the Administrative Court and speeding up the work of that court'.[84] In the event, the Home Office agreed a compromise: only fresh claim judicial reviews would be transferred initially.[85]

Precisely how tribunalised judicial reviews will operate remains to be seen. A widely touted advantage of the Upper Tribunal is its flexibility; Administrative Court judges can sit in the Upper Tribunal alongside Senior Immigration Judges; and special panels can be convened for important test cases. The transferred judicial reviews are to be heard by a combination of the Senior President of Tribunals, the UT Chamber Presidents, who are all High Court judges, and senior UTIAC judges who have been specially designated by the Senior President.[86] For the Government, this arrangement will provide a sufficiently robust mechanism to ensure that those cases which raise genuinely significant and complex issues will

---

2009); Home Office United Kingdom Border Agency, *Change to Our Policy on Judicial Reviews Challenges* (London, UKBA, 20 July 2009); *R (Medical Justice) v Secretary of State for the Home Department* [2010] EWHC Admin 1925. See further R Thomas, 'Judicial Review Challenges to Removal Decisions' (2008) 14(1) *Immigration Law Digest* 2.

[80] Tribunals, Courts and Enforcement Act 2007 ss 15–21. Cases may be transferred on an individual or class case basis.

[81] Supreme Court Act 1981 s 31A(7) (as inserted by the Tribunals, Courts and Enforcement Act 2007 s 19(1)).

[82] Hansard HL Deb vol 687 col GC 68 13 December 2006 (Lord Lloyd).

[83] Joint Committee on Human Rights above n 56 at [1.22]–[1.29]; House of Commons Home Affairs Committee, *Borders, Citizenship and Immigration Bill* (2008–09 HC 425) [63]–[78].

[84] President of the Queen's Bench Division above n 29.

[85] Borders, Citizenship and Immigration Act 2009 s 53.

[86] Lord Judge LCJ, *The Lord Chief Justice's Review of the Administration of Justice in the Courts* (London, The Stationery Office, 2010) 21.

continue to be heard by Administrative Court judges.[87] The Government's clear intention is that other classes of asylum judicial reviews will be transferred if the preliminary transfer of fresh claim judicial reviews is successful.[88]

Subsequent transfers are likely to include the various types of asylum satellite litigation, such as judicial review challenges against removal directions. Consider also those judicial review challenges which do not concern substantive asylum decision-making, but relate to the method or route of return proposed by the Home Office to effectuate the return of a failed asylum claimant. The Court of Appeal has held that as assessment of risk on return is a hypothetical exercise, the Tribunal is unable to consider contingent matters relating to the manner and method of return to a particular country; that is a matter for challenge by way of judicial review.[89] Given their general attitude toward immigration and asylum judicial reviews, Administrative Court judges are unlikely to relish the prospect of dealing with such challenges. Furthermore, as such challenges raise inherently factual issues concerning country situations for which there is limited expertise within the judicial system the preferable solution will be to transfer them to the UTIAC so that they can be handled by senior tribunal judges who have the requisite expertise. The broader picture is that Administrative Court overload has prompted the transfer of judicial review cases to the Upper Tribunal, a process that is likely to continue.

Asylum Review Decisions

A final point to note concerns the operation of the appeal process following the expiry of refugee status. Until 2005, it had been Home Office policy to grant indefinite leave to remain to refugees. However, the concept of surrogate protection under the Refugee Convention is envisaged as a temporary protection during a period of risk, not necessarily a permanent immigration status; granting indefinite leave to refugees precluded the operation of any procedure to consider the cessation of refugee status, as provided for in the Refugee Convention.[90] In 2005, Home Office policy changed: refugees would initially be granted temporary leave for a period of five years. After the expiry of that period, refugee status and the situation in the relevant country would then be reviewed, with the expectation

---

[87] Joint Committee on Human Rights, *Government Replies to the Second, Fourth, Eighth, Ninth and Twelfth Reports of Session 2008–09* above n 57 at 5–6.

[88] Hansard HC Deb vol 496 col 209 14 July 2009 (Minister of State for Borders and Immigration).

[89] *AG (Somalia) v Secretary of State for the Home Department* [2006] EWCA Civ 1342. See also *AM & AM v Secretary of State for the Home Department (armed conflict: risk categories) Somalia CG* [2008] UKAIT 00091 [20]–[32]. For instance, a Somalian claimant who has been found by an Immigration Judge not to be at risk on return in Somalia, may nonetheless claim that he would be placed in danger at Mogadishu airport following his arrival there or on the way home from Mogadishu; this latter decision concerning the method and manner of return is only challengeable by way of judicial review.

[90] *IA HC KD RO HG v Secretary of State for the Home Department (Risk—guidelines—separatist) Turkey CG* [2003] UKIAT 00034 [47]; Refugee Convention 1951, Art 1C.

that those no longer at risk would return home while those still at risk would be granted permanent status.[91]

Such a policy requires the Home Office to create another decision-making procedure to process reviews of those granted refugee status, and with it adverse decisions, and appeals against them. Since 2005, over 23,000 applicants have been granted asylum of which 8,000 will need to have their status reviewed in 2010. In 2009, it was noted that the Home Office had no process of keeping track of refugees after they have been granted asylum.[92] The Home Office has stated that it has been developing a process for reviewing the status of refugees after the end of the five year period of temporary leave had expired, though it remains to be seen how the procedure will operate in practice.[93] One practical problem is that individuals may lose contact with the Home Office or abscond when their five year temporary period of leave expires. Another issue is that if an individual's case is examined after five years and the Home Office concludes that it is safe to return, then this decision will attract a right of appeal and the whole appellate process will start again. If such appeals arise, then the principal issue will not be credibility, but whether or not country conditions have improved; country guidance could be specifically convened for such purposes. The fact that concerns over the lack of proper planning by the Home Office concerning reviews of asylum grants have been raised contributes to the general sense that the management of the decision-making and appeals system has sometimes been inadequate.

The Value of Onward Challenges

So much for organising onward challenges, but what value do they have? To what extent do they promote quality in decision-making? Are onward challenges a useful mechanism for assessing the quality of tribunal decision-making? To assess these questions, it is necessary to analyse the functions of onward challenges: retrospective error-correction; a deterrent function; and their prospective guidance function. The fourth legitimising function does not require analysis here; onward challenges are well-established and the Home Office is unlikely to attempt a re-run of the ouster clause episode. The other functions of onward challenges do, though, require analysis.

---

[91] Home Office, *Controlling Our Borders: Making Migration Work for Britain. Five Year Strategy for Asylum and Immigration* (Cm 6472, 2005) 22; Immigration Rules (1994 HC 395) r 339Q.

[92] NAO above n 66 at [2.38].

[93] See HM Treasury, *Treasury Minutes to the Twenty Eighth Report from the House of Commons Public Accounts Committee Session 2008–09* (Cm 7717, 2009) 23.

The Error-Correction Function

The ability of onward challenges to promote decisional quality through the retrospective correction of erroneous decisions depends upon the following factors: (i) the rate of onward challenge; (ii) the identity of the party lodging such applications; and (iii) the scope of onward challenge.

The first and second factors can be taken together. A high rate of challenge will enable reviewing judges to identify and correct more errors of law than if there is a low rate of challenge. The fact that in 2007–08, review applications were lodged in respect of some 56 per cent of initial appeal decisions means that reviewing judges will identify more errors of law in asylum decisions than in other tribunal systems. But the ability to detect errors of law will depend, to some degree, on which particular type of appeal decisions are challenged, which is determined by the party bringing such challenges. One feature of the asylum decision process is that a far higher proportion of onward challenges (89 per cent) are brought by unsuccessful claimants against adverse decisions when compared to the proportion brought by the Home Office against positive decisions (11 per cent). This is to be expected: more appeals are dismissed (75–80 per cent) than allowed (20–25 per cent).

Nevertheless, the higher propensity of unsuccessful claimants to challenge when compared with the much lower propensity of the Home Office can, to some extent, skew the ability to detect errors of law. Assuming that, all things being equal, errors of law are evenly distributed amongst all appeal decisions, whether allowed and dismissed, then the lower rate of challenge by the Home Office will mean that errors in allowed appeal decisions are less likely to be identified and corrected than those errors in dismissed appeal decisions. At the same time, the high rate of challenge by unsuccessful claimants enhances the ability of onward challenges in the asylum context to correct errors of law when compared with other tribunal systems.

Scope of Review

The third factor is the scope of review. The purpose of onward challenges is to detect errors of law rather than promote decisional quality. Nevertheless, there is a substantial overlap. A decision flawed by an error of law will not be of good quality, but the overlap is not complete; a decision not found to contain an error of law could, nevertheless, be of higher quality. A critical issue is the scope of review. A broad scope of review (decisions must be closely scrutinised for any error of law) widens the ability of reviewing judges to intervene while a narrow scope of review (decisions can only be upset if positively wrong in law) reduces it. This raises an enduring question of administrative law: what is the scope of error of law?[94] Do

---

[94] E Mureinik, 'The Application of Rules: Law or Fact?' (1982) 98 *Law Quarterly Review* 587; J Beatson, 'The Scope of Judicial Review for Error of Law' (1984) 4 *Oxford Journal of Legal Studies* 22; T Endicott, 'Questions of Law' (1998) 114 *Law Quarterly Review* 292; Z Chowdhury, 'The Concept of "Error of Law" and its Application in Immigration Cases' (2009) 15(2) *Immigration Law Digest* 8.

reviewing judges draw analytical distinctions between factual and legal issues before interfering or do they adopt a pragmatic approach by which they first decide whether to interfere and then, to justify such intervention, find an error of law?

Such questions cannot be de-coupled from the management of the adjudication process. If error of law is defined too broadly, the risk is that onward challenges may simply collapse into a re-run of the initial merits appeal with all the consequent duplication and money and time costs involved. The scope of error of law operates as a 'tool for regulating the incidence' of onward challenge.[95] But, if error of law is defined too narrowly, there is the risk that reviewing judges will be unable to correct clear errors; reviewing judges normally wish some scope to intervene.

Errors of Law

Which legal errors are most commonly encountered in practice? Making a legal error in terms of not applying the relevant legal rules correctly or making a material misdirection of law clearly qualifies; as does a procedural or other irregularity that affects the fairness of the proceedings. Such errors will normally invalidate the whole of the original determination. As we have seen, procedural errors—for instance, not adjourning an appeal when there were good reasons for doing so; a judge asking too many questions of an appellant; alternatively, a judge not properly testing an appellant's account in the absence of a Home Office presenting officer—do occur. Then there are errors of law concerning the handling of evidence and substantive decisional content: failing to take into account and/or resolve conflicts of fact or opinion on material matters; taking into account immaterial considerations; failing to make adequate or proper findings of fact or to give clear and proper reasons for such findings.

Failing to give proper or adequate reasons is perhaps the most frequently advanced ground of challenge. One purpose of reason-giving is to ensure that a party understands not only the outcome of a decision, but also the basis for the decision. Another is to enable the party to decide upon any consequential action (ie onward challenge) to take. A failure to give adequate reasons will be an error of law, but a reasons challenge will only succeed if the aggrieved party can demonstrate substantial prejudice.[96] A tribunal decision should not be set aside for inadequacy of reasons, unless the Tribunal had failed to identify and record the matters that were critical to the decision in such a way that a reviewing court is unable to understand why the decision was reached. At the same time, the absence of proper reasons justifying, for instance, adverse credibility findings will usually be sufficient to invalidate the decision because of the difficulty of determining whether, in the absence of proper reasons, the decision was valid.

---

[95] P Cane, *Administrative Law* (Oxford, Oxford University Press, 2004) 230.
[96] *South Bucks District Council v Porter* [2004] UKHL 33; [2004] 4 All ER 775 [36] (Lord Brown).

There are, though, reasons and reasons, some of which may be material to the decision and others which might not. If a reviewing judge goes too far in making requirements for proper reasons, then this can in effect result in overturning a decision simply because the reviewing judge does not like it. Alternatively, there is the risk is that the reviewing judge's search for adequate reasons can easily become a quixotic search for decisional perfection. As it is almost always possible to criticise or improve on any reason or other point made by a tribunal, it would be fatuous to expect perfection in any decision, all the more so in the light of the pressures on immigration judges.[97] However, as the Tribunal noted in 2001, 'there has in the past—and the Tribunal must take some of the blame for this—been too great a concern to see that every matter is dealt with by an adjudicator however unimportant or peripheral'.[98] The higher courts subsequently sought to put a stop to reasons challenges which simply attacked the lack of proper reasons on minor or secondary issues. As Brooke LJ put it in 2005, 'unjustified complaints . . . based on an alleged failure to give reasons, or adequate reasons, are seen far too often'; while each challenge must receive intense scrutiny, 'the practice of bringing appeals because the . . . Immigration Judge has not made reasoned findings on matters of peripheral importance must now come to an end'.[99]

A particular aspect of reasons challenges that arises frequently is the failure to make proper findings on particular issues and/or improper handling and assessment of the evidence. For instance, in one appeal, the judge had concluded that there had been no evidence that the appellant would be identified as a person demonstrating outside their country's embassy in London, but the appellant had relied upon a former embassy official who had asserted that such demonstrators would be identified; while the judge was bound to accept that evidence, he was obliged to explain its rejection.[100]

Restricting onwards challenges to error of law grounds precludes challenges against adverse factual findings, but there is no fixed distinction here.[101] The distinction between law and fact is not the result of any *a priori* division, but rather reflects a judicial policy as to where to draw the line between the public interest and the protection of private interests. The general position is that a reviewing judge will accept the factual findings of a lower tribunal, unless they are clearly wrong.[102] A poor factual decision will not be vitiated unless the reasons given are clearly inadequate or the findings irrational. The distinction between fact and law is, though, inherently malleable. A judge can hold that a factual finding was flawed because sufficient reasons were not given or that adequate findings were not made. The degree to which issues of fact can, and should, be turned into issues of law

---

[97] *HK v Secretary of State for the Home Department* [2006] EWCA Civ 1037 [59] (Neuberger LJ).

[98] *Slimani* above n 10 at [9].

[99] *R (Iran) v Secretary of State for the Home Department* [2005] EWCA Civ 982; [2005] INLR 633, 641–642 (Brooke LJ) (CA).

[100] Case 14.

[101] J Dickinson, *Administrative Justice and the Supremacy of the Law in the United States* (Cambridge, Harvard University Press, 1927) 55.

[102] See, eg, *P and M* above n 12 at 93 (Lord Woolf MR).

remains ambiguous. The temptation is for the reviewing judge who perceives there to be a manifest injustice to manufacture a legal error to justify intervention.[103]

This issue arises acutely in asylum cases because of the highly fact-sensitive nature of decision-making. At the same time, this ambiguity provides an avenue through which unsuccessful appellants may seek to upset adverse factual findings. The suspicion is that challenges against adverse factual findings, typically adverse credibility findings, but also assessments of country conditions, can be artificially constructed to re-open factual issues. While not unique to the asylum jurisdiction, attempts to dress facts up as law feature regularly. According to Laws LJ, the asylum appellate process is 'bedevilled' by 'the misuse of factual arguments, sometimes amounting to little more than nuance, and often points of small detail, as a basis for assaulting the legality of a decision'.[104]

The judicial dilemma is apparent: challenges essentially against factual findings can be a particularly difficult area for reviewing judges exercising an error of law jurisdiction, but close scrutiny is necessary given the error costs.[105] It would be simply wrong in principle to permit plainly defective decisions to stand, a point augmented in the context of asylum appeals with its lower standard of proof and serious consequences of incorrect decisions.[106] But extensive use of onward challenges uses up judicial resources and increases administrative costs and delays.

In addition to these familiar grounds of challenge, there are some errors of law particular to asylum jurisdiction. The failure to apply country guidance decisions without good reason has already been considered.[107] The courts have also held that a reviewing judge is enabled, indeed required, to intervene if there is a '*Robinson* obvious' point of asylum law in the appellant's favour which was not considered by the fact-finding judge.[108] To explicate, if when considering an initial tribunal determination, the reviewing judge finds that there is readily discernible an obvious point of refugee or asylum law favourable to the appellant which was not dealt with in the initial appeal decision, then reconsideration must be ordered, even though the point was not pleaded or otherwise advanced by the appellant. The point must be both obvious and have strong prospects of success. The duty on a reviewing judge to pursue a point of law not raised by the party

---

[103] According to J Laws, 'Law and Fact' [1999] *British Tax Review* 159, 162: '. . . the boundary between law and fact is not fixed . . . It depends on what the higher courts think *ought* to be a matter of law: or, more pointedly, what they think should be the subject of judicial control'.

[104] *AJ (Cameroon) v Secretary of State for the Home Department* [2007] EWCA Civ 373 [22] (Laws LJ); *FM (Iran) v Secretary of State for the Home Department* [2008] EWCA Civ 1540 [16] (Laws LJ).

[105] See, eg, *SS (Iran) v Secretary of State for the Home Department* [2008] EWCA Civ 310 [12] (Lord Neuberger). In *SA (Sri Lanka) v Secretary of State for the Home Department* [2008] EWCA Civ 614 [3] Sedley LJ noted that 'one is profoundly conscious . . . that the sanguine prognostications of a tribunal which dismisses an asylum appeal may well turn out to be false, with consequences for the appellant that one shudders to think of. At the same time it is the AIT . . . which is the fact-finding tribunal. This court can only consider intervening if there is an arguable error in the fact-finding, either an error of law or an error of logic'.

[106] *HK* above n 97 at [60] (Neuberger LJ).

[107] Asylum and Immigration Tribunal, *Practice Directions* (2007) [18.4].

[108] *R v Secretary of State for the Home Department, ex parte Robinson* [1998] QB 929, 946 (Lord Woolf MR) (CA).

whom the point favours is an unusual feature of an adversarial system and is best understood as an aspect of the need for anxious scrutiny and the underlying public interest.[109] A particular facet of the broader adversarial-inquisitorial debate, the courts have doubted whether the same obligation could ever avail the Home Office given the inequality of resources between it and the average asylum appellant.[110] Finally, the asylum jurisdiction has provided fertile ground for the development of other grounds of challenge, such as unfairness resulting from a mistake of fact.[111]

Closely linked to such scope of review issues is the requirement that errors of law be material to outcomes; errors of law which do not make any difference to the outcome do not matter.[112] An error of law will be immaterial only if, but for the error, the judge *must* otherwise have reached the same conclusion; if a different conclusion *might* have been reached, then the error will be material.[113] Furthermore, any party seeking to argue that an error of law is immaterial will have a high burden to discharge.[114] Most, though not all, errors of law will be material.

Determining whether errors of law exist is then frequently an essentially judgmental task influenced by a number of broader considerations; different reviewing judges may differ in identifying errors of law. The search for quality therefore has to distinguish between those borderline errors over which different reviewing judges might legitimately differ and those clear errors of law which are indicative of a lower quality of decision-making. Another factor is that senior judges are likely, through their overview of decisions and informal networking, to have an appreciation of the perceived quality of individual judges; inexperienced recent judicial appointees or judges known for producing lower quality decisions may have their decisions more closely scrutinised than more experienced judges.

The Rate of Error-Correction as a Quality Indicator and Decisional Quality

Despite the variable scope of review, what can the outcomes of onward challenges tell us about the quality of tribunal decisions? Consider the headline figure of successful challenges. In 2007, of the 3,573 reconsideration appeals decided, 1,381 (39 per cent) were allowed, that is, an error of law was identified and a decision allowing the appeal was substituted. However, this headline figure of successful challenges is not necessarily a reliable indicator of the quality of initial tribunal

---

[109] *GH (Afghanistan) v Secretary of State for the Home Department* [2005] EWCA Civ 1603 [15]–[16] (Brooke LJ).

[110] Ibid, [17] (Brooke LJ).

[111] *E and R v Secretary of State for the Home Department* [2004] EWCA Civ 49; [2004] QB 1044 (CA). See PP Craig, 'Judicial Review, Appeal and Factual Error' [2004] *Public Law* 788; R Williams, 'When is an Error not an Error? Reform of Jurisdictional Review of Error of Law and Fact' [2007] *Public Law* 793.

[112] Asylum and Immigration Tribunal (Procedure) Rules SI 230/2005 r 31(2); *R (Iran)* above n 99 at 640.

[113] *IA (Somalia) v Secretary of State for the Home Department* [2007] EWCA Civ 323 [15] (Keene LJ).

[114] *Detamu v Secretary of State for the Home Department* [2006] EWCA Civ 604 [14] (Moses LJ).

decisions for two reasons. The reconsideration process can involve the submission of fresh evidence. Facts, such as country conditions, can change and either party may want to argue that country conditions have improved or deteriorated. If a reconsideration decision is decided upon fresh evidence, then the outcome reached does not provide a reliable means of assessing the quality of the initial appeal decision. Secondly, the headline figure omits those cases in which the outcome of the cases remained unchanged, but in which the reasons for the initial determination were found wanting. Nonetheless, taking account of factors and the variability of the concept of error of law, it does not appear that the quality of decision-making is uniformly high.

This view is supported by the frequent errors identified in actual decisions. Frequent errors include the following: failure to make proper findings of fact; failure to give adequate or proper reasons; improper treatment of expert evidence; a failure to decide cases methodically and so on. For instance, in one case, a Senior Immigration Judge had dismissed an appellant's appeal on the ground that the appellant could internally relocate, but this ground had not been raised before the Immigration Judge. As a Court of Appeal judge noted in one case:

> this court has repeatedly pointed out that internal relocation is a serious issue which ordinarily requires not only notice, but evidence—including crucially the applicant's own evidence—and full argument. The Tribunal here has adopted the novel approach of expecting the applicant to have advanced an argument before the Immigration Judge against a proposition which had never been raised, and of then deeming her to have lost it. It is an approach which bristles with objections.[115]

Judges sometimes commit the most egregious errors, such as applying a previous tribunal decision which had been subsequently overturned. According to Sedley LJ:

> This is far from the first time in recent years that the AIT has either ignored or overlooked decisions of this court. It should never happen, and there is no logistical or other reason why it should . . . If the tribunal are to refer to an unargued decision, as they may legitimately do in support of an apparently uncontroversial point, it is incumbent on them to make sure that it has not been overset or departed from by a higher court.[116]

A common complaint is the poor drafting of determinations.[117] While senior tribunal judges and the higher courts at times trenchantly excoriate poor decisions by Immigration Judges, they also compliment well-written decisions. Overall, there is evidence of both good and inferior quality decision-making. If certain factors, such as the high rate of challenge and the temptation of senior judges to intervene when they disagree with the outcome, are held static, then there is certainly scope for the improvement of the substantive quality of appeal decision-making.

---

[115] Case 39.

[116] *YB (Eritrea) v Secretary of State for the Home Department* [2008] EWCA Civ 360 [8] (Sedley LJ).

[117] See, eg, *GO v An Immigration Officer, Heathrow (Right of appeal: ss 89 and 92) Nigeria* [2008] UKAIT 00025 [5] (the Immigration Judge had 'failed properly to carry out the task he had set himself; and his conclusions as a whole entirely lack reasons. The document simply fails to demonstrate that the judge has properly performed his judicial function in this case . . . we consider it to be well below the professional standard that could be expected by the parties or the taxpayer').

There may be several competing and overlapping explanations for variable decisional quality: the pressure on the judges; insufficient training and support; the pace of legal and factual change; and the variable contribution of representation to the determination of appeals. There may be other factors such as a judge's length of service: more recent appointees might not be sufficiently-well experienced in the jurisdiction and consequently make mistakes; alternatively, other judges may have worked in the jurisdiction for too long. Another factor may be whether or not a judge has either a full-time or a part-time appointment; as the majority of Immigration Judges are part-time, it may be that the case that such judges are not able to acquire a sufficient familiarity with all aspects of the jurisdiction. A further factor may simply be that not all individual judges are able attain a high degree of competency.

The Deterrent Function

What then of the deterrent function, the degree to which onward challenges induce first-tier judges to adopt a more careful approach when making their decisions? Given the high rate of onward challenge, judges are acutely aware that adverse decisions are likely to be challenged and subjected to close scrutiny (and, of course, some judges think that the review process should be more light touch). These factors may induce judges to prepare better decisions.

At the same time, there are some aspects of tribunal operations which militate against this. One is the degree to which judges become aware that their decisions have been overturned. Judges may decide to check whether their decisions are overturned or might be informed of this by their Designated Immigration Judge, but there is no formal process by which judges are automatically notified. Secondly, there is the issue of the extent to which judges are not only informed that a previous decision has been overturned, but also see the error of law decision. This can provide judges with a steady stream of reasoned feedback as to whether or not their decisions were capable of withstanding scrutiny and, if not, why not. However, for such a mechanism to operate properly it is necessary that the Tribunal's internal organisation possess the administrative capacity to ensure that each of the tribunal's 700 or so members receive copies of the relevant decisions, and this must be achieved in the context of a tribunal comprised of geographically dispersed hearing centres and tribunal members many of whom work part-time. The Tribunal's ability to achieve this has varied over the years. As one judge noted, the issue of feedback had been an ongoing issue in the Tribunal for many years, there having been periods in which judges received few onward decisions and periods in which they received most of them.[118]

Even when feedback does function properly, it cannot be guaranteed that it will in practice have a deterrent effect. Judges may have to accept the views of senior

---

[118] Immigration Judge interview 3.

judges but, as noted above, the scope of error of law is itself variable. Nevertheless, while the feedback mechanism be irregular, judges tend to become aware of the general view of senior judges as to how appeals should be determined, in particular the need for judicial fact-finders to provide clear and proper findings on factual issues and give proper and sustainable reasons for such findings.

Prospective Guidance

The third function of onward challenges is the prospective guidance function. By considering onward challenges against first-tier decisions, senior judges can obtain an extensive oversight of the issues and problems arising for decision. Guidance can promote certainty and uniformity. To be effective, it needs to be communicated to first-tier judges and representatives. Such guidance can be of different kinds: guidance on the interpretation and application of relevant legal rules and principles; procedural guidance concerning the hearing and determining of appeals; and other relevant guidance.

The Tribunal has developed a number of mechanisms to ensure uniformity of approach; country guidance has already been examined, but there are other forms of tribunal guidance, such as 'starred' determinations (legally binding guidance) and 'reported' determinations, which provide other generic guidance on issues.[119] As new issues arise—for instance, the approach to be taken by judges when presented with linguistic analysis evidence concerning an appellant's nationality?— senior judges issue new guidance.[120] More generally, the prospective guidance function will be a principal responsibility of the Upper Tribunal. That tribunal will issue at least three different forms of guidance: substantive guidance on the specialist legislative and administrative rules governing the particular appellate system; overarching guidance that develops a generic and coherent administrative law jurisprudence applicable to all tribunal jurisdictions; and practical guidance in relation to the decision-making process on matters of practice and procedure, not only in relation to first-appeals, but also with regard to initial agency decision-making.[121] With the transfer of asylum and immigration appeals to the Upper Tribunal, this guidance function is likely to develop further.

The task of issuing guidance has not, of course, been confined to the Tribunal. Asylum law is characterised by an extraordinary volume of judicial guidance and case-law from all levels—domestic and European—without parallel in any other area of legal practice. The national higher courts—the Court of Appeal and the Supreme Court—have increasingly been required to resolve issues of asylum law, and then there is the increasing involvement of both the European Court of Human Rights and the European Court of Justice.

[119] Asylum and Immigration Tribunal, *Practice Directions* (2007) [17]–[18].

[120] See, eg, *FS v Secretary of State for the Home Department (Treatment of expert evidence) Somalia* [2009] UKAIT 00004.

[121] G Hickinbottom, 'Upper Tribunal: A Forum to Clarify and Develop the Law' (2009) (Spring) *Tribunals* 3, 5.

Despite the importance of the prospective guidance function, problems can arise for a number of reasons. First, there is the risk that the guidance itself can be internally inconsistent. If this happens, then uncertainty is inevitable. Judicial dialogue can allow for different views by different panels to be expressed thereby enabling the Tribunal to arrive at a collective resolution of difficult or problematic issues. But such resolution can itself sometimes be elusive, take time, prompt further onward challenges, and thereby generate backlogs. A related problem is selective citation of guidance by the parties to support their cases. Given the volume of case-law and guidance, there can be considerable scope for the parties selectively to cite guidance in support of a position favourable to them, but without having to cite other contrary decisions.

The Tribunal has instituted procedures to ensure consistent guidance. Since 2006, senior judges have not been able to report their own decisions; that decision rests with the Tribunal's reporting Committee (consisting of the Deputy President and several senior judges) which acts as a filter designed broadly to ensure that cases that are reported are consistent with one another and existing higher court authority and contain guidance that is pertinent to Immigration Judges.[122] To end the practice of selective citation, the Tribunal introduced constraints upon relying on unreported determinations.[123] There has also been an effort by the Tribunal to make its case-law more interlinked or 'joined-up' so that it is clear how the new decision fits with previous decisions on the same issue. The impetus to promote certainty and uniformity therefore generates the trend for a centralised reporting system within the Tribunal. Nonetheless, there is much guidance issued and most Immigration Judges and representatives will admit to some difficulty in keeping abreast of it all.

Beyond the tribunal level, various problems can arise with effective guidance and case-law, in part because of the sheer volume of cases, the different courts involved (the Court of Appeal, the House of Lords/the Supreme Court, the European Court of Human Rights, and the European Court of Justice), and the growing complexity of asylum and immigration law, which has become increasingly intertwined with EU law and European human rights law. For instance, the problem of inconsistent guidance has not been limited to the Tribunal, but has extended to the Court of Appeal. One problem has been that guidance provided by the Court of Appeal has not always been internally consistent, coherent, or sufficiently detailed. As such judgments are binding on the Tribunal, any inconsistencies they possess can create major problems for lower-tier judges. Likewise, there has been a perceived lack of consistency between different House of Lords decisions on article 8 ECHR and between different opinions in the same case and unclear, incomplete, or equivocal guidance. In the context of the UTIAC, this is likely to change. As Sir Nicholas Blake has noted, 'one of the products of the Upper Tribunal system is that there is improved communication between the UT and the

---

[122] Asylum and Immigration Tribunal, *Practice Directions* (2007) [17.2]
[123] Asylum and Immigration Tribunal, *Practice Directions* (2007) [17.6]–[17.8].

Court of Appeal and some opportunity for dialogue about how and when our decisions are reviewed by the senior courts'.[124]

Other problems arise from time-lags within the production of guidance at different levels of the decision-making hierarchy. It can take time for the higher courts to produce guidance; meanwhile, ordinary appeals need to be determined. If such courts decide that the Tribunal has been determining appeals on the basis of erroneous legal rules and principles, then those appellants whose appeals have already been determined will naturally wish to attempt to overturn them if adverse. When the higher courts do give guidance, then this will have to filter down into the appellate system and may be the subject of further clarification by the Tribunal. The difficulties can be compounded if the relevant higher court does not itself provide uniform and authoritative legal guidance or if the Tribunal's subsequent interpretation and elucidation of that guidance is itself the subject of subsequent challenge.[125] Higher courts may also provide a gloss upon legal rules which may be the subject of further litigation as the parties seek to either expand or confine the scope of that legal rule or principle.

In summary, the guidance and case-law concerning asylum and immigration is voluminous, complex, springs from multiple sources, and is constantly developing. Issuing coherent and effective guidance can present challenges which increase with the number of different tribunals and courts (both national and European) involved, the pace of legal and factual change and its dynamic nature, and the nature of the subject-matter. The Tribunal's Reporting Committee gives it control over the number of guidance decisions the Tribunal issues and ensures that the guidance is uniform and certain. However, the proliferation of precedents from the higher courts can create challenges in terms of overall coherence and consistency and the time taken. There are, though, some practical solutions that might be able to resolve some of the difficulties by fostering closer interaction between different levels of the judicial structure. For instance, hybrid panels comprising both senior tribunal judges and Court of Appeal judges can be used to provide authoritative resolution of important legal and country guidance issues. Liaison judges can enable effective communication between different levels of the judicial structure and facilitate coordination, so that, for instance, the same issue is not repeatedly determined by the Tribunal and the Court of Appeal or that the Court of Appeal does not proceed to determine an important issue in ignorance of relevant, existing tribunal guidance. Given that the impetus behind the transfer of

---

[124] Blake above n 50 at 4.

[125] Cf *VNM v Secretary of State for the Home Department* [2006] EWCA Civ 47 [29]–[30] (Brooke LJ): 'One of the difficulties we have experienced in connection with this jurisprudence in recent years has been derived from our three-tier appellate system, whereby decisions of the House of Lords frequently disturb the authority of earlier decisions by this court and the IAT; and because the House of Lords does not speak with a single voice it sometimes takes time for the true meaning of a decision (or decisions) of the House of Lords to work its way through the system. Difficulties also arise because cases which appear to raise a common issue (such as internal flight relocation) are sometimes decided solely in relation to a claim under the Refugee Convention, sometimes in relation to a claim under Article 3 ECHR, sometimes in relation to an Article 8 claim, and sometimes in relation to a combination of the three'.

the jurisdiction to the First-tier and Upper Tribunals has been to reduce the asylum and immigration burden on the higher courts, new mechanisms for judicial interaction need to be developed to promote practical cooperation in the task of issuing effective and coherent guidance.

Assessing Onward Challenges and an Alternative

It has often been assumed that the level of cases challenged and the outcomes are the best measure of the decisional quality. The analysis presented here has offered a more nuanced understanding of the contribution of onward challenges to promoting and assessing decisional quality. The existence of onward challenges is insufficient by itself to ensure that a tribunal produces quality decisions. The effectiveness of such systems of challenge is dependent not just upon typical access to justice issues such as time limits and the presence of representation, but also upon a number of different factors: the actions or inactions of the parties concerned; the scope of review adopted; the attitudes of and coordination between judges at different levels of the appeal structure; and the internal organisation of the Tribunal itself. The upshot of this is that while onward challenges provide some opportunity to both detect and to stimulate quality decisions, they do not provide a comprehensive means of monitoring quality.

Should a more comprehensive alternative system be introduced in order to monitor quality? One alternative would be to institute a quality assurance system of appeal decisions. Such a system might operate as follows: adjudicative criteria would be formulated against which a representative sample of determinations would be assessed by senior judges and graded in terms of their quality. Recurring trends in determination quality could be identified and corrective action implemented so that general decision-making standards could be improved. Furthermore, internal quality assurance of draft determinations prior to their formal promulgation could reduce the frequency of poorly written determinations. It is likely then that a carefully designed and systematic quality assurance system would enhance overall decision-making quality in a more effective way than existing onward challenges. To some extent, a very rudimentary quality assurance process operates in some hearing centres by which Designated Immigration Judges read through determinations of newly appointed Immigration Judges and provide them with constructive feedback so that they can improve their decision-writing skills. The establishment of a more systematic quality assurance process is, however, outside the Tribunal's legal framework and requires more time and resources than the tribunal possesses. The principal option is then to continue with the task of enhancing the quality and consistency of guidance issued to Immigration Judges.

Tribunals, Courts and Decision-Making Quality

The final topic examined in this chapter concerns the broader relationship between the tribunal system and the higher courts, a subject that has attracted renewed interest since the creation of the First-tier and Upper Tribunals. The basic issue concerns the relative distribution of responsibility between the specialist tribunal and generalist higher courts. By considering the development of the broader relationship between the tribunal system and the higher courts, we can acquire further insight into the quality of tribunal decision-making.

The Judicial Hierarchy and Specialised Justice

It is apparent that decisional quality will depend not just upon the procedures used, the evidential material to be considered and so on, but also upon the quality and calibre of the decision-makers themselves. If so, then the hierarchies in which decision-makers function assume considerable significance. In the context of judicial hierarchies, the conventional assumption is that higher court judges possess a greater ability to produce decisions of higher quality than those lower down the judicial structure; the quality of decision-making only increases the higher up the judicial hierarchy a case proceeds. This superior ability of higher court judges is generally attributed to the nature of the qualifications, training, and experience that entry into their judicial office requires. If so, then quality in decision-making is a resource that needs to be tightly rationed as there is simply no means by which all appeals can be allowed to proceed up the hierarchy.

This conventional assumption is deeply embedded within our legal culture and is readily apparent from the views of legal practitioners, academics, and judges themselves as to the competence and quality of judicial decision-makers. It is also reflected and reinforced by the gradations of the judicial hierarchy and the distinction traditionally drawn between the 'superior' courts which supervise the decisions of 'inferior' tribunals. However, the reality of tribunal adjudication often reveals a couple of shortcomings in this point of view.

The first drawback is that the conventional approach pays insufficient attention to the different adjudicatory functions that are appropriately performed at different levels of the judicial hierarchy: fact-finding; error-correction; the production of country and other guidance; clarification of important questions of law; and, in appropriate cases, determining questions of legal policy. As these different judicial functions are allocated to different levels of the hierarchy, it is a mistake to assume that decisional quality only ever increases the higher up the hierarchy one goes. Fact-finding judges are accustomed to hearing particular types of appeals as part of their quotidian adjudicative responsibility and this experience may help them to solidify their understanding of the particular nature of the jurisdiction. By contrast, the insight of higher appellate courts into the nature of the fact-finding task may be limited because they sit at two instances removed from it. Instead, the focus of the higher courts is upon resolving important questions of law and their status ensures that their guidance is accepted as authoritative. By contrast, second-tier tribunals sit in-between the first-tier fact-finding and higher appellate level and have responsibility for both error-correction and the issuing of detailed, specialist guidance, such as country or other guidance.

A second, related shortcoming with the conventional view of the judicial structure is that the hierarchical view of courts and tribunals is cross-cut by the distinction between specialist and generalist judges. Tribunal judges specialise in a particular area in that they repeatedly deal with similar cases coming before them and tend to be viewed as possessing particular expertise. By contrast, higher courts are generalists in that they deal with appeals from across a broad range of areas of legal practice.

For these two reasons, it may be mistaken to assume that the decisions of the higher courts are necessarily superior to those of specialist tribunals. From an alternative perspective, high quality decisions are more likely to be produced by judges who specialise in a particular jurisdiction, especially when that jurisdiction experiences a high rate of legal challenge. However, claims to expertise need to be considered carefully because they may obscure rather than illuminate and can be used for self-serving ends. Furthermore, the benefits and costs of specialist and generalist approaches are not unmixed.

The critical issue is the extent to whether specialisation enhances decisional quality. It is generally accepted that specialisation and experience generates expertise in adjudication.[126] As asylum appeals depend heavily on the accuracy and reliability of the main fact-finding tribunal, specialisation in hearing appeals can produce expertise not just in the relevant legal rules, but also in the particular problems and difficulties and this is acquired through repeated and constant exposure to the jurisdiction. The diversity of the caseload can fill in the gaps in tribunal members' knowledge and enable them to acquire a rounded view of the jurisdiction.

Specialisation has other advantages, such as: familiarity with the particular problems and issues posed by a particular area of adjudication; and knowledge of how to handle expert evidence and country information. It can also enhance the decision-maker's ability to identify those lines of inquiry that the parties have not raised. From the perspective of the specialist tribunal judiciary, the risk may be that the non-cognoscenti may be persuaded to accept arguments that would otherwise have received short-shrift; for instance, Administrative Court judges and deputies who do not necessarily possess immigration law expertise may not make

---

[126] See SH Legomsky, *Specialized Justice: Courts, Administrative Tribunals, and a Cross-National Theory of Specialization* (Oxford, Clarendon Press, 1990) 7–16. Cf RE Wraith and PG Hutchesson, *Administrative Tribunals* (London, Allen & Unwin, 1974) 253: even if tribunal members are not selected because of their particular expertise, 'the very fact of being restricted to a narrow field means that they soon become expert in it'. See also HH Bruff, 'Specialized Courts in Administrative Law' (1991) 43 *Administrative Law Review* 329; P Cane, *Administrative Tribunals and Adjudication* (Oxford, Hart Publishing, 2009) 124–128.

informed decisions.[127] As has been noted above, generalist higher court judges can also produce judgments which are either at odds with each other or do not take into account settled tribunal case-law. In a specialist jurisdiction, generalist judges unaware of the nature of the specialist jurisdiction may appear to be out of their depth. Furthermore, specialisation has other significant advantages such as procedural efficiency; as specialist judges are highly familiar with the jurisdiction, they can deal with cases in a more timely way than generalist judges. Familiarity with the subject-matter can diminish the amount of time needed per case, an especially important consideration when there may be an incentive to lodge challenges for delay purposes.[128] In summary, specialisation by judges in a particular appellate context enables them to build up expertise, which will mature over time. This expertise will, in turn, advance the production of high quality decision-making.

Specialisation is not, however, without its disadvantages; perhaps the greatest is the loss of a generalist perspective. The risk is that specialist adjudicators will operate within their own silo. By contrast, generalist legal knowledge can ensure that general legal standards apply across the board so that those applied in one jurisdiction do not differ markedly from those applied in another. A further possible risk is that, because of their immersion within a particular jurisdiction, specialist judges may, over time, become case-hardened and jaded; by contrast, 'generalists can be expected to approach cases with fewer preconceptions than can those who have been buried in the particular field for an appreciable period of time'.[129] A related risk is that specialist judges may become so accustomed to operating at the coal-face of a particular adjudication process, that they find difficulties in distancing themselves or in taking a longer-term view when required to interpret or formulate a rule of general application. Hubris is another risk; specialists may become too convinced of their own ability and resent interference by the higher courts.

Clearly, there are subtle trade-offs between specialist and generalist approaches, some of which have been reflected in the debate over the transfer to FTTIAC and UTIAC. This transfer will enable specialist judges to deal with onward challenges and reduce the role of the higher courts. As we have seen above, one aspect of the compromise is made by the legislature and relates to the organisation of tribunal appeal systems, a trade-off which can be heavily influenced by caseload considerations. Another aspect concerns the approach of the higher courts themselves and the degree to which they are prepared to interfere with tribunal decisions. If a specialist tribunal demonstrates sufficient expertise, then this justifies less intervention by generalist higher courts and vice versa. Consequently, the legal doctrine governing onward appeals assumes a critical role in managing the division of responsibility.

---

[127] For instance, it has been known for Administrative Court judges deciding opt-in applications to order reconsideration on the basis of new factual evidence even though the jurisdiction is limited to error of law grounds, an outcome contrary to *CA v Secretary of State for the Home Department* [2004] EWCA Civ 1165; [2004] Imm AR 640 (CA).

[128] Legomsky above n 126 at 16–18 and 31–32.

[129] Ibid, 16.

Appeals to the Higher Courts

The relationship between tribunal and the higher courts has been a live issue for decades. Depending upon their predisposition, the higher courts can either subject tribunal decisions to close scrutiny or more or less leave them to get on with their task.[130]

Contemporary discussion of the second-tier tribunal-higher court relationship was initiated in 2001 in *Cooke* where Hale LJ explained that the Court of Appeal should approach appeals from decisions of the Social Security Commissioners with 'an appropriate degree of caution'.[131] This approach was justified given the highly specialised nature of the legal and administrative rules governing the particular system ('it is probable that in understanding and applying the law in their specialised field the tribunal will have got it right'), the experience and expertise of the tribunal members, and their awareness of the realities of tribunal life. Historically, few cases proceed from the tribunal system to the higher courts, a factor which has limited their exposure to such specialist areas and augmented the role of the second-tier tribunal.

But what of the attitude of the higher courts in asylum cases? Caseload and the importance of the issues at stake loom large as does decisional quality. In practice, the views of the higher courts have oscillated wildly. In 2001, the Court of Appeal declined to extend the *Cooke* approach to appeals from the IAT. Explaining that asylum appeals often raised complex issues of fact and law and that asylum and refugee law was then still developing, Brooke LJ noted that some IAT decisions were of 'uncertain quality'.[132] While properly reasoned and well-structured IAT determinations would normally mark the end of the road unless there was some uncertainty about the applicable law, the court recognised that asylum cases required the most anxious scrutiny. In the typically restrained language of appeal court judges, the statement was unprecedented and indicated strongly that, for the Court of Appeal, decisions produced by particular IAT panels were of poor quality.

But in 2005, the Court of Appeal had a volte-face: the *Cooke* approach did extend to asylum appeals after all.[133] Previous concerns as to variable decisional quality had been overtaken by a noticeable improvement in tribunal decision-making and the appointment of Administrative Court judges as Tribunal Presidents. Furthermore,

---

[130] See, eg, *Edwards v Bairstow* [1956] AC 14 (HL); *R v Preston Supplementary Benefits Appeal Tribunal* [1975] 1 WLR 625 (CA).

[131] *Cooke v Secretary of State for Social Security* [2001] EWCA Civ 734; [2002] 3 All ER 279 [16] (Hale LJ) (CA). The Social Security Commissioners determined second-tier appeals from initial social security appeals; this jurisdiction is now exercised by the Upper Tribunal (Administrative Appeals Chamber). See also *Napp Pharmaceutical Holdings Ltd v Director General of Fair Trading* [2002] EWCA Civ 796; [2002] 4 All ER 376 (Competition Appeal Tribunal); *Hinchy v Secretary of State for Work and Pensions* [2005] UKHL 16; [2005] 1 WLR 967 [30] (Lord Hoffmann) and [49] (Baroness Hale) (Social Security Commissioners); *Able (UK) Ltd v HM Revenue and Customs* [2007] EWCA 1207 [28] (General Commissioners, now First-tier Tribunal (Tax)).

[132] *Koller v Secretary of State for the Home Department* [2001] EWCA Civ 1267 [26] (Brooke LJ).

[133] *R (Iran)* above n 99 at 665–666 (Brooke LJ); *Akaeke v Secretary of State for the Home Department* [2005] EWCA Civ 947; [2005] Imm AR 701, 710–712 (Carnwath LJ) (CA).

onward challenges had been restricted to error of law grounds and the law was in a far more settled state than it had been in 2001. While the higher courts retained a vital role as final arbiters in relation to genuine issues of law and the overall fairness of the procedures, they would in future be more cautious before interfering with decisions on matters within the special expertise and competence of the Tribunal, which included not only the evaluation of the difficult and often harrowing evidence produced in support of individual claims, but more generally questions of general principle relating to the conditions in particular categories of claimant or particular countries. In 2007, Baroness Hale, describing the AIT as 'an expert tribunal charged with administering a complex area of law in challenging circumstances', stated that tribunal 'decisions should be respected unless it is quite clear that they have misdirected themselves in law. Appellate courts should not rush to find such misdirections simply because they might have reached a different conclusion on the facts or expressed themselves differently'.[134] This statement has subsequently been used by the Court of Appeal when it has refused to allow challenges against AIT decisions that otherwise lack merit or merely amount to an attempt to re-visit concluded findings or a complaint against adverse factual findings.[135]

From one perspective, the shift in the attitude of the higher courts (especially by the Court of Appeal) toward AIT decisions could be seen as an attempt to stem the flow of onward challenges. If so, then the attempt was unsuccessful because the proportion of onward challenges remained high; the transfer to the First-tier and Upper Tribunals was needed to deal with that problem. However, the recognition by the higher courts that the degree of caution doctrine applied in relation to asylum appeals can be seen as laying an essential foundation for reforming the jurisdiction and as an explicit recognition that the second-tier tribunal ought to be recognised as a specialist body.

The precise reach of this degree of caution doctrine is at present unsettled. For one Court of Appeal panel, this approach extends to decisions by a specialist tribunal on points of law as well as to its assessment of the facts.[136] Other appeal court judges have been more circumspect. A middle ground position has been articulated as follows: the courts should not 'pick over tribunal decisions in a microscopic search for error, and should be prepared to give Immigration Judges credit for knowing their job' but this does not mean that 'the standards of decision-making or the principles of judicial scrutiny which govern immigration and asylum adjudication differ from those governing other judicial tribunals, especially when for some

---

[134] *AH (Sudan) v Secretary of State for the Home Department* [2007] UKHL 49; [2008] 1 AC 678 [30] (Baroness Hale) (HL). The rationale for this approach is the specialist tribunal's expertise. A different rationale was articulated by Lord Radcliffe in *Edwards v Bairstow* above n 130 at 36: '[t]he reason is simply that by the system that has been set up the Commissioners are the first tribunal to try an appeal, and in the interest of the efficient administration of justice their decisions can only be upset on appeal if they have been positively wrong in law'.

[135] See, eg, *OD (Ivory Coast) v Secretary of State for the Home Department* [2008] EWCA Civ 1299 [11] (Touslon LJ); *BK (Democratic Republic of Congo) v Secretary of State for the Home Department* [2008] EWCA Civ 1322 [22] (Laws LJ).

[136] *AS & DD (Libya) v Secretary of State for the Home Department* [2008] EWCA Civ 289 [15].

asylum-seekers adjudication may literally be a matter of life and death'.[137] And, of course, some commentators would dispute the whole notion that the current immigration judiciary can properly be regarded as experts.[138]

The New Model of the Judicial Hierarchy

Nonetheless, the new approach seems here to stay and seems to imply a different model of the judicial hierarchy. As the Senior President of Tribunals has noted, the *Cooke* approach is striking because of 'its anti-hierarchical approach to the relationship between the courts and tribunals' which suggests that the courts are, in certain areas, less qualified than the tribunals they are reviewing.[139] The emerging idea is that the degree of caution doctrine emanating from the higher courts since *Cooke* will support the developing role of the Upper Tribunal in the context of the new model of the judicial hierarchy. The foundation of this new model is based not upon the formal level occupied by the relevant judge within the hierarchy, but upon the notion that a dedicated cadre of specialist judges can exist at more than one level of the hierarchy.[140] What matters is that those shaping the law in a particular area should be specialists. In some instances, this may mean that this responsibility rests principally with the specialist judges in the second-tier tribunal. In other instances, it will rests with specialist judges in the higher courts—depending on the nature of the issue and its legal and policy significance. If so, then the relationship between second-tier tribunals and the higher courts becomes more coordinate, with the higher courts more willing to recognise that they are not competent to overturn tribunal decisions on issues within the tribunal's area of special expertise.

An important aspect of the new model will be the function of the Upper Tribunal in producing guidance of use throughout the whole decision-making system.[141] In practice, the Upper Tribunal will enable greater flexibility when hearings important appeals. For instance, it will be possible to have lead cases heard by hybrid panels comprised of a mixture of both higher court judges and senior tribunals to ensure that the guidance produced is authoritative and informed by specialist experience, unlikely to be challenged, and thereby promote certainty and efficiency.

Furthermore, responsibility for shaping the law is unlikely to mean just the narrow task of interpreting the legal rules concerning a particular area of decision-making. Rather, in this context the approach taken to issues of 'law' is likely to be widened to include other guidance, such as factual guidance and other general guidance in relation to the decision-making process. As the Senior President has noted, if expediency and the competency of the Upper Tribunal are relevant, then,

---

[137] *Entry Clearance Officer, Mumbai v NH (India)* [2008] EWCA Civ 1330 [28] (Sedley LJ).

[138] See, eg, Z Chowdhury, 'The Doctrine of Deference to Tribunal Expertise and the Parameters of Judicial Restraint' (2009) 15(3) *Immigration Law Digest* 15.

[139] R Carnwath, 'Tribunal Justice—A New Start' [2009] *Public Law* 48, 57–58. See also *AA (Uganda) v Secretary of State for the Home Department* [2008] EWCA Civ 579 [42]–[52] (Carnwath LJ).

[140] See Hickinbottom above n 121 at 5.

[141] Tribunals Service above n 8 at [190]–[192]; Carnwath above n 139 at 56–58.

even though its jurisdiction is limited to error of law grounds, it will be able to venture more freely into the grey area separating fact from law than an ordinary court. 'Issues of law' can be interpreted as extending to any issue of general principle affecting the specialist jurisdiction so that the Upper Tribunal can use its expertise to shape and direct the development of law and practice in a particular field.[142] Country guidance provides the best illustration here.[143]

For some, the scope of these developments may, at least initially, appear to be too radical a departure from the customary division of responsibility between the tribunals and the courts. For Cane, the guidance function of tribunals 'has very significant implications for understanding the role of tribunals—especially second-tier tribunals'.[144] If the higher courts adopt heightened deference to tribunal decisions then, taken to an extreme, this approach 'could turn tribunals into a de facto system of administrative courts, effectively immune from control by the "ordinary" courts'.[145] It is apparent that the relationship between tribunals and the higher courts is being recast, but there seems little real prospect that tribunals will be exempt from higher court oversight or that the higher courts will no longer have any responsibility for interpreting and developing the law—certainly not, at least, in the asylum context. While the more restrictive test limits the scope for onward appeals from second-tier tribunals, it only puts such challenges on the same basis as appeals in other contexts rather than excluding them altogether. Even when this restriction is combined with the degree of caution now to be shown by the higher courts to those decisions made within the area of specialist knowledge of the second-tier tribunal, the higher courts will still have a jurisdiction to clarify appropriate and important points of law. The clear intention is to organise the decision-making hierarchy so that cases are determined at the most appropriate level and that only those cases that raise broader issues of legal principle proceed beyond tribunal level.

This approach combined with practical cooperation between the Tribunal and the higher courts—hybrid panels, closer judicial interaction—is likely to support the role of specialist senior judges located in the Upper Tribunal to issue more effective guidance. After all, the higher courts have traditionally declined to provide guidance that will be of assistance to both primary administrative decision-makers and lower-level tribunal judges, but tribunals have a different role as they are an integral and judicial part of the broader administrative process for implementing policy. If the decision-making process is understood in terms of this 'vertical integration', then there is a recognised need for tribunals to produce such guidance—not just for the benefit of first-tier judges, but for administrative agencies, representatives, and appellants as well.

In the context of asylum appeals, all of these changes raise a number of implications. It is likely that the UTIAC will continue to develop its specialist capacity

---

[142] Carnwath above n 139 at 63–64.
[143] *R (Iran)* above n 99 at 657–662 (Brooke LJ).
[144] Cane above n 126 at 199.
[145] Ibid, at 200.

to issue guidance for the benefit of both first-tier judges, appellants, representatives, and Home Office case-workers and that the higher courts will adopt a light touch scrutiny to Upper Tribunal decisions. To be effective, such guidance will need to be robust. Indeed, all the signals are that the UTIAC is conscious that it will have to earn its enhanced place within the judicial hierarchy. As Sir Nicholas Blake has noted:

> My vision for the Upper Tribunal is a body of case-law of high quality, consistency, and clarity so it will be a useful tool for all Immigration Judges and stakeholders. We must maintain and develop high standards of judicial decision-making and earn the respect of the Court of Appeal, the Supreme Court, the profession, and other stakeholders and ultimately politicians and the public.[146]

Furthermore, the Upper Tribunal is unlikely to be a narrowly focused adjudicative body; on the contrary, all the indications are that it will seek to integrate its specific adjudicative function with general public law norms and principles. It is possible that the UTIAC will take over other types of work, such as making declarations of incompatibility under the Human Rights Act 1998 and ruling upon the legal validity of the Immigration Rules.

Conclusion

This chapter has analysed various aspects of onward challenges: their organisation; their contribution to the assessment and promotion of quality in tribunal decision-making; and their operation in the context of the developing relationship between tribunals and the higher courts. As with much else in the asylum appeals process, the operation and organisation of onward challenges function within the context of a tension between the need to ensure that each case receives individual scrutiny and the competing pressures of timeliness and efficiency.

The design of onward challenge against asylum appeal decisions has been particularly susceptible to frequent legislative overhaul to cope with the caseload. If anything the willingness of policy makers constantly to re-shape the legal process of adjudication to ensure that appeals can be concluded within an appropriate timescale demonstrates the centrality of adjudication to the broader administrative process. The story of the development of onward challenges also illustrates two other aspects. First, the executive's desire to push the legal process to its absolute limits, and even to attempt to abolish judicial review altogether. The backlash against the ouster clause debacle illustrates the importance of onward challenges and provides a warning to any future government. The second aspect is the relative failure of policy makers who, when in retreat over the ouster, designed the 2005 appeals system. While the 2005 appeals system was introduced to reduce

---

[146] Blake above n 50 at 6.

the caseload of the higher courts, it only succeeded in increasingly it. Nonetheless, the 2005 appeals system did introduce some beneficial features, such as the development of country guidance and closer interaction between the two levels of the tribunal judiciary. The transfer of asylum and immigration appeals to the First-tier and Upper Tribunals is intended to develop these aspects further while simultaneously bringing a stop to onward appeals from the UT and to takeover responsibility for asylum and immigration judicial reviews.

The contribution onward appeals make to the quality of decision-making is mixed. Systems of onward challenge operate so as to correct errors of law, deter judges from making such errors, and to issue prospective guidance in order to promote uniform and good quality decision-making. However, the extent to which such systems effectively perform these functions is in practice dependent on many other factors such as the rate of challenge, the scope of the concept of error of law, the delivery of feedback throughout the tribunal, and the coherence of tribunal and higher court guidance. While systems of onward challenges are able to identify and correct errors of law in initial tribunal decisions, by their very nature, they are not designed to ensure that all tribunal decisions are of high quality.

The overall finding is that the quality of first-tier decision-making is mixed. A substantial amount of decision-making by Immigration Judges is of good quality, but there are errors of law in a sizeable proportion of challenged decisions. This might not be surprising given the pressure under which they operate and the variable scope of review by reviewing judges. Nonetheless, there is certainly scope for improvement.

Looking to the future, the transfer of asylum appeals to the First-tier and Upper Tribunals is likely to provide a stable, long-term setting for judicial appeals against immigration and asylum decisions. It will also give senior tribunal judges more authority with which to issue coherent guidance to first-tier judges. The transfer of asylum and immigration appeals is intended to reduce the burden of the asylum and immigration caseload on the higher courts. But it is important to distinguish between two types of litigation: reviewing and correcting errors in individual cases and resolving points of law of general importance. As the UTIAC's refusal of permission to appeal will mark the end of the process, the challenge is for the UTIAC to ensure that its decisions are respected. As regards transferred judicial review cases, it is likely that the UTIAC will, over time, assume responsibility for other categories of immigration and asylum judicial review litigation. The Court of Appeal's caseload will reduce, but it will retain its role in resolving important points of law. The tribunal-higher court relationship will continue to depend upon a number of factors: the perceived quality of the decisions of the UTIAC; its specialist expertise; and the willingness and desire of the higher courts to determine general issues of law.

9

Conclusion

THIS BOOK HAS presented an in-depth case-study of asylum adjudication. The purpose has been to analyse the effectiveness and quality of asylum adjudication and to examine the challenges posed by asylum decision-making. In a modern society, complex and competing demands are placed upon government across the many different areas of public policy. One of those demands is that individuals dissatisfied with primary administrative decisions be able to appeal against them to an independent tribunal. Given the scale of modern governmental activity, there are now many different individual tribunal adjudication systems at work. This book has only examined a single adjudication process—the asylum appeals process—which is itself only one aspect of the broader immigration appeals system. Nonetheless, asylum appeals raise many complex issues and problems concerning the operation, organisation, and development of the appeals process. This study has sought to cast some light upon this intricate and relatively under-explored part of the administrative-legal process and to contribute to wider debates on administrative justice.

Having undertaken a detailed analysis of the operation and functioning of asylum adjudication, this chapter concludes the book is in two sections. The first summarises the view taken here of both the nature of tribunal adjudication and of adjudicative quality. It also seeks to discern the broader lessons that can be distilled from this study of asylum adjudication. Some caution is required in this regard. Every legal-administrative process is unique in one way or other, and asylum adjudication is more atypical than most. Nevertheless, there are some aspects of this case-study of asylum adjudication which are potentially generalisable. Moving from administrative adjudication in general back to asylum adjudication in particular, the second section provides an overview of the strengths and weakness of the current system. It also considers how the effectiveness of the system of asylum adjudication could be improved and enhanced.

Evaluating Adjudicative Quality

Adjudication as a Legal Technique of Policy Implementation

It has conventionally been assumed that as adjudicative mechanisms, tribunals are concerned solely with dispute resolution and are separate from the broader administrative process. From this perspective, it is well-established that tribunals resolve disputes by enabling individuals dissatisfied with an initial administrative decision with the opportunity to appeal against that decision to an independent and judicial adjudicative tribunal. Tribunals comprise one process amongst many by which individuals can seek redress against poor decisions produced by administrative agencies. Accordingly, tribunals adjudicate and are not involved with administration.

This book has argued to the contrary that administrative tribunals are best understood to be the judicial, adjudicative component of a broader administrative process for implementing public policy. Tribunals administer public policy in individual cases. They must be institutionally separate and independent from the administrative agency, but nevertheless comprise part of the broader process for implementing government policy. By adjudicating upon disputes individuals have with an administrative agency, tribunals enable individuals affected by the administration of public policy to secure fairness by directing participating in the process of policy implementation.

This perspective has increasingly come to be accepted. With the growth of the modern administrative state, and its responsibility for implementing policy programmes across a diverse range of policy areas, adjudication has increasingly been adopted as one, though by no means the only, mechanism through which policy can be implemented. The advantage of this perspective is that it places tribunals within the context of the broader process of policy implementation and provides a more realistic standpoint from which to understand and examine them. It also means that the criteria for evaluating adjudication do not concern solely the degree to which they are to provide effective access to justice for their users, but also the degree to which the tribunal process is able to provide an effective mechanism for implementing public policy.

Individual tribunals are then a vital part of the broader administrative process. It is recognised, for instance, that while the asylum appeals system is independent of the Home Office, it is a crucial aspect of the wider decision-making process for administering immigration and asylum law and policy. More generally, the Senior President of Tribunals has deployed the neologism 'vertical integration' to capture the end-to-end nature of this broader process commencing with initial administrative decision-making, then the tribunal stage, and concluding with the higher courts.[1] This broader process is not confined to administrative and appellate

---

[1] R Carnwath, 'Tribunal Justice—A New Start' (a speech given to the Administrative Justice and Tribunal Council annual conference, November 2008) [17].

decision-making, but will also include other administrative justice techniques such as internal reviews, complaint handling, and ombudsmen investigations. The important point is that the overall process is designed in the public interest to achieve fairness and finality for individual appellants in the most efficient way possible. Within this context, the task of resolving disputes arising from administrative decisions made to implement social policy inevitably means that the adjudicative tribunal is itself also administering, and in some instances making, policy.

This perspective on tribunals is particularly apposite in relation to asylum adjudication. In this context, the underlying policy goal is to provide international protection to those individuals who would be at real risk of serious ill-treatment on return to their country of origin. However, the accomplishment of this policy goal requires accommodation with an equally pressing and important policy goal: that of maintaining immigration control. There is nothing particularly unusual in this underlying policy tension; public policy is rarely, if ever, problem-free. On the contrary, much policy is often informed by competing goals and the difficult task of seeking to balance competing goals is often in practice undertaken by the administrative process.

The Mix of Adjudicative Values

There are a number of values which inform the design and organisation of a tribunal adjudication system. This study has identified four principal values: accuracy, procedural fairness, cost-efficiency, and timeliness. These are supplemented by a wide range of other values, such as: accessibility; independence; impartiality; consistency; public confidence; openness and transparency, and tribunal expertise in both the subject-matter and the legal rules to be applied.

These values are internal to the nature of administrative adjudication itself. They correspond with different critiques of an adjudication process. Criticisms of adjudication tend to revolve around the failure of a particular adjudication system to fulfil certain values. Adjudication systems are variously criticised for not producing correct decisions, for not employing fair procedures, for excessive costs and delay, and for inconsistent decisions. These critiques, in turn, suggest the corresponding qualities which should characterise a well-functioning adjudication process: accuracy, procedural fairness, cost-efficiency, timeliness, and consistency. The task of designing and operating an effective adjudication process requires the right mix of a number of different values. Put together, these values comprise an analytical framework for evaluating adjudication.

As this study has demonstrated, assessing the degree to which such values are fulfilled in practice can be problematic. It is possible to measure the extent to which some values are fulfilled in practice. Values such as timeliness and cost are easily susceptible to quantitative measurement, but it can be difficult, and sometimes impossible, to measure other values. Accuracy is of central importance, but it is often intrinsically unquantifiable. Given the judgmental nature of fact-finding, the scope for decisional evaluation, and the frequent inability to assess decisional accuracy by reference to what happens after decisions have been taken, there can be no definitive or clear means for assessing decisional accuracy.

The organisation of adjudication requires that appeal procedures be designed to enable the parties to participate in the decision-making process. This requires a number of procedural choices to be taken in relation to different aspects of the process, such as the identity of the adjudicator, the nature of appeal hearings and the mode of the appeal procedure, the role of representation, reason-giving, and onward challenges. The procedural choices selected are designed to provide a fair procedure, but are also informed by other values, in particular, the cost-efficiency of the process and its timeliness.

These values often pull in different directions; a greater emphasis upon one value inevitably means less of an emphasis upon other values. Attaining an appropriate equilibrium between competing values is not a once-and-for-all-time task. Rather, the task of organising the adjudication process is often a continuing enterprise in which the design of the system responds to particular concerns that are raised in relation to its operation; for instance, cases taking too long to conclude, or costing too much, or the procedures used not being considered sufficiently fair. As regards asylum appeals, the task is not to design and organise a tribunal process which is able to ensure that every claimant so entitled is granted asylum irrespective of the costs imposed or of the time taken. Rather, it is to operate a system which is able to produce good quality decisions with the limited funds available and subject to the time limits imposed. Compromises and trade-offs are inevitable. Changes to advance a particular value can often only be purchased at the expense of other values. The desire for speed and cost-efficiency comes into tension with the corresponding need for fair procedures which produce accurate decisions. Consistency has to be balanced against the need for sufficient flexibility to consider individual circumstances.

These trade-offs are normally one of degree; they are necessary if some decision process is to function, but they are often problematic. It is normally possible to determine the consequence of a change to an adjudication process in terms of the enhanced throughput of appeals or a reduction in administrative costs. However, it is much more difficult, if not impossible, to assess whether such changes raise or lower levels of decisional accuracy.

The tension between competing values is particularly acute in the asylum context. As an important aspect of that broader administrative process for implementing policy, the tribunal is necessarily under pressure to fulfil competing values which, in turn, reflect the inherent policy tensions. The requirement to afford protection to those genuinely in need of asylum stems from the legal obligations of the state under refugee, asylum, and human rights law. Given the importance of the decisions, the adjudicatory values of accuracy and fairness emerge as especially important and insistent demands upon the adjudication process. At the same time, the legitimate desire of the state to maintain the integrity of its immigration controls requires that the adjudication process work quickly and achieves finality in decision-making. Furthermore, the overall costs of the adjudication process need to be kept with acceptable limits.

The advantage of this perspective is that it provides a realistic perspective from which to examine the work of tribunals. Tribunals are judicial institutions, but they are not informed by or to be assessed by solely legal values, such as fairness and legality. They are also under pressure to fulfil other goals such as efficiency and finality. Adjudicative quality has to be assessed both in terms of individual justice, but also in terms of effective policy implementation. An administrative adjudication process is only ever likely to work in an acceptable manner if it provides an effective means of implementing policy.

This perspective also helps to explain the development of adjudication processes. Such processes are not static, but fluid and dynamic; their design tends to respond to particular concerns relating to their operation in addition to the domestic political context. Adjudicative design is an incremental process by which policy makers seek to restructure and refashion the adjudicative process to ensure that it satisfies the values that they wish to advance. The operation and development of the adjudication process will be shaped by a wide range of different interests which have exerted varying degrees of influence: political pressures; the lobbying of interest groups, such as representative organisations; rulings of the courts; the number of appellants; and the attitudes of the parties toward the adjudication process. Understanding adjudication therefore requires an appreciation of the policy context and the nature of the crucial relationship between the administrative agency and the tribunal in addition to the complex interrelationships with other actors within the process, such as: the higher courts; expert witnesses; and representative organisations.

Despite its advantages, an inherent limitation of this perspective is that it cannot itself specify which particular mix of values a successful adjudication process needs to possess. All of the values identified are equally important. There is no *a priori* ranking of values. The competing pressures on an adjudication process will tend to emphasise all of these values. However, because of the tensions that arise, there has to be some way of reconciling different values in the practical implementation of the adjudication process. The critical issue is not whether or not an individual value should be considered relevant, but how much of a sacrifice of other values is required to secure that value? Such tensions are, in practice, resolved through the policy process. Indeed, it is probably unproductive to search for intellectually rigorous ways of resolving the tensions between competing values because the policy process exists for this purpose. In the context of the operation of an adjudication system, the policy context will usually, if not always, be of critical importance in influencing the design of an adjudication process and the weight accorded to one or more values over other values. Indeed, policy considerations will pervade the management and structure of appeal procedures in terms of the volume of cases to be determined, the caseload of the higher courts, and the costs of the process. The concept of adjudicative quality is, then, a function of a number of influences: the specific function of an adjudication process within the context of the broader/policy context; the balance struck between competing adjudicative values; the policy context and pressures in which an adjudication system operates; the development of an adjudication system overtime; and its actual day-to-day operation.

Law, Policy, and Adjudication

A further issue to consider is the implications of this for our understanding of the character of administrative law. It is common for legal scholars to understand law from a normative perspective as a body of legal values and principles external to the governmental process which are developed, principally, if not exclusively, by the courts, in order to impose legal controls over government.[2] From this perspective, law is understood as a means of controlling government. It is created through judicially developed principles. Furthermore, it is unrelated to the achievement of governmental purposes and policy goals.

Much debate has focused on whether this conception of law provides an adequate explanation for the practice of judicial review by the higher courts. There is no need to resolve this debate for present purposes. The point is that this conception of law cannot adequately explain the work of tribunals. This is because tribunals operate as adjudicatory mechanisms in the implementation of public policy. Judicial review is limited to the review of administrative decisions and policies, but tribunals are explicitly empowered to substitute their own decisions. Given the higher caseload of tribunals than the courts, tribunals come to play a critical role in the broader governmental process. More broadly, tribunals are involved in the administration and, to some extent, the making of public policy. Any conception of law which is separate and external to the work of administrative government is, therefore, inappropriate in relation to the work of administrative tribunals.

A more appropriate way to understand tribunals is by reference to an instrumental conception of law. Law—especially administrative law—is often used by government as a mechanism for implementing its policy goals. More specifically, as adjudicatory bodies, tribunals operate within the context of a broader administrative process. By doing so, tribunals are one institutional device by which affected individuals can participate in policy implementation. While tribunals provide individuals with a means of challenging administrative decision-making and hence a means of legal control over government, the responsibility for creating and managing appeal systems rests principally with government itself. Tribunal systems are also managed and funded by government.

---

[2] This is often referred to either as 'red light' theory or as normativist (whether of a conservative or liberal variant) public law theory. See respectively C Harlow and R Rawlings, *Law and Administration*, 3rd edn (Cambridge, Cambridge University Press, 2009) ch 1; M Loughlin, *Public Law and Political Theory* (Oxford, Clarendon Press, 1992).

The nature of the legal control provided by administrative tribunals is, then, the result of a policy of self-imposed constraint that government accepts and applies to itself through the creation of an appellate system. By establishing a tribunal process, government is voluntarily submitting itself to a legal discipline by which responsibility for taking final individual decisions rests with an independent adjudication process over which it can have no direct influence. The appropriate conception of administrative law for understanding the role of administrative tribunals is, then, one in which law is understood as a product of the policy process, but also one in which legal processes and techniques are themselves designed in order to further the achievement of policy goals.[3]

Having accepted the need for such a discipline, government must manage the appeals process to enable individuals to participate, while also ensuring that the process is an appropriate means of effectively implementing policy goals. The adjudication process may, therefore, have to be re-organised by government to ensure that the process can meet the government's policy goals. In other contexts, government may decide to withdraw appeal rights altogether as part of a broader reform of administrative policy. Furthermore, it is important to appreciate that the creation and management of a tribunal process is not concerned solely with the legal control of government. Tribunals are concerned with the legal control of government in the sense that, by creating an appeal system, government is bound by the tribunal's decision. But appeal processes also empower tribunals by giving them the responsibility for decision-making. Once a tribunal process has been established, it will operate as a self-imposed constraint that government has willingly subjected itself to; the tribunal process will simultaneously empower the tribunal to adjudicate.

The establishment of adjudication in the context of an administrative programme may generate its own momentum as tribunal members are allocated the responsibility for hearing and determining appeals. The insertion of adjudication into a specific administrative-policy context means that the agency has handed-over final responsibility for decision-making to the tribunal. But it has other implications. It will represent the insertion of law and legal techniques into the administrative process. To defend its decisions before the tribunal, the agency must devote necessary resources to this end; its failure to do so may be the result of limited resources, but will be seen by the tribunal as a threat to its neutrality and impartiality. The agency will also have to ensure that the individuals concerned have a fair opportunity to participate before the adjudicator. As tribunal decisions are binding on the parties involved, they cannot be circumvented by the agency through administrative (in-)action. The tribunal will assume particular importance as a crucial part of the broader governmental process and the agency will have to develop policy concerning the operation of the tribunal. The tribunal may also come to assume responsibility for the development of policy by issuing guid-

---

[3] RE Wraith and PG Hutchesson, *Administrative Tribunals* (London, Allen and Unwin, 1973) 17; C Stebbings, *Legal Foundations of Tribunals in Nineteenth Century England* (Cambridge, Cambridge University Press, 2006) 5.

ance as to how certain types of case ought to be handled. The agency may seek ways to reduce the number of appeals. The issue of agency learning from the tribunal feedback will also become a salient concern; to ensure that it is best able to make good decisions that can be defended before the tribunal, the agency will need to study the outcome of decisions and appreciate which types of reasons will and will not stand up before the tribunal.

The use of adjudication also has various implications with respect to the agency's management and influence over the adjudication process. Given its role in the broader policy implementation process, various aspects of the adjudication system will assume considerable significance for the administrative agency, such as the speed with which the tribunal processes appeals and the administrative costs taken up by the process. The questions to be asked of adjudication systems include the following: how should the adjudication process be organised so as to enable effective participation in the implementation of policy? How can the relationship between the agency and the tribunal be best handled so that it both maintains the tribunal's independence while also ensuring efficiency? How can the effectiveness of adjudication be enhanced in any particular area of administration?

Reconsidering Asylum Adjudication

We can now turn to consider the quality of asylum adjudication by considering the following questions. How effective and adequate is the present system, all things considered? Is there some alternative mechanism for implementing asylum policy other than adjudication which could be usefully substituted for the current system of asylum adjudication? If not, then how could the current tribunal process be re-designed or remodelled to enhance the effectiveness of adjudication in this context?

Appraising Asylum Appeals

Established in 1993, the asylum appeals system is, compared with other tribunal systems, a relatively young jurisdiction. The central dynamic of the appeals process is the tension that arises from the need to afford each appeal close scrutiny and the high rate of onward challenge against adverse decisions. The overall tension is between the quality of substantive decision-making and the need to process a large volume of cases within the context of scarce resources and in accordance with per-formance targets. The unusual feature of asylum appeals has been the exception-ally high rate of onward challenge. This has overwhelmed not just the tribunal itself, but also the higher courts. This in turn has prompted frequent structural reforms of the tribunal and its relationship with the higher courts.

Any balanced appraisal of the quality of this appeals process must recognise both its positive and negative aspects. On the credit side, the appeals system is independent of the executive and is staffed by experienced judges. The process is accessible and appeal hearings are heard through fair procedures. This provides appellants with an appropriate degree of protection and enables them to participate in the decision-making process. Immigration Judges have access to different sources of country information. Over time, Immigration Judges acquire experience in the handling of appeals and they build up their knowledge of conditions in countries of origin. The system provides a degree of publicly funded representation and some representatives are of high quality and competence. Reasoned, written decision must be produced and can be reviewed for any error of law. While under pressure to determine appeals expeditiously, Immigration Judges do the best they can under challenging circumstances. They benefit from the assistance and judicial leadership of Senior Immigration Judges, who are recognised as specialists. Country guidance promotes quality, efficiency, and consistency in the assessment of country conditions. Finally, the structure of this appeals jurisdiction has been subject to various changes over recent years, some of which have been of negative value. Nonetheless, the transfer to the First-tier and Upper Tribunals should provide the jurisdiction with a stronger and more secure legal structure and make it more difficult for any short-term, politically motivated restructuring. This restructuring of the appeals process will augment the position of the senior judges and enable them to have closer communication and dialogue with the higher courts.

Putting these positive aspects to one side, the appeals system labours under various constraints. The appeals process is frequently afflicted by the difficulties incurred by low level administrative incompetence. Appellants are entitled to be represented, but legal aid restrictions have increased the number of unrepresented appellants. The Home Office does not attend a substantial proportion of hearings. Even when both parties are represented, the standard of representation can be variable. There is a continuous risk that the ability of appellants to participate in the process may be compromised because of the difficulties of translation. Given the large number of judges involved, there is the constant risk of inconsistent and disparate decision-making. There is also a pervasive ambivalence as to the appropriate mode of appeal procedure (adversarial, interventionist, or enabling?). Opinion within the immigration judiciary itself seems evenly split between those who would favour a more interventionist approach and those would prefer to retain the traditional adversary process. There is, though, little evidence of a decisive shift either way, perhaps because the issue is so central to the adjudication process, yet also difficult to resolve fully.

The ability of Immigration Judges to assist unrepresented appellants is variable. The role of expert evidence is weakened by the fact that it is obtained and presented by a party to the appeal process; the Tribunal is unable to commission its own expert evidence. The politically-driven emphasis upon the timely dispatch of appeals may sometimes operate so as to the hamper the effectiveness of the appeals process. Immigration Judges face pressures arising from the volume of their caseload and the requirement of rapid decision-making which inevitably compromises proper and mature consideration of complex and demanding decisions. Consequently, poorly written determinations may be overturned and have to be re-determined, thereby lengthening the decision process and increasing costs. The concerns over quality are heightened because of the political and caseload pressures and the acute nature of the subject-matter. While the Tribunal is generally staffed by experienced judges, the quality is not even throughout. Finally, the system of onward challenges has placed a considerable burden on the higher courts. The appeals structure has experienced many changes, not all of which have proved to be either beneficial or well-thought through. It remains to be seen whether or not this recurrent problem will be resolved by the transfer to the First-tier and Upper Tribunals.

There are several reasons for the difficulties experienced by the asylum adjudication system. The political pressures are more acute than elsewhere. The design and restructuring of the process has proved to highly sensitive to fluctuations in the caseload. The imperative to process appeals quickly is more intense than elsewhere. There is also the concern that negative media and political perceptions of asylum claimants may adversely affect decision-making. There is a high rate of onward challenge and the absence of any real scope or willingness by the parties to settle or mediate appeals. Finally, there is the lingering sense that the work put into the hearing and determination of appeals may, in practice, make little difference as enforcement—the removal of failed appellants—continues to run at a comparatively low rate. Underlying all of these difficulties is, of course, the inherently problematic task of determining who is in need of asylum.

Alternatives to Adjudication

How, then, might be the asylum adjudication procedure be reformed to ameliorate some of the difficulties identified? An initial point to consider is whether there is an alternative to adjudication. The principal alternatives are: complaint mechanisms (whether to the administrative agency or to elected representatives); ombudsmen investigations; and judicial review. Like adjudication, all of these techniques enable some degree of participation in the decision-making process. But none of them offers the full range of benefits as adjudication, that is: an independent judicial process which enables a full factual assessment of individual circumstances, commands the confidence of the parties, facilitates participation, and which produces authoritative decisions which determine that individual's entitlement to a particular status. Complaint processes and ombudsmen investigations provide individuals with a means for achieving the redress of grievances and for uncovering maladministration, but they do not provide a mechanism for making authoritative determinations of entitlement or status. Likewise, judicial review focuses upon legality and precludes detailed factual assessment. None seem viable alternatives to adjudication.

Neither do more radical alternatives to adjudication such as the replacement of individualised decision-making altogether seem to present much of a way forward.

For instance, it is possible to envisage asylum decision-making is undertaken through the making of rules which recognise specific categories of person as being in need of asylum. Alternatively, individualised decision-making could be substituted by lottery. But both options seem offensive to our sense of justice as they preclude precisely the individualised assessment of each case. For as long as an asylum decision process is wedded to the notion of individualised determination of status, then there is no real alternative to adjudication.

Remodelling Asylum Adjudication

If adjudication is to be retained, how then might the current appeals process be improved? This question is fundamental, but also problematic. If the adjudication process was organised differently, then would this actually enhance its overall quality and effectiveness? How might change to one aspect of the process—the adoption of non-adversary procedure, for instance—affect other aspects? What, if any, unintended consequences might result from a restructuring of the process? Furthermore, reform must be implemented in the context of a working system, which itself constrains the ambition of such reforms. But, there is now a statutorily enshrined requirement to consider how to develop innovative methods of dispute resolution.[4] The following prescriptions are, then, put forward not as detailed blueprints for reform, but as possible options for enhancing and re-designing asylum adjudication. Three types of gradated reform can be envisaged, each involving a progressively higher degree of organisational change: relatively minor reform; an intermediate set of reforms; and major re-organisational reform of the appeals process.

From one perspective, radical reform is unlikely; it is more realistic to envisage incremental change over time; the asylum appeals process is, like most, path-dependent. The transfer of asylum appeals to the First-tier and Upper Tribunals represents a secure foundation for the jurisdiction and is likely, assuming no major change, to provide the institutional framework of the appeals system for the foreseeable future. Within this new structure, there are plenty of improvements that could enhance the operation of the appeals process.

The first set of relatively minor reform proposals could, then, include the following. The Home Office could commit itself to enhanced levels of representation and higher standards of administrative competence in initial decision-making and the representation of appeals. It could also enhance its feedback mechanisms by which it collects and analyses data concerning allowed appeals and feed such results back to caseworkers. The Home Office could also institute performance targets concerning not just the speed, but also the quality, of initial decisions and enhance its internal quality assurance processes. Access to the provision of legal advice and representation could also be enhanced and the regulatory system

---

[4] Tribunals, Courts and Enforcement Act 2007 s 2(3)(d).

overseeing immigration representatives augmented. The Tribunal could undertake more extensive and enhanced training for Immigration Judges and institute more robust mechanisms to enable comprehensive feedback to Immigration Judges from onward challenges. Detailed guidelines could clarify the judge's role in represented and non-represented appeals. The Tribunal could examine whether, and, if so how, to move to a process by which asylum appeals were heard not by a single Immigration Judge, but by a panel of two or three judges. Amended procedural rules could enable the Tribunal to instruct expert witnesses. The Tribunal could also continue with its efforts in ensuring better cooperation and coordination between itself and the higher courts to ensure that the right cases get decided at the right levels of the judicial hierarchy. These proposals could be introduced within the current appeals framework.

The second set of proposals would include a greater range of reforms to the current appeals process, but stopping short of more radical reform. This range of reforms could include a number of other options which could be advanced to reform the appeals process, many of which have been considered in the preceding discussion: increasing legal aid funding to ensure that all appellants were represented before appeal hearings; relaxing the time limits and performance targets imposed upon the Tribunal; moving more decisively from an adversarial toward a more fully inquisitorial mode of appeal procedure, and the establishment of an independent country information centre to collect and disseminate country information. These proposals would require greater public expenditure and a larger degree of organisational change than the first set of possible reforms.

The third option is major re-organisational reform of the appeals process. The first two options envisage some improvements, but retain the basic structure of the adjudication process which determines appeals against initial administrative decisions. An alternative way of proceeding might be to reconsider this basic relationship between initial administrative decision-making and the tribunal stage. A familiar feature of the organisation of tribunal systems is that appeals are only commenced by individuals who have received an initial negative administrative decision. In the asylum context, given the high rate of challenge, this arrangement induces a degree of inefficiency and duplication. A substantial number of appellants are successful, but only after having gone through the stress and anxiety of the appeal process. Furthermore, there are concerns over the robustness of both positive and negative initial decisions.

An alternative way of organising decision-making would, then, be to assimilate initial administrative decision-making within the current appellate system. This could be achieved by retaining adjudication, but inserting it at the initial decision stage rather than by way of appeal and by embedding it within an administrative structure. This adjudication function would continue to be judicial in nature and be characterised by oral hearings conducted in public and heard by independent judges specialising in asylum cases. The jurisdiction would also still be essentially judicial, though it would be an initial, not appellate, jurisdiction.

Such a change should enhance overall procedural efficiency; while the caseload would increase (because all claims would be adjudicated upon), the level of repeat decision-making would reduce. Onward challenges would be limited to error of law grounds. Furthermore, as the tribunal decision would be the only fact-based decision, decision-making targets could also be modified to reflect this. More importantly, adjudication should also provide a better standard of decision-making than current Home Office decision-making.

In such an initial adjudicative system, the adjudicator could take responsibility for active case-management throughout the process. Hearings would be distinctly non-adversarial, but inquisitorial, and proceed without representation. The adjudicators could make their own inquiries through direct questioning of claimants, commissioning of medical reports, and by instructing dedicated country information staff and country experts to research detailed queries. Furthermore, claims could be heard by multi-disciplinary panels combining legal expertise with country and medical expertise. If structured appropriately, this remodelled composition could enable decision-makers to contribute their different attributes when hearing and determination claims. An adjudication process like this would need to operate within an administrative support structure that would undertake the processing of claimants, see to their support needs, and collect the essential content of their claims. This administrative structure would be directed largely to collecting the details of claimants' accounts rather than the making and defending of decisions. It would also assist adjudicators in managing an end-to-end process and have a unit specialising in the collection of country information which decision-makers would draw upon.

This proposal is not without its possible objections. One might be that closer assimilation of administration and adjudication would run counter to the notion of proportionate dispute resolution, that is, that the focus should be upon targeting those cases where a tribunal hearing is the best option, but otherwise seeking to reduce formal adjudication. But if adjudication provides a better means of decision-making than straightforward administration in such a crucially important area as asylum, then using it throughout could enhance overall decisional quality.

Another objection might be that closer assimilation of adjudication and administration risks undermining judicial independence; the current system is politically vulnerable and its anchoring with the tribunal system is necessary to protect judicial independence. The political threats are not unreal and adjudication needs to be properly insulated. However, there may be little reason why adjudication could not be properly insulated within a reformed asylum determination agency. Judicial appointments would not be handed over to the Home Office and while the Home Office will still wish to agree targets as regards processing times, the parent government department would continue to be the Ministry of Justice. There is no reason why it could not be possible to devise appropriate arrangements by which judges could adjudicate on initial claims and operate within an administrative framework and remain independent.

To summarise, the assimilation of the current system of initial administrative and appellate tribunal decision-making could produce an adjudication process which is both cost-effective and produces robust, defensible decisions that command the respect of all parties to the process. While the appeals process certainly has its weaknesses, it is not so afflicted with such difficulties so as to erode its legitimacy altogether and to require the establishment of an altogether different process. Perhaps the biggest stumbling block is a cultural one by which it is assumed that administration and adjudication are distinct tasks that must be kept wholly separate and distinct. A willingness to rethink and remodel adjudication as a means of enabling individuals to participate in policy implementation is an essential preliminary step to enhancing its effectiveness and quality.

Looking to the future, the challenge for the asylum appeals process will continue to depend upon a number of factors: global migratory pressures; the volume of claimants and appellants; the political salience of asylum; and future constraints on public spending. The process will remain under pressures to fulfil competing adjudicative values. The subtle and the complex challenges of delivering and organising effective administrative justice are unlikely to diminish.

BIBLIOGRAPHY

1 Books and articles

Adler, M, 'A Socio-legal Approach to Administrative Justice' (2003) 25 *Law & Policy* 323.
—— 'Tribunal Reform: Proportionate Dispute Resolution and the Pursuit of Administrative Justice' (2006) 69 *Modern Law Review* 958.
—— 'Fairness in Context' (2006) 33 *Journal of Law and Society* 615.
—— and Gulland, J, *Tribunals Users' Experiences, Perceptions and Expectations: A Literature Review* (London, Council on Tribunals, 2003).
Aegis Trust, *Lives We Throw Away: Darfuri Survivors Tortured in Khartoum Following Removal From the UK* (London, Aegis Trust 2007).
Alexander, SB, 'A Political Response to the Crisis in the Immigration Courts' (2006) 21 *Georgetown Immigration Law Journal* 1.
Allars, M, 'Neutrality, the Judicial Paradigm, and Tribunal Procedure' (1991) 13 *Sydney Law Review* 377.
Allison, JWF, 'Fuller's Analysis of Polycentric Disputes and the Limits of Adjudication' (1994) 53 *Cambridge Law Journal* 367.
Amnesty International, *Get It Right: How Home Office Decision-making Fails Refugees* (London, Amnesty International, 2004).
Anker, D, 'Determining Asylum Claims in the United States: An Empirical Case Study' (1992) *New York University Journal of Law and Social Change* 433.
Arthurs, HW, *'Without the Law': Administrative Justice and Legal Pluralism in Nineteenth Century England* (Toronto, University of Toronto Press, 1985).
Asylum Aid, *Still No Reason At All* (London, Asylum Aid, 1999).
Baillot, H, Cowan, S and Munro, VE, 'Seen but Not Heard? Parallels and Dissonances in the Treatment of Rape Narratives across the Asylum and Criminal Justice Contexts' (2009) 36 *Journal of Law and Society* 195.
Barber, M, *Instruction to Deliver* (London, Politico's, 2007).
Baldwin, J, Wikeley, N and Young, R, *Judging Social Security: The Adjudication of Claims for Benefit in Britain* (Oxford, Clarendon Press, 1992).
Baldwin, R, *Rules and Government* (Oxford, Oxford University Press, 1995).
—— and Hawkins, K, 'Discretionary Justice: Davis Reconsidered' [1984] *Public Law* 570.
Bannerman, L, 'High-rise Asylum Seekers Plumb Depths of Despair' *The Times* (13 March 2010).
Barnes, J, 'Expert Evidence—The Judicial Perception in Asylum and Human Rights Appeals' (2004) 16 *International Journal of Refugee Law* 349.
Beatson, J, 'The Scope of Judicial Review for Error of Law' (1984) 4 *Oxford Journal of Legal Studies* 22.
Berger, P and Luckman, T, *The Social Construction of Reality* (London, Penguin, 1991).

Bingham, T, 'The Judge as Juror: the Judicial Determination of Factual Issues' (1985) 38 *Current Legal Problems* 1.

Blake, CG, 'Immigration Appeals—The Need for Reform' in A Dummett (ed), *Towards a Just Immigration Policy* (London, Cobden Trust, 1986).

—— 'Judicial Review, Second Tier Tribunals and Legality' in M Partington (ed), *The Leggatt Review of Tribunals: Academic Seminar Papers* (University of Bristol, Faculty of Law, Working Paper Series No 3, 2001).

Blake, N, 'The Arrival of the Upper Tribunal Immigration and Asylum Chamber' (Tribunals Service, 11 February 2010).

—— and Fransman, L, *Immigration, Nationality and Asylum under the Human Rights Act 1998* (London, Butterworths, 1999).

—— and Husain, R, *Immigration, Asylum & Human Rights Law* (Oxford, Oxford University Press, 2003).

Blom-Cooper, L, (ed), *Experts in the Civil Courts* (Oxford, Oxford University Press, 2006).

Bögner, D, Herlihy, J and Brewin, CR, 'Impact of Sexual Violence on Disclosure During Home Office Interviews' (2007) 191 *British Journal of Psychiatry* 75.

Bohmer C and Shuman, A, *Rejecting Refugees: Political Asylum in the 21st Century* (London, Routledge, 2008).

Bridges, L, 'Legality and Immigration Control' (1975) 2 *British Journal of Law and Society* 221.

—— Mészáros, G and Sunkin, M, *Judicial Review in Perspective*, 2nd edn (London, Cavendish, 1995).

Bruff, HH, 'Specialized Courts in Administrative Law' (1991) 43 *Administrative Law Review* 329.

Buck, T, 'Precedent in Tribunals and the Development of Principles' (2006) 25 *Civil Justice Quarterly* 458.

—— Bonner, D and Sainsbury, R, *Making Social Security Law: The Role and Work of the Social Security and Child Support Commissioners* (Aldershot, Ashgate, 2005).

Burn, S, *Successful Use of Expert Witnesses in Civil Disputes* (Crayford, Shaw and Sons, 2005).

Buxton, R, 'Application of Section 13(6) of the Tribunals, Courts, and Enforcement Act 2007 to Immigration Appeals from the Proposed Upper Tribunal' (2009) 14 *Judicial Review* 225.

Cameron, HE, 'Risk Theory and "Subjective Fear": The Role of Risk Perception, Assessment, and Management in Refugee Status Determinations' (2008) 20 *International Journal of Refugee Law* 567.

Cane, P, *Administrative Law* (Oxford, Oxford University Press, 2004).

—— 'Understanding Judicial Review and Its Impact' in M Hertogh and S Halliday (eds), *Judicial Review and Bureaucratic Impact: International and Interdisciplinary Perspectives* (Cambridge, Cambridge University Press, 2004).

—— *Administrative Tribunals and Adjudication* (Oxford, Hart Publishing, 2009).

Care, G, 'The Judiciary, the State and the Refugee: the Evolution of Judicial Protection in Asylum—A UK Perspective' (2005) 28 *Fordham International Law Journal* 1421.

Carnwath, R, 'Tribunal Justice—A New Start' (a speech given to the Administrative Justice and Tribunal Council annual conference, November 2008).

'Tribunal Justice—A New Start' [2009] *Public Law* 48.

Carver, N, (ed), *Home Office Country Assessments: An Analysis* (London, Immigration Advisory Service, 2003).

—— (ed), *Overview of the 2004 Reports* (London, Immigration Advisory Service, 2004).

Chowdhury, Z, 'The Concept of "Error of Law" and its Application in Immigration Cases' (2009) 15(2) *Immigration Law Digest* 8.

—— 'The Doctrine of Deference to Tribunal Expertise and the Parameters of Judicial Restraint' (2009) 15(3) *Immigration Law Digest* 15.

Clayton, G, 'Home Office Guidance and Zimbabwe' (2009) 15(2) *Immigration Law Digest* 21.

Cohen, J, 'Questions of Credibility: Omissions, Discrepancies and Errors of Recall in the Testimony of Asylum Seekers' (2002) 13 *International Journal of Refugee Law* 293.

Connelly, M, 'Refugees and Asylum-seekers: Proposals for Policy Changes' in A Dummett (ed), *Towards a Just Immigration Policy* (London, Cobden Trust, 1986).

Constitutional and Administrative Law Bar Association, *Response to UK Border Agency Consultation: Immigration Appeals, Fair Decisions, Faster Justice* (London, ALBA, 2008).

Coulter, C, 'Call for Review of up to 1,000 Rejected Asylum Applications' *The Irish Times* (20 March 2008).

Cowan, D and Halliday, S, *The Appeal of Internal Review: Law, Administrative Justice and the (Non-) emergence of Disputes* (Oxford, Hart Publishing, 2003).

Craig, PP, 'Judicial Review, Appeal and Factual Error' [2004] *Public Law* 788.

Craig, S, Fletcher, M and Goodall, K, *Challenging Asylum and Immigration Tribunal Decisions in Scotland: An Evaluation of Onward Appeals and Reconsiderations* (Glasgow, University of Glasgow, 2009).

Crawley, H, *When Is a Child Not a Child? Asylum, Age Disputes, and the Process of Age Assessment* (London, ILPA, 2007).

Crépeau, F and Nakache, D, 'Critical Spaces in the Canadian Refugee Determination System: 1989–2002' (2008) 20 *International Journal of Refugee Law* 50.

Daintith, T and Page, A, *The Executive in the Constitution: Structure, Autonomy, and Internal Control* (Oxford, Oxford University Press, 1999).

Davis, KC, *Discretionary Justice: A Preliminary Inquiry* (Urbana and Chicago, University of Illinois Press, 1969).

—— *Administrative Law Treatise Vol 2* (California, KC Davis Publishing, 1979).

Davis, ML, 'The Value of Truth and the Optimal Standard of Proof in Legal Disputes' (1994) 10 *Journal of Law, Economics and Organization* 343.

Dickinson, J, *Administrative Justice and the Supremacy of the Law in the United States* (Cambridge, Harvard University Press, 1927).

Douglas, M and Widavsky, A, *Risk and Culture: An Essay on the Selection of Technological and Environmental Dangers* (Berkeley, University of California Press, 1982).

Downs, A, *Inside Bureaucracy* (Boston, Little Brown, 1967).

Dummett A and Nicol, A, *Subjects, Citizens, Aliens and Others: Nationality and Immigration Law* (London, Weidenfeld and Nicolson, 1990).

Dunsire, A, *Administration: the Word and the Science* (London, Martin Robertson, 1973).

Duxbury, N, *The Nature and Authority of Precedent* (Cambridge, Cambridge University Press, 2008).

Dwyer, D, *The Judicial Assessment of Expert Evidence* (Cambridge, Cambridge University Press, 2008).

Ekman, P, *Telling Lies: Clues to Deceit in the Marketplace, Politics, and Marriage* (New York, Norton, 2001).

Einhorn, BJ, 'Consistency, Credibility, and Culture' in J Ramji-Nogales, AI Schoenholtz and PG Schrag (eds), *Refugee Roulette: Disparities in Asylum Adjudication and Proposals for Reform* (New York, New York University Press, 2009).

Bibliography

Elcock, HJ, *Administrative Justice* (London, Longmans, 1969).

Endicott, T, 'Questions of Law' (1998) 114 *Law Quarterly Review* 292.

Ensor, J, Shah, A and Grillo, M, 'Simple Myths and Complex Realities—Seeking the Truth in the Face of Section 8' (2006) 20 *Immigration, Asylum and Nationality Law* 95.

Farmer, JA, *Tribunals and Government* (London, Weidenfeld and Nicolson, 1974).

Feeley, MM and Rubin, EL, *Judicial Policy Making and the Modern State: How the Courts Reformed America's Prisons* (Cambridge, Cambridge University Press, 1999).

Ford, R, 'Home Office Ignored Judge Over Deportation' *The Times* (27 August 2004).

—— 'Home Office "Disregarded Law"' *The Times* (8 April 2006).

—— 'Mother of Three Was Deported After Court Ruled She Could Stay' *The Times* (16 August 2006).

—— 'Our Asylum Failure "Has Spread Misery and Division"' *The Times* (21 October 2008).

—— 'Minister Admits: We Got It Wrong On Immigration' *The Times* (3 November 2009).

Fordham, M, 'Common Law Illegality of Ousting Judicial Review' (2004) 9 *Judicial Review* 8.

Frank, J, *Law and the Modern Mind* (New York, Brentano's, 1930).

—— *Courts on Trial*, rev edn (New York, Atheneum , 1963).

Fuller, LL, 'The Forms and Limits of Adjudication' (1978) 92 *Harvard Law Review* 353.

Galanter, M, 'Why the "Haves" Come Out Ahead: Speculations on the Limits of Legal Change' (1974) 9 *Law and Society Review* 95.

Gearty, C, *Principles of Human Rights Adjudication* (Oxford, Oxford University Press, 2004).

Genn, H, 'Tribunals and Informal Justice' (1993) 56 *Modern Law Review* 393.

—— and Genn, Y, *The Effectiveness of Representation at Tribunals: Report to the Lord Chancellor* (London, Lord Chancellor's Department, 1989).

Gibb, F, 'Extra Judges Drafted in to Hear Immigration Appeals: Asylum Backlog Delays Other Cases "for a Year"' *The Times* (15 December 2008).

Gibney, MJ, *The Ethics and Politics of Asylum: Liberal Democracy and the Response to Refugees* (Cambridge, Cambridge University Press, 2004).

Gilliespie, J, 'Expert Evidence in Asylum Cases' (2001) 15(2) *Immigration, Asylum and Nationality Law* 88.

Glossop, B, 'Immigration Judges' Visit to Ethiopia' (2008) 14(4) *Immigration Law Digest* 38.

Good, A, 'Expert Evidence in Asylum and Human Rights Appeals: an Expert's View' (2004) 16 *International Journal of Refugee Law* 358.

—— '"Undoubtedly an Expert"? Country Experts in the UK Asylum Courts' (2004) 10 *Journal of the Royal Anthropological Institute* 113.

—— *Anthropology and Expertise in the Asylum Courts* (London, Routledge-Cavendish, 2007).

Goodwin-Gill, GS and McAdam, J, *The Refugee in International Law*, 3rd edn (Oxford, Oxford University Press, 2007).

Griffith, JAG, 'Tribunals and Inquiries' (1959) 22 *Modern Law Review* 125.

—— and Street, H, *Principles of Administrative Law*, 2nd edn (London, Pitman, 1957).

Halliday, S, *Judicial Review and Compliance with Administrative Law* (Oxford, Hart Publishing, 2004).

Hansen, R, *Citizenship and Immigration in Post-war Britain: The Institutional Origins of a Multicultural Nation* (Oxford, Oxford University Press, 2000).

Harding, J, *The Uninvited: Refugees at the Rich Man's Gate* (London, Profile Books, 2000).

Harlow, C and Rawlings, R, *Law and Administration*, 3rd edn (Cambridge, Cambridge University Press, 2009).

Hastings, C, Ralph, A and Johnston, I, 'Asylum Seekers Win Right to Stay Because of "Shambolic" Immigration Hearings' *The Telegraph* (18 April 2009).

—— and K Dowling, 'Home Office Surrenders to Migrants' *The Sunday Times* (25 April 2010) 4.

Hathaway, JC, *The Rights of Refugees under International Law* (Cambridge, Cambridge University Press, 2005).

Hay, C, McKenna, K and Buck, T, *Evaluation of Early Neutral Evaluation Alternative Dispute Resolution in the Social Security and Child Support Tribunal* (London, Ministry of Justice Research Series 2/10, 2010).

Helton, AC, *The Price of Indifference: Refugees and Humanitarian Action in the New Century* (Oxford, Oxford University Press, 2002).

Hepple, B, 'Aliens and Administrative Justice: the Dutschke Case' (1971) 34 *Modern Law Review* 501.

Herlihy, J, Scragg, P and Turner, S, 'Discrepancies in Autobiographical Memories— Implications for the Assessment of Asylum Seekers: Repeated Interviews Study' (2002) 324 *British Medical Journal* 324.

—— and Turner, S, 'Should Discrepant Accounts Given by Asylum Seekers be Taken as Proof of Deceit?' (2006) 16 *Torture* 81.

Hickinbottom, G, 'Upper Tribunal: A Forum to Clarify and Develop the Law' *Tribunals* (2009) (Spring) 3.

Hirsch, A, 'Asylum Tribunal Apologies for Questioning Academic's Evidence' *The Guardian* (27 October 2008).

Hood, CC and Margetts, HZ, *The Tools of Government in the Digital Age* (Basingstoke, Palgrave Macmillan, 2007).

Houle, F and Sossin, L, 'Tribunals and Guidelines: Exploring the Relationship Between Fairness and Legitimacy in Administrative Decision-making' (2006) 49 *Canadian Public Administration* 282.

Huber, S, Pettitt, J and Williams, E, *The APCI Legacy: A Critical Assessment: Monitoring Home Office Country of Origin Information Products* (London, IAS, 2010).

Immigration Law Practitioners' Association, *The Detained Fast Track Process: A Best Practice Guide* (London, ILPA, 2008).

—— *ILPA Briefing House on the Borders, Citizenship and Immigration Bill: Transfer of Judicial Reviews & Appeals to the Court of Appeal* (London, ILPA, 2009).

Independent Asylum Commission, *Report of Interim Findings* (London, IAC, 2008).

International Association of Refugee Law Judges (IARLJ): Country of Origin Information— Country Guidance Working Party, 'Judicial Criteria for Assessing Country of Origin Information (COI): A Checklist' (2009) 21 *International Journal of Refugee Law* 149.

Ison, TG, ' "Administrative Justice": Is It Such a Good Idea?' in M Harris and M Partington (eds), *Administrative Justice in the 21st Century* (Oxford, Hart Publishing, 1999).

James, D and Killick, E, 'Ethical Dilemmas? UK Immigration, Legal Aid Funding Reform and Caseworkers' (2010) 26 *Anthropology Today* 13.

Jobson, L, 'Cultural Differences in Specificity of Autobiographical Memories: Implications for Asylum Decisions' (2009) 16 *Psychiatry, Psychology and Law* 453.

Jones, CAG, *Expert Witnesses: Science, Medicine, and the Practice of Law* (Oxford, Clarendon Press, 1994).

Jordan, A, 'Country Information: The United Kingdom and the Search for Objectivity' (a paper presented at the IARLJ conference, Budapest, November 2005).

Jowell, JL, *Law and Bureaucracy: Administrative Discretion and the Limits of Legal Action* (New York, Dunellen Publishing, 1975).

—— 'Judicial Deference and Human Rights: A Question of Competence' in P Craig and R Rawlings (eds), *Law and Administration in Europe* (Oxford, Oxford University Press, 2003).

—— 'Parliamentary Sovereignty under the New Constitutional Hypothesis' [2006] *Public Law* 562.

Juss, S, *Discretion and Deviation in the Administration of Immigration Control* (London, Sweet & Maxwell, 1997).

Kagan, M, 'Is Truth in the Eye of the Beholder? Objective Credibility Assessment in Refugee Status Determination' (2003) 17 *Georgetown Immigration Law Journal* 367.

Kälin, W, 'Troubled Communication: Cross-cultural Misunderstandings in the Asylum Hearing' (1986) 20 *International Migration Review* 230.

Kaplow, L, 'The Value of Accuracy in Adjudication: An Economic Analysis' (1994) 23 *Journal of Legal Studies* 307.

Kenney, DN and Schrag, PG, *Asylum Denied: A Refugee's Struggle for Safety in America* (Berkeley, University of California Press, 2008).

Kuhn, TS, *The Structure of Scientific Revolutions,* 3rd edn (Chicago, University of Chicago Press, 1996).

Kushner, T and Knox, K, *Refugees in an Age of Genocide: Global, National and Local Perspectives during the Twentieth Century* (London, Frank Cass, 1999).

Landa, MJ, *The Alien Problem and its Remedy* (London, King & Son, 1911).

Laws, J, 'Law and Fact' [1999] *British Tax Review* 159.

Le Sueur, A, 'Developing Mechanisms for Judicial Accountability in the UK' (2004) 24 *Legal Studies* 73.

Legomsky, SH, *Specialized Justice: Courts, Administrative Tribunals, and a Cross-National Theory of Specialization* (Oxford, Clarendon Press, 1990).

—— 'Learning to Live with Unequal Justice: Asylum and the Limits to Consistency' in J Ramji-Nogales, AI Schoenholtz and PG Schrag (eds), *Refugee Roulette: Disparities in Asylum Adjudication and Proposals for Reform* (New York, New York University Press, 2009).

Loughlin, M, *Public Law and Political Theory* (Oxford, Clarendon Press, 1992).

Lustig, SL, 'Symptoms of Trauma Among Political Asylum Applicants: Don't be Fooled' (2008) 31 *Hastings International and Comparative Law Review* 725.

Macdonald, IA, *Immigration Law and Practice in the United Kingdom,* 7th edn (London, LexisNexis, 2008).

MacIntrye, H, 'Imposed Dependency: Client Perspectives of Legal Representation in Asylum Claims' (2009) 23 *Journal of Immigration, Asylum, and Nationality Law* 181.

McKee, R, 'Legal Diary' (2010) 13(1) *Immigration Law Update* 14.

McKeown, MM and McLeod, A, 'The Counsel Conundrum: Effective Representation in Immigration Proceedings' in J Ramji-Nogales, AI Schoenholtz and PG Schrag (eds), *Refugee Roulette: Disparities in Asylum Adjudication and Proposals for Reform* (New York, New York University Press, 2009).

Macklin, A, 'Truth and Consequences: Credibility Determination in the Refugee Context' in *The Realities of Refugee Determination on the Eve of a New Millennium: The Role of the Judiciary* (1998 Conference of the International Association of Refugee Law Judges).

—— 'Refugee Roulette in the Canadian Casino' in J Ramji-Nogales, AI Schoenholtz and PG Schrag (eds), *Refugee Roulette: Disparities in Asylum Adjudication and Proposals for Reform* (New York, New York University Press, 2009).

McAdam, J, *Complementary Protection in International Refugee Law* (Oxford, Oxford University Press, 2007).

March, JG and Simon, HA, *Organizations,* 2nd ed (Oxford, Blackwell, 1993).

Mashaw, J, *Bureaucratic Justice: Managing Social Security Disability Claims* (New Haven, Yale University Press, 1983).

Memon, A, Vrij, A and Bull, R, *Psychology and Law: Truthfulness, Accuracy and Credibility* (Chichester, Wiley, 2003).

Millbank, J, ' "The Ring of Truth": A Case Study of Credibility Assessment in Particular Social Group Refugee Determinations' (2009) *International Journal of Refugee Law* 1.

Mintzberg, H, *The Structuring of Organizations: A Synthesis of the Research* (Englewood Cliffs NJ, Prentice-Hall, 1979).

Moorhead, C, *Human Cargo: A Journey Among Refugees* (London, Vintage, 2006).

Moxon, S, *The Great Immigration Scandal* (Exeter, Academic Imprint, 2004).

Mullen, T, 'Reflections on *Jackson v Attorney-General*: Questioning Sovereignty' (2007) 27 *Legal Studies* 1.

Mureinik, E, 'The Application of Rules: Law or Fact?' (1982) 98 *Law Quarterly Review* 587.

Newman, M, 'Tribunal Experts Fear Attacks on Integrity' *Times Higher Education* (6 November 2008).

Nonet, P, *Administrative Justice: Advocacy and Change in a Government Agency* (New York, Russell Sage, 1969).

Ogus, A, *Costs and Cautionary Tales: Economic Insights for the Law* (Oxford, Hart Publishing, 2006).

Painter, C, 'A Government Department in Meltdown: Crisis at the Home Office' (2008) 28 *Public Money & Management* 275.

Palmer, JRB, Yale-Loehr, SW and Cronin, E, 'Why Are So Many People Challenging Board of Immigration Appeal Decisions in Federal Court? An Empirical Analysis of the Recent Surge in Petitions for Review' (2005) 20 *Georgetown Immigration Law Journal* 1.

Partington, M, 'Restructuring Administrative Justice? The Redress of Citizens' Grievances' (1999) 52 *Current Legal Problems* 173.

Pearl, D, 'Immigration and Asylum Appeals and Administrative Justice' in M Harris and M Partington (eds), *Administrative Justice in the 21st Century* (Oxford, Hart Publishing, 1999).

Peiris, GL, 'Judicial Review and Immigration Policy: Emerging Trends' [1988] *Legal Studies* 201.

Pettit, J, 'The Problem with Country of Origin Information (COI) in Refugee Status Determination' (2007) 13(1) *Immigration Law Digest* 13.

Pirouet, LM, *Whatever Happened to Asylum in Britain? A Tale of Two Walls* (Oxford, Berghahn, 2001).

—— 'Materials Used in Making Asylum Decisions in the UK' (2003) 93 *African Research & Documentation* 29.

Pöllabauer, S, 'Interpreting in Asylum Hearings: Issues of Role, Responsibility and Power' (2004) 6 *Interpreting* 143.

Polyani, M, *The Logic of Liberty: Reflections and Rejoinders* [1951] (Indianapolis, Liberty Fund, 1998).

Porter, B, *The Refugee Question in Mid-Victorian Politics* (Cambridge, Cambridge University Press, 1979).

Posner, RA, 'An Economic Approach to Legal Procedure and Judicial Administration' (1973) 2 *Journal of Legal Studies* 399.

Prasad, R, 'The Asylum Lottery' *The Guardian* (25 January 2002).

Pressman, JL and Wildavsky, A, *Implementation,* 3rd edn (Berkeley, University of California Press, 1984).

Prosser, T, 'Poverty, Ideology and Legality: Supplementary Benefit Appeal Tribunals and their Predecessors' (1977) 4 *British Journal of Law and Society* 39.

Public Law Project, *Action on Administrative Court Delays* (London, Public Law Project, April 2008).

Quayum, M and Chatwin, M, 'A Fair-handed Approach?' (2003) 153 *New Law Journal* 533.

Ramji-Nogales, J, Schoenholtz AI and Schrag, PG (eds), *Refugee Roulette: Disparities in Asylum Adjudication and Proposals for Reform* (New York, New York University Press, 2009).

Randall, C, 'An Asylum Policy for the UK' in S Spencer (ed), *Strangers and Citizens: A Positive Approach to Migrants and Refugees* (London, Rivers Oram Press, 1994).

Ranger, T, 'The Narratives and Counter-narratives of Zimbabwean Asylum: Female Voices' (2005) 26 *Third World Quarterly* 405.

Rawlings, R, 'Review, Revenge and Retreat' (2005) 68 *Modern Law Review* 378.

—— 'Modelling Judicial Review' (2008) 61 *Current Legal Problems* 95.

Redmayne, M, *Expert Evidence and Criminal Justice* (Oxford, Oxford University Press, 2001).

Rehaag, S, 'Troubling Patterns in Canadian Refugee Adjudication' (2008) 39 *Ottawa Law Review* 335.

Rhys Jones, D and Verity Smith, S, 'Medical Evidence in Asylum and Human Rights Appeals' (2004) 16 *International Journal of Refugee Law* 381.

Richardson, G and Genn, H, 'Tribunals in Transition: Resolution or Adjudication' [2007] *Public Law* 116.

Robinson, GO, 'The Making of Administrative Policy: Another Look at Rulemaking and Adjudication and Administrative Procedure Reform' (1970) 118 *University of Pennsylvania Law Review* 485.

Robson, WA, *Justice and Administrative Law: A Study of the British Constitution,* 3rd edn (London, Stevens, 1951).

Rousseau, C, Crépeau, F, Foxen, P, and Houle, F, 'The Complexity of Determining Refugeehood: A Multidisciplinary Analysis of the Decision-making Process of the Canadian Immigration and Refugee Board' (2002) 15 *Journal of Refugee Studies* 43.

Rubin, EL, *Beyond Camelot: Rethinking Politics and Law for the Modern State* (Princeton/ Oxford, Princeton University Press, 2005).

Rycroft, R, 'Communicative Barriers in the Asylum Account' in P Shah (ed), *The Challenge of Asylum to Legal Systems* (London, Cavendish Publishing, 2005).

Sainsbury, R, 'Administrative Justice: Discretion and Procedure in Social Security Decision-Making' in K Hawkins (ed), *The Uses of Discretion* (Oxford, Oxford University Press, 1992).

Schauer, F, 'Giving Reasons' (1995) 47 *Stanford Law Review* 633.

Schuster, L, *The Use and Abuse of Political Asylum in Britain and Germany* (London, Frank Cass, 2003).

Sedley, S, 'Asylum: *Can the Judiciary Maintain its Independence?* (a paper presented at the International Association of Refugee Law Judges World Conference, Wellington, New Zealand, April 2002).

Shapiro, DL, 'The Choice of Rulemaking or Adjudication in the Development of Administrative Policy' (1965) 78 *Harvard Law Review* 921.

Showler, P, *Refugee Sandwich: Stories of Exile and Asylum* (Montreal, McGill-Queen's University Press, 2006).

Simon, HA, *Administrative Behavior*, 4th edn (New York, Free Press, 1997).

Smillie, JA, 'The Problem of "Official Notice": Reliance by Administrative Tribunals on the Personal Knowledge of Their Members' [1975] *Public Law* 64.

Somerville, W, *Immigration Under New Labour* (Bristol, Policy Press, 2007).

Spencer, IRG, *British Immigration Policy Since 1939: The Making of Multi-Racial Britain* (London, Routledge, 1997).

Stebbings, C, *Legal Foundations of Tribunals in Nineteenth Century England* (Cambridge, Cambridge University Press, 2006).

Steele, J, *Risks and Legal Theory* (Oxford, Hart Publishing, 2004).

Steiner, N, *Arguing About Asylum: The Complexity of Refugee Debates in Europe* (New York, St Martin's Press, 2000).

Sterett, S, *Creating Constitutionalism? The Politics of Legal Expertise and Administrative Law in England and Wales* (Ann Arbor, University of Michigan Press, 1997).

Stevens, D, *UK Asylum Law and Policy: Historical and Contemporary Perspectives* (London, Sweet & Maxwell, 2004).

Stockton, P, *Proportionate Dispute Resolution: What are the Options?* (a paper given at a Nuffield Foundation Administrative Justice Seminar, 23 January 2006).

Storey, H, 'EU Refugee Qualification Directive: a Brave New World?' (2008) 20 *International Journal of Refugee Law* 1.

Sunkin, M, 'What is Happening to Applications for Judicial Review?' (1987) 50 *Modern Law Review* 432.

—— 'Withdrawing: A Problem in Judicial Review?' in P Leyland and T Woods (eds), *Administrative Law Facing the Future: Old Constraints and New Horizons* (London, Blackstone, 1997).

Supperstone, M, Stilitz, D and Sheldon, C, 'ADR and Public Law' [2006] *Public Law* 299.

Sweeney, JA, 'Credibility, Proof, and Refugee Law' (2009) 21 *International Journal of Refugee Law* 700.

Talbot, T, 'Credibility and Risk: One Adjudicator's View' (2004) 10(2) *Immigration Law Digest* 29.

Thomas, R, 'Asylum Appeals Overhauled Again' [2003] *Public Law* 260.

—— 'The Impact of Judicial Review on Asylum' [2003] *Public Law* 479.

—— 'Immigration Appeals for Family Visitor Refused Entry Clearance' [2004] *Public Law* 612.

—— 'Assessing the Credibility of Asylum Claims: EU and UK Approaches Examined' (2006) 8 *European Journal of Migration and Law* 79.

—— 'After the Ouster: Review and Reconsideration in a Single Tier Tribunal' [2006] *Public Law* 674.

—— 'Judicial Review Challenges to Removal Decisions' (2008) 14(1) *Immigration Law Digest* 2.

—— 'Refugee Roulette: a UK Perspective' and SH Legomsky, 'Learning to Live with Unequal Justice: Asylum and the Limits to Consistency' in J Ramji-Nogales, AI Schoenholtz and PG Schrag (eds), *Refugee Roulette: Disparities in Asylum Adjudication and Proposals for Reform* (New York, New York University Press, 2009).

Travers, M, *The British Immigration Courts: A Study of Law and Politics* (Bristol, Policy Press, 1999).

Travis, A, 'Home Office Ignored Court Injunction on Deportation' *The Guardian* (16 August 2006).

—— 'Reid Warns Judges Not to Block Iraqis' Deportation' *The Guardian* (5 September 2006).

Troup, E, *The Home Office* (London, Putnam's, 1925).

Trueman, T, 'Reasons for Refusal: An Audit of 200 Refusals of Ethiopian Asylum-seekers in England' (2009) 23 *Journal of Immigration, Asylum, and Nationality Law* 281.

Twining, W, 'Taking Facts Seriously' in *Rethinking Evidence: Exploratory Essays,* 2nd edn (Cambridge, Cambridge University Press, 2006).

Vincenzi, C, *Crown Powers, Subjects and Citizens* (London, Pinter, 1998).

Vrij, A, *Detecting Lies and Deceit: the Psychology of Lying and the Implications for Professional Practice* (Chichester, Wiley, 2000).

Weber, M, *Economy and Society* (Berkeley, University of California Press, 1978).

Williams, R, 'When is an Error not an Error? Reform of Jurisdictional Review of Error of Law and Fact' [2007] *Public Law* 793.

Woolf, H, 'A Hotchpotch of Appeals—the Need for a Blender?' (1988) 7 *Civil Justice Quarterly* 44.

—— 'The Rule of Law and a Change in the Constitution' (2004) 63 *Cambridge Law Journal* 317.

Wraith, RE and Hutchesson, PG, *Administrative Tribunals* (London, Allen and Unwin, 1973).

Yeo, C (ed), *Country Guideline Cases: Benign and Practical?* (London, Immigration Advisory Service, 2005).

—— 'Country Information, the Courts, and the Truth' (2005) 11 *Immigration Law Digest* 26.

Zahle, H, 'Competing Patterns for Evidentiary Assessments' in G Noll (ed), *Proof, Evidentiary Assessment and Credibility in Asylum Procedures* (Leiden/Boston, Martinus Nijhoff, 2005).

2 Official publications

Advisory Panel on Country Information, *Terms of Reference* (APCI, 2005).

Aspden, J, *Evaluation of the Solihull Pilot for the United Kingdom Border Agency and the Legal Services Commission* (London, UKBA, 2008).

Asylum and Immigration Tribunal, *Report of a Working Party* (AIT, 2005).

—— *Practice Directions* (2007).

Brooke, H, *Should the Civil Courts be Unified? A Report by Sir Henry Brooke* (London, Judicial Office, 2008).

Bowman, J, *Review of the Crown Office List: A Report to the Lord Chancellor* (London, Lord Chancellor's Department, 2000).

Brooke, H, 'A Last Word' in *Court of Appeal Civil Division—Review of the Legal Year 2005–2006* (London, Court of Appeal, 2006).

Cabinet Office, *Capability Review of the Home Office* (London, Cabinet Office, 2006).

—— *Security in a Global Hub: Establishing the UK's New Border Arrangements* (London, Cabinet Office, 2007).

Carnwath, R, Senior President of Tribunals, *Third Implementation Review* (London, Tribunals Service, July 2009).

—— *Practice Statement: Immigration and Asylum Chambers of the First-tier Tribunal and Upper Tribunal* (London, Tribunal Service, 2010).

—— *The Senior President of Tribunals' Annual Report: Tribunals Transformed* (London, Tribunals Service, 2010).

Children's Commissioner for England, *The Arrest and Detention of Children Subject to Immigration Control* (London, Children's Commissioner for England, 2009).

Collins, A, Statement by Collins J, Lead Judge of the Administrative Court, *Administrative Court List* (London, Administrative Court, April 2008).

Complaints Audit Committee, *Annual Report 2007/08* (London, UKBA, 2008).

Council on Tribunals, *Annual Report 2004/2005* (2004–05 HC 472).

Courts Service, *Delays in the Administrative Court* (London, HMCS, November 2007).

—— *Overview of Current Position in the Administrative Court* (London, HMCS, July 2008).

Cox, A, 'Asylum & Immigration Tribunal: Case Management Review (CMR) Project' in Administrative Justice and Tribunal Council, *Adjust* (December 2007) available from www.ajtc.gov.uk.

Department for Constitutional Affairs, *Government Response to the Constitutional Affairs Select Committee's Report on Asylum and Immigration Appeals* (Cm 6236, 2004).

—— *Transforming Public Services: Complaints, Redress and Tribunals* (Cm 6243, 2004).

—— *The Asylum and Immigration Tribunal—The Legal Aid Arrangements for Onward Appeals* (London, DCA, CP 30/04, 2004).

Deputy Chief Adjudicator, *Guidance Note on Unrepresented Appellants Who Do Not Understand English* (IAA, 2004).

European Commission, *Proposal for a Regulation Establishing a European Asylum Support Office*, COM (2009) 66.

—— *Proposal for a Minimum Standard for the Qualification and Status of Third Country Nationals or Stateless Persons as Beneficiaries of International Protection and the Content of the Protection Granted*, COM(2009) 551.

—— *Proposal for a Directive on Minimum Standards on Procedures in Member States for Granting and Withdrawing International Protection*, COM(2009) 554.

Franks Committee, *Report of the Committee on Administrative Tribunals and Enquiries* (The Franks Report) (Cmnd 218, 1957).

HM Treasury, *2007 Pre-Budget Report and Comprehensive Spending Review: Meeting the Aspirations of the British People* (Cm 7227, 2007).

—— *Treasury Minutes to the Twenty Eighth Report from the House of Commons Public Accounts Committee Session 2008–09* (Cm 7717, 2009).

Home Office, *Report of the Committee on Immigration Appeals* (Cmnd 3387, 1967).

—— *A Report on the work of the Immigration and Nationality Department* (London, Home Office, 1984).

—— *The Government Reply to the Third Report from the Home Affairs Committee* (Cmnd 9626, 1985).

—— *The Government Reply to the Second Report from the Home Affairs Committee Session 2003–04 HC 218: Asylum Applications* (Cm 6166, 2004).

—— *The Government Reply to the Fifth Report from the Home Affairs Committee Session 2005–06 HC 775 Immigration Control* (Cm 6910, 2006).

—— *A Points-Based System: Making Migration Work for Britain* (Cm 6741, 2006).

Home Office, *Simplifying Immigration Law: The Draft Bill* (Cm 7730, 2009).
—— *Draft Immigration Bill 2009* (Cm 7666, 2009).
—— and Lord Chancellor's Department, *Review of Appeals: A Consultation Paper* (London, Home Office and LCD, 1998).
Home Office Immigration and Nationality Directorate and Department for Constitutional Affairs, *New Legislative Proposals on Asylum Reform* (London, Home Office, 2003).
—— *Process Communication: Revised Instructions for Handling Injunctions Against Removal* (London, IND, 16 August 2006).
—— *Background Note to Revised IND Policy on Handling JR Challenges to Removal Decisions* (London, Home Office, 2006).
—— *Background Note to Revised IND Policy on Handling JR Challenges to Removal Decisions* (London, Home Office, 2006).
—— *Fair, Effective, Transparent, and Trusted: Rebuilding Confidence in our Immigration System* (London, Home Office, 2006).
—— *Change of Policy Relating to the Circumstances in Which Removal Will be Deferred Following Challenge by Judicial Review* (London, IND, 2007).
—— *Asylum Process Guidance: Conducting the Asylum Interview* (Home Office, 2007).
Home Office United Kingdom Border Agency, *Consultation: Immigration Appeals—Fair Decisions; Faster Justice* (London, Home Office UKBA, 2008).
—— *New Policy on Judicial Reviews that Challenge Removals* (London, UKBA, 9 January 2009).
—— *Zimbabwe: Operational Guidance Note* (London, Home Office, 2009).
—— *Jamaica: Operational Guidance Note* (London, UKBA, 2009).
—— *Immigration Appeals: Response to Consultation—Fair Decisions; Faster Justice* (London, Home Office UKBA and Tribunals Service, 2009).
—— *Customer Strategy 2009–2012* (London, UKBA, 2009).
—— *Oversight of the Immigration Advice Sector: Consultation Response* (London, UKBA, 2009).
—— *Asylum Process Guidance, Medical Evidence (Non-Medical Foundation Cases) and Medical Foundation Cases* www.ukba.homeoffice.gov.uk/sitecontent/documents/policyandlaw/asylumprocessguidance/consideringanddecidingtheclaim/.
House of Commons Constitutional Affairs Committee, *Asylum and Immigration Appeals* (2003–04 HC 211).
—— *Legal Aid: Asylum Appeals* (2004–05 HC 276).
House of Commons Home Affairs Committee, *Refugees and Asylum, with Special Reference to the Vietnamese* (1984-85 HC 72).
—— *Asylum Removals* (2002–03 HC 654).
—— *Asylum and Immigration (Treatment of Claimants, etc.) Bill* (2003–04 HC 109).
—— *Asylum Applications* (2003–04 HC 218).
—— *Immigration Control* (2005–06 HC 775).
—— *Borders, Citizenship and Immigration Bill* (2008–09 HC 425).
—— *Monitoring of the UK Border Agency* (2008–09 HC 77).
—— *Managing Migration: The Points Based System* (2008–09 HC 217).
House of Commons Public Accounts Committee, *Returning Failed Asylum Applicants* (2005–06 HC 620).
—— *Management of Asylum Applications* (2008–09 HC 325).
House of Commons Public Administration Select Committee, *User Involvement in Public Services* (2007–08 HC 410).

House of Commons Work and Pensions Committee, *Decision Making and Appeals in the Benefits System* (2009–10 HC 313).

House of Lords Economic Affairs Select Committee, *The Economic Impact of Immigration* (2007–08 HL 82).

House of Lords European Union Committee, *Handling EU Asylum Claims: New Approaches Examined* (2003–04 HL 74).

House of Lords Merits Committee, *What Happened Next? A Study of Post-Implementation Reviews of Secondary Legislation* (2008–09 HL 180).

Hyde, S, *A Review of the Failure of the Immigration and Nationality Directorate to Consider Some Foreign National Prisoners for Deportation* (London, IND, 2007).

Immigration Appellate Authority, *Asylum Gender Guidelines* (London, IAA, 2000).

—— *Adjudicator Guidance Note No 3:Pre-hearing Introduction* (IAA, 2002).

—— *Adjudicator Guidance Note No 5: Unrepresented Appellants* (IAA, 2003).

Independent Chief Inspector of the UK Border Agency, *Report July 2008—September 2009* (London, OCIUKBA, 2009).

—— *Asylum: Getting the Balance Right? A Thematic Inspection: July—November 2009* (London, OCIUKBA, 2010).

—— *First Annual Report of the Independent Advisory Group on Country Information* (IAGCI) (London, OCIUKBA, 2010).

Joint Committee on Human Rights, *Asylum and Immigration (Treatment of Claimants, etc.) Bill* (2003–04 HL 35 HC 304).

—— *The Treatment of Asylum Seekers* (2006–07 HL 81 HC 60).

—— *Government Response to the Committee's Tenth Report of this Session: The Treatment of Asylum Seekers* (2006–07 HL 134 HC 790).

—— *Legislative Scrutiny: Borders, Citizenship and Immigration Bill* (2008–09 HL 62 HC 375).

—— *Government Replies to the Second, Fourth, Eighth, Ninth and Twelfth Reports of Session 2008–09* (2008–09 HL 104 HC 592).

Judge LCJ, *The Lord Chief Justice's Review of the Administration of Justice in the Courts* (London: The Stationery Office, 2010).

Judicial Working Group, *Justice Outside London* (London, Judiciary of England and Wales, 2007).

Leggatt, A, *Tribunals for Users: One System, One Service. The Report of the Review of Tribunals by Sir Andrew Leggatt* (London, The Stationery Office, 2001).

Lord Chancellor's Advisory Committee on Legal Education and Conduct, *Improving the Quality of Immigration Advice and Representation: A Report* (London, Lord Chancellor's Department, 1998).

Ministry of Justice, *Judicial and Court Statistics 2006* (Cm 7273, 2007).

—— *Judicial and Court Statistics 2007* (Cm 7467, 2008).

—— *Judicial and Court Statistics 2008* (Cm 7697, 2009).

—— *Judicial Salaries and Fees 2008–09* (London, Ministry of Justice, 2008).

Moorhead, R and Sefton, M, *Litigants in Person: Unrepresented Litigants in First Instance Proceedings* (London, DCA Research Series 2/05, 2005).

Morgan, B, Gelsthorpe, V, Crawley, H and Jones, GA, *Country of Origin Information: A User and Content Evaluation* (London, Home Office Research Study 271, 2003).

National Audit Office, *Getting it Right, Putting it Rights: Improving Decision-making and Appeals in Social Security Benefits* (2002–03 HC 1142).

—— *Improving the Speed and Quality of Asylum Decisions* (2003–04 HC 535).

National Audit Office, *Returning Failed Asylum Applicants* (2005–06 HC 76).

—— *Management of Asylum Applications by the UK Border Agency* (2008–09 HC 124).

—— and Audit Commission, *Delivering Efficiently: Strengthening the Links in Public Service Delivery Chains* (2005–06 HC 940).

Northern Ireland Human Rights Commission, *Our Hidden Borders: The UK Border Agency's Powers of Detention* (NIHRC, 2008).

O'Loan, B, *Report to the United Kingdom Border Agency on 'Outsourcing Abuse'* (London, UKBA, 2010).

Office of the Immigration Services Commissioner, *Annual Report and Accounts 2008–09* (2008–09 HC 627).

PA Consulting Group, *Asylum and Immigration Tribunal: Analysis of Judicial Time* (London, PA Consulting Group 2007).

Parliamentary and Health Service Ombudsman, *'Fast and Fair?' A Report by the Parliamentary Ombudsman on the UK Border Agency* (2009–10 HC 329).

Philips LCJ, *The Lord Chief Justice's Review of the Administration of Justice in the Courts* (2007–08 HC 448).

President of Appeal Tribunals, *President's Report: Report by the President of Appeal Tribunals on the Standards of Decision-making by the Secretary of State 2007–2008* (Tribunals Service, 2008).

President of the Queen's Bench Division, *Response of the President of the Queen's Bench Division to the UK Border Agency Consultation on Immigration Appeals* (London, RCJ, 2008).

Tribunal Procedure Committee, *The Tribunal Procedure (Upper Tribunal) Rules 2008— Consultation on Rule Amendments for Asylum and Immigration Upper Tribunal Chamber* (London, Tribunals Service, July 2009).

Tribunals Service, *The AIT Review Report April 2006* (London, DCA, 2006).

—— *Transforming Tribunals: Implementing Part 1 of the Tribunals, Courts and Enforcement Act 2007* (London, Ministry of Justice, 2007).

—— *Annual Report and Accounts 2008–09* (2008–09 HC 599).

United Nations High Commissioner for Refugees (UNHCR), *Handbook on Determining Refugee Status* (Geneva, UNHCR, 1992).

—— *Istanbul Protocol: Manual on the Effective Investigation and Documentation of Torture and Other Cruel, Inhuman or Degrading Treatment or Punishment* (UNHCR, 9 August 1999).

—— *Country of Origin Information: Towards Enhanced International Cooperation* (Geneva, UNHCR, 2004).

—— *Quality Initiative Project: A UNHCR Review of the UK Home Office Refugee Status Determination Procedures* (London, UNHCR, 2005).

United States Government Accountability Office, *US Asylum System: Significant Variation Existed in Asylum Outcomes across Immigration Courts and Judges* (GAO-08-940, September 2008).

Waller, Lord Justice, 'A First Word' in *Court of Appeal Civil Division—Review of the Legal Year 2006–2007* (London, Court of Appeal, 2007).

Woodhouse, S, *The Annual Report of the Certification Monitor 2005* (London, IND, 2005).

Woolf, H, *Access to Justice: Final Report* (London, HMSO, 1996).

INDEX